On Tragedy and Transcendence

On **TRAGEDY** and **TRANSCENDENCE**

An Essay on the Metaphysics of Donald MacKinnon
and Rowan Williams

Khegan M. Delport

FOREWORD BY
Graham Ward

◆PICKWICK *Publications* · Eugene, Oregon

ON TRAGEDY AND TRANSCENDENCE
An Essay on the Metaphysics of Donald MacKinnon and Rowan Williams

Copyright © 2021 Khegan M. Delport. All rights reserved. Except for brief quotations in critical publications or reviews, no part of this book may be reproduced in any manner without prior written permission from the publisher. Write: Permissions, Wipf and Stock Publishers, 199 W. 8th Ave., Suite 3, Eugene, OR 97401.

Pickwick Publications
An Imprint of Wipf and Stock Publishers
199 W. 8th Ave., Suite 3
Eugene, OR 97401

www.wipfandstock.com

PAPERBACK ISBN: 978-1-5326-9776-0
HARDCOVER ISBN: 978-1-5326-9777-7
EBOOK ISBN: 978-1-5326-9778-4

Cataloguing-in-Publication data:

Names: Delport, Khegan M., author. | Ward, Graham, 1955–, foreword.

Title: On tragedy and transcendence : an essay on the metaphysics of Donald Mackinnon and Rowan Williams / by Khegan M. Delport ; foreword by Graham Ward.

Description: Eugene, OR : Pickwick Publications, 2021 | Includes bibliographical references and index.

Identifiers: ISBN 978-1-5326-9776-0 (paperback) | ISBN 978-1-5326-9777-7 (hardcover) | ISBN 978-1-5326-9778-4 (ebook)

Subjects: LCSH: MacKinnon, Donald M. (Donald MacKenzie), 1913–1994. | Williams, Rowan, 1950–. | Metaphysics. | Philosophical theology.

Classification: BT40 .D45 2021 (print) | BT40 .D45 (ebook)

09/30/21

Scripture quotations are from New Revised Standard Version Bible, copyright © 1989 National Council of the Churches of Christ in the United States of America. Used by permission. All rights reserved worldwide.

For Alease A. Brown (1970-2020†)

οὔτοι συνέχθειν, ἀλλὰ συμφιλεῖν ἔφυν
(Sophocles, *Antigone* 523)

Contents

Foreword by Graham Ward | ix
Preface | xiii

1 **Introduction** | 1
　The Scope　1
　On Beginning in the Middle　6
　The Argument　13

2 **On the Not-So-Ancient Quarrel of Tragedy and Christianity** | 18
　On 'Tragedy' and 'the Tragic'　18
　On Poets and Philosophers　23
　On Christianity and the Tragic　27

3 **Tragedy and Transcendence: On Theological Coherency** | 39
　On Divine Transcendence and Aseity　40
　On Tragedy and Transcendence: Modern Inversions　50

4 **Donald MacKinnon I: On Critical Antiphony** | 64
　On Donald MacKinnon and the Question of Difficulty　64
　David Bentley Hart: The Tragic as Sacrificial Economy and Metaphysical Consolation　72
　John Milbank: The Tragic as Transcendental Limitation and Sublime Speculation　76

5 Donald MacKinnon II: On Aporetics and Apophatics | 89
Aristotle's Aporeticism: On Substance   92
Kant's Agnosticism: The De-Ontologizing of Analogy   101

6 Donald MacKinnon III: Between Tragedy and Metaphysics | 118
Plato the Moralist   119
The Irreducibility of the Ethical   125
The Transcendence of the Tragic   138
Critical Evaluation   155
Summary   164

7 Rowan Williams I: On Metaphysics and Poetics | 168
The Metaphysical Poetics of Rowan Williams   169
   On Creativity   172
   On Language   183
   On Analogy   189
Without Substance: Augustine and the Problem of Evil   196

8 Rowan Williams II: The Tragic within Grace, or On the Politics of Estrangement | 206
On Learning   207
The Self in Fragments: On Tragicomic Augustinianism   209
Tragedy and Estrangement   224

9 Conclusion | 250

Bibliography | 267
Author Index | 293
Subject Index | 299
Scripture Index | 303

Foreword

At the University of Cambridge, the undergraduate course in English Literature is divided into two parts (Tripos I and Tripos II). The first part covers a chronological curriculum from the study of Chaucer to contemporary fiction. The second part is made up of two Special papers (on subjects like the Novel) and two compulsory papers: what was called "Practical Criticism" or textual appreciation and the Tragedy paper. Every year, students demand to know why there is a compulsory paper on tragedy. Why not comedy? And, I'm sure, the responses from tutors in my time are fairly similar to what tutors tell the students today: that Tripos II aims to allow students to show the breadth and depth of their knowledge in areas recognized over several centuries to be key to the study of literature. Tragedy raises the most profound and the most perplexing of questions about the nature and destiny of being human, which demands some knowledge of the whole of the western canon of literature, philosophy *and* religion.

I want to begin here for two reasons. First, many of the theological thinkers whose work is examined in this book studied or worked at the University of Cambridge, among them MacKinnon, Eagleton, Williams and Milbank. They were acquainted with the major debates on tragedy around that time between George Steiner (whose views on the subject were primarily literary) and Raymond Williams (whose views on the subject, given his left-wing politics, refused to separate literature from tragic social events and conditions). MacKinnon was embroiled in these debates. Secondly, anyone taking up the challenge tragedy poses for literature, philosophy and theology, has to grapple with an enormous body of writing with heavy-weight cultural baggage. As a subject to write about, this one is not for the faint-hearted. It is very easy to get overwhelmed, if not by the volume of work, then by the profundity of the questions raised. And it is to the enormous credit of Dr. Delport that he has the courage and conviction not only to labour in this necessarily interdisciplinary area, but to articulate clearly the central questions that the tragic poses for Christian faith, and then tackle them. The erudition required has to equal the intellectual tenacity demanded.

Having sat in lectures given by Raymond Williams and sat the Tragedy paper, I first came to write about tragedy, from a theological perspective, having come to know George Steiner. Later, having presented a paper on Steiner's views, I came to know the retired and quite reclusive Donald MacKinnon. Though he had long departed from the Divinity School at Cambridge, legends of his Scottish eccentricities were still very much in circulation. But when I came to write about MacKinnon I had something of a surprise: I was rejected by the editors of US journals on the grounds that no one in the States really knew the work of MacKinnon. He was not a scholar of sufficient importance outside certain debates in the UK. In fact, it further surprised me, when I then met a South African doctoral student at Stellenbosch University (the author of this book) who told me he was researching MacKinnon's theology. It is somewhat sobering now, given Rowan William's tribute to MacKinnon in *The Tragic Imagination* and this volume, to appreciate some theological writings (and theologians) have to wait a long time for their importance to be widely recognized. For MacKinnon's theological reflections, as this study shows, were and still are seminal—twenty-seven years after his death. I hope he's having a chuckle over that.

MacKinnon was not one to eschew difficulty, and as Delport rightly states, "Tragedy is about the denial of easy answers and quick fixes" (71). This fact, as I said, qualified it to be compulsory for Finals in English Literature. Some overriding sense of fate or providence (both, though in different ways, concerned with what transcends us) disrupts, and disrupts profoundly, any settling scenarios for the contingent. And from this disruption emerges questions of meaning or meaninglessness, guilt and punishment, propitiatory sacrifice and senseless suffering. Literature, particularly drama, is only giving expression to the questions we all live with in the face of events we all either witness, directly or indirectly. Drama dramatizes: staging the agonies and even brutalities of a wrestling all of us are exposed to, religious or non-religious. If there's some truth in the words of Forrest Gump's mother—"life is like a box of chocolates . . . you never know what you're goin' to get"—then tragedy takes away some of the sugar and fat, and replaces it with slivers of glass and lacings of poison. And MacKinnon's work engages in that wrestling, knowing that Christians are not taken from the world, but given to it. There's something very Pauline in his dogged attention to suffering and evil. In a very perplexing claim to the church in

Colossae, Paul describes how he suffers with them, helping "to complete, in my poor human flesh, the full tale of Christ's afflictions still to be endured, for the sake of his body which is the church" (Col 1:24 NEB). We can quibble about the translation, but suffering is never far from Paul's experience of being a Christian, as it wasn't from MacKinnon's theology.

What we have of that theology is mainly fragments: essays, lectures, two monographs. Nothing systematic. But these are densely written, erudite and insightful pieces composed in the "borderlands of theology" (as one of the collections of his essays is entitled). However complex the thought expressed, and however abstract, his wrestling is with the concrete: the sheer difficulty of engaging the detail theologically. His pursuit was for theological honesty, and because of that, whatever the criticisms of his Aristotelian or Kantian presuppositions, his rejection of analogy and lack of a doctrine of participation (and creation) that follows from it, he raised questions that speak now and still preoccupy. And not just about whether Christianity has to engage with the tragic or about the nature and perplexity of evil. Of all I gained from reading MacKinnon, foremost was method: how to do theology. Or, more precisely, how dogmatics and Scriptural interpretation cannot divorce themselves either from ethics or metaphysics; philosophy more widely, hermeneutics and moral reasoning. There is no pure theology. There is no pure philosophy either. And that's what MacKinnon's successor, Nicholas Lash taught me, in his seminars on Wittgenstein. MacKinnon's wrestling with difficulty and tragic suffering leads us away from a God who we think we know. His refusal to accept cheap theological escape routes like "mystery" or even *apophasis*, served to make plain the need to distinguish between the unthinkable and the apophatic—what is not accessible to human understanding and *theologia negativa*—in the face of events that remain disturbingly inexplicable, even in (especially in) Scripture.

What continues to impress me about MacKinnon's work is its longevity. That says something about the sheer honesty of his thinking. With David Bentley Hart (a student of John Milbank's), MacKinnon has now crossed into the US, and with this book by Khegan Delport then he is being engaged within a South African context. Surely, this longevity and fertilization of the theological imagination is a sign of true pedagogy. This book stands in that line of questioning opened by MacKinnon, and like the interlocutors treated here, it clarifies, critiques and attempts to advance, theological reasoning. "Advance" is not the right word, if by that we mean progress. Advance, theologically, is the handing on of what has been handed on to us, through the tradition and the rethinking and remolding of that tradition in new contexts. The tragic occurs, we name it, and literature gives expression to it. It occurs in the lives of Christians and their experience of living in a world in which suffering is all too evident. Of course, new contexts continually open new possibilities for reworkings of the Scriptures and the Christian tradition. We are far from the Second World War, and the British context in which MacKinnon was formed as a theologian as atrocity upon atrocity came to light. If nothing else, we have come through postmodernism and embarked now on post-colonial critiques of Western culture hegemony, and decolonizing strategies. Some echoes of which inevitably, and rightly, feature in Delport's book. But what I sense is the same desire to be unflinchingly honest. Atrocity still comes to light.

This is a brave book. Ambitious, yes, in the range of material it covers, but even though its focus is on the "grammars of transcendence" (251) with respect to classical theology, it remains throughout brave *and* pertinent. He reaffirms Rowan Williams' "attachment to the negativity of the tragic [which] cautions him against any eschatological cancellation of the tragic" (p. 256), but it is exactly here that the honesty kicks in: the appeal for great clarity and detail. It is not only the Devil that's in the detail: with the tragic it is also God.

Graham Ward

Regius Professor of Divinity
University of Oxford

Preface

It is a kind of comic irony that my first attendance of theatrical tragedy should happen after I wrote a dissertation on the tragic. This might seem somewhat odd to those raised near the likes of the West End, or Broadway, or the Market Theatre, or the Baxter. I admit that this is a mildly embarrassing factoid, but I find some comfort in that there is nothing historically unprecedented about this. The birth of tragic theory for good or ill coincides with a decline in performances of staged tragedy. One could be somewhat flippant and say something like the Owl of Minerva only flies at dusk (as Hegel would have it), but such a narrative of decline is not the whole story. It is true that with the rise of the novel and private reading, the textuality of tragedy comes to hold priority, stimulating a surge in philosophical exploration. And in many ways, this essay on transcendence and tragedy is a continuation of this trajectory. The reasons for this on my part, however, are highly idiosyncratic and contingent: I come from a decidedly middle-brow family; attendance of the theatre or even musical concerts was (and still is) decidedly rare. Moreover, my teenage years were spent in a small town, hours away from any major metropolitan district. Also, it is not irrelevant to add that the theatre can be a rather costly affair, something out of the price range for the majority of South Africans—never mind as a normal family outing. In short, for the majority of my life, going to the theatre would have been rather eccentric.

In any case, on 21 September 2019 I decided to go to watch a tragedy with a friend of mine. A local production of Mark Fleishman's new play *Antigone (not quite/quiet): "Ninganiki Okungcwele Ezinjeni"*[1] was premiering at

---

1. IsiXhosa for "Give not unto dogs sacred things," an allusion of course to Matt 7:6, but also a poem by S. E. K. Mqhayi—which is central to the third part of the play's triptych.

the Baxter for a limited time. It formed part of a series of events hosted by the Centre for Theatre and Performance Studies at the University of Cape Town. I did not know quite what to expect, but from the given title and the hand-outs, one had suspicions this was going to be a rather deconstructive affair—like *King Lear* à la Godard, or Lee Breuer's *The Gospel at Colonus*, and so on. It was a wonderfully 'faithless' adaptation: one part self-agonizing soliloquy (Ismene), one part dance choreography (Antigone), and one part multimedia presentation (Tiresias).[2] The first dramatizes Ismene (a white woman) coming to terms with her betrayal of Antigone, and her conflicting emotions of self-justification. Ismene is emblematic of the collective psyche of white South Africa, poised between acceptance and denial. She is caught in a tragic and destructive "middle" that is not resolved by the end of the first act.[3] Her failure to act has wide ramifications, for her betrayal is not of an individual, or of the blood-bond; instead, she has forsaken a future collective, the generations of mostly black youth who are still to come. Unlike the original play, this "Antigone" is represented by a chorus rather than a single character—a troupe of *toyi-toying*[4] singers and dancers.[5] They are symbolic of the post-1994 generation and those disenchanted with "rainbowism."[6]

A deep pessimism is visible in this play. Its mood is crepuscular and apocalyptic, especially in the third act. Tiresias's foreboding invocation of Mqhayi is a prophetic threat: "The days of reckoning are coming / Days of inquiries and cross-/ examinations / Of being prodded with a weapon / When you can be over-thrown / without reserve."[7] Who exactly is going to do the overthrowing is not entirely clear, but it is centred on the imagery of Mbambushe, a mythical and nebulous dog-human, who returns periodically to sow havoc in the nation. All of this is not comforting for us: the future imaged is not Panglossian. The atmosphere and the music are darkly ambient and unsettling. In confirmation of this disconcerting undertone, at one point the chorus of singers release a punning, bitter re-imagining of Silenus: "*Better not to be born free.*"[8] It is at this point that art, philosophy and life are drawn together provocatively.

   2. Tiresias is portrayed as a *sangoma*—a Zulu word for a traditional healer.
   3. The language of "middle" is drawn from the work of Gillian Rose.
   4. A form of dancing usually associated with protest in South Africa.
   5. It is not at all unprecedented to depict inter-racial conflict as a problem of inter-familial violence in South African theatre, as can be seen in Yael Farber's *Molora*.
   6. An allusion to Archbishop Desmond Tutu's famous designation of South Africa as a "rainbow nation."
   7. Mqhayi, "U-Mbambushe"; the translation is by Phyllis Ntantala, and is taken from the play's hand-out.
   8. The so-called "born free" are those born after 1994 or were too young to

I mention this play and this story because the trajectory of this study might, at first glance, seem to be removed from contextual elements, being an exposition of a European tradition of theology and metaphysics. But this distance in idiom does not necessarily imply a disconnection of content. Transcendence and tragedy, I believe, have transcultural resonance. Tragedy is just as real for my continent of Africa as anywhere else, and maybe even more so. Tragedy staged or otherwise is not merely a Western importation, but one that has been creatively indigenized on the continent for decades. There is already sizable scholarship on the reception of classical tragedy in Africa, and it continues to grow as more tragedies are produced.[9] From Soyinka to Fugard, from Rotimi to Osofisan, across the expanse of the continent and its diaspora, the re-imagination of the tragic for Africa continues. These bear witness to the continuing reality of post-colonial violence, failed states, and setbacks related to transitional justice.[10] Situations like these, in countries like South Africa and others on the continent, lend themselves to tragic interpretations. There is something fitting in their mutual relating and juxtaposition; and when one combines this factor with the massive historical influence of Christianity on the continent, for good and bad, these questions become even more pertinent. Donald MacKinnon and Rowan Williams's implication of Christ and the Church in a tragic paradigm has resonance with such experience, even though it touches little upon African experience as such. Essential for them is the way that staged tragedy attempts to represent those destructive and fatal contiguities that connect us to one another and the world. On their reading, we are not free to invent ourselves in whatever manner we choose, apart that is from a matrix of implication and effect, and the immanent restrictions that we are born into. Tragedy provokes us to reflect on these limits, suggesting not so much that we are doomed to inevitable outcomes, but that actions can come at a cost. This is a question that tragedy raises for us, both theologically and philosophically.

For example, when one hears a statement like "*Better not to be born free,*" it is hard not to pick up deeper ontological questions. It speaks to the problem of hopelessness, a sense of lost futurity, an echo reverberating across millennia. More and more, in the times of recessions and pandemics, there is a growing sensibility that cultural death and failed promises are intrinsic

---

remember the period of legal apartheid. I say "legal" because many would argue that unofficial, neo-apartheid structures remain embodied in institutions until the present day—most clearly evidenced in the persistent racialized geography of South Africa.

9. Cf. Goff and Simpson, *Crossroads in the Black Aegean*. On the reception of Greek tragedy in South African theater more generally, see Smit, "The Reception of Greek Tragedy," and also Dominik, "Reception of Greek Tragedy."

10. On this, one can consult Scott, *Conscripts of Modernity*.

to the social functioning of late capitalism, a "cruel optimism" to reference Lauren Berlant.[11] These are global affects that cannot be narrowed down to one segment of the North Atlantic. Tragic ideas are not ghettoized concepts, and are certainly not cloistered within Eurocentric "discursive regimes."[12] There are events that impact us globally, of which the impending climate crisis is the most obvious. It is of course possible to overemphasise the importance of this tradition especially within Occidental criticism (Ochieng has provocatively spoken of "the fetishization of tragedy"[13]). Observing the mass of literature on the tragic, as well the philosophical reception of its themes, one could say there is some basis for this concern. There are certainly many other registers into which human experience and art can be encompassed. Tragedy should not be hypostatized into some catch-all experience, a totality into which all the disparities of daily life and practice should be included. We should be wary of a "tragic theory of life." Much of this will be repeated and emphasized in the study to follow. My main point here, however, is that ontological questions, including options such as "pessimism," are certainly not enclosed within a Western enclave—which remains a disparate tradition even in its own setting.[14] Within critical theory, "Afropessimism" is a living and influential option, and has produced a significant amount of reflection and discussion in recent times.[15] While I will not enter explicitly into a discussion of these ideas, one of the questions I will ask here is whether "ontological pessimism" is a necessary outcome of the tragic imagination. Does respect for tragedy imply an account of transcendence which is necessarily threatening and destructive? And if we configure a "transcendence" that bypasses this option, then what do we say about history, which so often is experienced as afflictive? Does the arc of the universe bend towards justice or is this simply a deceptive fantasy? Are there deeper grounds for hope and redemption, or is pessimism the only realism? This is a vital query, because it appears recurrently in secular disputations of the relation between Christianity and the tragic, as seen in the likes of Christopher Hamilton and Simon Critchley (amongst others).[16]

---

11. Berlant, *Cruel Optimism*, 23–49.

12. The language of "discursive regime" or "discursive field" is taken from Foucault's *The Archeology of Knowledge*, 119–32.

13. Ochieng, *The Intellectual Imagination*, 200.

14. See Thacker, *Cosmic Pessimism*.

15. Scholars influential in this turn include Nahum Chandler, Saidiya Hartman, Fred Moten, Orlando Paterson, Jared Sexton, Hortense Spillers, Calvin Warren, Frank Wilderson III, and Sylvia Wynter.

16. I am thinking of Hamilton's *A Philosophy of Tragedy* and Critchley's *Tragedy, the Greeks and Us*.

Many might think that an emphasis on tragedy leads towards the latter proclivity, that is, towards ontological despair. This would naturally be the impression if one read someone like Schopenhauer. However, this is not a foregone conclusion. In many ways, the bipolarities of hope and despair are *internal* to tragic representation. If we put aside for the moment ideas of "absolute tragedy," as offered by George Steiner, one can see how tragedy dramatizes both of these options. There are plays that appear unremitting, that offer scarce consolation. *The Persians* ends in catastrophe for Xerxes at the Battle of Salamis: his mother Atossa opines "When waves of trouble burst on us, each new event / Fills us with terror; but when Fortune's wind blows soft / We think to enjoy the same fair weather all our lives. / Now, ringed with fears, in every threat I see Heaven's wrath; / My ears are dinned with notes that bear no healing spell."[17] One could also think here of Euripides's *The Women of Troy*, *The Bacchae* and *Medea*. However, *The Oresteia* portrays an ordeal of suffering pedagogy, where internecine conflict is gradually realized as an unsustainable option. Here something is gained: a moral growth in the perception of justice and mutual recognition beyond violent reprisals. In this sense, Aeschylus dramatizes the dictum of *Agamemnon* that we have to *"suffer to be wise"* (*pathei mathos*).[18] Similar polarities could be found in the other ancient dramatists: Sophocles's *Ajax, Trachiniae, Electra*, as well as his Theban trilogy—the undoubted masterpiece of Attic tragedy—all contain deeply unsettling elements. But even a cursory reading of *Oedipus Tyrannus* and *Oedipus at Colonus* will show that the expulsion and pollution of the blinded protagonist are not the conclusion in this rather sad story. Even in *Oedipus at Colonus* there is the marked transition from the nihilistic desperation of the Chorus's earlier commentary, like when they say "Not to be born is best,"[19] towards something much more affirmatory ("Well, no more sound, / raise no more lamenting: / these things are bound / firmly to this ending.").[20] This is only a very short sample of the Greek corpus, but in summary what it tells us is that tragedy is not always as "tragic" as we imagine it to be. As I hope

---

17. Aeschylus, *The Persians* 581–618, in *Prometheus Bound, The Suppliants, Seven Against Thebes, The Persians*, 139. However, since this forms part of a trilogy (the other parts of which have been lost), we do not know how Aeschylus planned to end the larger drama. There is a strong likelihood that it would have ended with a somewhat less lugubrious tone. On this, see Wise, "Tragedy as 'An Augury of a Happy Life.'"

18. Aeschylus, *Agamemnon* 163–86, in *The Oresteian Trilogy*, 48. In South Africa, this narrative has been re-imagined in Yael Farber's *Molora*, which juxtaposes Aeschylus's *Oresteia* to a fictional re-telling of the Truth and Reconciliation Commission.

19. Sophocles, *Oedipus at Colonus* 1211–38. This translation is taken from *Sophocles, The Three Theban Plays*.

20. Sophocles, *Oedipus at Colonus* 1777–79. The translation is taken from *Sophocles: Four Tragedies*.

to show in this essay, it is precisely a departure from the particularity of tragic texts that creates problems further down the road in its reception, and leads to certain tensions which will have to be unpacked. Tragedy, like life, resists the systems and categories we place on it.

It is a persistent theme of this study that tragedy is not merely reflective of the stage or the writing desk, but the stuff of everyday reality, and especially the quotidian tragedy of the Two-Thirds World. I have already indicated that the reason tragedy speaks to us both aesthetically and philosophically across continents is because it touches upon the real conflicts and unforeseen consequences of human action, events which can never be eliminated, at least this side of finitude. This will be a pressing concern as we look at the figures of Donald MacKinnon and Rowan Williams, because, as churchman of differing stripes, they were both concerned with the theological question of how Christianity is able to speak to a world in which these things happen, without evasion and without cheaply-acquired reductions. They are convinced that a truthful meditation on suffering was not in fact negated by the Christian faith, but sustained and transformed by its basic teachings regarding creation and the cross. Rather than implying avoidance, for them Christianity provides resources for some kind of meaningful perseverance through the surd and aporetic perplexities of human loss. It is a theme that runs throughout their scholarly output. As I will argue, I think that Williams maintains the balance somewhat better than MacKinnon; but nevertheless it is clear that both have attempted to reiterate these issues through their careers, with varying degrees of emphasis. But what is central for both of them is that tragedy is not just an intellectual or aesthetic affair. To stay within this register alone would just be another avoidance of the tragic itself.

This was impressed on me rather violently later on the same night that I went to the theatre. On my drive home from the Baxter, not far from the suburb where I live, I came across a minibus accident that had just happened. Several cars had stopped. The minibus was on its right side, mangled, with its front lying partially in the road. I stopped, parked near the curb, and put on my emergency lights. There were no police vans, emergency response vehicles, or fire services in sight. A small crowd had already formed. From what I could piece together, the taxi had lost control and collided head-on with a tree, with such impact that it crushed the front of the van, spun around, and landed on its side. Ostensibly, no other motor vehicles were involved. Several people were still inside the minibus—all black women and men. Shrapnel was dispersed all around the grassy pavement and in the adjacent road that led to a local storage company and car dealership. There was a woman, lying prone near the tree in question; she had either been ejected during the crash or had crawled their on her own. She was alive and communicative, but barely moving. The tree stood there, partially stripped by the collision, but still stout and unsparing in its rigidity. I then noticed what others already saw: that there was young man trapped beneath the minibus. The full weight of the bus was on him along with the passengers still inside. He was non-responsive. "O Lord Jesus, he's dead!" one woman cried. She had seen similar scenes before: the everydayness of death. The crowd was discussing what we should do next. "Break the window," some shouted. There was an emergency exit at the top of the minibus. Not wanting to be bystander, I retrieved a wooden implement from my car. By the time I returned, however, the window was broken. Still no one appeared to be moving inside. I do not know if there was communication with the wounded, but the sudden consensus was that the bus needed to be hoisted. A young man's life was at stake.

There were risks: besides the precarity of lifting a minibus, there were people in the vehicle, possibly dead or with life-threatening injuries. Common wisdom says that one should wait for paramedics to arrive before moving anyone. But there was a human being trapped. The choice was: either wait for the experts to arrive or try to lift the minibus ourselves. Neither choice was perfect. Pushing the bus upwards would move those still inside, possibly injuring them further, while leaving the bus as it was would certainly make things worse for the man still being crushed. Was this a tragic choice? Within a few seconds, and after some hard lifting, the minibus bounced as it came down again on its wheels. Those inside ricocheted about before the bus came to a standstill. There was no response from the passengers. An arm dislodges, hanging lifelessly out of the compacted frame. It was the driver's. I could see the young man was unencumbered now. He was motionless, except for a ruptured artery. A fountain of blood was pumping intermittently: the stream formed a dark puddle and started to flow down the curb. I went around to the other side to the taxi door and peered inside. Did I see something move, or had a limb just come to its natural resting place? I am still not sure. I then noticed that the local community-watch were on the scene, gently telling the woman near the tree not to move. She was still communicating but clearly traumatized. She kept her movements to a minimum. She was able to do so. Those inside were not as lucky. We had already decided for them. Soon thereafter the police and paramedics arrived and I departed from the scene. I have no idea who survived and who did not. I heard reports later of several deaths.

I am left with the question: was the decision to move the minibus right? Was the man not already deceased? Did we worsen the injuries of several passengers to save someone who might have already been dead? What if someone had a severe spinal injury and was left paralyzed by our actions?

Was it worth the risk? Then again, who knows? Possibly no-one had spinal injuries and maybe the movement of bodies did no further damage. Maybe the risk was worthwhile, to save the life of one person. Of course, they all could have been dead already. I do not have the answers. Ideally the experts should have got there sooner. But should we have just stood around, waiting? Would that have been responsible? Now I tell this story not to invoke the narrative of a tragic hero thrust into impossible circumstances. I do not know if there were any heroes in this awful story. And yet it does point us to something substantially tragic, to those times where there are no harmless options, where our choices can come at the expense of others—and even our own lives. What I do know is that at this moment, tragedy had descended from the stage and confronted me directly.

And little did I know that there was another tragedy brewing beneath the surface. This would be the last night I would see my friend Alease Brown alive. She had graduated with her PhD earlier that year, the same as me. We had attended the production of *Antigone* together. She was a postdoc and was thriving in her position. She had recently written a paper on Persephone. We spoke about it before we went inside to the watch the performance. We did not see each other again after that night. I walked away as she waited for her Uber. We had made plans to meet up again but never got around to it, even though we live in the same city. We had kept in contact through the usual channels, still hoping to catch up, to hear how postdoc life was treating her. And then in the following March, I was informed that she had passed away. She had recently returned from a long stint in New York, and on her way back she had passed through Athens. It was during Lent, before the hard lockdown hit South Africa during Covid-19. A few weeks after returning, she started to feel ill. What began as an irritating headache had turned into hospitalization, and finally ended in death. It was sudden and unexpected. I had no idea of any underlying health conditions. I was informed that she had died of a genetic blood condition more prevalent in those of African descent. You are born with it, you do not contract it, and you die relatively young. There is no cure for it. I was obviously taken aback by the news. She was at the beginning of her academic career; so much left undone. The cosmic lunacy of it all was impressed upon me. It seemed like such a waste: to reach a lifetime goal only to be snuffed out. But then something else came to mind: this was a congenital and terminal condition. It is a disease that will eventually kill you. You do not know when exactly, but it will. Like the proverbial Sword of Damocles, it is always hanging around. Yet despite this chronic prognosis, she nevertheless upended her whole life. She left behind a promising law career and began to study theology. She moved to South Africa, adopting it as her own. She probably knew she would die young, but that did not stop her. She did not allow the logic of death to govern her life decisions. For me there is a beautiful, albeit tragic grandeur in all that: the willingness to risk everything without a guarantee of completion or success. This is very poignant for me. It reminds one of Antigone in her determination to bury her brother. There is something Greek in this decisiveness, a sense that some things are worth doing even if failure is highly probable. But Alease was a Christian, she also believed in miracles. She believed in resurrection, in Good Friday and Easter. She came from a tradition of the blues, but also of the spirituals. It was a deeply hopeful act. I am reminded of Luther's willingness to plant a tree on the eve of the apocalypse, of saying "yes" when everything screams "no." Maybe she thought: is a medical prognosis the end of the story? Like Carl Theodor Dreyer's masterpiece *Ordet* (1955), who knows whether one's prayers might not be met by the seemingly impossible gift of reprieve, of a life beyond the terminal sentence of death? Alease lived in this tension, seemingly until the end.

For the past few pages, I have spoken about tragedy as a description of the stage, of thought and of life. In many ways, this study seeks to move between these poles of experience. It stems from where my headspace has been for the past several years, especially since the beginning of my postgraduate studies. Along the way, I have many people I need to thank. Special thanks should be given to Prof. Robert Vosloo for his gracious accommodation and direction, most notably in the final stages of preparation of the doctoral research. Additional thanks should also go to my examiners of the original dissertation upon which this book is based, namely Prof. Dion Forster, Prof. Danie Veldsman and Dr. Stephen Martin, for their patient and often insightful commentary. I also cannot avoid thanking my cohort of fellow PhD students for their support and friendship, here in particular Dr. Marnus Havenga, Dr. Calvin Ullrich, and (soon-to-be Drs.), Louis van der Riet and Helgard Pretorius. Dr. Selina Palm also deserves mention for her honest and realistic advice throughout my PhD journey. I must also thank the various anonymous peer-reviewers who have looked over previous iterations and portions of this text, and who have helped to sharpen the argument of the book. Additional thanks must be given to the team at Wipf & Stock, and especially Dr. Charlie Collier for his guidance in the final stages of the manuscript preparation. And I must express my heartfelt thanks to Prof. Graham Ward for providing the Foreword to the book.

In terms of resources, I must also express my gratitude to the librarians at the Theology Library (University of Stellenbosch) for their unfailing assistance in providing books and inter-loan articles upon request. I also recall the help granted by Prof. Mike Higton and Dr. Benjamin Myers in the early period of my postgraduate research, particularly as regards their provision of hard-to-find texts penned by Rowan Williams. Dr. André Muller also deserves mention for granting me access to some early drafts of his biography of Donald MacKinnon, as well as several other documents he was editing. In the exploratory phases of the research, he sharpened my reading of MacKinnon and thoughtfully indicated the directions I should follow. All mistakes in interpretation, however, remain my own.

I would also like to express my thanks to Stellenbosch University for granting permission to re-publish my doctoral dissertation in the revised format here presented. Additionally, I would acknowledge and thank John Wiley and Sons and Cambridge University Press for allowing me to reprint material published in *The Heythrop Journal*, *Modern Theology*, and the *Journal of Anglican Studies* in Chapters Five and Eight.

Second-to-last, I would like to express gratefulness to my grandparents for their spiritual and material support, and their constant belief that I would see the process through. And lastly, I cannot avoid thanking my parents for their love and assistance throughout all my studies and research up till now.

This book, for the all reasons given above, is dedicated to the memory of the late Dr. Alease A. Brown.

1
Introduction

The Scope

The argument of this book is premised on the interconnections between Christian metaphysics and what has come to be called the philosophy of the tragic. It is the questions surrounding this relation that will animate our discussion, and is something that I hope to clarify a bit more in this extended essay. What will become clearer as we move forward is that this work aims to address some tensions that arise in the juxtaposition of Christianity and the tragic. More specifically, it will be centered on 'transcendence,' and how a more 'classical' or 'orthodox' metaphysics is able to account for, or at least reckon with, the tragic. A relationship between these discourses cannot be assumed to be harmonious, and so it is my task to suggest why this might be the case, and how they might be correlated, both conceptually and existentially. Its central argument is that there are accounts of transcendence that hinder an appropriation of the tragic, at least as regards classical theology. This is exemplified in the debate between, on the one side, David Bentley Hart and John Milbank, and on the other, Donald MacKinnon and Rowan Williams. It is this particular debate, and its wider context, that will form the center of this study.

Here our trajectory is not concerned, primarily, with a Christian metaphysics *in toto* but rather with a specific tradition, that is, with what has been called *classical orthodoxy*.[1] It is this point of departure that will

---

1. In our sense, 'orthodoxy' has a special linkage to the classical tradition and the question of transcendence (e.g., aseity, *analogia entis*, etc.), as well as other *regula fidei* linked to the Ecumenical Creeds. And yet, there is another conception of 'orthodoxy' presumed also, one which works at a meta-structure, and not simply at the level of

inflect our language of transcendence, and how we relate the tragic to its contours. By working within a more classical tradition of Christian metaphysics, I am going forward with specific assumptions in regard to the nature of God and the matrix of beliefs connected to it. Here the language of 'transcendence' is particularly emphasized as being central to the grammar of classical orthodoxy, and therefore accrues an elevated place in this discussion. Consequently, this adopted framework provokes special challenges to conceptual reconciliation—or what could be called systematic coherency—which will need to be addressed if one is going to try and relate the classical language of transcendence to the tragic and the overtones it has accrued, especially in recent times.

Both 'transcendence' and 'tragedy' are multivalent and require longer expositions, but here already I can give some preliminary definitions. For instance, we see that the language of 'transcendence,' in everyday usage, often concerns the liminality associated with transition—as seen in the intersections between past, present and future, or moving from somewhere to somewhere else. In a slightly more rarified sense, 'transcendence' references experiences which frustrate reduction or 'elevate' us to some degree, those moments of wonder and terror where our senses are uplifted, overloaded and destabilized, like when one contemplates the immensity of nature or has an ecstatic experience of some kind. In more extreme cases, they can signify those experiences of *intractability* or *non-negotiability* within the world, indicating those events that transport us or shock us into new modes of awareness—the tragic included. As I hope to show later, tragedy is an example of this phenomenological resistance, precisely to the degree it reveals what cannot be repressed or evaded, namely, the world's untameablity. But transcendence also betokens realities that are *not* experienceable in

---

specific dogmas. Here as elsewhere, our conception is influenced by Rowan Williams: this position does not equate 'orthodoxy' with a carapaced traditionalism or conservatism—as if we could somehow repristinate a bygone era *without* changing the meaning of the tradition in the process. Williams's account is *not* concerned with this variety of conservatism. His account is an open-ended, humble—even kenotic—account of the handing-over of church tradition, one that includes the necessity of fabrication and invention within the continuation of ecclesial identity. It could be called a "traditioned creativity" (to use Jeffrey McCurry's terms), and implies both the *faithful* transmission and the *imaginative* continuation of the church's identity—*faithful* because it is attentive to the church's historical and spiritual identity, and *imaginative* because it knows that the art of continuation cannot be achieved without the risks and joys of re-thinking the tradition within changing contexts. For more details on this, see Williams, "What is Catholic Orthodoxy?"; Williams, "Does it Make Sense"; Williams, "The Nicene Heritage"; Williams, "The Seal of Orthodoxy"; Williams, *Arius*, 1–25, 233–45. For secondary literature, see McCurry, *Traditioned Creativity*; Myers, "Disruptive History"; Myers, *Christ the Stranger*, 43–49. More generally, see Brown, *Tradition and Imagination*.

the mundane sense of the term, and are rather concerned with questions of *meaning*, with that which *creates* experience (that is, religions, myths, philosophy, etc.). In this sense, we can speak of experiences as having a 'metaphysical' or even 'transcendental' scope.[2] Furthermore, in this study, 'transcendence' is placed within the specific context of a classical account of Christian language regarding 'divine being' (e.g., aseity, impassibility, analogical participation,[3] the convertibility of being and goodness),[4] with the aim of showing that this tradition expresses a level of penetration that is not often recognized by revisionists. These questions will come into focus, especially when I discuss the work of Rowan Williams.

To state things concisely, the central question of this book is this: can a classical doctrine of transcendence account for the seriousness and often disturbing singularity of tragedy? This main question implies sub-questions which will also have to be addressed: are there conflicts between these representations of experience? And if there are, where do they lie? Are they substantial or the product of miscomprehension? As I progress, a couple of these tensions will become more apparent: on the one hand, there could be a query about whether classical metaphysics takes tragedy seriously, since (as has been prosecuted by some) it absconds from historicity.[5] Such interrogation might conclude that this language operates more like an 'ideology' than responsible discourse. On the other hand, an objection might arise regarding the acceptance of 'the tragic' or 'tragic theology,' since respondents could argue that this implies a rejection or a limitation of Christian orthodoxy. In summary: one could argue either that the implications of tragedy should be curtailed or re-imagined—because it remains too refractory and inassimilable—or one should reject classical orthodoxy as an unnecessary hindrance.

And yet the question remains: are these the only two options available, sheer acceptance or rejection? As I argue, the answer should be a qualified

---

2. Though not to be equated here with the Kantian sense of the term, as we will see later.

3. By 'participation,' I am referring to that "constitutive structure whereby a being or beings share to varying degrees in a positive quality or perfection that they receive from a donating source that alone enjoys the fullness of this quality of perfection," in Sherman, "A Genealogy of Participation," 82.

4. A description of this metaphysical vision can be found in Hart's essays, "No Shadow of Turning: On Divine Impassibility," 45–69; "The Destiny of Christian Metaphysics," 97–112; and "The Hidden and the Manifest: Metaphysics after Nicaea," 137–64; all in Hart, *The Hidden and the Manifest*.

5. On 'historicity,' see Koselleck, "'Space of Experience' and 'Horizon of Expectation': Two Historical Categories," in *Futures Past*, 255–75; Hartog, *Regimes of Historicity*; Carr, "On Historicity." For a more theological perspective, see Balthasar, *A Theology of History*, and Williams, *Why Study the Past?*

no. Rather I suggest a possible third way beyond the extremes of simple acceptance or rejection. But to do this, several things will have to be accounted for: (1) it will have to argue that Christianity, even in its more traditional variety, is not opposed to the tragic, and is able to account for its challenges. For the purposes of this study, it will do so by localizing this tension on an area of deep importance for the classical orthodox tradition, namely, its grammar of transcendence. In this way, it provides a node of concentration for what is otherwise a daunting and complex tradition, showing how its language of transcendence impacts its reception of the tragic. (2) It will have to express sensitivity to the aporias of contingency, since it is precisely these factors which give the tragic its edge, and provides fodder for the critics of orthodoxy. And (3) it will also need to demythologize certain entrenched perspectives on the tragic, which for understandable reasons are often associated with the unremittingly catastrophic. It needs to address these concerns because if they remain in place, they express an incompatibility with a Christian account of redemption. As regards my argument, I will suggest that a 'MacKinnonesque' position, as modified by Williams, is one that is able to address these concerns, insofar as it takes historicity and tragedy seriously within a more-or-less orthodox position, while simultaneously addressing the particularity of tragic experience. In this study, I hope to see if such compatibility is a workable and coherent one within the theological assumptions here adopted.

Returning to the over-arching tensions as regards tragedy and transcendence, it appears beneficial to anticipate some of my arguments, so that we can concretize some of the debates I am referencing. On the one hand, one can see that a 'transcendence' which avoids historicity evades the problem, since finitude—in theatre and in life—remains an essential trait of the tragic; any theology which avoided this factor would remain unable to address or absorb the insights of tragedy. In terms of an 'orthodox' response, one would then have to show that aseity (and the analogy of being[6]) are not opposed to the experience of time and development. On the other hand, if history and its tragic outcomes are transcendentalized then this produces conclusions which a classical theology would want to caution against. As I suggest later, a traditional or classically-orthodox metaphysics would reject three interrelated revisions that are occasioned by this acceptance: namely, *the concept of a suffering God, the rejection of evil-as-privation,* and *the (post) modern aesthetics of the sublime.*

---

6. Especially after Aquinas, Catholic theology has tended to read 'transcendence' within an analogical metaphysics that conjectures a participation of finite being within God's infinite act of being. This does not imply a reduction of God to finitude, but rather a similarity within an ever-greater dissimilarity.

Of course, in a genealogical perspective these are distinct phenomena that have arisen in different historical stages, and so are not reducible to each other. But it will be argued,[7] that they are connected and converge within their substance. For instance, it argues that *the concept of a suffering God* ultimately 'ontologizes' suffering and evil,[8] and that this move has metaphysical implications, insofar as it tacitly opposes *evil-as-privation*. Firstly, this is because the transcendent good is conceived as mutable and therefore not infinite, as modified or placed 'over-against' contingency and evil; and, secondly, evil is granted a status of its own that is independent of the Good, since it exists as 'something,' whereas classically-orthodox metaphysics has asserted that evil has no existence of its own. On this account, evil or suffering becomes a 'substance' in itself, replete with a distinct existence, being no longer reducible to an ontological perversion. This revision, moreover, renders 'Being' as both good and evil (e.g., Manichaeism), or as 'beyond good and evil' (e.g., Nietzschean-postmodern tragic sublime[9]), since once you ascribe a discrete 'existence' to evil, then 'evil' becomes an expression of 'Being.' Once 'evil' and 'suffering' are given a non-parasitic 'existence'—to the extent that they *exist* in a univocal sense to other existents—then this grants them an independence that is equal with the Good. This is irreconcilable with a classical metaphysics which says that the Good is convertible with Infinite Being. If one accords 'being' to evil, then it is hard to avoid an equiprimordiality of evil with the Good. It is this conclusion that suggests there is an *ontological pessimism* within such a tragic vision, since now 'Being' is severed from any special affinity to the Good, a move which promotes an 'ontological violence' and a politics based on the irreconcilability of human goods (á la Hobbesian liberalism).[10] And it is this 'pessimism'—as witnessed in the writings of George Steiner—that supports ideas of unremitting disaster as belonging to the essentially tragic, and buttresses arguments that Christianity and the tragic are finally opposed.[11]

7. Rowan Williams's arguments in this regard which will be detailed in Chapter 3 and Chapter 7.

8. This is not to say that *all* suffering is reducible to evil. There are varieties of suffering which are linked to the natural impingements of finitude, and are by-no-means evil as such.

9. See Critchley, "The Tragical Sublime," 169–85.

10. Here my argument is in large agreement with the work of John Milbank and others (e.g., Adrian Pabst). However, it should be said that this is not an exclusive explanation; there is a multitude of causation, both historical and intellectual, for any political tradition.

11. As regards 'tragedy' as such, we are not bound to this schema. For in Hegel's reading (as read by Rowan Williams), tragic conflict is not a question of irresolvable dualities, but rather "one-sidedness." 'Goods' are not mutually opposed, as in the usual

It is at this moment that the debate between our main discussion partners becomes intelligible. All of them, Hart and Milbank, MacKinnon and Williams, serve as representatives of theological orthodoxy, specifically as regards the theme of transcendence. However, it is the differences between them as regards 'the tragic' that require explanation; such an explanation pivots around MacKinnon, and the others's responses to him, since he is a figure central to the *modern*[12] theological debate surrounding 'the tragic.' It is in the critical reception of his work, and the particular tradition he mediates (e.g., Kantianism), that many of the key contentions will be adjudicated.

However, it appears helpful to speak briefly regarding method and my own situatedness in this argument.

On Beginning in the Middle

A word on method and assumptions: as a theologian, one has to begin somewhere, and that 'somewhere'—as Rowan Williams has suggested—is "the middle of things."[13] One begins where one is at, where one is located, within all the 'middles' this implies. Any theology is 'placed' and cannot pretend otherwise; even the most systematic or interlaced arrangement can never be totally "self-referential" or "auto-poetic."[14] One should emphasize this once more: theologies arise within contexts and the interplay between locations and their informing traditions (their history, culture, language, religiosity, etc.). Every theology has 'orthodoxies,' since theologies—no matter how radical, venerable or established—cannot erase this limitation. Without this factor, we would be unable to say anything with coherency or fidelity. On the one hand, this is an existential necessity since we cannot step out of our own skins, so to speak. But on the other this reality intimates a theological truth also: that out knowledge of God is always socially and historically mediated. As finite beings, our rationality is sequential and diachronic, and so (because of this) theological language is a *learned* discourse, and is entwined with those habits that cultivate it. Or to adopt Marxist

---

reading. Instead, they are misrecognised as being ultimate. 'Reconciliation' is about learning to recognize my good as bound to yours, and it is the refusal of this that occasions tragic conflict.

12. In this study, the language of 'modern' is often a circumlocution for 'contemporary.' However, it is also clear (especially after Chapter 3) that 'modern' carries with it overtones of 'modernity' as well.

13. Williams, "Prologue," in *On Christian Theology*, xii.

14. The language is drawn from Michael Murrmann-Kahl, "*Mysterium trinitatis*," 1–16.

phraseology, orthodoxies are "produced,"[15] and gather their viability as they capacitate the traversal of 'symbolic capital' across diverse contexts and strata.[16] But because these 'texts' and 'contexts' are continuously produced and appraised, they are neither value-neutral nor 'natural.' They are living and vibrant systems fabricated through historical signs and material practices, semantic densities that are subject to time and alteration.[17] Theological reflection occurs within this flux, and the often "unsystematized speech" that is awakened within it.[18] Once more, as theologians we are placed within 'the middle.' We are unable to erase those "life-worlds" (*Lebenwelten*) and "backgrounds" (*Umwelten*) that shape us—including the present author. As a white African male, a descendent of European colonizers and refugees, I am shaped by Western tendencies of thought. This can be discerned, for example, in my metaphysical and genealogical proclivities, my preference for 'historicism,' as well as my choice of subject-matter, which is dominated by North Atlantic, Euro-American men. However, one should also stress that being placed in a country like South Africa makes one sensitive to questions which might not be readily apparent in others. The daily admixture of joy and despair, of laughter within the *vallis lacrimarum*, that is experienced everyday by a majority of black and brown South Africans, cannot be lost on any sensitive commentator. Tragedy, real or fictional, is not just a Hesperian phenomenon. In this light, my study is contextual, personal and 'biographical,' in the sense that it exhibits what Williams has called the "lived incoherence" of theological writing, a factor which reminds us of "the inescapable place of repentance in all theological speech worth the name."[19] Alluding to this should not, however, act as an alibi for ersatz or hazy argumentation, but should rather remind us of the angularity of its composition.

Locatedness and particularity are intrinsic to know where one is speaking from. We cannot escape our 'middles.' But then how does one retain rigor or accountability? What approach should we take to maintain 'objectivity'? Here, I will adapt some concepts used by Vincent Brümmer[20] (and others[21]) to unravel my method and assumptions presupposed in this study. Firstly, as previously stated, my argument works within a trajectory of

15. Certeau, *The Writing of History*, 17–113.

16. Bourdieu, "The Production of Belief: Contribution to an Economy of Symbolic Goods," in *The Field of Production*, 74–111.

17. Ward, *How the Light Gets In*, 131–35.

18. Cf. Williams, "Prologue," xii–xiii.

19. Williams, "Prologue," xvi.

20. See Brümmer, "The Intersubjectivity of Criteria in Theology," in *Brümmer on Meaning and the Christian Faith*, 453–70.

21. Brand, *Speaking of a Fabulous Ghost*, 38–57.

classical and orthodox metaphysics, and therefore aims to express *continuity* within this stream. I work within this 'tradition,' one that traces its origins to those scriptural and patristic sources that provided the early seed-bed for Christian thought.[22] This specificity establishes the limits and objectivity of the work, insofar as it projects not just any object, but a particular one. But I know that one cannot simply repeat formulae without an awareness of how such language works in the present, and the overtones this might or might not carry due to changed circumstances and historical resonance.[23] This suggests that translation and 'non-identical' repetition remain essential for the process of handing-over, and that Christian 'identity' does not persist apart from this, and assists us with understanding the theological criterion of *relevance*—the ability to speak to one's time—or what McCurry has called *traditioned creativity*. To quote Rowan Williams "orthodoxy" (or tradition) remains "something still future," which "means that a briskly undialectical rhetoric" of "conserving" or "defending" any "clear deposit of faith may come less easily to us," since "Orthodoxy continues to be made."[24] Therefore, we cannot make the assumption that holding strictly onto dogmas or scriptural language will guarantee faithfulness to the tradition. On the contrary, sometimes one requires a leap of imagination, a rupture within language, to maintain identity within the present.

Moreover, I do not assume a homogenous tradition devoid of diverse streams and counter-arguments, as well as persecuted or minority voices. I presume a complex tradition, and affirm an existential requirement that different historical periods or contexts might require a shifting or pragmatic emphasis of one stream over another. This addresses the problem of practical *adequacy*: that the "symbolic capital" of one or another stream might change or dissipate—depending on its historical location. As the past shows, repressed traditions may become 'orthodoxy' and mainline traditions 'heretical' insofar as they are able to, or fail to, open deeper ranges of meaning and *coherency*.[25] This point is important to stress: throughout this study in particular I will note again and again the ideal of a 'systematic' coherence as regards the relation between classically-inclined Christian metaphysics and 'the tragic.' Such coherency is applicable to the question of its internal theological consistency, but also has connection to other regimes of knowledge. Ideally, it should offer an aesthetic and persuasive power, a

22. Brümmer's reflections in "The Identity of the Christian Tradition," in *Brümmer on Meaning and the Christian Faith*, 375–89 for a philosophical account of 'tradition.'

23. See Lash, *Theology on the Way to Emmaus*, 55–58, for more on this.

24. Williams, *Arius*, 24–25.

25. As Williams says, heresy is largely about "a major reduction in the range of available sources of meaning" ("What is Catholic Orthodoxy," 16).

capacity to account for diverse experiences and language-games within a comprehensive vision.[26] In other words, it should exhibit *credibility*. If it fails to do so, or demonstrates a lack of coherency with available knowledge, its epistemic plausibility will suffer as a consequence. This does not necessarily mean that such a position is completely wrong or misguided, since novel hypotheses might propose a vision at odds with current sciences, and still be finally more correct (Galileo is an example of this).[27] Still, theological traditions should aspire to an elegance of explanation, and not incoherency. This applies not only to the principle of non-contradiction, but touches on broader theological themes as well.

For example, from its inception Christian orthodoxy has constituted an attempt to garner a 'world,' and an intelligible arrangement of how we are situated in it. For Christianity, this 'world' assumes unity and rationality, since God is one and not divided. For this reason, the narrative of redemption cannot be localized in an exclusionary way, because that would imply that God's dealings with creation were not reflective of the divine nature. The possibility of a radically *different* path towards salvation would imply there was a *different* god, thus undermining Oneness. If God's actions were fundamentally disparate, one could not confess the deity of the biblical traditions. Apart from this metaphysical unity, the acclamation of 'truth' would be rendered dubious, since now there would be no trans-historical 'sense' in which the world could be 'read.' It is this drift towards sense-making, of having a unified sense of 'world,' that inspired the early Christians to construct narratives about themselves, and the universe they inhabited.[28]

Coherency and *credibility* also touch upon another area, namely what Brümmer calls *intersubjectivity*. This aspect privileges accountability between discourses, and the necessity of a continuing encounter, so they will not become isolated and insular in their scope. In other words, our argument will have to balance a desire for the 'systematic' while also maintaining a sense of 'realism,' an awareness that it is not reducible to an internal "language game."[29] It must remain alert to its finite and perspectival nature, and the particular tradition it works within. Of course, such an argument desires to demonstrate the intellectual resilience of this tradition in particular, but it does not try to be exhaustive or all-encompassing. It represents *an* argument

---

26. My theology of persuasion is influenced by Hart, *The Beauty of the Infinite*, and Milbank, *Theology and Social Theory*.

27. See Feyerabend, *Against Method*.

28. Williams, "Origen"; Williams "Defining Heresy," 324–27. Also, cf. Williams, "The Unity of Christian Truth," in *On Christian Theology*, 16–28

29. For a critique of an 'intertextual' theology, see Williams, "The Judgement of the World," in *On Christian Theology*, 29–43; Dehart, *The Trial of the Witnesses*.

situated within a very specific debate, and in our case, on the relation between the grammars of transcendence and the tragic. In this context, however, there remains the question of how one retains 'realism' or 'objectivity'—here assuming the theological requirement that our language gives us "*access to something other than itself.*"[30] Here *intersubjectivity* assists with the external criteria of 'objectivity' in terms of responsibility and accountability to other language-games. However, Christianity has its own internal resources of 'objectivity' that are unique to its 'object,' namely God.

Speech about God should demonstrate real transcendence. And yet how does religious speech show this? One suggests that theological speech moves in the right direction to the degree that it does what it *says* it does.[31] Its argumentation, its style and form, should bear witness to the peculiarity of its object. As Williams suggests, theology cannot claim a "total perspective" because "there can be no conversation with a total perspective."[32] Consequentially, language about God must express "dispossession"—to use another phrase of Williams[33]—if it is to demonstrate its integrity, an integrity that "*declines the attempt to take God's point of view.*"[34] For him, "the truth of a religious claim is a matter of discovering its resource and scope for holding together and making sense of our perceptions and transactions without illusion."[35] This move relates itself to the criteria of unity and coherency. But it must therefore express accountability to its transcendent object, and should not remain stuck within a self-immunizing system. For Williams, theological language articulates 'realism' insofar as it is "done in ways that are open to continuing scrutiny and revision." Thereby, it "shows that we are serious about the extra-mental by certain features of our linguistic behaviour," and "by the exposure of our representations to response and correction or expansion, by behaving as though they were accountable to something more than their own inner logic or the convenience of the speaker."[36] It must evidence a transparency, a dispossession, a willingness "to *display* modes of arguing and interpreting rather than to advance a single system."[37] In this light, one may paraphrase Gadamer:

---

30. Williams, "'Religious Realism': On Not Quite Agreeing with Don Cupitt," in *Wrestling with Angels*, 247. However, the entire chapter is instructive in this regard.

31. For this argument, see Williams, "Theological Integrity," in *On Christian Theology*, 3–15.

32. Williams, "Theological Integrity," 5.

33. Williams, "Theological Integrity," 8–12.

34. Williams, "Theological Integrity," 7.

35. Williams, "Theological Integrity," 14.

36. Williams, *The Edge of Words*, 77.

37. Williams, "Prologue," xvi.

when it comes to the question of theological argumentation, *the truth is in the method*. Or to put it differently, the question of *how* one argues is intrinsically related to *what* one argues.

So while this study hopes to bypass any gestures towards "totalization,"[38] and is therefore resigned to the "lived incoherence" of particularity, one should emphasize that it remains committed to larger questions of *meaning* that are essential for theological argumentation.[39] It has a regard for those 'systematic' aporias that arise within the juxtaposition of thought-worlds, while holding onto a vision of 'integrity' or 'coherence' that is intrinsic to sense-making. Theology can never be parochial or ghettoized: the situatedness of all regimes of discourse does not necessitate reductionism. This is because any 'context' is always-already situated in a more comprehensive 'text' that prohibits closure,[40] since every cultural production is encoded within a scope that cannot be pre-emptively foreclosed. Therefore, any index apart from its setting of intelligibility risks mystification, since singularities are not comprehended without their placing. Instead, the imagining of a 'context' involves connecting 'life-worlds' to a whole, to an intuited 'totality'—or in the case of theology, to a sense of the divine. It is this intuition that remains essential for 'systematic theology,' insofar as it brings all existence into the remit of the divine light. To quote Aquinas: "in sacred science, *all things* [my italics] are treated of under the aspect of God: either because they are God Himself or because they refer to God as their beginning and end."[41] If this is true, then reality has its *raison d'être* in divinity, since every existent is dependent on God and reflects God as cause. 'Systematic theology' is therefore inextricably connected to the logic of creation, insofar that it traces the multiplicity of existents to a divine plenitude.[42] It is this assumption that motivates the drive within 'systematic theology' towards imagining 'the whole'—a *théologie totale* (Sarah Coakley). And it is this

---

38. My understanding of "totalization" is drawn from the realm of critical theory, and to some extent coheres with the understanding of the term as found in Adorno and Levinas. For a brief and critical discussion of the idea of 'system' in relation to "totalization," see Adorno, *Negative Dialectics*, 24–28.

39. See Brümmer, "Spirituality and the Hermeneutics of Faith." On the history of the term 'sense,' see the entries in Cassin, *Dictionary of Untranslatables*: Burgee, "Common Sense," 152–54; Cassin et al., "Sense / Meaning," 949–67; and Libera, "Sensus Communis," 967–68.

40. This I take to be Derrida's central contribution.

41. Aquinas, *Summa Theologiae*, I.1.7.

42. Williams, "What is Systematic Theology?," and Webster, "Principles of Systematic Theology."

which gives systematics its inter-disciplinary tendency, its desire to connect 'sacred doctrine' to diverse fields of study.[43]

It is therefore an assumption of this study that the practice of systematic theology requires a 'metaphysic,' that is, an attempt to think the multiple in its dependency on the One and, contrariwise, to show the One as reflected in the Many. In other words, it should account for this reality of divergence, while making conjectures regarding their interconnections within a prior unity. Admittedly, the language of 'metaphysics,' and especially after Martin Heidegger, has received a significant amount of bad publicity. One only mentions "ontotheology"[44] and there is a clamor to be distanced from it. According to Heidegger, it is by considering 'Being' as the *Grund* of 'beings' that we, on the one side, forget the question of Being itself, and, on the other, ultimately include God within a causality that denies real transcendence.[45] In the wake of this diagnosis, modern theology has castigated 'metaphysics' as promoting an abstract deity with precious resemblance to the living God of revealed theology (e.g., Karl Barth). Or to adopt an even stronger version, it has been argued that 'metaphysics' aims to construct an idolatrous God *within* finite 'being,' and therefore that the God of metaphysics (or ontotheology) cannot be the 'God' of the Christian tradition (e.g., Jean-Luc Marion). These criticisms are not without merit, and this study is in solidarity with several of its concerns. Nonetheless, it must be said that the history of 'metaphysics' is rather variegated, and cannot be reduced to Heideggerian genealogy.[46] One must remain alert to the ruptures within medieval metaphysics and thereafter, and avoid

---

43. See Graham Ward's chapter in "What is an Engaged Systematics?" in Ward, *How the Light Gets In*, 115–44. Also see Coakley's reflections on systematics as a *théologie totale* in *God, Sexuality, and the Self*, 33–65.

44. As is well known, the term was invented by Kant, and thereafter taken up by Heidegger: "Transcendental theology either thinks that the existence of an original being is to be derived from an experience in general (without more closely determining anything about the world to which this experience belongs), and is called cosmotheology; or it believes that it can cognize that existence through mere concepts, without the aid of even the least experience, and is called ontotheology" (Kant, *The Critique of Pure Reason*, A 632 = B 660).

45. Heidegger, "The Onto-Theo-Logical Constitution of Metaphysics," in *Identity and Difference*, 42–74.

46. Boulnois, "Quand commence l'ontothéologie?"; Boulnois, *Être et représentation*; Boulnois, *Métaphysique rebelles*; Courtine, *Suarez et le système de la métaphysique*; Libera, "Genèse et structure des métaphysique médiévales," 159–81; Esposito, "Heidegger, Suárez e la storia dell'ontologia"; Esposito, "The Hidden Influence of Suárez," 117–34; Esposito, "Suárez and the Baroque Matrix of Modern Thought," 124–47; Grondin, *Introduction to Metaphysics*; Honnefelder, "Der zweite Anfang der Metaphysik"; Honnefelder, *Scientia transcendens*; Lamanna, "Ontology between Goclenius and Suárez."

overly-linear narratives of decline. 'Metaphysics' has multiple histories of "disruption"[47] that require re-narration. As regards my own metaphysical assumptions, however, I can say that they remain more-or-less classical and Thomistic in their temperament. For if Oliva Blanchette is correct, then a Thomistic metaphysics already states that it is only from *particular* beings that a meaning of 'Being' is extrapolated, since to the degree that any contingent entities *are*, they give an aperture into the *to be*. For Aquinas, the richness of being, of the *to be*, means that the multitude of beings 'intensively' reflects that infinite being in which all things live, move, and have their being.[48] This already exceeds Heidegger's history of metaphysics, and probably absolves Aquinas from charges of ontotheology.[49]

Since I have now "recollected" some of the characteristics of the theological method,[50] we may move onto a schematic of my argument.

The Argument

In terms of our chapter outline, the majority of this study centers upon a critical exposition of Donald MacKinnon's *The Problem of Metaphysics* (1974) and Rowan Williams's *The Tragic Imagination* (2016). Why I have decided, methodologically, to focus on these texts will become clear as we go on. But simply stated, one can say that MacKinnon, even until the present day, remains a significant discussion partner within the theological conversation on the tragic. Therefore, it appears logical that our discussion focus on the book where his most mature presentation appears. Much of this same reasoning could be adduced for choosing *The Tragic Imagination*. To date, it constitutes Williams's only monograph-length consideration of this question—which is why it has received a prominent place in this study.

Chapter 2 investigates where the tensions between orthodox Christianity and the tragic *might* have arisen. Here I argue that a retrojection of conflict onto abstract terms such as 'Christianity' and 'the tragic' fails to address those peculiar strategies employed by early and medieval Christians. Our exposition is however premised upon a prior story, namely the placement of Attic tragedy within the debate between the poets and the philosophers (e.g., Plato). Thereafter, I discuss how 'tragedy' was transmuted into

47. For this language, see Foucault, *The Archaeology of Knowledge*, 1–33.

48. Blanchette, *Philosophy of Being*, 83–144; Te Velde, *Aquinas on God*, 65–93.

49. For an argument showing that Aquinas should not be classed under ontotheology, see Marion, "Thomas Aquinas and Onto-theo-logy," 288–311.

50. See Brümmer, "Philosophical Theology as Conceptual Recollection," in *Brümmer on Meaning and the Christian Faith*, 433–52.

the Christian period, here suggesting that any hard rejection of 'tragedy' as such is rare, and that when 'tragedy' *is* criticized it is due to an alignment with anti-theatrical sentiments which were not exclusively Christian. On the contrary, the patristic and medieval periods display a variety of responses to tragic themes, many of which are positive and creative. Thus it appears that the tensions between Christianity and the tragic only really become marked in the *modern* theological scene, which suggests that there are other more recent developments at hand which have produced them. This is exemplified within the proposals of some literary critics (e.g., George Steiner), and in the contemporary reception of Donald MacKinnon (e.g., David Bentley Hart and John Milbank).

In Chapter 3, I attempt to display where these moments of tension lie. It is suggested that a central problematic is the configuration of transcendence, particularly as regards to divine aseity. Thereafter, it suggests that the *modern* fabrication of a tension between Christianity and the tragic is manifest within three tendencies, all related to the nature of 'transcendence.' Most pointedly, it is connected to *the invention of the tragic* within European classicism and philosophy. Of these tendencies, it is particularly (1) *the concept of the Kantian sublime* (e.g., Schiller) and (2) *a metaphysic of the suffering Absolute* (e.g., Schelling and Hölderlin) that provides a lucid connection between 'the tragic' and transcendence, and moreover how such trends create problems for aseity. These in turn are related to another trend which argues that an acceptance of the tragic implies (3) *a rejection of the Platonic-Augustinian notion of evil-as-privation* (e.g., Kathleen Sands, George Steiner), and with it any ontological priority of goodness. It is then suggested that a more classical metaphysics will have to address these developments.

Chapter 4 exposits the contemporary theological debate on the tragic, especially as this has occurred in the critical reception of Donald MacKinnon in David Bentley Hart and John Milbank. Hart's criticisms of MacKinnon are not exclusively addressed to MacKinnon but to tragic drama as such, which he reads as proposing a "sacrificial totality." But as regards MacKinnon himself, Hart argues that reading the gospel tragically ends-up misrepresenting the radicalness of Christ's resurrection, and intimates a vision that tacitly advances the ontologization of violence. Milbank's critique is related but more expansive: he would agree with Hart on the question of ontological pessimism and violence, since MacKinnon categorically rejects the *privatio boni*. However, he also brings an emphasis on MacKinnon's Kantianism in a way that implicates him in a politics of liberalism and a post-Schillerian aesthetics of the sublime. It is this latter tendency, so Milbank claims, that is connected to MacKinnon's rejection of a Catholic doctrine of analogy, a move which in turn hinders MacKinnon from relating the historical to the metaphysical.

Chapter 5–6 aims to address these critiques to see whether they hit their mark. To do this, I engage in an extensive reading of Donald MacKinnon's *The Problem of Metaphysics*. I begin by analyzing MacKinnon's encounter with Aristotle and Kant's metaphysics before moving onto his reading of Plato and Kantian ethics, thereafter turning to his reflections on the tragic. Our conclusions are mixed: overall, I confirm Milbank's critique of MacKinnon, but express disagreement as regards the tragic. In the end, nonetheless, I suggest that MacKinnon is finally unable to coherently relate the immanent to the transcendent, that is, in a way that is able to affirm the ultimate goodness of Being. I think he remains entrenched, unwittingly, in a modern regime of the sublime. This is due to his Kantianism and his apparent rejection of the *analogia entis*, as well as the concept of evil-as-privation.

Our next two chapters (7–8) will gravitate towards the contributions of Rowan Williams, who in our estimate provides the most admirable synthesis of the tensions I have been addressing. On the one hand, he expounds an analogical metaphysics that includes historicity, as seen in his reflections on poetics, language and analogy. Moreover, unlike MacKinnon, Williams is completely committed to the *privatio boni* and divine non-passibility, a move which assists him in avoiding the critiques of Hart and MacKinnon. On the other hand, he provides a riposte to Milbank and Hart as regards tragedy, thereby showing how the story might be more complicated than Milbank and Hart's conclusions appear to imply.

In my final chapter, there is a summary of my argument. In terms of our most pertinent question (namely '*can a classical account of transcendence affirm the tragic?*'), my argument suggests that Williams provides a correction and supplementation to MacKinnon's approach. Firstly, he avoids Hart and Milbank's critiques of divine suffering—as well as their accusations of ontological violence and pessimism—as being incompatible with an orthodox perspective. Secondly, his affirmation of the *privatio boni* refuses an absolutization of evil, which MacKinnon's position was unable to sufficiently counter-act. Moreover, his acceptance of a modified Augustinianism at this point denies any order or meaning to evil and suffering per se. Such enables Williams to do at least two things: (1) it refuses any theodicy which grants meaning to *all* suffering, as if evil could be 'justified' as an alignment with the best of possible worlds. On the contrary, evil and suffering *as such* have no necessary ordering towards the truth, and therefore should not be assumed as having meaningfulness. However, (2) such a perspective does not exclude the ability of human beings to *create* meaning out of suffering and tragedy, specifically in the way that trauma becomes representable between relational agents. Additionally, Williams's clear denial of an eschatological cancellation of tragedy, and his suggestion that the risen body includes its wounds, is able to maintain (in a different fashion) what MacKinnon dubbed "the transcendence of the tragic" or what Paul Janz calls "the finality of non-resolution." Because of this, one could say then that Williams affirms the *negativity of the tragic*, while including an amelioration of its finality. Thirdly, Williams's conceptual superiority over MacKinnon becomes clearer as regards the contemporary sublime. As will be argued, MacKinnon's metaphysics was ultimately unclear in his postulation of the convertibility of goodness with being, and that this was linked to his rejection of the *privatio boni*. However, because Williams clearly endorses the evil-as-privation doctrine, and cogently defends Augustine's position against its critiques, it appears that Williams does not fall into the tradition of sublimity that conceptually ails MacKinnon. It is at this juncture where my study tries to make a unique contribution: it seeks to relate Williams's analyses, specifically within *The Tragic Imagination*, to his larger metaphysical enterprise, and to questions that were not addressed in the constraints of that work. Moreover, it draws out his implicit critique of Kantian sublimity and its postmodern iterations, as this is found in its assertions of the unthinkability and unspeakability of pain—implications which he did not substantially tease-out in *The Tragic Imagination*. However, and despite all of the benefits of Williams's position, his conclusions have not been uncriticized, and so in the conclusion I will detail some of the critiques and some of the questions which might be left open.

As I make our transition to the next chapter, here is a revision of what I have discussed: at the beginning, I outlined our theme as this was related to the supposed tensions between a classical account of 'transcendence' and 'the tragic.' There I hinted how this debate is incarnated within the contemporary discussion between Hart, Milbank, MacKinnon and Williams. I then suggested a structure for the development of this argument, specifically as it proceeds through a critical reception of MacKinnon's work, and its supplementation by Williams. Thereafter, I disclosed my assumptions as regards method, here drawing upon Vincent Brümmer and Rowan Williams. Moreover, I suggested (after Williams) that transparency and dispossession should become intrinsic to theological argumentation. I also stated how the method of 'systematics' requires a 'metaphysics,' specifically as this seeks to relate the particularity of contexts to a wider scope of intellectual integrity and coherency.

In the following chapter, I address my understanding of tragic drama, with a particular focus on how tragic themes were appropriated by Plato and patristic-medieval thinkers. This is done with the aim of discerning where the supposed tensions between Christianity and the tragic are focused. In it, I suggest that things might be more complicated than the common narrative might suggest, and that the opposition between Christian theology and tragedy might be a confabulation of modern critics and theologians. This is important for our task insofar as it relates to our attempt to investigate where the tensions between Christianity and the tragic are to be located, and whether they remain valid within the current discussion. Our sense from reading the literature is that the enduring suspicions of tragedy within Christianity are related to an unstable Platonic evaluation of theatre in general. Moreover, these voices are not magisterial but rather minor when compared to the deluge of positive or neutral receptions among pre-modern Christian writers. The history suggests, therefore, that there is by-no-means a necessary contradiction between Christian language and tropologies of the tragic. However, it does raise the question where these tensions have arisen in the past. In this regard, I suggest that it is among modern critics that there have been developments that have tended to reify and essentialize 'Christianity' and 'the tragic' into mutually-exclusive visions, a move not required by the availing evidence. This insight, in the light of our general argument, will assist us exploring the relationship between the classical tradition of orthodoxy and 'tragedy' in the broadest sense of that term, and our question regarding their conceptual reconciliation.

2

On the Not-So-Ancient Quarrel of Tragedy and Christianity

This chapter will attempt to lay-out a definition of 'tragedy' and 'the tragic.' In doing so, it seeks to problematize the opposition between the performative and the reflective as regards tragic drama. It suggests that 'tragedy' at its origins was engaged in contemplation (*theoria*), and was always-already amenable to philosophical readings. Thereafter, our deconstruction is strengthened through an analysis of Plato, with the purpose of showing that his contribution is unstable, a fact which renders his vituperations against the tragic (and theatre more generally) as open to immanent critique. After that, I offer a brief account of the reception of tragedy within patristic and medieval thinkers, showing that there is by-no-means a single strategy of response in this regard. 'Tragedy' and 'the tragic' were deployed in multiple ways by diverse thinkers, and was not received in a negative light by the majority. This then raises the question as to where the perceived tensions between Christianity and the tragic arise. Here already there is a sense that the opposition might be a relatively recent creation, and could have a lot to do with the *modern* invention of 'the tragic,' as well as reductive readings of Christian tradition *and* the tragic. This idea is developed more in Chapter 3, but already there are some intimations of this development.

On 'Tragedy' and 'the Tragic'

At the outset one can say that the language of 'tragedy' has a history and, moreover, is an effective history. One could even suggest that 'tragedy' has in diverse ways stimulated the turn to 'history' in both ancient and modern times.¹ Already then, Attic drama connected the typologies of mythic folklore to politico-juridical debates within the ancient city, being traceable to the "invention"² of theatre in fourth century Athens (around 534 BCE).³ As is now well-known, the etiology of tragedy has been sourced within the City Dionysia, and was linked to Dionysos and the sacrificial cult in ancient Greece, even though the exact nature of this causality remains murky.⁴ We cannot avoid the religious element within the genesis of tragedy, and will return to it again. But it must be emphasized here that tragedy also served as a paradigm of political engagement, one which sought to expose the fragility of the Athenic city-state, as it was formed during an important period of cultural transition. This was revealed within those liminalities between 'legal' traditions that emphasized personal responsibility under law, and those 'archaic' and 'heroic' traditions (stemming from Homeric theology) that sought to assert the often-inscrutable justice of the gods, and (in particular) the excessiveness of Dionysos.⁵ Here the mythological foundations of the πόλις were no longer immune from investigation and critique, but were migrated into the terrain of political scrutiny. Within this movement, it was particularly the hero who was subject to interrogation: in tragedy, she or he ceases to be a *model* to be simplistically emulated, but a *problem* to be represented (Vernant). This politicizing trend can also be seen in the way that tragic art ascribed a greater importance to human agency than earlier mythical presentations which did not disclose this sensitivity.⁶ Such emphasis on human volition (not to be understood in the post-Enlightenment

---

1. For the modern period, see Leonard, *Tragic Modernities*, 72–107.

2. In the words of Vernant, even though tragedy was thoroughly informed by its context and historical 'moment' within Athens, it should still be considered as an 'invention' not fully reducible to its immediate background. For this, see Vernant, "The Historical Moment of Tragedy in Greece: Some Social and Historical Conditions," in Vernant and Vidal-Naquet, *Myth and Tragedy in Ancient Greece*, 23–28.

3. Else, *The Origin and Early Form of Greek Tragedy*.

4. Burkert, "Greek Tragedy and Sacrificial Ritual." On the general religious ethos that informs Attic tragedy, see Halliwell, "Human Limits and the Religion of Greek Tragedy."

5. Vernant, "Tensions and Ambiguities in Greek Tragedy," in Vernant and Vidal-Naquet, *Myth and Tragedy in Ancient Greece*, 29–48. Here one could mention the point raised by Paul Veyne regarding the importance of heroic legends, and how belief in such legends was less subject to the acids of cynicism than even the Olympian deities. This means that the subjection within tragic drama of ancient heroes to moral ambiguity should not be taken lightly, in light of the importance attached to them. See Veyne, *Did the Greeks Believe in Their Myths?*

6. For more on the conception of human volition within Greek tragedy, see Vernant, "Intimations of the Will in Greek Tragedy," in Vernant and Vidal-Naquet, *Myth and Tragedy in Ancient Greece*, 49–84.

sense of an individual will, but as a contributing factor within the matrix of divine-human causalities[7]) has a connection to the democratic impulse that informed early drama—a factor obfuscated somewhat since Aristotle's *Poetics*.[8] The political function of tragedy within this context was to tease out the dangers within the "civic ideology" of the Athenic state,[9] even though it cannot be separated from the ideological drive to establish consensus within its ranks also.[10] Nevertheless, by representing this *agon*, tragedy contributed to the democratic project within ancient Greece, as can be seen, for example, in its emphasis on the presentation of conflict and the balancing of interests within the *demos* of the city (e.g., *The Oresteia*). This is evidenced by all of the great tragedians associated with the golden age of its development, including Aeschylus, Sophocles, and Euripides.[11]

The historicist etiology of Greek tragedy assists to hold in check an overly-generalized recounting of Attic drama,[12] tendencies which (amongst others) stem from the *long dureé* of de-politicized readings of tragedy, as well as Kantian traditions of subjective aesthetics.[13] Such contingencies were combined with the priority of private reading during eras of intense speculation regarding the tragic form, since tragedies were not widely performed in Europe until rather late in its history.[14] This lesson needs to be absorbed, because there has been a tendency to underplay the context that eventuated in the tragic form. Nonetheless, we should not acquiesce to those who militate against its universalizing thrust.[15] One sees from early on that tragedy already invited reflection and abstraction. Within the substance of the drama itself, the tragic Chorus—who are by-no-means simply bystanders in the action or an 'ideal' audience—provide contemplative diatribes on the action being witnessed, often drawing conclusions that are not peculiar to the characters in question, but relate to human experience

---

7. Cf. Lesky, "Decision and Responsibility in the Tragedy of Aeschylus."

8. Rösler, *Polis und Tragödie*; Hall, "Is There a *Polis* in Aristotle's Poetics"; DuBois, "Toppling the Hero."

9. On the function of tragedy in regard to the 'civic ideology' of Athens, see Goldhill, "The Great Dionysia and Civic Ideology."

10. Longo, "The Theater and the Polis," 12–19.

11. Euben, *The Tragedy of Political Theory*, 67–163.

12. For examples, scholars such Michelle Gellrich have pointedly shown how 'tragedy' often escapes the confines of 'tragic theory.' For this, see *Tragedy and Theory*.

13. Gadamer, *Truth and Method*, 37–49.

14. Goldhill, "Generalizing About Tragedy," 45–65.

15. For instance, see Leonard's comments in *Tragic Modernities*, 166, where she pushes back against the historicizing trend represented by Vernant, suggesting that "the tragic" should also "put tragedy into question."

more collectively,[16] as seen in the Ode to Man (*Antigone* 332–75) and the Chorus's assertion that Oedipus is an instructive paradigm of human unhappiness generally (*Oedipus Tyrannus* 1524–30).[17]

Additionally, the content of 'tragedy' was already generalized within antiquity (as in Aristophanes's *Frogs* and Aristotle's *Poetics*), and by the time of the Roman historian Cassius Dio (c. 150–235 AD) one could already be apply 'tragedy' to historical events, such as Nero's murder of his mother.[18] What this says is that 'tragedy' and 'the tragic' already had developed a degree of formalized content by this time, and that this trend—while certainly exacerbated in the modern period—is not completely unique or unprecedented. One could add to this Charles Segal's comments: he says that Oedipus (or tragedy) has "always be torn between the historicists and the universalizers," and that both sides need "to rescue the work from the other."[19] Similarly, the Cambridge-based classicist Simon Goldhill has spoken of "a double attentiveness" within our reflection on tragedy, one that needs to "pay due attention to the specific socio-political context of ancient drama, while recognizing the drive towards transhistorical truth in the plays'[s] discourse and in the plays'[s] reception." This means that "tragedies and 'the tragic' are in a productive and dialectical tension," and continually need to be placed alongside one another in order for this relation to be beneficial.[20] He goes on to say that because "drama itself is committed to dialogue, to a play or contest of different voices," this means that "the tension between locatedness and generality is integral to Greek tragedy."[21] This is why there is a need to maintain a balance between treating ancient or modern tragedies as "texts," on the one hand, and our ever-changing cultural deployments of them as "scripts" on the other.[22] "Scripts" are linked to "performances," and are tied to our "culturally produced horizons of expectation." While evidencing a "historical

---

16. See Gould, "Tragedy and Collective Experience," and the response by Goldhill, "Collectivity and Otherness."

17. For the so-called 'Ode to Man,' see Segal, "Sophocles' Praise of Man and the Conflicts of the 'Antigone.'" On the Chorus's reflection in *Oedipus Tyrannus*, Kamerbeek writes that "Oedipus' fate is represented as paradigmatic of the human condition, but in such a way that the misery of the man Oedipus is not lost sight of, nor his greatness," in Kamerbeek, *The Plays of Sophocles, Part IV*, 222.

18. I draw this example from Poole, *Tragedy*, 14.

19. Segal, *Sophocles' Tragic World*, 142.

20. Goldhill, *Sophocles and the Language of Tragedy*, 165.

21. Goldhill, *Sophocles and the Language of Tragedy*, 261.

22. Goldhill, *Sophocles and the Language of Tragedy*, 262–63.

contingency," a script "exceeds the process of its performance," and does not ever achieve "the status of an ordinary or fixed object."[23]

One can conclude then that tragedy exhibits a simultaneous tendency towards the particular and the universal, towards the abstractive and the concrete—which is a philosophical gesture. From a hermeneutical perspective, Gadamer has similarly argued that the temporality of an aesthetic consciousness implies a non-identical repetition of an artwork's presence in the here and now. The work becomes "contemporaneous" with our own time, and includes us within it.[24] The same can be said for "the tragic," since it contains "no unchanging essence" to which we are objectively referred, but is made present in multiple forms and to which response is invited.[25] Gadamer says that tragedy is self-involving in this sense because its very definition is included in the "*effect . . . on the spectator.*" But this immersive experience is not merely individualized or subjective, but includes a transformative ecstasy whereby the spectator is temporarily taken outside of themselves through an experience of "commiseration" and "apprehension" (to adapt Aristotle's terms). This provides release and reconciliation with the truth of reality,[26] namely, a discovery of that "tragic suffering" that is "truly common" to the human lot.[27] Thus there is a dynamic interplay in the "tragic pensiveness"[28] of ancient drama, between the *theatrical* moment of ritual immersion (*theoros*) and the *theoretical* moment of reflective contemplation (*theoria*).[29] Once more, we can see how a hard opposition between tragedy and philosophy is tenuous.

However as this dynamic is translated beyond the sphere of theatre as such, one could say (with Larry Bouchard) that there must be a focus on the particularity that 'tragedies' assume—whether they are real or fictional—in order to make responsible generalizations. In applying this observation, our definition of 'tragedy' or 'the tragic' will have an open-texture that makes allowances different and changing concepts of "the tragic as an existential or religious dimension."[30] As a result, this hermeneutical

---

23. Goldhill, *Sophocles and the Language of Tragedy*, 263.

24. Gadamer, *Truth and Method*, 119–25. Gadamer is attempting here to overcome the emphasis on 'alienation' and 'subjectivity' that have characterized aesthetics since the time of Kant and Schiller. See pp. 37–101 for his deeply perceptive reading of this trajectory. For what follows, also see Tate, "Transcending the Aesthetic," 34–50.

25. Gadamer, *Truth and Method*, 125.

26. Gadamer, *Truth and Method*, 126.

27. Gadamer, *Truth and Method*, 128.

28. Gadamer, *Truth and Method*, 127.

29. Gadamer, *Truth and Method*, 122.

30. Bouchard, *Tragic Method and Tragic Theology*, 244.

circle will, in turn, feed back into our definition of tragedy *qua* tragedy, or even expand the meaning of 'the tragic'.[31] This means that there will be interplay between the different manifestations of the tragic, between "the literary, the philosophical, and the vernacular" (here adopting Felski's terms[32]). According to Felski, the "literary" aspect refers to the textual-aesthetic productions of tragic themes (e.g., Aeschylus, Sophocles, Euripides, Shakespeare, Racine, etc.), while "the philosophical" refers to abstract reflections on 'the tragic' (e.g., Plato, Aristotle, Schiller, Hegel, Nietzsche, etc.). Finally, "the vernacular" speaks to that everyday sense of the term, as when we refer to this or that event as being 'tragic.' Such a judgement will also have to be context specific, since not all suffering or death should be deemed tragic.[33] One could say that the tragic expresses a sort of "relativity," since what might destroy one person might not have the same effect on another.[34] Ultimately, the particular circumstances that actualize events should be taken into account. This will assist us in making distinctions between different kinds of pain. Without such distinctions, 'tragedy' as a term would be too diffuse, lacking heuristic usefulness.

In summation, this back-and-forth movement between tragedy as *discourse* and tragedy as *empirical history* appears advantageous for a capacious account of tragic experience,[35] and moreover seems to be internal to the conceptualization of 'the tragic' itself.

On Poets and Philosophers

But if this movement towards the contemplative is already present within tragic drama, then what is one to say about the debate between the poets and philosophers, or, more specifically for our purposes, the debate between

31. Bouchard wonders whether events like Hiroshima and the Shoah can really be classified as tragedies rather than just "events, brutal facts, of such enormity as commonly to provoke the sense that they are different from ordinary events, beyond the grasp of reason" but then backtracks a little by saying that maybe these events change the way we perceive what 'tragedy' or 'the tragic' even means, and writes that "there has never been much warrant for demanding that tragedies comport to sacrosanct formulas" (*Tragic Method and Tragic Theology*, 249).

32. Felski, "Introduction," in Felski, *Rethinking Tragedy*, 2–4.

33. See Bernhardt, "Die Erfahrung des Tragischen als Herausforderung für Theologie," 258–59.

34. Dalferth has spoken of "the relativity of evil" in the sense that evil is always the perversion of something (*von etwas*) for a particular individuals (*für jemanden*). For more detail on this argument, see Dalferth, *Malum*, 86–88.

35. I take this distinction from Janz and his discussion of Donald MacKinnon in *God, the Mind's Desire*, 171–73.

theology and tragedy? The debate has come to be exemplified in concrete terms by Plato's expulsion of the poets from the ideal city. But as we will see things are not quite so simple as far as Plato is concerned.

Against commonplace reductions, one should say that Plato's objections to the poets are only partially based upon the critique of Homeric theology. If this was the main concern of his invective, Plato would be hardly different from Xenophanes, Heraclitus, Pythagoras and the tragic poets (like Euripides), who all in one way or another expressed distaste for an anthropomorphic religion. Plato assumed this as a matter of course, but this is not where the weight of his emphasis lies: his deeper problem with poetry is both more subtle and more radical. His critique can be summarized as follows: while philosophy is concerned with truth, poetry is linked to imitation (*mimesis*). Poetry is about 'appearances' (*doxa*), with the 'look' of things rather than the discovery of things-in-themselves. It is a variety of sophism because it does not attempt to reflect upon the meaning of 'the just' or 'the good,' but is content with the 'opinions' (*doxa*) of the *hoi polloi*. Much like the Sophists, it makes the weaker argument appear stronger through aesthetic embellishment. It does not question the perceived world, but imitates, repeats, and represents it. As a consequence, it promotes the degradation of society and the self, because in being concerned chiefly with a distracting and affective presentation, one can become alienated from a truthful awareness and introspection.

The mimetic impulse then, for Plato, does not concern itself with self-examination, or the moral formation of citizens, but rather surrenders us to the complacency of the present order. Its aesthetic is finally an anaesthetic, a dulling of moral sensibility. Through imitation, one is distanced from ethical personhood, because one aims to imitate 'the other' rather than engage in self-knowledge (*gnōthi seavton*). But since any representation of 'the other' remains at the level of surfaces, the enterprise is rendered doubly superficial, since one is *not* concerned with the thing-in-itself, that is with 'truth,' because 'truth' becomes simply a matter of persuasion and aesthetic adornment. 'Truth' is reduced to mere 'opinion.' It follows then that even if poets give assurance of their afflatus, they are still not concerned with the discovery of truth. They remain unable to put forward a reliable procedure whereby truth might be sought. They mystify rather than clarify their particular *gnosis*. And even if they chance upon wisdom, this would be through happenstance rather than through a maieutic process. Since it could not be *followed* or *taught*, it would therefore be unreliable as a *paideia*. For Plato, poetry—in the broadest sense of any aesthetic representation—ultimately encourages intellectual indolence, a collective enthusiasm rather than critical efficacy.[36] In summary, poetry sits lightly on the question of truth, because *mimesis*, as Plato says, remains "far removed from the truth" (*The Republic* 598b).[37]

But one has to ask: what about Plato's conception of tragedy specifically?[38] On this there are some scattered references throughout Plato's texts: *Philebus* 50b refers to the tragic and comedic aspects of life, as they imply a living fluctuation between pain and pleasure, while *Cratylus* 408b–d implies that the tragic is associated with the 'human' side of the god Pan, and therefore with falsehood. The implication of this is that tragedy fails to give us veridical access to the divinity in its purity, since it locks us into a limited perspective of the material world. Then there is a well-known passage in *Laws* 817b that describes the encounter between the city's lawmakers and a group of tragic actors, in which the guardians describe their ideal as superseding tragic theatre, since they have fashioned the city-state in accordance with "the finest and noblest life," that is, a "tragedy" which is the "best we can create." Another reference can be found in *Phaedo* 115a in which Socrates adopts the position of a tragic character who is destined with a certain kind of death (in this case, suicide by hemlock).

But Plato's most stringent treatments of tragedy are to be found in *The Republic*, especially in Books II, III, and X. There he makes many of the arguments I have mentioned above; but in addition to the critique of *mimesis*, one can mention the following, namely: tragedy's negative portrayal of the gods as the causes of evil (379a–c), its teaching that death is to be feared (386a–387c), that the death of loved ones is a loss of paramount scope (387d–388d), and its intimation that the just and happy life are not necessarily correlated (392b). The most pertinent critique however, as mentioned already, is the tendency for the poets to collapse reality into a form of representation. This impacts on the ethos of the city-state, since those who imbibe tragic emotions will equate such *pathos* with truthfulness. Emotions become disconnected from rational discernment, because the audience is immured in the lamentation that is connected to the experience of death (cf. 605a–d, 606a–b); but this immersion in pity and despair shows that we take death too seriously, and human life also (cf. 604b–c). Ultimately, the real danger of tragedy for Plato, in the words of Stephen Halliwell, is that "emotional responses to tragedy are the carriers of implicit values and thus hold the potential to generate,

---

36. This reading relies upon the excellent essay of Gadamer, entitled "Plato and the Poets," in *Dialogue and Dialectic*, 39–72.

37. Quotations are taken from Plato, *Complete Works*.

38. This paragraph relies on Halliwell, "Plato's Repudiation of the Tragic," 332–49. Also see Critchley, *Tragedy, the Greeks and Us*, 137–82.

or intensify, a tragic sense of life,"³⁹ values which are, in the estimation of Plato, unprofitable for our knowledge of the Good. Imitations that are seen and practiced from youth will become a part of one's nature (395c–d), and Plato worries that tragic theatre does not put forward images worth imitating. Tragedy corrupts those who are nurtured on its vision, making them to more liable to manipulation by tyrants; and therefore it should be excluded from the ideal city he seeks to construct.

It is worth mentioning in passing that such a view is opposed to Aristotle's appreciation of *mimesis*, and tragedy in particular. As he famously said, tragedy is an "imitation of an action that is serious and also, as having magnitude, complete in itself," which in its enactment involves "incidents arousing pity and fear, wherewith to accomplish its catharsis of such emotions" (*Poetics* 1449b22–31).⁴⁰ Aristotle was also more nuanced than Plato as regards suffering and happiness, since he allowed that "the intermediate kind of personage"—a person having good and bad traits—could through their hidden "fault"⁴¹ endure a tragic "discovery" and "reversal" of fortunes (1452b31–38; 1452b10–13; 1452a22–b9). For Aristotle, it appears that imitation had an instructive and phronetic role for the listeners and readers—even if not presented as a spectacle (1453b1–11). For Aristotle, tragedy provides us with a universality that transcends the actors, since it is able to show us (in a delimited arrangement) the connections between actions and their outcomes; it thereby could act (at least on one reading) as a pedagogical measure for those who lack the practical experience that comes with age.⁴² On the moral worth of tragic poetry then, it would seem that Aristotle and Plato could not appear more different.

But this is not the whole story: as already seen above, in Book VII of the *Laws*, Plato considers the ideal city-state as the best kind of "tragedy." As Catherine Pickstock comments, the ideal city-state for Plato is "the true tragedy, not because what occurs there is rueful or dreary, but because the

---

39. Halliwell, "Plato's Repudiation of the Tragic," 345.

40. The translations are taken from Barnes, *The Complete Works of Aristotle*. For a more in-depth philological treatment, see Marx, "La véritable catharsis aristotélicienne," who tries to show that the original function of the *pathēmatōn katharsin* in Aristotle was concerned with the balancing of pity and fear within the context of the ancient theory of humours. However, also compare this with the excellent essay of Jonathan Lear, who contests this kind of reading. See Lear, "Katharsis."

41. For more on *hamartia* and *atē* in Aristotle and elsewhere, as well as the intimate connection between them, see Dawe, "Some Reflections on *Ate* and *Hamartia*."

42. Donini, "*Mimesis* tragique et apprentissage de la *phronesis*," 38–51. This reading is not accepted by Lear in "Katharsis," and appears to be seconded by Critchley in *Tragedy, the Greeks and Us*, 190–92.

city is where the battle of good against evil actually takes place."[43] This alone might imply that Plato works with a looser definition of tragedy that allows for a more positive appreciation of its content. This is especially noticeable in Plato's modes of argument, which can only be tenuously distinguished from theatrical or dramatic presentations.[44] Additionally pertinent is his reference, throughout his writings, to various myths and imagery which are essential to his dialogues. To be sure, this imagery is bracketed by the claim that the philosopher may return to images only after she has grasped the truth that they represent.[45] But their usage should nonetheless give us pause when it comes to evaluating his ultimate position vis-à-vis the tragic—and poetry more generally. In addition to this, there also have been several intelligent attempts to read Plato as a tragic philosopher: whether this applies to his account of reason, and its inability to convince those opposed to it,[46] or his understanding of *eros* as a never-to-be-accomplished search for unity.[47] One could also mention his account of the philosopher-king who must rule in the ideal city, but who is nonetheless condemned to play the dirty and mendacious games of politics in order to rule in the present.[48] And there is the question of whether tragedy as such, with its agonies of moral deliberation, does not already anticipate the dramatic aporias that Plato was deeply concerned with—a fact which intimates that Greek tragedy might have opened the way for Socratic philosophy.[49] Moreover, the suggestion could be made that this ambiguity, both in regard to the content and structure of Plato's philosophy, is echoed in the history of its countervailing receptions.

On Christianity and the Tragic

These tensions will continue to play out in the reception of tragedy, and the theatrical, within some quarters of Christendom. But I will suggest that their supposed opposition is more of a *modern* invention than intrinsic to the subject matter at hand. A full description of this topic is not possible in the space given, and so is here very restricted and eclectic in its scope. But nonetheless, from the representative examples given, it appears that the interaction of Christian theology with tragedy has not followed a linear

43. Pickstock, "Justice and Prudence," 279.
44. Tarrant, "Plato as Dramatist."
45. Cf. Schindler, *Plato's Critique of Impure Reason*, 283–336.
46. Roochnik, *The Tragedy of Reason*.
47. Hyland, "Philosophy and Tragedy in the Platonic Dialogues."
48. Harman, "The Unhappy Philosopher."
49. Kuhn, "The True Tragedy," parts 1 and 2.

mode of development. There is a critique of tragedy that belongs within a wider antipathy towards pagan theatre, as seen in Tertullian, Novation, John Chrysostom, and Augustine—a movement that reached its apogee in Puritan iconoclasm.[50] The decline of theatre in the East and West has been connected by some to the dissemination of Christian culture, especially after the reign of Constantine, as seen in the marked decrease in theatre construction in the period that succeeded it. However, the evidence is ambiguous, and might even reflect changing attitudes towards the theatre among pagans themselves.[51] Nevertheless, even if there was a special causality between Christianity and the decline of theatre, this would apply to all dramatic presentation and not just tragedies.

Additionally, many patristic, medieval and post-Reformation thinkers (as we will see shortly) did *not* express an especially antagonistic relationship to tragedy per se. In fact, the most stringent assertions of a contradiction between Christianity and the tragic have been made in the *modern* period, and appear to be predicated on a presumed antithesis between the respective metaphysics of Christianity and tragedy. It has been argued, especially by certain literary critics, that these two visions cannot be reconciled. For instance, I. A. Richards has said that "[the] least touch of any theology which has a compensating Heaven to offer the tragic hero is fatal."[52] George Steiner has persisted on similar lines when he says that since tragedy is concerned with absolute and irremediable loss, while Christianity is about eschatological recovery, their reconciliation remains unachievable.[53] Karl Jaspers also has concurred insofar as he says that "The believing Christian no longer recognizes genuine tragedy,"[54] a view repeated by D. D. Raphael[55] and Laurence Michel.[56] All of these are significant figures of influence, who have contributed to the perceived irreconcilability of Christian language and the tragic. But it can be argued that these modern critics and philosophers are working within a rather simplistic characterization that does not account for the complexity of these respective traditions, of both Christianity and the tragic. Chief among them is George Steiner, who in many ways remains a key pivot within this development. Steiner is particularly interesting

50. Barish, "The Antitheatrical Prejudice."
51. Barnes, "Christians and the Theater," 315–34.
52. Richards, *Principles of Literary Criticism*, 230–31.
53. Steiner, *The Death of Tragedy*; Steiner, "Tragedy, Pure and Simple," 534–46; Steiner, *No Passion Spent*, 129–41; Steiner, "Tragedy, Reconsidered."
54. Jaspers, *Über das Tragische*, 48: "Der glaubende Christ anerkennt keine eigentliche Tragik mehr."
55. Raphael, *The Paradox of Tragedy*, 37–69.
56. Michel, "The Possibility of a Christian Tragedy."

because he remains theologically literate, and was a close friend of Donald MacKinnon. However, he has been seriously criticized for his tendency to essentialize the tragic via the cipher of "absolute tragedy." For Steiner, "absolute tragedy" concerns sequences of resolute catastrophe and dereliction, events beyond any hope of restoration or amelioration. However, and because of this decision, Steiner also ends-up re-reading the canon of tragic literature through this lens, and as a result excludes significant examples that do not match up to his standard of the absolutely tragic. Here the 'idea' reigns supreme, and diversity is removed through an exclusionary focus. Now it is of course possible that these critics are correct regarding their opposition of Christianity and tragedy, in regards to their specific visions of the world. Whether they are correct or not is something that will become clearer as this study progresses. But in light of the historical evidence to be given shortly, it appears that this conclusion is by-no-means obvious. And if this history paints a more variegated picture, then the assumption of an opposition between Christianity and the tragic cannot be assumed to have substantial pedigree. If anything, it suggests that an assumption of hard and exclusionary opposition is something modern.

In more recent times, theologians such as David Bentley Hart and John Milbank have, in a more nuanced fashion, expressed a continuing opposition between Christianity and the tragic. For his part, Hart is influenced by the readings of someone like George Steiner, who he quotes approvingly in *The Beauty of the Infinite*. However, the anti-tragic reading of Christianity is not consistently upheld by all. One can see this in the nuanced comparisons given by Terry Eagleton who remains sharply critical of the anti-tragic reduction of Christianity and Marxism.[57] Moreover, amongst modern theologians, there has been a more commodious approach to tragic tropes and metaphors—a fact which is undoubtedly connected to a profounder sensitivity to human catastrophe, especially after the debaucheries of the twentieth century. In this vein, Christian theology has undergone a significant transformation, one in which a greater willingness to connect Christianity and the tragic can be seen, as is noticeable in several contemporaneous attempts to re-imagine the divine as a suffering entity. As regards the influence of tragic themes in modern theology, the list is continually expanding.[58] One could mention especially also collected volumes such as

---

57. Eagleton, *Sweet Violence*; Eagleton, *Hope without Optimism*.

58. See especially Balthasar, *The Glory of the Lord*, 101–54; Balthasar, "Tragedy and Christian Faith," 391–411; Bouchard, *Tragic Method and Tragic Theology*; Farley, *Tragic Vision and Divine Compassion*; Quash, *Theology and the Drama of History*; Quash, "Christianity as Hyper-Tragic," 77–88; Rasche "Das Phänomen des Tragischen"; Simon, *Pity and Terror*; Toole, *Waiting for Godot in Sarajevo*; Tracy, "On Tragic Wisdom,"

Christian Theology and Tragedy: Theologians, Tragic Literature, and Tragic Theory (2011), edited by Kevin Taylor and Giles Waller, and also older volumes such as *Christ, Ethics and Tragedy: Essays in Honour of Donald MacKinnon* (1989), edited by Kenneth Surin. Here it can be remarked that both of these volumes are deeply influenced by Donald MacKinnon. This indicates that he has a central place in the current debate regarding the perceived tensions between Christianity and the tragic, and that if one wants to deal with this relation, then MacKinnon remains a deeply important and controversial figure—but more on that later.

However, the appropriation of 'the tragic' within Christianity is not a recent development; on the contrary, tragedy has linkages to the Judeo-Christian tradition from early on. And as I will argue, its reception is more variegated than modern portrayals would imply. To start with, scholars have noticed the similarity of biblical stories to tragic narratives, particularly within the Deuteronomistic History (Saul, David, etc.), with some even suggesting a reliance on Hellenistic sources.[59] One also cannot leave out Old Testament examples like Job, Lamentations or the Suffering Servant of Deutero-Isaiah, that is, in terms of substantial affinity if not actual dependence.[60] One can also detect Hellenistic influence in the earliest sample we have of Jewish playwriting: the *Exagōgē* by Ezekiel the Tragedian (dated in the second century BCE), and of which only fragments have survived.[61] Entering the Christian epoch, however, we discover a variety of receptions that are worth detailing.[62]

13–24; Tracy, "Horror and Horror"; Ward, "Tragedy as Subclause"; Ward, "Steiner and Eagleton"; Williams, *The Tragic Imagination*.

59. Exum, *Tragedy and Biblical Narrative*; Römer, "Why Would the Deuteronomists Tell about the Sacrifice of Jepthah's Daughter?"

60. Theodore of Mopsuestia (c. 350–428), for instance, already in his day thought that the Book of Job was patterned after Greek tragedy. During the Medieval period, theologians made comparisons between Job and Aeschylus's *Prometheus Bound*, often reading it and as a pre-figuring of the suffering undertaken by Christ and the martyrs. In the Renaissance, the Jewish scholar Leone De'Sommi (in 1556) postulated—incorrectly—that the theatre of the Occident was drawn from Hebrew sources rather than Greek, and that the Book of Job was ultimately if not the origin then at least the greatest early example of the tragic form. The Reformer Theodore Beza even turned it into a stage play. For these details, see Pietropaolo, "Whipping Jesus Devoutly," 399–401.

61. A translation of this text can be found in Ezekiel the Tragedian, "*Exagōgē*," in Charlesworth, *Old Testament Pseudepigrapha: Volume 2*, 803–19. For details on this, one can consult Davies, "Reading Ezekiel's *Exagoge*."

62. For most of what follows, see Symes, "The Tragedy of the Middle Ages," 335–69. Also cf. Kelly, *Ideas and Forms of Tragedy from Aristotle to the Middle Ages*, 23–27, for some of the examples given. At the time of this writing, I have been unable to consult Paul M. Blowers' recent major monograph on the patristic reception of the tragic, but

It should be admitted, by way of contextualization, that the Latin Fathers did not have much first-hand knowledge of tragedy: most of what they referenced were commonplace ideas regarding the genre, and was not by-and-large the result of an encounter with the Greek texts themselves (though there are significant exceptions, as with ninth century Irish scholar Sedulius Scotus). The exposure they did have, especially in medieval times, was due to the revival of Seneca and not primarily Aeschylus, Sophocles or Euripides. Such was not a new problem, since already in the fourth century BCE—as can be already seen in Aristotle's *Poetics*—there is a significant amount of historical uncertainty regarding the origins of tragedy and its ideal form of production. This obscurity constitutes one explanation for the diversity of responses to the tragic genre, and theatre more generally. Another factor is the perceived detrimental influence of theatre on society: much like Plato, Tertullian and Augustine were perturbed about the societal effects of tragic drama (and Greek culture more generally, including its philosophy). The huge majority of negative references to tragedy within the early church stem from this trajectory—especially Tertullian and those who continued to reference him (e.g., Lactantius). Tertullian's contributions, which are the most vociferous within ancient Christianity, were shaped by theatre's connections to pagan rituals, and were thus primarily motivated by its affiliation to idolatry, and its provocation of base emotions. Augustine's influential aversion to theatre was tied to its assumed connection to deception, as seen in his commentary on the Sermon on the Mount, where he equates thespianism with hypocrisy (*hypocrita*), or when he criticizes staged tragedy in *The Confessions* (especially Book III) as promoting a kind of voyeurism of suffering and not true Christian pity. But while these strains of interpretation were influential—as can be seen in the way such writings were co-opted after the Reformation—they certainly were not the only readings offered by ancient and medieval Christianity. Moreover, these critiques are directed at ancient drama *in toto*, and not simply tragic drama. They would have had just as much aversion to comedies, satyric-interludes or childhood pantomimes.

Overall, the Christian usage of tragic themes in this period is either neutral or positive in its appropriation. Augustine himself seems to have presented a nuanced view, one that was deeply sceptical of pagan theatre, on the one side, while exhibiting a Christianized version of tragedy as original sin on the other. He also appeared to grant some leeway, under the influence of Aristotle, to ideas of staged tragedy giving some instruction in compassion

---

all indications of its main arguments only seem to strengthen my argument that the supposed opposition between ancient Christianity and the tragic is spurious. See Blowers, *Visions and Faces of the Tragic*.

for human suffering. He still expresses a deep Platonic worry about the effects of theatrical representation, but somewhat mitigates this through an acknowledgement of its pedagogical function.[63] Some Byzantine writers (e.g., Cassiodorus) could argue that theologians (such as the Cappadocians) had imitated or quoted Greek poetry and tragedy in their writings, and others like Ambrose of Milan had also made favorable comparisons between the Psalmist and the lyric of Attic tragedy (Bede made similar concessions regarding the Canticles). Beyond literary conceits, however, there are appropriations which sought to apply tragedy to actual historical events: people such as Fréculf and Rupert of Deutz described the history of the Jews in tragic terms—especially the destruction of Jerusalem in 70 CE as recounted by Josephus.[64] The beheading of John the Baptist, and the bacchanal surrounding his execution, is categorized in Euripidean imagery by Peter Chrysologus and Paschasius Radbertus. The poet Prudentius once described the martyrdom of St. Romanus as a "tragedy," and Boethius (even more significantly) called the incarnation a *'tanta tragoedia'*—a term which certainly alludes to the reversal of Christ's *fortuna*. One can also find examples where war, and especially internecine conflict (national or otherwise), is described in the language of "tragedy" (e.g., Peter the Deacon and Williams of Malmesbury). This idiom was eventually translated into an ecclesial context, as seen in the way that "the tragic" was used to describe church schisms, here exemplified by Irenaeus's lost treatise on the Nestorian crisis (which was entitled 'Tragoidia'). This specific trend is continued in several church fathers: in some, "tragedy" is used to describe the schismatic crises of the church, as seen in the letters of Pope Leo I and Pope Gelasius I. Such a trajectory is also noticeable, and more problematically, in the anti-Judaic tractates of this period, where the "heresies" of the Jews are subjected to critical scorn by Christian teachers, and are described also as "tragedies."

What these references confirm is that already from early on Christian teachers were able to use the language of the tragic in more expansive terms than is often realized. However, this is not the end: there were some significant liturgical and sacramental deployments within a couple of medieval thinkers which are particularly striking as well: Aribo Scholasticus could compare "harmonious" and "inharmonious" music with "tragedy" and "comedy" respectively, and even more suggestive is that writers (e.g., Sicard of Cremona) could compare the liturgical order of service to the

---

63. See Blowers, "Augustine's Tragic Vision," and Rigby, *The Theology of Augustine's Confessions*, 115–29. As we will see later, Rowan Williams espouses a similar view of Augustine.

64. Fréculf even postulated that the etiology of tragedy was to be found in the period of the Babylonian exile.

structure of Greek drama, in which each of the various clergy occupied a role. Peter of Blois argued that stories of tragic misfortune could actually inspire repentance and self-examination among penitents, and that tragedy could have a transformational effect on its audience. A remarkable text is also found in *Gemma animae* of Honorius Augustodunensis where he seeks to conceptualize the Catholic Mass as a "tragedy" in which the participants, through ritual signs, postures and utterances, are invited to repeat the narrative of Christ's suffering in the present. Domenico Pietropaolo even argues that the Mass, after Honorius, could be read as providing the ontological rationale for Christian tragedy, constituting a "sacramental catharsis" for participants within the drama of the Eucharist.[65] Finally, it would be remiss not to mention here the 'Christos Paschōn' (Ξριστός πάσχων) or 'Christus Patiens,' (originally attributed to Gregory Nazianzus, but now dated to the eleventh or twelfth century) which re-imagines the story of Pentheus in the language of Christian sacramentality, with the severed body of the tragic hero now being replaced with a crucified and sacramental body. It is certainly this theatrical aspect of Christian liturgy which inspired the mystery and passion plays of later periods. After the Reformation, it was Philipp Melanchthon, in his *Corhortatio* (1545) who—drawing upon the revived interest in the *Poetics* after the publication of Alessandro Pazzi's translation (1536)—promulgated an Aristotelian and Christianized reading of tragedy with the aim of asserting a moral symmetry between actions and consequences.[66] All of these examples drawn from the history of the Christian church, while certainly not being comprehensive in scope, give an indication of the complexity of reception.

In light of these appropriations, the question needs to be asked: why the perceived tension between Christianity and tragedy? If our previous narrative has demonstrated anything it is that Christianity has provided a diversity of strategies in appropriating or rejecting the tragic, and that there is not *one* method of appropriating it. What this suggests is that a projection of a supposed tension between Christianity and the tragic could be a largely *modern* invention that is not connected to the substance of the tradition. Then again, it might not resolve the problem completely. One would still need to address the *normative* claims of those theorists who assert incompatibility, precisely because there might substantive issues raised that were not noticed by earlier generations. Are these visions

---

65. Pietropaolo, "Whipping Jesus Devoutly," 404. Also see the larger commentary on the *Gemma animae* in 401–2, which has some rather wonderful insights regarding the Mass as grounding the ontological possibility of tragic drama for the Christian church.

66. Lurie, "Facing Up to Tragedy," 442–44.

contradictory because Christianity imagines happy endings while tragedy only disastrous ones? Or does it lie within the different religious perspectives that characterize Greek religion and Judeo-Christianity respectively? Or can one say that the conflicts only lie between a *specific* kind of Christianity and particular sorts of tragedy?

Of these questions, it is the last possibility that appears the most penetrating. That is because conclusions about whether there is any conflict will imply a judgement that is generally informed but also context-specific, one that is related to *particular* tensions or contradictions that arise within their juxtaposition. If one speaks about 'Christianity' or 'tragedy' in general, one is bound to a level of abstractness that is not helpful for making adjudications. It depends on *what* Christianity you are speaking of, and *which* tragedy you are referring to. If someone, for instance, proposes a mode of confident or triumphalist religion, then one could conclude that this will sit rather uneasily with the tragic. Similarly, if one proposes that tragedy *qua* tragedy is about unmitigated disaster, then this will not cohere with Christianity as traditionally understood. But if one relaxes these extremes, can one conclude that the contradictions remain? Possibly not, but that does not necessarily resolve the tensions completely, because even if one could put forward an account of tragedy that was more congenial to Christian assumptions, or put forward a less triumphalist account of Christianity, one still might not have not addressed other concerns—as can be seen in the contributions of David Bentley Hart and John Milbank, who will be discussed in Chapter 3.

One can exemplify this in the following way: it appears that some modern theologians who incorporate tragedy within theology are able to do so with greater alacrity because they have problems with traditional accounts of divine aseity and transcendence, insofar as they allow suffering to enter the Godhead (e.g., Balthasar, MacKinnon, Bulgakov, etc.). Within this theological stream, others take a leap and describe the trinity *ad intra* as an eternal tragedy of suffering love, initiated through a temporalization of divinity within the cross and resurrection of Christ. This move necessitates a transcription of dramatic categories—of alienation and reconciliation—onto the divine life as such (e.g., Moltmann), which means that they are more open to the idea that God is subject to change and contingencies, in distinction from the 'apathetic' God of so-called 'classical theism.'[67] Such

---

67. I am aware that 'classical theism' is a pejorative term in modern theology and that it has been heavily chided in recent times (e.g., Eberhard Jüngel, John Caputo, Richard Kearney, Jean-Luc Marion, etc.). I am not sure always however what it actually refers to, since the reference often shifts. Is one referring to the entire metaphysical (or 'ontotheological') tradition that has now, supposedly, been discarded by

amenability implies a connection between the doctrine of God's transcendence, and one's willingness or not to absorb the tragic. This is so because if tragedy is concerned with historicity and suffering, then it follows that if God is ontologically implicated in these dynamics, then one has less anxiety about the problem of tensions. However, if one is predisposed to a more orthodox accounts of divine aseity (e.g., David Bentley Hart, John Milbank), then there does seem to be a corresponding suspicion that incorporating 'the tragic' or a 'tragic theology' into Christianity will lead to doctrinal aporias. But this is not a complete picture since there are still other thinkers, who also assume God's aseity, but who remain nonetheless more open to the insights that tragedy might provide (e.g., Graham Ward, Rowan Williams, etc.). The fact that these latter thinkers are more disposed to accept tragedy as a theological trope implies that a more classical rendering of God might *not* be opposed to such a procedure. But if this is the case, where does the problem lie then? Without being reductionist, it seems that the central problematic might not just be an abstract problem,

---

post-Heideggerian thought? If this is the case, then it has flaws as regards to historical genealogy (as I have suggested earlier). To take one example: one could query whether the priority of 'possibility' over 'actuality' (endorsed by Jüngel, Caputo, Kearney) is not itself a continuation of modern metaphysics since Scotus and Suárez. Strictly-speaking, it is this tradition which is the most 'ontotheological' and 'metaphysical' of them all (as Marion confirms). On top of this, one could suggest that the 'omni-God' of absolute power, which they reject, has more affinity for the nominalist conceptions of *potentia absoluta* than the God of the classical tradition. Similar criticisms have been directed towards Kearney by William Desmond (see William Desmond, "Maybe, Maybe Not," 55–77). However, it can be said Marion should not be placed within the same trajectory. But even his more nuanced approach appears not to appreciate the complexity of early Christian thought, especially as regards its analogical re-conception of 'being,' insofar as it resisted modeling the divine 'being' after finite causality. This has been pointed out by David Bentley Hart, John Milbank, and Rowan Williams.

But returning to Caputo, Jüngel, and Kearney once more, it appears that they might have slightly different *foci* in relation to 'classical theism.' For his part, Jüngel continues a Lutheran-Barthian opposition to 'metaphysics' in general, and Aristotle in particular. Moreover, he is critical of Thomism insofar as it proposes an overly-negative account of divinity, one that excludes any cognoscibility and speakability of the divine nature. However, one should point out here Te Velde's excellent monograph entitled *Aquinas on God*, which argues that Thomas escapes a 'classical theism' of this kind. As regards Kearney and Caputo, one wonders (as Fergus Kerr suggests) whether their proposals are not largely a poetically-inclined reaction to the 'neo-scholastic apologetics' of manual Thomism (see Kerr, Review of *Reimagining the Sacred*, 325–27). But if this is so, what does one make of the *ressourcement* tradition of *nouvelle théologie* (Lubac, Balthasar, Ratzinger, etc.) which is also opposed to Baroque neo-Thomism insofar as it constituted, for them, a departure *from* the classical and patristic vision? One could suggest then that if by 'classical theism' one is referring to the dry and rationalistic traditions of the neo-scholastics, then one is referring not to the 'classical' or 'Thomistic' tradition, but rather to an early modern development.

but much like Plato's Socrates is also centred on a figure. That figure, I would suggest, is Donald MacKinnon, a thinker who has served (over several decades) as the catalyst in the discussion of tragedy and transcendence within the contemporary theological scene. In other words, it appears that this debate is not simply focused on conceptual tensions that have arisen in recent times, but that they are concretized (at least for modern theology) within the reception of a specific person.

Donald MacKinnon (1913–1994) was a Christian philosopher who had a seminal impact on British academia in the latter half of the twentieth century. Already then, theologians, philosophers, playwrights, and intellectuals absorbed his teaching, many of whom went on to have a significant impact on the intellectual culture of the British Isles. Some of these include heavyweights such as Philippa Foot, Mary Midgely and Iris Murdoch, the playwright Tom Stoppard, the literary critic George Steiner, and, more pertinently for our immediate purposes, theologians such as Fergus Kerr, Nicholas Lash, and Rowan Williams. MacKinnon also had a seminal impact more generally, and has been credited with reversing the tide of British theology against the liberalism of 1960s towards a more intellectually robust and subtle defense of theological orthodoxy.[68] This trajectory can be further seen in other theological movements such as Radical Orthodoxy, which in many ways trace their lineage to the influence of MacKinnon at Cambridge. Central figures such as John Milbank and Graham Ward have admitted as much.[69]

But one could ask: why should MacKinnon have a centrality in this discussion? Firstly, he was a thinker who, by all accounts, has had the greatest impact in the revived interrelation of tragedy and theology. It was a question which he was intensely engaged with, as his academic output will show. Furthermore, even beyond his students, his influence on this question is wide-spread, as can be seen in his reiterating presence within volumes such as *Theology and Tragedy: Theologians, Tragic Literature, and Tragic Theory*—never mind the books and research dissertations that have been written on similar themes. Secondly, MacKinnon broadened the question of the tragic to include not only tragedy as a literary genre, but also the larger questions of time and historicity and their bearing on moral deliberation, seeking to show the connection of the tragic to the questions of life. Thirdly, his teaching had an influence not only on the orthodoxy of his students, but also on their reception of tragic themes. It is not coincidental

---

68. On this see, Williams, "John A. T. Robinson (1919–1983)," in *Anglican Identities*, 103–20.

69. Cf. Goosen and Kruger, "Radical Orthodoxy," 5, 9.

that it is from these thinkers—all with links to Cambridge—that some of the most intelligent defenses and critiques of 'tragic theology' have arisen. Rowan Williams's influence on John Milbank is well-known—more generally but also on the question of the tragic—and Milbank in turn has had a significant influence on David Bentley Hart, who both spent significant periods at the universities of Cambridge and Virginia. It is particularly the latter two thinkers who have provided the most trenchant responses to his influence as regarding the tragic. Therefore, since MacKinnon has had such a central place within these debates, one concludes that he should serve as a lodestar in our discussion.

But the question remains: what is the substance behind their differing responses? Why is it that theologians who are very similar in many other regards, come to different conclusions regarding the tragic, and ultimately the reception of MacKinnon's work itself? And if these differences are significant, can they be ameliorated? Admittedly, some questions have already been addressed by Rowan Williams in *The Tragic Imagination* (2016) for example. But it is arguable that Williams, while dealing with many of the significant areas of conflict (as put forward by Steiner, Milbank and Hart), does not deal with *all* of their substantial disagreements. This is where this book tries to make some kind of contribution. Continuing disagreements occur for instance within the following areas, namely: (1) the arena of *metaphysics*, especially as it relates to transcendent being and historicity, (2) the question of *genealogy*, as it relates to the impact of Kantianism on the reception of tragic themes (and its impact in turn on MacKinnon himself), and (3) its connection to *politics*, especially as regards the impact of ontological pessimism on socio-political arrangements.

All of these tendencies, I will argue, are related to the configuration of *transcendence*, specifically as regards transcendent goodness and aseity. With this in mind, the central question of this book can be posed again: within the modern theological context and debate, can one reconcile a classical account of infinite and transcendent goodness—as put forward by Hart, Milbank and Williams—with the insights of the tragic? This problem raises the question of coherency, with all its intellectual, doctrinal and spiritual overtones. Or more specifically: what kind of Christian metaphysics provides the greatest level of cogency in relation to questions of transcendence, without repressing the difficulties that the tragic exposes. It is to these questions that we turn to in the next chapter.

In this chapter, I suggested that a supposed opposition between Christian theology and the tragic does *not* have a deep history within the tradition; rather, the reception of the tragic is more diverse and complicated than a homogenous narrative allows. Our argument was both conceptual and historical: it tried to ask where the node of the contention really lies, with the aim of reaching our central question. Our query, broadly-speaking, is concerned with the relationship between classical Christianity and the tragic, and as we will see shortly, how this is centred on the problem of transcendence. But at this stage, our method was more probing, asking where and why perceptions of conflict might have arisen. To do this I began the chapter by discussing tragedy itself, as well as the debate between Plato and the poets. There I suggested that the tensions, while not without substance, are not immune to deconstruction both from *within* tragedy and Plato himself. As we saw, tragedy is not opposed to philosophy and Platonism is not irreconcilable with tragedy. Moreover, even though Platonism did influence some early Christian rejections of ancient drama, it was not decisive in its impact throughout. This raises the question once more of where the real tensions lie in the debate. Here I wagered that the tensions, specifically as regard classical Christianity and the tragic, might be more recent than ancient in origin. I suggested that such assertions of contradiction might be traceable to tendencies within literary criticism, which has sometimes espoused a more strenuous opposition between Christian theology and tragedy. In this light, I mentioned John Milbank and David Bentley Hart as being possible inheritors of this recent trajectory. It was in this setting that I introduced Donald MacKinnon, and the importance he has had in the debate regarding the theology and the tragic, here specifically as regards the question of transcendence. But at this stage, many of these questions have been left open-ended and await development within the chapters to follow.

But one question seems especially pertinent at the moment: what do I mean by a classical account of 'transcendence'? In the next chapter, I hope to provide some answers with the aim of showing their connection to the research question. I also hope to render lucid some of the interconnections between 'transcendence' and 'the tragic,' with purpose of deepening our thesis that the supposed abrasiveness between classical metaphysics and the tragic has been strengthened by modern developments.

3

Tragedy and Transcendence

On Theological Coherency

This chapter aims to lay bare some of the theological assumptions which will be advanced in this book. As was intimated previously, it appears that claims of an incompatibility between 'Christianity' vis-à-vis 'the tragic' depends upon how one substantiates those terms. There it was wagered that the assertion of contradiction might be a more recent phenomenon in intellectual history, bound up with proximate trends in the relatively recent past. However, the reason for this development was only hinted at: on the one hand, the opposition between Christianity and the tragic was exacerbated by some literary critics who might be working with a rather jaundiced conception of Christian theology—which is illuminated when one compares their swift juxtapositions with the more elaborate comparisons of someone like Terry Eagleton. But on the other hand, this admission did not resolve the issue completely, because some modern theologians—who are fully apprised of Christianity's complexity—still remain adamant that irreconcilable tensions persist.

Exemplary of this trend are David Bentley Hart and John Milbank. Our suggestion as to why this is so was sought within their continued commitment to a classical metaphysics and Christian orthodoxy, with a particular regard for their espousals of aseity and transcendence. Of course, these suggestions are only anticipations of a more complete exposition of their work, and the tensions these *might* create when compared with a more tragically-slanted theology. Because of this, conclusions cannot be asserted as of yet. However, what can be stated here at the outset is that I remain in agreement with many of the concerns of these authors, more generally, including what is to my mind their nuanced repetition of a classically-informed metaphysics. I am persuaded that Hart and Milbank are neither pious reactionaries nor practitioners of fusty mystification, but thoughtful exponents of a renewed orthodoxy within our so-called 'postmodern' epoch. Because of this, I assume a significant amount of their insights, as will be seen in the developing argument. However, there are some clear disagreements on my part, especially (as we shall see) as regards the applicability of tragic themes to Christian orthodoxy. It will become apparent in what is to follow that I have a great sympathy for the account of Donald MacKinnon as this has been critically supplemented by the scholarship of Rowan Williams. Both of these thinkers, within differing degrees of acceptance, show adherence to a more classical 'orthodoxy' while at the same time remain deeply informed by the insights of the tragic. But what are my assumptions regarding that loaded term 'classical metaphysics,' especially as regards the problem of transcendence? And why is there a continuing perception that Christianity and the tragic are finally conflictive? In this chapter, I seek clarity regarding the terminology of 'transcendence,' here with the assistance of Rowan Williams and John Webster. I outline how this tradition has construed the metaphysics of transcendence, with the aim of articulating, against misconstructions, what it really affirms and what it does not. Such remains important for 'coherency' and sense-making, since systematic theology remains implicitly committed to the idea of an ultimately rational order, one that is predicated on the unity and simplicity of divine action. But since it is this classical tradition in particular which has expressed a marked tension regarding tragedy and theology in recent times, it is important to analyze *why* these tensions have arisen, with the purpose of asking whether they can be ameliorated. This tension can be most clearly seen in three trends that have developed in the *modern* deployment of 'the tragic,' all of which have a connection to the ontological topology of transcendence, namely: *the post-Kantian sublime, the idea of a suffering God,* and *a rejection of the* privatio boni.

On Divine Transcendence and Aseity

My purpose is not to give a comprehensive treatment of divine aseity. Rather, it is attuned to whether a reading of God's transcendent goodness is suitably pared with *the negativity of the tragic*, that is, with the way that tragedy challenges and even undermines overly-harmonious perspectives of order within the cosmos. Here already, the demand of 'coherency' becomes stringent, as will become recognizable shortly. But it is worthwhile at the outset to establish the doctrinal contours of a classical account of divine transcendence, so that I may give clarity on what I am speaking about.

At the outset, it should be said that 'transcendence' has several valences which need to be clarified, and which are by no means univocal, especially between diverse epistemic regimes (e.g., literature, religion, philosophy, psychology, aesthetics, etc.).[1] Using Karl Jasper's terms, one might say that 'transcendence' generally pertains to our encounters with liminality and limit-situations.[2] In our own register, one could say that 'transcendence' in its more stringent sense has to do with what is *non-negotiable* or *intractable* within experience, with those events that arrest and carry us beyond ourselves or resist phenomenological reduction. However, a lexicon of 'transcendence' also presupposes that we speak of 'immanence', since we cannot understand 'transcendence' without grasping what it is transcendent *to*. Moreover, these concepts are asymmetric because it is firstly 'transcendence' that allows us to understand the distinction initially, and is what gives 'immanence' its sense of being derived *from* something. This means that immanence-as-such remains semantically indecipherable apart from its connection to transcendence. This distinction is a useful one, but some more are required: since all projections of transcendence remain within the immanent, one needs to make a distinction not only between the *transcendent-as-such* (e.g., the Absolute, the One, God, etc.) and *immanent-as-such* (e.g., the cosmos, created beings, history etc.), but one must also distinguish between the transcendent and immanent as it appears *within* the immanent-as-such. Ingolf Dalferth has framed this distinction as *absolute* and *relative* forms of transcendence.[3] *Absolute* transcendence speaks to those realities that exist independently from *relative* transcendence, those apart from which no immanence could be postulated (e.g., God, the Unmoved Mover, etc.). *Relative* transcendence encapsulates those moments of transcending *within* the immanent world, as seen paradigmatically within religious practices, moments of self-transcendence or rituals of transition (e.g., conversion, *rites de passages*, falling in love, etc.). Such transitions occur in the movement between events of anticipation and events of transformation, those passages between ignorance and knowledge. Self-transcendence is *relative* because regardless of the magnitude of elevation, it always remains within immanence. This is not to say that

---

1. See Dalferth, "Ereignis und Transzendenz," for the differing 'grammars' of transcendence that occur in an interdisciplinary context.

2. For more reflection on this, see Bornemark, "Limit-situation."

3. Dalferth, "The Idea of Transcendence," 146–88. However, our distinction has a slightly different resonance since it does not share Dalferth's anti-Platonism or his Reformed antipathy towards the *analogia entis*.

relative transcendence is incapable of intimating *absolute* transcendence, but rather that its speculative grasp is always non-absolute.[4]

The above clarifications should help us, but one can register some complications—not only for the sake of accuracy but because it also anticipates some themes that will be engaged later. These complications relate to the contrastive *dualism* that is presupposed in transcendence-immanence language. The first concern is that, genealogically-speaking, 'immanence' has its first occurrence in Diderot's *Encyclopédie*.[5] This rather late occurrence should give pause before we impose such language on older traditions. Such a suspicion is deepened further when we realize that the earliest definition of the transcendence-immanence duality is found in Immanuel Kant, namely in his *Critique of Pure Reason*. There his treatment of this duality, within the 'Transcendental Dialectic,' served to delimit the metaphysical reach of the rational powers. Kant's transcendentalism had a seminal impact on this usage within German Idealism and in the so-called *Pantheismusstreit*—a trajectory that found its way into the interpretation of ancient philosophy and early Christianity. This schematic was certainly creative, and instituted a significant amount of original thinking and research. But one cannot avoid the conclusion that this paradigm, in retrospect, also led to a misreading of ancient categories of thought, especially as regards modernity's secularizing division between the immanent and the transcendent.

The second concern is an explicitly theological one: the grammar of aseity is misconstrued within a dualistic or conflictive approach, as has been argued by John Webster and Rowan Williams.[6] Webster distances a more traditional account of divine aseity from an approach that establishes content through a contrast with contingency.[7] He reckons, here following the principle of *Deus non est in genere*, that aseity should not be understood as "primarily a comparative or contrastive concept," since "the content of the term cannot be determined simply by analysis of the difference between God and contingent creatures."[8] On the contrary, the doctrine of aseity references "the glory and plenitude of the life of the Holy Trinity in its self-existent and

---

4. I have also consulted the typology of Stoker contained in "Culture and Transcendence," 5–28. As per the type of 'transcendence' here presented—understood as aseity, analogical participation, etc.—I think that it traverses Stoker's categories of "immanent transcendence," "radical transcendence," and "transcendence as alterity."

5. For what follows, see Zachhuber, "Transzendenz und Immanenz," 23–54.

6. To put it simplistically: in these two essays, Webster focuses more on the trinity while Williams more on divine oneness. Neither is to the exclusion of the other, but is simply a question of emphasis.

7. Webster, "Life in and of Himself," 107–24.

8. Webster, "Life in and of Himself," 108.

self-moving originality," "its underived fullness." It is this plenitude which is "the ground of [God's] self-communication."[9] Such grammar is obscured when *aseitas* becomes about whether "contingent reality is to be secured by a ground of existence beyond itself." On this model, aseity is "inseparably attached to, and expounded in terms of, the contingency of the world," leading to a "curious irony" in that the "divine self-existence itself becomes a derivative concept."[10] With this move, the language of aseity appears less a matter of doxological affirmation, and is instead reduced to a functional causality (such as Descartes's *causa sui*, that *bête noire* of Heideggerian genealogy). Here, divinity is understood impersonally, being "reduced to the bare self-positing cause of created reality."[11] In contrast to this, aseity must be conceived triunely: "God *a se* is the perfection of paternity, filiation, and spiration in which he is indissolubly from, for, and in himself and out of which he bestows himself as the Lord, Saviour, and partner of his creature."[12] In this light, the trinitarian structure of aseity can be concisely expressed in this way: "*God is from himself, and from himself God gives himself*... Aseity is *life*: God's life *from* and therefore *in* himself."[13]

Nonetheless, while we must predicate aseity of the divine triunity, as regards aseity as a "personal property," this belongs only to the Father: "although all the persons of the Trinity are *a se* according to essence, the Father alone is *a se* according to person."[14] What Webster means is that while the Son is eternally generated he does not share the Father's innascibility—even though such does not imply ontological inferiority, because there is no implication of coming into existence, a temporal before or after.[15] Conceptualizing triune relations so implies that there is no distinction between God's eternal self-distinction and eternal self-giving *in se* and his existence as being *a se*.[16] And it is this distinction *ad intra* which is

9. Webster, "Life in and of Himself," 107–8.

10. Webster, "Life in and of Himself," 110. It is for this reason that Webster is critical of the language of God as *causa sui* and *ens necessarium* (117–19)—the *causa sui* because it implies a notion of temporal causation, a postulated 'before' which preceded actualization, which obviously creates problems for any affirmation of divine eternity or immutability—the *ens necessarium* because it remains too entwined with a contrastive and functional approach, since the language of 'necessity' always implies a necessity *for* something. On this point, Ebehard Jüngel's statement that God is 'more than necessary' most certainly lies in the background.

11. Webster, "Life in and of Himself," 113.

12. Webster, "Life in and of Himself," 113.

13. Webster, "Life in and of Himself," 114.

14. Webster, "Life in and of Himself," 115.

15. Webster, "Life in and of Himself," 116.

16. Cf. Webster, "Life in and of Himself," 123: God's life is about "*inseity* as much as *aseity*."

the ontological basis for the divine mission *ad extra*, because while "aseity differentiates the divine Son from creatures, it is also at the same time the ground of his saving gift."[17]

Rowan Williams's reflections are framed by an awareness of the "impatience" surrounding language of divine oneness and aseity.[18] For this stream, an orthodox conceptualization of divine unity imagines God as "a solitary transcendent individual" within an "abstract theism." This schema, so the story goes, promotes a "thinking of the unity of the divine nature" that gives "a kind of priority to some reality lying behind the concrete relationality of God to God as Trinity."[19] In this light, revisionist theologians have advocated "a more obviously immanentist account" of a divinity who acts as "an endlessly resourceful manager of suffering and change."[20] But Williams wonders whether these tendencies have internalized the implications of their revisions, and he also doubts whether these count as accurate readings of the tradition. He asserts that the classical rendering of transcendent being, on the contrary, has included many of the concerns its critics raise. Moreover, Williams is also not insensitive to how the language of 'being' invokes controversial resonances within "the politics of discourse."[21] Nonetheless, he asserts that the postmodern rejection of metaphysics capitulates even more blatantly to these temptations, especially as regards the question of power. In the name of rejecting hierarchical models of deity,[22] they have left the dynamics of power intact, rather than undermining their premises.

---

17. Webster, "Life in and of Himself," 121.

18. Williams, "God," 75.

19. Williams, "God," 75.

20. Williams, "God," 76. He goes on to say that "A suffering and mutable God (such as is said to be found in the Bible) must be, in a very strong sense, a psychological subject comparable to ourselves; an immanent God is not obviously a subject in anything like this sense. The virtues of the mutable God are sometimes argued in terms of the need to say what must be said about God's compassion; but this is difficult to state intelligibly if God's subjectivity is not, at the level that matters, different from the totality of the experience of contingent subjects" (Williams, "God," 76).

21. Williams, "God," 86.

22. "Revisionist models of divine life in terms of passibility and so on have commonly been innocent or simplistic about [the politics of discourse]. The typical protest on behalf of emancipatory concerns has been that the traditional view sets in philosophical concrete a hierarchically ordered model of reality in which mind is privileged over feeling, spirit over body, male over female and so on; God's transcendence (including, for some writers, the doctrine of creation *ex nihilo*) as expressed in the classical 'attributes' places God in irreconcilable opposition to a world of chance and vulnerability. God becomes a metaphysical transcription of unexamined power structures in the world" (Williams, "God," 86).

Now advocates of the revisionist model claim that they have the Bible on their side, which appears to portray God as having anthropomorphic traits. Williams does not respond to these claims extensively in this essay (though Thomas Weinandy does in a monograph referenced by him[23]). He does nonetheless engage with the scriptural tradition: for instance, he argues that the Old Testament portrays a God whose "claims on the human community are not the claims of a divine monarch to worship only, but are identical with the claims of justice between human agents and strangers."[24] This is because "God is not an object competing for attention," since "to know God is to be involved in the entire range of actions specified by law," as exemplified in the way in which the knowledge of God is paralleled to Israel's commitment to compassion (*hesed*). For Israel, there is no religious sector cordoned off from the rest of its life: one's cultic dedication to YHWH is inseparable from the enactment of reciprocity. God's being is not a thing amongst others, but is that which gives meaning to the whole: "God's relation to the chosen community is thus *not* an element in the community's life," and is rather the creative principle of community as such.[25] As regards the New Testament, and especially Pauline language of the weakness of the cross, Williams thinks that the identification of God with suffering tends to obviate the rhetorical overtones of Paul's texts, flattening the shocking analogies found in the texts.[26]

The implication to be drawn from all of this is that divinity cannot be spoken of in terms of "finite activity, as a contingent and interdependent reality."[27] It was for this reason that early Christianity (drawing on Platonic categories) spoke of God as "beyond being," insofar as divinity was "characterised primarily by the stripping away of the attributes of contingent agency,"

---

23. Weinandy, *Does God Suffer*, 40–82. I am aware of the critical debate surrounding Weinandy's work. See Sarot, "Does God Suffer?"; and Weinandy, "Does God Suffer?" However, also see the analysis of the biblical tradition in Gavrilyuk, *The Suffering of the Impassible God*, 37–46.

24. Williams, "God," 77.

25. Williams, "God," 78.

26. Williams, "God," 86–87: "Paul's language is professedly a way of asking where we might expect to discern God in the world's experience, and displaying how God's actual presence upsets those expectations. To read it as endorsing a projection onto God of the vulnerability of subjects in the world is, ironically, to remove the upset by removing the paradox. If God as such is vulnerable in the sense that we are, God becomes a case of contingent possibility and discerning God in the cross of Jesus or in the action of grace in the poor, the voiceless, the failed and the spiritually incompetent is no longer surprising. What has been changed by the emancipatory move in theology is the locus of power and of suffering, not the nature of power relations themselves."

27. Williams, "God," 78.

as seen especially in someone like Pseudo-Dionysius. This was done because finite action always implies a blending of initiation and "passivity," something that cannot be ascribed to God.[28] The same could not be said for God, who since Aquinas, with biblical and patristic warrant, has been understood as "pure act" (*actus purus*).[29] More expansively, this teaches that:

> Divine action can be 'pure' only if it is in no sense in 'negotiation' with specific agencies. And so far from this leaving us with a God uninvolved in creation's life—as the polemic of revisionist theologies so often suggests—this allows some grasp of what is being claimed in saying that God is 'pure' *giver* (and therefore that any talk of God's favour or grace or goodwill must be a way of honouring the primacy of God's action rather than a drama of seeking and winning a desired reaction).[30]

The idea of God-as-pure-act is an alternative to the theological revisionism of modernity, in which God is paralleled to finite agency, because if God changes or suffers, then we have to concede that there are finite agencies that are "external to the agency of God." This remains so "even if we grant that God is in some way the ultimate source of their existence," whereby divine creativity "bestows on them a life on the other side of an ontological frontier such that they may [also] modify not only each other but their source." This paradigm, at first glance, appears to offer respite for North Atlantic post-theism. However, its comes at a price: "If the source is in this way modifiable, is it still possible to say that it is unequivocally the source of the meanings constructed or enacted in the world? And if it is not to be thought of as source, it has to be thought of as standing with, negotiating with or even contesting other possible meanings." And does this not, ultimately, presuppose the conflictive model that revisionists want to avoid? How is this distinguishable from what Milbank has described as "ontological violence"?[31] If this is the case, then it has deleterious

---

28. Williams, "God," 78–79.
29. Williams, "God," 81.
30. Williams, "God," 82.
31. "[T]o claim that the divine action can be trusted to prevail (following some varieties of process thought which privilege the resourcefulness of love while allowing a kind of passibility to God) is only to claim that, in the long run, God has more resource than other agents. The story remains one of contest and victory rather than the complex convergence imagined by classical theology and spirituality between growth in integrity and actualization as a creature and conformity with the 'will' or 'purpose' of God. And thus conversion, sanctification and so on become precisely the kind of issues they are regularly represented as being in modern, emancipatory theological rhetoric: they are about power, who has it and who doesn't, who has more of it, what counts as power and so on" (Williams, "God," 83).

implications for the spiritual life,[32] and also promotes a metaphysics that ontologizes conflict, for:

> [I]f there is no guaranteed 'triumph' for God, if contest is perpetual and unresolved, we are stuck with a metaphysic (the fact that it is commonly presented as a kind of alternative to metaphysics is irrelevant) in which what is unambiguously good has no necessary relation to how things fundamentally are, or are thinkable. Good becomes a function of the will, separated from 'nature', as in the familiar forms of debased Kantianism, and from intellect. If the former problem (God as an agency confronting others) tends to a reduction of God to an item in the world, the latter allies the reality of God to the workings of an 'inner' life, detaching God from the processes of learning that take place in a material and historical environment. In plainer terms, while the former interprets God's existence as being on the same footing as that of contingent realities, the latter moves towards evacuating talk of God's existence of all content.[33]

There is a lot in here which will re-appear again in this study: if God is the subject of change or suffering *in se*, then one could suggest that we have baptized competitive violence, since the Good has no necessary linkage with reality, but only 'goods' that are produced without any ontological basis for harmonization. In this quotation, we can see that this matrix of assertions—the problems of passibility, ontological violence, evil-as-privation, the primacy of the will, and the Kantian sublime—have a connection to the question of aseity. Without it, so Williams argues, the Good itself becomes de-natured, and God is conceived within a regime of the sublime that denies the deity's transcendent goodness and perfection. Moreover, it places God within the scope of ontotheology, since (on this model) God acts like a finite cause. On the traditional account, God as creator (who is not in competition to creatures) brings everything into a 'natural' relation to the Good, without hereby denying the freedom of creatures.[34] To enter into the Good is to

32. "If God comes to be characterised as an agent among agents . . . [i]t is not clear how [the practice of] contemplation can be conceived . . . as an embodiment of the other in the self, since two agencies are bound to be confronting each other within a contested 'territory.' When one triumphs, that constitutes a clear representation or inscription of God within the world. Once again, there is an underlying issue about power, about the risks of identifying some area of the world's discourse unambiguously with God" (Williams, "God," 84).

33. Williams, "God," 84–85.

34. In speaking this way, I am echoing figures like Maximus the Confessor who spoke of a 'natural' and 'rational' orientation towards the good, which then is elected (or not) through an exercise of the 'gnomic' will. On this, see Bradshaw, "St. Maximus the Confessor on the Will," 143–57.

become more creaturely and more human. However, if one conceives God as subjected to temporal process, then that means that the divine nature also is subjected to that same historical logic, and the Good is no longer considered as unchangeable. But now since the world has no metaphysical or 'necessary' connection to goodness, this means that there is no created aptitude for this, in the sense that finite being now has no more 'natural' affinity for either goodness or evil. It is purely a matter of voluntary and affective imposition, one way or the other.

This excursus on aseity and transcendence has served to outline their contours, as it has appeared within the classical tradition of theology. What we have seen is that if our concept of aseity is diminished or misread then the grammar of theology is fundamentally changed. If God is mutable or suffers *in se*, then this has some significant consequences: if the Good, which is convertible with Infinite Being, does not hold some kind of eschatological finality or priority in relation to evil, then goodness no longer has a more intrinsic position in reality, and evil (or material conflict) ascends into an equivalency with the Good. Beatitude as a result becomes less a moral attuning to reality, and rather a voluntary imposition. And since there is no necessary connection between goodness and being itself, the universal compass of the Good is unsustainable. There are other problems also: if God is the not the infinite source of all things, but rather an eternal manager of change 'outside' of God—since there is an externality which is not included within divine infinity—then can we even speak of 'creation' as *creatio ex nihilo*? One must admit that it remains difficult, as confirmed by contemporary process thought (e.g., Catherine Keller, Mary-Jane Rubenstein, etc.). Moreover, a denial of a non-rivalrous aseity creates Christological aporias also, since God and humanity are imagined as actors working *within* the same plane of reality. If God is an entity within the universe whose actions come into 'conflict' with human agency, then the grammar of the hypostatic union is altered. God and humanity exist alongside each other within Christ—which is a Nestorian conclusion. Such a model also raises problems for divine providence, since the divine and human agencies are understood as mutually restrictive or competitive.

Aseity might alleviate these problems: since God is the transcendent cause of everything, we should not understand God as being in opposition or *other* to reality itself. Because God is not in competition with anything, and is not hindered by material restriction, God remains infinitely close to every creature. Moreover, omnipotence should not be construed as a power *over* or *against*.[35] Instead, God's creative activity is aimed at our flourishing:

---

35. Cf. Schmutz, "The Medieval Doctrine of Causality," 203–50, who argues that

it is a power *for* us.[36] God's desire is not opposed to our nature as created beings, but is in accord with our *telos*. And since the Good is identical with Infinite Being, the Good is not a resource which is expended the more it is enacted, but is expanded through communication.[37] In addition other problems are also softened: *creatio ex nihilo* no longer resonates with the imagery of a cosmic overlord who exerts power *over* us, as if this power surrendered us into complete passivity. One could also argue that a non-competitive transcendence ameliorates the aporias of Christological doctrine: if God and creatures are not in competition for ontological 'space,' then there is no question of God existing alongside the humanity of Christ.[38] Similar comments can be related to the providential causal-joint, because now it is no longer a question of conflict, but rather an intensification of freedom.

Hopefully what has been said above gives a sense of how the language of 'transcendence' will be used in this study. The above exposition has served to articulate the centrality of this teaching for theological orthodoxy. But there is a query which needs further treatment, namely: what does *tragedy* have to do with *transcendence*? Related to this is the question as to why Christian orthodoxy, in its affirmation of aseity, would create tensions vis-à-vis 'the tragic'? Here we see once more that some of the difficulties that have arisen are connected to modern trends, and are by-no-means necessary developments.

---

the conflictive model of divine-human agency is linked to a decline of the Neoplatonic notion of *influentia* and a simultaneous assertion of the doctrine of *concursus*.

36. See Rowan Williams's generally excellent "On Being Creatures," in *On Christian Theology*, 63–78. He argues that 'creation' is not about an overweening agency, but is precisely creative in the sense that it opens up new possibilities of relation. Since there is nothing prior to creation, except God, the act of bringing-into-being does not exert power *over* anything since there is nothing there which exists 'outside' of God.

37. Dante's *Purgatorio* XV.49–75 has some wonderful things to say here: "Because your human longings point to where / portions grow smaller in shared fellowship, / meanness of mind must make bellows sigh. / If love, though, seeking for the utmost sphere, / should ever wrench your longings to the skies, / such fears would have no place within your breast. / For, there, the more that we can speak of "ours", the more each one possesses of the good / and, in that cloister, *caritas* burns brighter . . . How can it be that good distributed / to many owners makes, in that respect, / each one far richer than if few had shared . . . The Good that—infinite beyond all words—/ is there above will run to love like rays / of light that come to anything that shines. / It gives itself proportioned to the fire, / so that, as far as *caritas* extends, / eternal Worth increases over it. The more there are who fix their minds up there, / the more good love there is—and more to love—/ and each (as might a mirror) gives to each." This translation is taken from Robin Kirkpatrick's Dante, *The Divine Comedy*.

38. See the concise and perceptive treatment of this theme in Tanner, *Jesus, Humanity and the Trinity*; Riches, *Ecce Homo*; and Williams, *Christ the Heart of Creation*.

On Tragedy and Transcendence: Modern Inversions

Our definition of transcendence has emphasized the aseity of God and the convertibility of the infinite good with such transcendence. But the question remains: why is this important for our discussion of tragedy and theology? As an initial salvo, I will attempt to sketch three nodes of potential conflict, especially within the modern period: (1) *the aesthetics of the sublime* and *the theory of the tragic*, (2) *the question of history* and transcendence, specifically as it concerns *the historical suffering of the Absolute*, and (3) *the problem of conflicting goods* and its connection to a rejection of *evil-as-privation*.

From its origins, tragedy has been tied to a religious backdrop that projects transcendence (e.g., the gods, necessity, etc.). Attic tragedy was concerned about what could not be mastered or controlled, in other words with the transcendent and the intractable (the Homeric tradition). At the same time, tragedy concerns the instauration of *law* within Athens, which occasioned a transition to critical reflection and legal order (the Solonic tradition). Tragedy tapped into this liminality and period of transition, along with its ambiguities.[39] This "tension," which as Vernant says is "never totally accepted nor entirely obliterated," ultimately "makes tragedy into a questioning to which there can be no answers." Within this "tragic perspective," human beings and their actions come to be seen "not as things that can be defined or described, but as problems. They are presented as riddles whose double meanings can never be pinned down or exhausted."[40] In other words, tragedy did not uncritically inherit Homeric traditions nor did legality completely repress the Dionysian. Stephen Halliwell has spoken about how Greek tragedy resists those attempts to "secure and coherent understanding" of "the religious concerns and mentality of its characters."[41] He writes that "The gestures of tragedy's own people towards unified explanations of their world are reenacted by interpreters seeking to identify

---

39 "[T]he tragic writers are prone to the use of technical legal terms. But when they use this terminology it is almost always to play on its ambiguities, its vagueness, and its incompleteness. We find terms used imprecisely, shifts of meaning, incoherences and contradictions, which betray internal clashes and tensions at the very heart of a system of legal thought that lacks the elaborated form of that of the Romans. The legal terminology is also used to convey the conflicts that exist between legal values and a more ancient religious tradition, the beginnings of a system of moral thought already distinct from the law although the boundaries between their respective domains are not yet clearly drawn" (Vernant, "Tensions and Ambiguities in Greek Tragedy," in Vernant and Vidal-Naquet, *Myth and Tragedy in Ancient Greece*, 38).

40 Vernant, "Tensions and Ambiguities in Greek Tragedy," 38.

41. Halliwell, "Human Limits and the Religion of Greek Tragedy," 170.

and *circumscribe* a stable centre of significance in concepts," including ideas such as "fate, god-sent derangement, inherited 'guilt', divine malevolence, the conflict of freedom and necessity, the punishment of hybris, or perhaps some final theodicy beyond the realm of suffering." These concepts do not have finality since "tragedy itself often dramatizes the inconclusive value of these and other religious ideas which find expression in its characters' discourse of reflection and emotion." Moreover, even when there is insight, this temporary respite is "rare and precarious," and can "never certify its penetration into the designs of gods."[42]

Consequently, "tragic experience is most religious precisely at the points where determinacy and wholeness of explanation prove most elusive,"[43] which coheres with our previous usage of terms such as *negativity*, *non-negotiability* and *intractability* in relation to some instances of transcendence. This applies to actors on the stage and the audience too, because there is no "tragic equivalent to the (ostensibly) omniscient voice of the epic narrator." Discernment remains locked within the drama, so that "tragedy's religious ideas are mediated through the claims and judgments of those involved in, or close to, the action of the plays."[44] We thus do not have access to the transcendent agencies that inform our choices, but can only engage in speculations of their influence.[45] This does not mean that characters avoid self-transcendence: Oedipus does not remain in ignorance but seeks to know. "Sophoclean *daimonic* heroes are mortals who cannot but go beyond the mortal human measure into a realm closer to the immortal gods in order to reach whatever tragic knowledge may be available by the journey into that unknown."[46] Or to quote Halliwell again: "the tragic-heroic rises above the level at which human lives are absorbed in the patterns of the natural world or in the routines of social being," reaching thereby to "'the more-than-human.'"[47] Tragedy dramatizes the impulse towards revelatory disclosure, however disastrous or beneficial such knowledge might be. However, there is no necessity that the outcome of tragedy has to be destructive, since tragedy does not provide certainties of this kind, but rather dramatizes them in

---

42. Halliwell, "Human Limits and the Religion of Greek Tragedy," 170.
43. Halliwell, "Human Limits and the Religion of Greek Tragedy," 172.
44. Halliwell, "Human Limits and the Religion of Greek Tragedy," 170.
45. "Tragic figures possess, or come to, a consciousness that the directions of their lives point to agencies beyond their own knowledge or control. Yet this consciousness grows from, and enlarges, a feeling of the integrity of human experience in its own right" (Halliwell, "Human Limits and the Religion of Greek Tragedy," 170).
46. Tracy, "Horror and Horror," 761–62.
47. Halliwell, "Human Limits and the Religion of Greek Tragedy," 174.

an ironic fashion.[48] One could suggest that tragedy most clearly expresses transcendence here, within what I have previously called *the negativity of the tragic*—that intractability which refuses consolatory systems.

This is somewhat related to, but distinct from, Aristotle's statement that "tragedy" reaches towards something more universal than "history," and is thereby more philosophically inclined (*Poetics* 1451b5–b26). Philosophical expansion is certainly present in the likes of Aristotle and Aristophanes, and (as we saw earlier) is implicated within tragic drama itself. But it is clear that this universalizing scope of tragedy is most stringent within modernity,[49] especially after the so-called *la querelle des anciens et des modernes* (ca. 1792). To give a somewhat potted summary of these developments, what I am calling *the modern invention of the tragic* began more-or-less in France and Germany in the seventeenth century. This self-reflexive turn in Europe towards Attic drama was instigated by an intense study of Aristotle's *Poetics* (revived in the Renaissance) and also by the French Revolution which brought into the zeitgeist a sensibility for dawning emancipation. Tragedy in this cultural remit became a horizon of significance in which modernity achieved a self-understanding. Joshua Billings has argued that a duality appears within the literary criticism of this period: on the one hand, there is a transition towards *historicization* and classical philology, which emphasized the peculiarity of ancient tragedy in comparison with eighteenth-century norms.[50] But on the other hand, tragedy was also subjected to *universalization*, a movement that became epitomized in the philosophy of the tragic (in the works of Schelling, Schlegel, Hegel, Hölderlin, and Nietzsche). Initially, this development centred on whether the so-called tragic effect—or Aristotelian catharsis—exhibited transhistorical significance, and became a site of debate regarding the continuity or discontinuity between ancient and modern tragedies. Following this aggrandizing trajectory, the tragic gradually assumes a more metaphysical and ontological stature.

48. "The experiences of tragic-heroic men and women appear to defy unwavering belief in divine morality, yet the imagination which endows gods with quasi-human passions and attachments, and pictures them as drawn to involvement in human destinies, is for this very reason unable to suppose that the divine simply transcends the realm of goodness, love, or pity. In its ethical substance, as in its entire vision of the dealings between men and gods, Greek tragedy attains no final certainties—neither the sheer pessimism of a mechanical determinism, nor the consoling pledge of a supreme theodicy" (Halliwell, "Human Limits and the Religion of Greek Tragedy," 178).

49. See the studies found in Billings and Leonard, *Tragedy and the Idea of Modernity*. Also see Leonard, *Tragic Modernities*.

50. Billings, *Genealogy of the Tragic*. In France, this tendency was exemplified by Rochefort and in Germany by Romantics like Herder.

A watershed moment in this reception is the arrival of Kantian aesthetics, especially as regards its prioritizing, after Descartes and Locke, of the subjective representation of an aesthetic object.[51] The subjectivization of taste in Kant's philosophy (as Gadamer says) programmatically "denies taste any *significance as knowledge*," so that "nothing is known of the objects judged to be beautiful," and rather "only that there is a feeling of pleasure connected with them a priori in the subjective consciousness."[52] The Kantian concept of taste, within the Third Critique, is a formalist gesture which proposes that "the specific contents of taste are irrelevant to its transcendental function," because "Kant is interested only insofar as there is a special principle of aesthetic judgment, and that is why he is interested only in the *pure* judgment of taste."[53] Connected to this subjectivity of taste, over-against an externalized object, is the more general trope of 'alienation' that came to dominate modern aesthetics, whereby the "poetry of aesthetic reconciliation must seek its own self-consciousness against the prose of alienated reality."[54] Within this schema, Kant (and Schiller after him) held that beauty could only be characterized of things *as they appear to us*, and not to things-in-themselves, which were "sublime." This is related to the fact that Kant—in the wake of Edmund Burke[55]—accomplished a deeper separation between the categories of the sublime and the beautiful,[56] a move that issued a departure from the tradition of Pseudo-Longinus.[57] This meant that the beautiful could only be placed within the fleeting passage of the sensible, which for Kant was thoroughly pre-determined by natural laws. Beauty was ephemeral and depthless, concerned with pleasant arrangement of sensory inputs, and not the sublime and formally transcendental truths of reason.

For our purposes, this alteration is important for at least two reasons. Firstly, it is salient because the modern concept of the sublime (as mediated via Kant and Schiller) promoted the emergence of a noumenal transcendence that could only be formally grasped by reason. Why this is important

---

51. Gadamer, *Truth and Method*, 37–49.
52. Gadamer, *Truth and Method*, 38.
53. Gadamer, *Truth and Method*, 39.
54. Gadamer, *Truth and Method*, 72. On 'alienation' in Kant, cf. Bernstein, *The Fate of Art*, 17–65.
55. Burke, *A Philosophical Enquiry*; Gasché, ". . . And the Beautiful?," 24–36.
56. Kant, *The Critique of the Power of Judgement*, 5:244–78. Also see Guyer, "Kant's Distinction between the Beautiful and the Sublime"; Guyer, "The German Sublime after Kant," 103–5; Doran, *The Theory of the Sublime from Longinus to Kant*, 202–85.
57. See Longinus, "On the Sublime." Also see Deguy, "The Discourse of Exaltation (Μεγαληφορειν)," 5–24; Doran, *The Theory of the Sublime from Longinus to Kant*, 27–94; Séguy-Duclot, "Généalogie du sublime."

will become clearer later in this study. But what is illuminating now is that as an acceptance of the post-Kantian sublime became more widespread, specifically as regards its disconnection from any beautiful order, the idea of transcendence becomes to be associated with categories of unthinkable and unpresentable, equated with what cannot be cognized or communicated—especially by the poststructuralist, *soixante-huitard* generation (e.g., Derrida, Lacoue-Labarthe, Lyotard, Nancy, etc.).[58] The sublime transforms into something like the Lacanian Real or the Lyotardian *The Thing*, whose "presence as unpresentable to the mind" is one that "always withdrawn from its grasp," and "does not offer itself to dialogue and dialectic."[59] In Lacoue-Labarthe the sublime comes to be conceived as *the presentation of non-presentation*,[60] and in Nancy as *the presentation of presentation itself*.[61] This tendency (as we will see) remains incompatible with an account of metaphysical analogy, which proposes an ontological and axiological participation of the finite within the infinite, and the possibility of symbolization of the divine, within in the context of an infinitely-resourceful plenitude and apophatic suspension.[62] The postmodern continuation of Kantian metaphysics, ultimately, proposes a formalist metaphysics, a gesture of un-concealment that presents nothing, that is, *nothing-in-particular* apart from the suspension of meanings.[63]

58. For Lyotard, the "sublime is the feeling that something will happen, despite everything, within this threatening void, that something will take 'place' and will announce that everything is not over. That place is mere 'here', the most minimal occurrence" (Lyotard, *The Inhuman*, 84). It is a "presence," an "instant which interrupts the chaos of history and which recalls, or simply calls out that 'there is', even before that which is has any signification." Such sheer happening, without available content, is the meaning of sublimity within the Lyotardian lexis. Parsed thus, it reduces being-as-event to a formalist gesture without specificity, since "being is not meaning" but a pure *there is* (Lyotard, *The Inhuman*, 87). Speaking in "The Sublime and the Avant-Garde" (Lyotard, *The Inhuman*, 90), Lyotard says that the sublime does not concern a *quid* but simply a *quod*, that is, *ein Ereignis* (an event), an *es geschieht* (It happens). Besides Kant, Heideggerian notions of Being-as-*Ereignis* and Being-as-*Anwesen* certainly lie in the background here. On the Lyotardian sublime and its metaphysics, see Gasché, "The Sublime, Ontologically Speaking." For postmodern accounts of the sublime see Johnson, "The Postmodern Sublime." For a critique, see Kearney, *Strangers, Gods and Monsters*, 88–100; and Rancière, *The Future of the Image*, 109–38.

59. Lyotard, *The Inhuman*, 142.

60. Lacoue-Labarthe, "Sublime Truth (Part 1)"; Lacoue-Labarthe, "Sublime Truth (Part 2)." On the similarity and differences between Lacoue-Labarthe's and Lyotard's conceptualizations of the sublime, and their mutual indebtedness to Heidegger, see Peperstraten, "The Sublime and the Limits of Metaphysics."

61. Nancy, "The Sublime Offering," 25–53.

62. Milbank, "Sublimity," 211–34.

63. This is arguably a part of the Suárezian trajectory of metaphysics which was continued through Kant to Heidegger; see Blanchette, "Suárez and the Latent Essentialism

In Lyotard, the sublime names the rupture of the instantaneous, while for someone like Nancy the sublime traces a limit or contour that commences a beginning, an opening towards freedom. Like Kant, they also exclude any intellection of the sublime object (the *Ding-an-Sich*) which for Lyotard cannot be presented to the mind without a subjective and sacrificial incapacitation. The object—or *The Thing* as Lyotard calls it—cannot be dialectically engaged or confronted, but suspends any all interaction and affinity. Nancy appears to be an even greater transcendentalist since he excludes any cognizable object beyond the tracing of a limit. Such openness is presented to freedom as an *offering*, a gift that is promised but never received. Here the approximation to Being-as-such does not intimate transcendence but simply *no-thing* in particular. The deduction here is that there is no ontological reciprocity within Being-in-itself—no gift-reception or givenness but only their un-ending deferral—nor is there any mode of analogical correspondence between the finite and the infinite, since the mind is always-already exiled by Being's *presentation* (*Anwesen*) and *event* (*Ereignis*).[64] It is a sheer happening, an advent without arrival, a presentation without re-presentation. The importance of this becomes legible in Chapter 8 where I talk about whether there are varieties of tragic suffering and pain that are finally unthinkable and unspeakable, within the question about we can bring pain into speech or whether we are relegated only to silence. Following Rowan Williams and Gillian Rose, I will question the viability of this position, along with this postmodernist construal of the tragic sublime.[65]

Intrinsically connected to this story, turning now to our second point, is how this cultural shift in modernity affected readings of the tragic itself, which were now conceptualized through a post-Enlightenment sense of the autonomy of the subject. These tendencies were stimulated through the political changes in France (as I have mentioned above), as

---

of Heidegger's Fundamental Ontology"; Courtine, *Suarez et le système de la métaphysique*, 521–38.

64. On the metaphysical problems surrounding this, see Milbank, "The Thing That is Given."

65. To see the relevance of this to the interpretation of tragedy, let me reference one contemporary example: Karl Heinz Bohrer has argued that the essentially tragic concerns that suddenness, that *appearance* of sheer horror without reconciliation, an epiphany which he thinks is contemporized through the *Unheimlichkeit* of a Baudelairean poetics. One registers overtones of Heidegger's *Sein-zum-Tode* and *Anwesen* within his own arguments, which place in question Bohrer's aversion to philosophies of the tragic. This quotation is instructive: "the event of tragedy as a form of *appearance* that is so extreme in its terror and so abrupt in its temporal termination that it fulfills the phenomenological conditions of a visitation" (Bohrer, "The Tragic," 37). On the general slippage between the Kantian sublime and "the monstrous" or "horrific" (*Ungeheuer*), see Rogozinski, "The Sublime Monster."

well as the advent of Cartesian philosophy. Under this inspiration, Kant and Schiller's deployment of the distinction between the *mathematical* and *dynamical* sublime helped to solidify the *modern* opposition between freedom and necessity, usually with an emphasis on heroic individualism.[66] For Kant and Schiller, the *mathematical* sublime concerns experiences of magnitude, as when the faculty of cognition is unable to grasp the manifold. This in turn inspires the powers of reason to imagine a totality that would encompass this immensity. The *dynamical* sublime refers to those feelings of being overpowered and deprived of one's capacity to act. For Kant, this disenfranchisement of the will agitates the subject to assert itself over-against this countervailing power. This post-Critical opposition between freedom and determinism is here paralleled with the noumenal and phenomenal distinction: even though the subject is submitted to biological and historical necessity in the world of appearances, within the noumenal sphere one remains transcendentally free.[67] This schema was eventually taken up within Schiller's criticism, and thereafter dispersed into classical scholarship. This Kantian version of the sublime, and its influence on the reception of the tragic, continues until recent times within the writings of Walter Benjamin, Martin Heidegger, and more recently in the likes of Slavoj Žižek.[68] Trends such as these have been discussed in Michelle Gellrich's genealogical critique of "tragic theory," which argues that Kant's transcendental deduction of freedom has produced individualist and anachronistic interpretations of Attic tragedy. Since *dynamical* sublimity

---

66. One cannot abstract the new configurations of the sublime and tragedy from the broader cultural suasions towards individualism and industrial capitalism. For example, Burke's language of 'heroism' in his discussion of the sublime can be read as a part of this developing matrix. This has been noted by E. J. Clery: "Burke sees labour as an act of mastery, an overcoming of difficulty that gives rise to a heroic sense of self. The taste for the sublime would, in this sense offer a moral foundation for economic individualism" (Clery, "The Pleasure of Terror," 175). However, it should be added that Burke's account of sublime needs to be placed within the context of "*self-preservation* and *society*," since it is within this societal encapsulation that the "*pain* or *danger*" (Burke, A Philosophical Enquiry, 35–36) associated with one's precarity is linked to the bonds of human "sympathy" (Burke, A Philosophical Enquiry, 41). Burke, of course, was drawing here on the Scottish Enlightenment's tradition of 'moral sentiments' (e.g., Adam Smith).

67. Several of Schiller's texts on tragedy can be found in *Sämtliche Werke*, Band 5. The most important ones are *Über den Grund des Vergnügens an tragischen Gegenständen* (1792), *Über die tragische Kunst* (1792), *Vom Ehabenen* (1793), *Über das Pathetische* (1793), and *Über das Erhabene* (1801). On Schiller's reception of the Kantian sublime, and its impact on his understanding of the tragic, see Beiser, *Schiller as Philosopher*, 238–62; Billings, *Genealogy of the Tragic*, 75–104; Hughes, "Schiller on the Pleasure of Tragedy"; Robertson, "On the Sublime and Schiller's Theory of Tragedy."

68. See Young, *The Philosophy of Tragedy*, 188–262.

concerns an autonomous subjectivity, those who are indebted to it (consciously or unconsciously) tend to repeat an exegetical one-sidedness, creating popular impressions (that have not significantly subsided) that tragedy is primarily concerned with the lonely, suffering hero.[69]

Overall what is important to register is that after the Kantian moment the tragic receives a greater speculative adornment, even reaching to theological vantages. In the philosophies of Schelling and Hölderlin, the idea of *the speculative tragic*[70] comes to project an ultimate reality (or absolute) that is subjected to contradiction and suffering.[71] To be sure, both of these thinkers express significant differences from Kant and Schiller since, as metaphysical idealists, they were less constrained by the restrictions of Kantian transcendentalism. However, they remained nonetheless indebted this tradition particularly as regards the moral economy of the sublime. Schelling—who was arguably the first to propound a "philosophy of the tragic"[72]—argued that tragedy enacted a speculative reconciliation between freedom and necessity, or what he called "criticism" (á la Kant) and "dogmatism" (á la Spinoza). He sought to do this through a historicization of the subject-object schema (e.g., the Ego in its struggle against a recalcitrant environment) as this was folded into those moments where the opposition between necessity and self-determination were combined in an instant of experienced identity, thereby intimating their asymptotic harmonization within the Absolute. On the one hand, we can see this as simply a continuation of the Kantian opposition between freedom and natural law, here specifically mediated through Schiller—who was hugely significant for Schelling's aesthetics. But on the other hand, Schelling's concept of the sublime was less enamoured with the noumenalism of Kant, and as a result was quite willing to speak of the speculative identity between freedom and necessity within the Absolute, a move that certainly transgressed the prescribed limits of Kantian metaphysics. Because of this,

---

69. Gellrich, *Tragedy and Theory*, 243–67. This in turn impacts how one reads concepts like tragic necessity; as Raymond Williams writes, modern interpretations of Greek tragedy tend to have "abstracted a general Necessity" from the choral context of Greek tragedy, pitting it "within and against it suffering individuals, summed up as the tragic hero," whereby the "mainspring of the action is then seen as the isolation of this hero" (Williams, *Modern Tragedy*, 39–40).

70. On tragedy and the birth of "the speculative," see Lacoue-Labarthe, "The Caesura of the Speculative," in *Typography*, 208–35.

71. David Krell's *The Tragic Absolute* gives an expansive treatment of this theme in Schelling and Hölderlin (amongst others).

72. As Peter Szondi has famously said: "Since Aristotle, there has been a poetics of tragedy. Only since Schelling has there been a philosophy of the tragic" (Szondi, *An Essay on the Tragic*, 1).

the interrelation of the sublime and the beautiful was less conflictive for Schelling, since it theorized a speculative enfolding of the infinite within the finite, the formless within form, which enabled him to comprehend, within the confines of his broader system, the linkage between the sensible and the super-sensible. Such a logic was unfurled within 'the tragic' to the extent that the 'ethos' (*Gesinnung*) of the tragic persona (e.g., Oedipus) was able to demonstrate its capacity for the divine, its ability to unite a consciousness of liberty with destiny.

Similarly, Hölderlin conceptualized the sublime as a manifestation of the Absolute, but here through the mediation of *paradox*, here specifically considered as a type of intellectual intuition of the primordial whole. Tragic sublimity concerns the agitation of polar extremities so that through this confrontation of opposing aspects the infinite will appear under the "sign" of finitude. Only through the "negative presentation" of weakness and evacuation—an absolute nothingness or pure meaninglessness—does the original, preconscious unity of the Absolute manifest itself within time. For Hölderlin, the intuition of totality shows itself within the continuing partition that distinguishes objects from others, but precisely in a manner that these specific differences coincide with their arche-unity. The world of finitude gestures towards the Absolute as far as this division—in its vibrant and suffering elements—is able to maintain this connectedness. The most exemplary moment of this progress concerns the dialectic of self-identity: my knowledge of myself can only be concluded through mediating concepts, as far as my subjectivity does not coincide with itself but comes into my consciousness through self-reflection. It is through difference and conflict, and their coincidence within a paradoxical unity, that we achieve an "intellectual intuition" of the whole, a process which can never be completed within time—á la ontotheology—but only continually suspended. This suspension, or caesura, is simply another name for the sublime, which is here manifest as *the speculatively tragic* or what could be called *the tragedy of the speculative*. The converse of Hölderlin's suspended dialectic is that the Absolute cannot present itself within time as anything other than a fragmented order, as a totality which is always-already subject to the disintegrations of history. The suffering and division of the immanent is thereby mirrored within transcendent being, namely God.[73] David Krell summarizes this developing tragic metaphysic as one in which "all gods and every God, including the God of faith and the Spirit of absolute knowing, is subject to the same ambiguity and is on the same bumpy ride as the rest

---

73. This account of Schelling and Hölderlin is taken from Billings, *Genealogy of the Tragic*, 80–88, 123–32, 133–58, 189–221; Courtine, "Tragedy and Sublimity"; Courtine, "Of Tragic Metaphor."; Balfour, "Paradoxen."

of us. Suffering is written into the script. Languishing is of the essence."[74] Adopting Heideggerian language, one could say that this imaging of 'the speculative tragic' implies what could be called *ontotheology of suffering*: for Schelling and Hölderlin, the One is not self-identical or simple but ruptured and traumatized, always-already from the ages of the world.

From a more explicitly theological angle, what should be brought to attention is that this speculative trajectory is present in modern dogmatics also. Jürgen Moltmann is exemplary, as can be seen in his stridency against divine impassibility, as most famously expounded in *The Crucified God*.[75] This monograph has few explicit references to tragedy as such,[76] but the overall thematic of transcendental dereliction and 'godlessness' certainly places Moltmann within a Schellingesque trajectory.[77] In *God in Creation*, there are references to the tragic quality of a creation that is subject to "futility."[78] Elsewhere, he also makes mention of tragedy in reference to Miguel de Unamuno while discussing the mystical idea of "the sorrow of God" (*congoja*).[79] However, Moltmann's most affirmative statement on the tragic is in relation to the Russian mystical philosopher Nicholas Berdyaev.[80] Moltmann endorses the conjecture of a "tragedy in God" in which God struggles for freedom within time, so that "the tragedy of human history is God's own tragedy too."[81] The sublimation of the tragic into the Godhead has shades of speculative idealism, and carries with the conceptual tensions we have mentioned already apropos divine passibility.[82] What can be gleaned however from is that a passibilist account

74. Krell, *The Tragic Absolute*, 14.
75. Moltmann, *The Crucified God*.
76. Moltmann, *The Crucified God*, 221–22; 267–68; 303–7.
77. Bouchard places Moltmann's theology of the cross within the *agon* of a "negative dialectic" (Adorno), which is Bouchard's own rubric for tragic experience; cf. Bouchard, *Tragic Method and Tragic Theology*, 229–34; 250–51.
78. Moltmann, *God in Creation*, 68.
79. Moltmann, *The Trinity and the Kingdom*, 36–42.
80. Moltmann, *The Trinity and the Kingdom*, 42–47.
81. Moltmann, *The Trinity and the Kingdom*, 42.
82. I will not rehash my arguments once more, but will rather give a quotation from Moltmann's contemporary, and fellow political theologian, Johann Baptist Metz. Concerning the theological popularity of divine passibility, and its account of atonement, Metz has the following to say: "Is not a reconciliation with God at work here that is too speculative, too proximate to Gnosis, achieved too much behind the back of the human history of suffering? Is there not also and especially for theologians that negative mystery of human suffering which will not allow itself to be made sense of in anyone's name? How is discourse on the suffering God not just a sublime duplication of human suffering and human powerlessness? And from another direction: How is

of divine transcendence does make the inclusion of divine tragedy or suffering conceptually 'easier.' Contrariwise, it appears that a more traditional account of aseity creates more difficulties. However, it also proposes that these tensions might have been exacerbated by a *modern* genealogy of the tragic that incorporates the post-Kantian sublime and the absolutization of suffering found in German Idealism. Nonetheless, simply asserting this genealogical connection does not resolve the problem which has been raised within modernity, namely that of *historicity*. A question is therefore presented: how is one to relate historicity and classical metaphysics if historicity remains an indubitable aspect of tragic experience? This will have to be addressed as I progress further.

Another contention of classical metaphysics is the ontological primacy of the good over evil. Since Plato and Augustine, the so-called *privatio boni* has claimed that 'evil' does not have its own 'existence' or 'being' but is traceable to a perversion of the good. However, in recent times this doctrine has been found wanting by some, especially by theorists who lean towards Kantian ideas of radical evil, and also by those who in the wake of twentieth century totalitarianisms and exterminations consider it to be existentially inadequate. Against Plato and Augustine, Kant connects the ethical not to the natural desire for the transcendent good, but to the self-legislating law that establishes non-heteronomous moral criteria. For Kant, it is this posture that places normative responsibility within the hands of human agents, who are to subject themselves to categorical legislation. But as Milbank has argued,[83] Kantianism proposes a pure formality of law that has no intrinsic orientation to good or evil. Rather, as a kind of pre-actualized possibility,

---

language about a solidaristic God who suffers with us not just a projective duplication, under the anonymous pressure of a socially prevalent ideal of solidarity (just as earlier, in feudal societies, God was represented as the unapproachable king and lord)? In any event, is not the classical doctrine of analogy (concerning the *maior dissimilitudo* that holds between God and world) violated? How can the language of the suffering God, or of suffering between God and God, avoid leading to an eternalization of suffering? Do not here God and human being end up under the weight of a quasi-mythical universalization of suffering, which finally overcomes even the impulse that resists injustice? Or perhaps in this language of the suffering there is too much of Hegel, too much sublation of the negativity of suffering into the conceptually comprehended self-movement of absolute spirit and, therefore, too much reduction of suffering to its concept? In this language of the suffering God, does not something like a secret aestheticization of all suffering secretly come into play? Suffering, which makes us cry out or finally fall wretchedly silent, knows no majesty. It is nothing great, nothing sublime; at root it is something entirely different from a powerful, solidaristic suffering-with [*Mitleiden*]. It is not simply a sign of love; rather, it is much more a horrifying sign of no longer being able to love. It is that suffering which leads into nothingness if it is not a suffering unto God" (Metz, "Suffering unto God," 619).

83. Milbank, *Being Reconciled*, 1–25.

freedom is that catalyst which enacts the distinguishability between good and evil as such; and because of this, freedom persists within an un-decidable sublimity that is disconnected from natural determination or teleology, since freedom cannot be phenomenologically deduced from sensibility. For Kant, the criteria for discerning a perverted will from a good will can only be adjudicated in relation to its commitment to duty, specifically as it counteracts or is contra-purposive to the self-interests of individuals. But problems arise at this juncture: since we cannot ever be certain that we are acting out of ethical duty or self-interest at any particular moment, we can only prove adherence by consciously acting *against* our self-interest—which is why Kant favours heroic sacrifice as the paramount demonstration of freedom.[84] Moreover, since there is no deeper connection between goodness and the will, and evil as such is accorded co-priority with the good, evil could just as well be counted as a veracious expression of 'being' since both are equally truthful accounts of reality. Once more, 'being-as-such' becomes equipoised between goodness and evil and maybe even persists beyond this opposition altogether in an unfathomable abyss—as seen in Schelling's metaphysics of a divinity that pre-exists both goodness and evil.

This analysis gains relevance for our discussion of the tragic as I consider the work of someone like Kathleen Sands, who attempts to affirm tragic theology at the expense of privation theory.[85] Sands will be discussed again in Chapter 7, but for now it is worth tracing the outlines of her argument to illuminate their present connections. Sands's contribution to tragic theory is found in her disavowal of any idea of a transcendent and metaphysical Good, specifically as bequeathed through the Augustinian tradition. For her this is reducible to "moral dualism,"[86] an assertion of a "good" separated from the entanglements of time and tragedy. For Sands, there is no ethical action that is devoid of the potential for tragic consequences,

---

84. It is for this reason that Kant—particularly after Lacan's seminal essay—has been associated with Sade. See Lacan, "Kant with Sade," 645–68. It is therefore not surprising that Kant's doctrine of the sublime is associated with a sacrificial logic: for Kant, "power" of the dynamically sublime "makes itself aesthetically knowable only through sacrifices" (Kant, *Critique of the Power of Judgement*, 5:271). Commenting on this, Milbank has spoken how for Kant "the element of displeasure within the sublime experience is a sign of the necessary *sacrifice* of the pleasurable, which is the only possible mode of access to the purely moral domain" (Milbank, "Sublimity," 218–19). It is this move in turn which has promoted a Lyotardian, Derridean ethic of *"absolute self-sacrifice without return"* (Milbank, "Sublimity," 230).

85. Sands, *Escape from Paradise*. Also, see Sands, "Tragedy, Theology, and Feminism in the Time after Time." Sand's arguments have been repeated in Keshgegian, *Time for Hope*, 96–127.

86. Sands, *Escape from Paradise*, 17–36.

and therefore all moral reasoning has to take into account the temporal and interconnected quality of every action. We cannot transcendentally extract the good from the bad; and any attempt to do so simply succumbs to the Manichaean temptation to divide and exclude. Alternatively, so she writes, "the good" (with a small 'g') should be exposited as radically contingent and non-metaphysical, as an "immanent good" rather than a "transcendent" one.[87] This requires us (and especially women) to acknowledge "the absence of a limitless and transcendent good," and "take responsibility for sin and grace into [our] own hands."[88] At this juncture, Sands works with an either-or logic: either you accept tragedy, and acknowledge the finality of non-compossible goods, or you reject tragedy for the sake of Augustinian dogmas. You cannot have it both ways.

On this point, Sands's contributions certainly deserve to be taken seriously, even if they probably present a skewed reading of Augustine (as we will see later). Moreover, she is not alone: George Steiner has argued that "absolute tragedy" rejects any Platonic-Augustinian metaphysics. In his words, it proposes a "heretical" vision of the world, since "absolute tragedy" imagines that there is an "innate evil" within things, a "manichean dialectic," and that the tragic is best exemplified within a *"performative mode of despair."*[89] On this point, Steiner is deferential to the traumas of post-war Judaism and an ontological pessimism traceable to Schopenhauer.[90] But what these assertions raise, once more, is whether the question of transcendence (and specifically the ontological priority of the Good) might come into potential conflict with an affirmation of the tragic. But it also suggests a possibility that some of the supposed tensions between Christianity and the tragic have a more recent origin, and are traceable to post-Holocaust philosophical affinities for radical evil—and maybe not the tragic as such.

At this stage of the book, the questions given are left somewhat open-ended, since a larger argument is needed to address them. But what can be said now is that there are central affirmations of Christian orthodoxy—such as divine aseity, analogy and the primacy of the Good—that *could* present issues for an incorporation of tragedy within theology, especially after its contemporary reconfigurations. Whether or not these tensions can be addressed is the exploration of this study. So in order to adjudicate this, I have decided to examine Donald MacKinnon, and those critically engaged with him, since the tensions discussed hitherto play themselves out in his *oeuvre*, and in the

---

87. Sands, *Escape from Paradise*, 43–54.
88. Sands, *Escape from Paradise*, 143.
89. Steiner, "A Note on Absolute Tragedy," 155.
90. McDowell, "Silenus' Wisdom and the 'Crime of Being.'"

sceptical commentary they have occasioned. Crucial for MacKinnon are the relation between the tragic and transcendence; more than any other theologian or moralist in contemporary times, he emphasized the importance of tragedy for Christian theology. And so in the following chapter, I will introduce MacKinnon, putting forward the general outlines of his theology and method, as well as the criticisms of him crystallized in writings of David Bentley Hart and John Milbank. The chapters that come thereafter should be read as a response that is shaped by this critical reception.

In this chapter, I gave an outline of the classical teaching regarding transcendence and aseity. I then suggested that this teaching sits in tension with some tenets of the modern idea of the tragic, and in particular its connections to *the Kantian sublime, a suffering absolute* and *a rejection of evil-as-privation*. In the following chapter, and those to follow, we will see how these questions re-appear within a modern theological debate between Hart, MacKinnon and Milbank. It is to these interactions that I now turn.

4

Donald MacKinnon I

On Critical Antiphony

This chapter constitutes our initial foray into the work of Donald MacKinnon. It attempts to interpret his basic theological posture, and how this impacts our structure of argumentation. After delineating a skeletal outline of his theological output, it will attempt a detailed reading of his most stringent critics. This moment is profoundly important for such a study, since it is these dissensions that will serve as a catalyst for the following chapters, as they attempt a response to such questions. As will be seen, such a response will be constituted by a mixture of confirmation, qualification, and contestation.

On Donald MacKinnon and the Question of Difficulty

There is a sense in which Donald MacKinnon's scholarly testament defies simple description or reduction,[1] but if one could hazard a workable dilution

---

1. Brian Hebblethwaite writes of MacKinnon that "it is virtually impossible to summarize his views. He founded no school. His colleagues and pupils simply learned from him how to ponder and probe a whole range of metaphysical, theological, and ethical issues relentlessly, without evasion, and in depth" (Hebblethwaite, "Donald MacKinnon," 455). Also cf. Surin, "Donald MacKinnon," in Surin, *Christ, Ethics and Tragedy*, ix–xi. On p. ix he says the following: "MacKinnon's work is characterized by a vast erudition, and his mode of thought is profoundly interrogative (rather than affirmative). In theological matters, he refuses to take up substantive positions, and prefers instead to 'map' the ramifications of the espousal of such positions. This task is invariably undertaken with great subtlety and a deep respect for the complexities of the subject matter

it would be less a single dogma (philosophical, theological or otherwise) than a certain transparency to 'difficulty.' It has been commented upon that MacKinnon's style resists systematic formulation: "His was a trust in the fragment, in the incomplete torso, in that which sprang resoundingly and at risk from provocations, the calling occasioned by the immediate moment or setting." So says George Steiner, a close friend and colleague (who dedicated his *On Difficulty and Other Essays* to Donald and Lois MacKinnon).[2] Such should not be understood to mean that MacKinnon had a piecemeal or dilettantish approach. Instead, one should read this tendency as part of his commitment to an intellectual integrity that refused to trivialize phenomena, especially those rebarbative aspects that defy cheap circumscription (e.g., evil, the tragic).[3] Accordingly, the prose of MacKinnon's argumentation displays a "tortuous thoroughness"[4] rather than an air-tight systematic flourish. These sentiments have been echoed by Paul Murray, who describes his method as "a rigorously self-critical fallibilism."[5] This posture stems from his distaste for easy answers when complex questions are implied, and his resistance to the idea that the world is beholden to epistemic closure or attempts at 'finalization'—hence the language of 'difficulty.'

What is meant by 'difficulty'? In an essay on "the difficulty of reality,"[6] the philosopher Cora Diamond defines this as "experiences in which we take something in reality to be resistant to our thinking it, or to be painful in its inexplicability,"[7] or as "the apparent resistance by reality to one's ordinary modes of life, including one's ordinary modes of thinking." She goes on to say that "to appreciate the difficulty is to feel oneself being shouldered out of how one thinks, or how one is supposed to think, or to have a sense of

---

treated. The reader is always left with the impression that what matters for MacKinnon is precisely what is left unsaid, though, typically, this too is somehow indicated in his texts. A thinker who prefers to create an agenda (as opposed to dealing with one that has been pre-set), to articulate problems (as opposed to resolving them), to use speech to register (rather than to subdue) the complexity of 'realia', is very likely to produce a body of work that demands further exploration and elaboration."

2. Steiner, "Tribute to Donald MacKinnon," 5.
3. Cf. Williams, "Obituary," 31–32.
4. MacKinnon, *A Study in Ethical Theory*, 197. These are MacKinnon's own words that he used to describe the style of Joseph Butler (a moralist for whom he had great esteem), but they are apposite regarding MacKinnon himself as well.
5. Murray, "Theology in the Borderlands," 368.
6. Diamond, "The Difficulty of Reality." For some commentary on this essay, see Mulhall, *The Wounded Animal*, 65–94. For a theological perspective, see Hauerwas, "Bearing Reality."
7. Diamond, "The Difficulty of Reality," 45–46.

the inability of thought to encompass what it is attempting to reach."[8] The avoidance of such difficult knowledge is described by Diamond as "deflection," as a failure to imaginatively inhabit "bodies," resulting in them being treated as "mere facts" without moral relevance.[9] Such knowledge is overwhelming, and without imaginatively inhabiting such "exposure" (in which we recognize it as "*our* exposure . . . in a shuddering experience of death and life held together"[10]), we risk closing in upon ourselves, failing to yield to what we know (as Stanley Cavell said of Shakespeare's Othello[11]). However, Diamond is perceptive enough to realize that "difficulty" does not only apply to our experiences of alienation and suffering, or what Stephen Mulhall calls "disvaluation."[12] She also makes reference to the experiences we have of beauty and a deeper ordering within a backdrop of inhumanity, and pays tribute to the idea that miraculous occurrences also can shock us into new modes of being and perception.[13] She quotes the poet Czesław Miłosz, who once said that beauty "should not exist."[14] Diamond's point is that if suffering and evil resists easy description, then goodness does so as well. And as Mulhall has said elsewhere: "Some difficulties in reality . . . are *not* ones we would wish to wish away" (italics mine).[15]

The above statements help us with our heuristic definition of 'difficulty.' But at this stage it remains open whether MacKinnon is able to account for both sides of this problematic with equal dedication, especially as regards 'the problem of evil' and what could be called 'the problem of the good.' A surface reading of MacKinnon's overwhelming preoccupation with evil might lead one to think that this habit approached the level of the obsessive. The reasons for this temperament are surely manifold. Biographical factors are of course determinative,[16] but they are not my main concern here. I have already mentioned MacKinnon's concern for intellectual 'integrity,' but one could say also that such integrity is predicated on a preference for 'realist' and 'pluralist' accounts of philosophy, against British currents of idealism and monism. MacKinnon's 'realism' does not finally exclude creative receptivity, but he remained strenuous in asserting the priority of 'discovery'

---

8. Diamond, "The Difficulty of Reality," 58.
9. Diamond, "The Difficulty of Reality," 59.
10. Diamond, "The Difficulty of Reality," 73.
11. Cavell, *Disowning Knowledge in Six Plays of Shakespeare*, 141.
12. Mulhall, *The Wounded Animal*, 87.
13. Diamond, "The Difficulty of Reality," 60–64.
14. The phrase is taken from a poem entitled "One More Day."
15. Mulhall, *The Wounded Animal*, 88.
16. The ongoing work of André Muller deserves attention in this regard.

over 'construction,' and rejected any pre-eminence of ideation over the truthful disclosure of reality.[17] Such 'particularist' and 'realist' leanings are confirmed by his friends and students (e.g., George Steiner[18] and Nicholas Lash[19]), and can be seen in his various interactions with dialogue-partners, from R. G. Collingwood to more *avant garde* figures like Vladimir Lenin and Teilhard de Chardin—much to the irritation of some who knew him.[20] MacKinnon was concerned throughout his career with "the true service of the particular,"[21] which (while not rejecting larger metaphysical placement) sought to attend faithfully, and truthfully, to the exigencies that form the substance of the moral life. Particularly poignant was the reality of suffering, as well as the stubborn presence of the tragic in human affairs. But while he was "deeply fascinated by pain" (in the words of George Steiner[22]) he was rarely sentimental in his judgments, and rejected vague invocations of 'the tragic sense of life' as a hindrance to critical thinking and ethical mobilization. Nonetheless he performed a kind of "painful apostolate"[23] in which he, through the very contortedness of his witness, sought "to *enact* certain recognitions."[24] His character and prose can be read performatively, indicating a transparency to the many-sidedness of the real—as demonstrated in a multitude of styles and sources that are commandeered to bolster his persuasive enterprise. Certainly, MacKinnon's agonizing in this area can seem to be too stringent, a bit too non-conciliatory. Cornelius Ernst once remarked (in a review of MacKinnon) upon "an indulgence in 'problems' for their own sake, a sense that one's moral being is somehow heightened by the mere fact of having become problematic."[25] Similar criticisms are echoed by other

17. A précis of MacKinnon's position can be found in MacKinnon, "Further Reflections," in MacKinnon and Lampe, *The Resurrection*.

18. Cf. Steiner, "Tribute to Donald MacKinnon," 2.

19. Cf. Lash, *Theology on Dover Beach*, 4.

20. See Kerr, "Comment."

21. This phrase is taken from MacKinnon, "Evil and Personal Responsibility."

22. Steiner, "Tribute to Donald MacKinnon," 2.

23. The phrase is taken from an essay on Kierkegaard by MacKinnon in *Borderlands of Theology*, 125.

24. Surin, "Some Aspects of the 'Grammar' of 'Incarnation' and 'Kenosis': Reflections Prompted by the Writings of Donald Mackinnon," in Surin, *Christ, Ethics and Tragedy*, 96. Cf. Surin, "Some Aspects of the 'Grammar' of 'Incarnation' and 'Kenosis,'" 109n15 for some discussion of this point.

25. Ernst, "Ethics and the Play of Intelligence," 326. It should be said that such a risk was already acknowledged by MacKinnon. On this, see MacKinnon, *A Study in Ethical Theory*, 234–35. He also spoke against a certain "intellectual masochism" whereby the theologian "shows himself ready to assent to arguments simply because they seem to make faith harder for him" (MacKinnon, "Philosophy and Christology," in *Borderlands*

interpreters of MacKinnon, including John Milbank whose reading I shall elaborate in due course. But with this in mind, one could phrase the tension so: is MacKinnon's peculiar agony merely an indulgent revelry in "the beastliness of things,"[26] or is it a meditation on Christ's vigil at Gethsemane, as it was poised between a trust in divine response and the dark epiphany of human betrayal?[27] It is to such questions, and the adequacy of MacKinnon's answers, that I shall turn in the following chapters.

The awareness of difficulty and his non-systematic or fragmented style leaves one with the problem of beginnings.[28] His preoccupation with the 'difficult' and 'the particular' does create some problems for formulating a straightforward method of interpretation. By and large, his proclivity was for the essay, rather than the extended dilations of a monograph. However, there are two exceptions: *A Study in Ethical Theory* (1957) and *The Problem of Metaphysics* (1974). Both studies are important, since they provide a larger canvass for presentation, and in some sense bring together many of the scattered expostulations found in his essays and shorter writings. Our preference, however, leans towards *The Problem of Metaphysics*, for the following reasons: (1) it was MacKinnon's last monograph and therefore provides a better vantage for reading his mature thought. (2) *A Study in Ethical Theory* leans, though not absolutely, towards being a historical account of other thinkers (Bentham, Butler, Kant, Hegel), and therefore should not be

---

of Theology, 66).

26. MacKinnon, *A Study in Ethical Theory*, 242.

27. Kerr, "Remembering Donald MacKinnon," 269.

28. Timothy Connor has written, in a different context, of the risks involved in interpreting MacKinnon's thought. He has said, "Any attempt to anchor the exposition of [his thought] in what MacKinnon actually wrote inevitably runs the risk of untangling in ploddingly exegetical fashion the complex skein of his thought and flattening out the often turbulent form in which it is expressed. In addition, a thinker whose theological work is so markedly occasional and allusive and set so angularly and tersely against the backdrop of several argumentatively-rich and exegetically-thick theological and philosophical *oeuvres* is difficult to summarize. Moreover, MacKinnon invites interpretation as a disciple of one or more major figures, particularly Karl Barth and Hans Urs von Balthasar in theology and Joseph Butler and Immanuel Kant in moral philosophy. Yet the attempt to trace tributaries of influence which themselves interweave and overlap leads all too often to a vast penumbra of thought whose thematic range and density MacKinnon only rarely exposed to detailed critical exposition. Only the most selective reading could ever locate him as a Barthian or Kantian *tout simple*. Further, it must be said that if polemic rarely serves clarity of expression, in MacKinnon's case it leads in specific texts to one-sided overstatements of positions which are often mollified in related writings of the same period. If concern for balanced representation of his thought has led us to develop a synthetic account of strands of argument from across a wide variety of his works, care has been taken not to present MacKinnon's thought as tidier or more settled than it actually is" (Connor, "From Galilee to Jerusalem to Galilee," 13–14).

given the same status as his more constructive ventures. And lastly, (3) the later text addresses more explicitly the themes of tragedy and metaphysics, and therefore is deemed to be more pertinent for our present task. It is for these reasons that I have decided to focus in detail on this later text, which will provide not only a window into MacKinnon's mature thinking, but will also give a framework in which to order our presentation of a thinker who seems to resist such tidiness.

However before I discuss this specific monograph in detail, it seems necessary to place its exegesis within the context of its reception. And so it is important at this stage to step back to clarify the context of my argument. My aim here is directed towards interpreting MacKinnon's approach to the question of metaphysical transcendence, and its connection to the tragic. What should be salient though is that I am trying to read MacKinnon in light of the most important criticisms of his work; inevitably, this means that the argument is slanted towards the questions raised by such criticisms. The two figures who will be engaged are David Bentley Hart and John Milbank. Both of these thinkers are critical of his work, but they also have criticisms that reach beyond MacKinnon himself and address larger questions. So their criticisms should be seen in the developing argument as a whole, and not just in the current chapter. This is because they have views that evince pertinence on larger questions which are the concern of this study, namely, that of tragedy and a classical rendition of Christian metaphysics. They reach beyond MacKinnon and deserve a wider engagement than can be contained in this chapter alone. This means that, throughout the argument, I will be glancing backwards towards the criticisms expounded here, with the hope of addressing some of the lingering concerns which may remain. This implies that my consideration of their arguments is taken in stages, some of which extend beyond the present chapter. One result of this methodological choice is that in order to present my take on MacKinnon's work, it seems that I am obliged to present the arguments of MacKinnon's interlocutors *before* I represent his own positions on this question in detail. Such an ordering will provide clarity and direction regarding the emphases and turns in my argument. And since an appreciation or criticism of their interpretations of MacKinnon can only be properly evaluated once the evidence is laid out, there will be periodic repetitions of their readings when an informed rebuttal or confirmation of their views can be encountered.

I will turn to these views shortly, however one more thing needs discussion: since Hart and Milbank assume some knowledge of MacKinnon's work, I will briefly (and inadequately) give a summary of his intellectual tendencies. Overall, MacKinnon's proclivity was towards a moral realism[29] that sought to place human agency within a resolutely attentive mode of awareness. He prioritized the fact that our knowledge of the world, while having an undeniably constructive element, was nonetheless fundamentally premised on an openness to objective reality, to the fact that we first *discover* before we *create*. Our being is placed within an ontological receptivity that defines us as human beings, that is, having a sense of being generated out of something that exceeds selfhood. We are not self-created, and therefore because we are limited beings, it follows that we are dependent on a reality that exceeds immediate grasp. Coming to an awareness of this condition is essential if we want to enter our creatureliness. And to say that we are 'created' means, additionally, that we exist within *time*, that we are *historical* beings who are subject to an irreversible flow of development. Our agency is placed within this context, which necessitates that actions also take place within limitations that constrain all forms of human activity. It is for this reason that MacKinnon has a particular affinity for Kantian metaphysics, since it sought to place limits upon the mind's capacity for transcendent knowledge. Our knowledge is transcendentally curtailed, insofar as it remains limited by the incapacity to know things-in-themselves. It also explains MacKinnon's perennial adherence to Joseph Butler's ethical vision, which treated the question of morality within a persistent focus on the particularity of human nature. For MacKinnon, it is this attempt to overcome this limitation that constitutes our drift towards sinfulness, because by doing so we deny our time-bound nature.

This concern for limitation and finitude also explains MacKinnon's preference for *the particular*, as seen in his rejection of idealism for a variety of critical realism. For MacKinnon, rather than imposing alien structures upon reality, one must patiently and creatively allow the *realia* to manifest themselves rather than pre-empting their disclosure. This does not however imply sheer passivity, but necessitates that one cultivate certain habits of perception that will assist one in recognizing and discerning the truth when it manifests itself. Much like an artist or poet—MacKinnon uses the example of Paul Cézanne—one needs to hone a set of material capacities in order to allow the work to speak, for it to take on a life of its own in a way that exceeds the objective willing of the persona. Thus one must allow the particularity of things to show themselves, rather than imposing a pattern which misprisions them. It is for this cause that MacKinnon rallies against any philosophical *monism* that collapses singularity into an all-embracing totality. Here the influence of G. E. Moore is decisive,

---

29. See Bowyer, *Donald MacKinnon's Theology*, 32–43.

especially as regards his rejection of F. H. Bradley's account of "internal relations." This is intrinsically connected to MacKinnon's realism, since the drive to establish 'a whole' once more implicates the philosopher in the conceits of idealism, in an attempt to impose a totalizing pattern upon the intractable diversity of the world. This is why MacKinnon's metaphysics is best described as a form of *pluralistic realism*.[30]

All of this helps to contextualize MacKinnon's penchant for tragic motifs, and is especially enlightening as regards his rejection of religious theodicy. Tragedy is about the denial of easy answers and quick fixes: its vision is one of human beings existing in a world of unforeseen consequences. Our actions create effects that exceed our control, and sometimes imply innocent suffering that defies any just rationale. Thus any attempt to explain away or curtail suffering implies a denial of reality. This is why MacKinnon has little patience for theodicies that seek to impose patterns and meaning upon narratives of suffering, since this drive to justify suffering, in the words of Rowan Williams, is ultimately "an attempt to forget it as suffering, and so a quest for untruthfulness."[31] MacKinnon is opposed to any metaphysics that seeks to plot tragedy within a larger order of justification. But he is also radically opposed to a metaphysical relativism that denies meaning altogether. Without values, such as the dignity of human freedom, the substance of tragedy becomes altered beyond recognition, since without a non-trivial form of valuation, one could not say *why* tragedy and loss is so violating, why it is so *difficult*. It is for this reason that MacKinnon can speak of "the transcendence of the tragic" as a metaphysics, while also being a kind of anti-metaphysics as well. One cannot impose any confident order upon the rebarbative nature of the tragic, but one also cannot deny transcendent order altogether, because without it 'tragedy' itself would cease to be a problem. For MacKinnon then, this interplay remains a continuing issue for metaphysicians, unless one tries to avoid 'tragedy' altogether.[32]

One hopes that the last few paragraphs have given us an adequate sense of the general trend of MacKinnon's philosophy. Such will assist us then as I engage with the critiques lodged at it—a subject which will occupy the remainder of this chapter.

---

30. Cf. MacKinnon, *The Problem of Metaphysics*, 32.

31. Williams, "Trinity and Ontology," in *On Christian Theology*, 155.

32. Following after Kant, MacKinnon had an affinity for "the moral argument for the existence of God"; see Bowyer, *Donald MacKinnon's Theology*, 17–26.

David Bentley Hart: The Tragic as Sacrificial Economy and Metaphysical Consolation

Any cursory reading of Hart's *The Beauty of the Infinite* will encounter its profuse conviction and sometimes alienating volubility.[33] Such rhetoric is deliberate since Hart is not content to demurely hand over the socio-cultural realm to a 'neutral' and secularizing discourse. For him, any supposed neutrality is already to have capitulated to a particular telling of the human story, and so is a thoroughly ideological gambit. Taking cues from John Milbank, he would argue that such a tale is a historically-constructed and contingent interpretation of the world, and therefore not insuperable or inevitable. This sentiment betrays a significant awareness of postmodern accounts of how language and narrative structure our reality, and also underlies his concern for a 'rhetorical' turn in relation to the communication of Christian truth.[34] This theological conviction makes his treatise a kind of anti-Nietzschean manifesto, an unashamed affirmation of the infinitude of beauty.

Hart's treatment of tragedy occurs in the section entitled "The Consolations of Tragedy, the Terrors of Easter" (373–94).[35] The overarching concern of his argument is to distinguish between two orders of "beauty," namely that of Christ's self-donation, and, contrastively, the supposed harmony of Attic tragedy. For Hart, these constitute two different and "opposed" aesthetic visions of the world, since the perspective of Greek tragedy belongs to "[t]he sacrificial regime of the totality" as well as an "economy of violence" in which human sacrifice is given "aesthetic necessity" and "moral symmetry" (373). This constitutes Hart's initial criticism of interpreting the gospel through the lens of tragedy. The second one is that the tragic vision, in Hart's opinion, fails "to take suffering seriously enough" (373), and serves as a "consolation" that is unable to really account for the gravity of evil and suffering. Both of these criticisms underlie Hart's rejection of any kind of "tragic theology." For him "every tragic wisdom is in fact far too comforting to grasp what has occurred in Christ," and "it can scarcely, at the last, inspire any ethos but one that hovers disquietingly between resignation and masochism (or even sadism)" (374).

33. See Hart, *The Beauty of the Infinite*. Hart has some similar reflections on tragedy and antique culture in "God or Nothingness," 55–76.

34. Hart nonetheless distinguishes his "narrative" approach from other "postliberal" theologies that are placed more within the Barthian tradition, especially as regards their rejection of 'metaphysics.' Hart remains an unabashed 'Christian Platonist' and is a champion for the classical tradition. For explicit statements of his persuasion on this matter, see Hart, "Response to James K. A. Smith, Lois Malcolm and Gerard Loughlin."

35. He has more recently returned to this topic in his response to Rowan Williams's *The Tragic Imagination*. For this, see Hart, "The Gospel According to Melpomene."

Underlying Hart's rejection of "tragic theology" is his distaste of any preference for a "suffering God" (374–75).[36] For Hart these are theologies of "masochism" to the extent that they cede ontological "positivity" to suffering and evil. Hart refuses any such "positivity" because, firstly, "theology must insist upon 'historicizing evil,'" treating it as "the superscribed text of a palimpsest, obscuring the aboriginal goodness of creation" (384). Hart is clear then in his affirmation of the *privatio boni*: evil is not a "thing" or "entity," but rather a privation of goodness. It follows then that a denial of divine impassibility for Hart leads to an undermining of the goodness and metaphysical transcendence of God, and renders evil an ontological necessity (since not even God, as the being of all beings,[37] can avoid the scope of its advancement). Such a perspective also romanticizes suffering, since for Hart there exists no intrinsic connection between suffering and existential betterment: "suffering is only suffering and nothing more: it is not creative, it does not inspire love but destroys it . . . pain is essentially parasitic, a privation of being, capable of enriching or perfecting nothing" (375).[38] In Hart's estimate, "the gospel of divine *apatheia* as revealed in Christ" (375) is glad tidings, since it refuses any divine declension before the reality of suffering. God is not altered by the dialectic of evil or finitude but rather, eschatologically-speaking, is able to take creation beyond evil altogether (Hart is a proud exponent of the *apokatastasis panton*).[39]

For Hart then, "tragic theology" is damaging precisely because it is *too* conservative, too constrained in its aesthetic receptivity to account for the world-altering event of God's saving action. On the contrary, the "sacrificial logic" of tragedy ultimately resigns us to injustice, rather than prompting a resistance to the structural evils of society. Speaking of Attic tragedy, Hart says that "tragedy does not encourage; it offers no promise and seems heroically devoid of mystification; it may endow its protagonist

---

36. Also see 155–67, 354–60. One can also consult Hart, "No Shadow of Turning: On Divine Impassibility," in *The Hidden and the Manifest*, 45–69.

37. That Hart considers God to be 'being' itself is presupposed in his strenuous assertion for the *analogia entis* (which is essential for Hart's entire argument in *The Beauty of the Infinite*). However, Hart has shown in his more recent writings that the idea of God-as-Being is fundamental to the metaphysical and religious traditions more generally, and is not just confined to Christianity and the lineage of Western metaphysics. For this, see Hart, *The Experience of God*, 87–151. For a summary of his take on the *analogia entis*, see Hart, "The Destiny of Christian Metaphysics," in *The Hidden and the Manifest*, 97–112. See also Hart, "Notes on the Concept of the Infinite."

38. It is also worth mentioning that Hart is very critical of the various enterprises of theodicy, as can be seen in *The Doors of the Sea*, as well as in his beautifully sombre tale "A Voice from the Emerald World," in Hart, *The Devil and Pierre Gernet*, 89–122.

39. Hart, "God, Creation, and Evil"; Hart, *That All Shall Be Saved*.

with a certain tragic grandeur, but only one that ends in the embral glow of his or her holocaust." For him, tragedy does not "pretend to penetrate the mystery of evil . . . there is an inscrutable inevitability in the malignity of things that human freedom, far from averting, can only serve" (376). This has theological underpinnings because evil within the antique Greek mind was to be superimposed onto the Olympian realm: "Attic tragedy often locates evil in no particular place, but in a tension between human culpability and divine malice," one in which "the tragic is older than the gods" themselves (377). Hart therefore questions references to the "tragic wisdom" which might be gained, for example, from the Chorus's contemplation of undue suffering. He wonders whether the outcome is less the gaining of "wisdom" than rather an "emotional exhaustion" that is unable to counteract "the invincible violence of being" (379). He examines (briefly) some Greek tragedies (e.g., *The Oresteia*, *The Bacchae*), and comes to the conclusion that they do not contradict his assertion that "the religious dynamism of Attic tragedy" entails "the form of a closed circle," that "it reinforces the civic order it puts into question, by placing that order within a context of cosmic violence" (380).

An exposition of Donald MacKinnon and Nicholas Lash becomes pertinent now: regarding Lash, Hart argues that he "more or less collapses Easter into Good Friday in such a way that the former takes on the character of simply a second perspective upon the latter," "a speculative return to the cross," constituting its "most inward meaning" (382). Particularly worrying for Hart is "the way [that such a] reading makes knowledge and spiritual comfort the fruit of an annihilation of finite form" (387), turning it into a quasi-pagan *auto-da-fé*. For Hart, Lash's reading of resurrection implies an eternalization of the cross, a move he rebuffs by saying that "to reinterpret the resurrection as the speculative inner fold of the crucifixion is also an attempt to moderate the aesthetic affront of Easter" (389). This implies a denial of the radicalness of Easter, and thus underwrites a perpetual return to "the Same" (387–88). Hart rejects identifying the cross with the resurrection, and argues rather that "the resurrection occurs apart from the crucifixion, after the crucifixion, in time, and . . . vindicates not the cross but the Jew who died there" (391).

Regarding MacKinnon, he wonders if one "might ask whether MacKinnon . . . has not read the story of the crucifixion in the light of Attic tragedy as read tragedy in Christian terms" (383). Read so, it implicates the story of Jesus in the trajectory of Olympian metaphysics in which violence is ultimately "mystified" (384), as exemplified in the case of the tragic hero who is scapegoated for the cause of civil harmony (the influence of René Girard is explicit here). He expands this by saying that

"Tragedy universalizes the form of the splendid hero," but that this figure is ultimately "excluded, pushed to the margins," and that "his suffering cannot inaugurate a new *civitas*, but only restores the balance of the old order." Thus the hero "ventures into the void, and so affirms once again that beyond the city walls there is only void." The hero, therefore, "dwells always in that penumbral region between *the sublime and the beautiful, guarding the boundaries of both*" (385; italics mine). Referencing Lash's and MacKinnon's tragic realism—a realism that seeks to disillusion us of world-denying fantasies—Hart suggests (on the contrary) that "Tragedy is not . . . an art of disenchantment" because "metaphysical solace is precisely what the tragic is" (386). Tragedy, rather than being a rupture of bloated expectations, is precisely too "optimistic." In distinction from this, the narrative of cross and resurrection is able to affirm both the horrific quality of evil, as well as the "insane expectation that what is lost will be given back" (392). For Hart, the resurrection is a truly irruptive event, whereas tragic wisdom is resigned to a world of hopeless circumambulation.

As seems clear from the above, Hart is strenuous in his assertion that the adoption of a specifically tragic perspective within Christian theology can only imply a confirmation of exclusionary political systems, in which human beings are sacrificed for social harmony. On this point, Hart's refusal seems clear. However, all of this does not mean that he is rejecting tragedy as a poetic form outright (cf. 375–76), nor that he is homogenizing all tragedy under the same "sacrificial logic" (he does not think that Shakespeare or Calderón can be painted with the same brushstrokes[40]). Nor does this imply that Hart is unable to sympathize with the pathos and grandeur of Greek religion,[41] or that Christ cannot be understood as a "tragic" figure in his own right.[42] Nonetheless, and despite these qualifications, it is the specifically Greek incarnation of tragic consciousness that remains problematic for Hart. For him, it is embroiled in the sacrificial economy of Olympian religion and ritual, and cannot account for the radical novelty of the Christian gospel. And it is precisely this 'Greek' trajectory which he claims to find in

40. Cf. Hart, "Response from David Bentley Hart to McGuckin and Murphy."

41. See for example his short story entitled "The House of Apollo," in *The Devil and Pierre Gernet*, 64–88.

42. In *Atheist Delusions*, Hart has mentioned in passing that "Try as we might, we shall never really be able to see Christ's broken, humiliated, and doomed humanity as something self-evidently contemptible and ridiculous; we are instead, in a very real sense, *destined* to see it as encompassing the very mystery of our own humanity: a sublime fragility, at once tragic and magnificent, pitiable and wonderful" (Hart, *Atheist Delusions*, 173). It should however also be said that his rather bleak view of Greek religion and culture (including tragedy) remain intact. On this, see Hart, *Atheist Delusions*, 129–45. Also cf. Hart, "Baptism and Cosmic Allegiance."

both Lash and MacKinnon's appropriation of tragic themes. With Lash, we have a 'Hegelian' collapse of the resurrection into the crucifixion, and with MacKinnon we have the gospel being read as a Greek tragedy (with all its implied 'sacrificial' overtones).

I will not enter here into an interpretation of Lash's theology of the cross (or contest Hart's reading of Hegel). Rather, my focus is on Donald MacKinnon, and the influence he initiated. Since I have yet to expound MacKinnon's thought in more detail it seems expedient at this stage not to get into a deep examination of the content and form of Hart's critique, since this is the burden of what is to come in later chapters. What can be said at this stage (by way of foretaste) is that Hart's judgments seem to have a rather sweeping character to them, one that renders his arguments vulnerable in relation to detail. His rather brash examination of MacKinnon, without regard to his complexity, seems to undermine the durability of his critique. Such a tendency is also apparent in his treatment of the Greek tragedians. Does his heuristic of 'sacrificial totality' have universal sway in this regard? One could ask whether this illuminates plays such as *Philoctetes, Oedipus at Colonus* or even *The Eumenides*. On his estimate, these plays are rather odd tragedies. Much like the essentialization of the tragic as found in George Steiner (who Hart quotes at length), he seems to be rather reductive in his approach to Greek tragedy and ostensibly cites little recent scholarship on the matter. It is also worth asking whether Hart is sufficiently aware of the Kantian trajectories he incarnates, as when he speaks of the tragic hero as one who dwells between "the sublime and the beautiful, guarding the boundaries of both" (385). Is this not an anachronistic poetics? Can it historically account for the fact that this language is *precisely* the product of a post-Kantian aesthetic of the tragic? These are questions I would pose to Hart. As mentioned earlier, my questions are tentative and require deeper argumentation. However, they serve to give an indication of where my trajectory is leading.

John Milbank: The Tragic as Transcendental Limitation and Sublime Speculation

Milbank's riposte to MacKinnon is different, but cognate with Hart's disagreements. Milbank is less focused than Hart on how we interpret Greek tragedy, and is more concerned about how the tragic moves within MacKinnon's thought both philosophically and ethically. His most sustained critique of MacKinnon is found in a collection of writings penned in honour of MacKinnon,⁴³ which was later re-titled "A Critique of the Theology of Right."⁴⁴ The burden of Milbank's essay is to question the Kantian legacy within theology in the name of a revived Thomism.⁴⁵ Of particular concern are the "transcendentalist" assumptions that have migrated uncritically into theological thought. Milbank desires to counteract these tendencies by advocating a renewed focus on theology as "metaphysics" and as a form of "historicism," which he attempts through a Thomistic-inspired and postmodern 'repetition' of the *analogia entis* (here understood a paradoxical participation of creatures in the divine perfections). Such notions (as seen in his more recent work) are strongly inflected by a Christian Neoplatonism that seeks to relate notions of analogical participation to 'theurgic' accounts of liturgy and human creativity.⁴⁶

It is for these reasons that Milbank considers Kantian metaphysics to be dubious, since by confining access to the transcendent only to the practical will (and not 'reason'), Kant renders transcendence as 'beyond' the aegis of discernment, making it unable to adjudicate between rival metaphysical claims, or to articulate a positive account of collective and distributive justice. Such transcendental "agnosticism" is the political foundation for liberalism, since a "theology proceeding in the wake of transcendentalism is partially reducible to a liberal rights ideology" (7).⁴⁷ Such a political vision is often assumed to be agnostic regarding transcendent values, but such a perspective *already* assumes a secularized and heterodox theology, as Milbank stresses continuously.

43. Milbank, "Between Purgation and Illumination," 161–96.

44. Milbank, "A Critique of the Theology of Right," in *The Word Made Strange*, 7–35. My quotations shall be taken from this later version. The pagination is found in the text.

45. The rejection of the Kantian delimitation of metaphysics is pervasive in the writings of Milbank (and Radical Orthodoxy more generally), for a sample and summary of this critique, see Milbank, "Knowledge," 21–37; Milbank, "The Soul of Reciprocity, Part One," 371–83; Milbank, "The Invocation of Clio," 13–21; Milbank, "The Grandeur of Reason and the Perversity of Rationalism," 368–73; Milbank, "Hume Versus Kant."

46. For a fuller exposé of Milbank's retrieval of metaphysics, see Milbank, "Only Theology Overcomes Metaphysics," in *The Word Made Strange*, 36–52; Milbank, "Only Theology Saves Metaphysics," 452–500; Milbank, "The Double Glory, or Paradox Versus Dialectic," 110–233; Milbank, *Beyond Secular Order*, 19–113; Milbank, "Manifestation and Procedure," 41–117. For some secondary literature on Milbank's metaphysics, see Bengston, *Explorations in Post-Secular Metaphysics*, 53–74, and the very good summary found in Venard, "The Litany of Truth."

47. One can consult here especially Milbank's critical work on the Western discourse of rights and liberalism. For more, see Milbank, "On Complex Space," in *The Word Made Strange*, 268–92; Milbank, *Being Reconciled*, 162–211; Milbank, "Against Human Rights"; Milbank, "Dignity Rather than Right"; Milbank, *Beyond Secular Order*, 114–269; Milbank and Pabst, *The Politics of Virtue*.

Milbank's metaphysical concerns are immediately apparent in this essay: he initiates it by diving into a portrayal of theological analogy, particularly construed as "participation." Such participation' implies a truthful speculation of divine being through the capacities of human language; but it is also apophatic since divine nature can never be comprehended. Milbank is critical of Eberhard Jüngel who (he argues) conflates negative theology with a kind of Kantian transcendentalism, in which the ultimate "cause" of things can only be construed as an indefinite "as if," lacking eminent attribution. Milbank contests Jüngel's 'agnostic' reading of Aquinas as overemphasizing the "analogy of proportion" (e.g., A/B: C/D) while neglecting Aquinas' more "mature" statements affirming the "analogy of attribution" (e.g., A/B: C/B).[48] In this later version, creation has an analogous relation to being—with God as the medium of such relation—and not some prior known proportion into which God and creation are inserted. Such a construal of analogy maintains "a dynamic ontological tension," in which created being's analogical naming of God draws incrementally towards God. Milbank argues that Kant's use of the analogy of proportion implies "a specifiable, fixed, precisely known sort of relation of God to the creation," since "God is only related to creation as efficient cause—he '*constructs*' the world outside himself as an artisan manufactures a clock" (9). This implies that Kant's metaphysics is ultimately more "dogmatic" than Aquinas,' in the sense that while Aquinas is more "agnostic" regarding God's relation to the world, Kant is much less so (despite him being more chary, than Aquinas, regarding God *in se*). His position is confirmed further when one examines the metaphysical lineage that underpins Kant's "phenomenalism" (e.g., Leibniz and Wolff) whereby noumena are unknowable, and yet are fixed by the boundedness of pure reason (9). For Kant, things-in-themselves remain without content, constituting a "sublime" speculation whereby "one is brought up against the margin of organized, formal, 'beautiful' experience, and at this margin becomes overwhelmed by the intimation of the materially formless, and infinitely total" (10).[49] Kant's "dogmatism" asserts an aprioristic division of the metaphysical realm from phenomena, and the categories of understanding from "things-in-themselves." But such a

---

48. For more on this see, Landry, "L'analogie de proportion chez saint Thomas d'Aquin"; Landry, "L'analogie de proportionnalité chez saint Thomas d'Aquin"; Millet, "Analogie et participation chez Saint Thomas d'Aquin"; Montagnes, *The Doctrine of the Analogy of Being according to Thomas Aquinas*; Hütter, "Attending to the Wisdom of God," 209–45.

49. For more on Milbank's critique of the modern aesthetic of sublimity, see Milbank, "The Sublime in Kierkegaard," 68–81; Milbank, "Beauty and the Soul," 1–9; Milbank, "Sublimity," 211–34.

standpoint already implies the conceit of a metaphysical spectator who is able to survey the interrelations within being, determining from 'outside' where the 'phenomena' ends and the 'noumena' begins. Furthermore, it assumes a scheme-content dichotomy in which categories apply only to the epistemological surface of things, rather than to ontological depth. Such a move is objectifying in the sense that it places the observer 'above' the fray of metaphysical entanglement, in the name of rational delimitation. For Milbank, these are unfounded assumptions which assume a panoptic contemplation of things that is both ahistorical and dogmatist. Such a procedure is predicated largely on a "metaphysics of the sublime," in which "one can step up to a boundary where one 'sees' that phenomenal categories no longer apply, and where one grasps, with necessity, that there are things-in-themselves, even if one can give no content to them" (11).

The political implications of this metaphysics for Kant's ethics is that freedom is understood in a largely formalist sense, in which each individual is understood to have an unalienable, negative liberty vis-à-vis other agents.[50] However, such freedom is ultimately without content, and can only be politically guaranteed by the state, and ontologically inferred from a law-giving, unknowable God who ordains permanent and unchangeable statutes of 'nature' that are read off by the rational subject.[51] Such a notion of freedom for Milbank exemplifies the tradition of liberalism, whereby the concept of freedom comes to be treated in a purely 'negative' sense, without including more substantive notions of how freedom is to be understood as collective negotiation and interrelation. Milbank thinks that Kant remains largely within this liberal tradition, but he does not disregard some countervailing instances where Kant might want to push beyond it (though Milbank thinks these are finally unsuccessful).

His discussion of Kant weaves back into a reflection on Aquinas,[52] where he is critical (though appreciative) of the work of David Burrell.

---

50. This language of negative freedom is drawn from the analyses of Isaiah Berlin in "Two Concepts of Liberty," in *Liberty*, 169–78.

51. Milbank considers this to be a move within the 'Baroque' tradition of scholasticism that stems from Francisco Suárez. More generally speaking, one can infer from this essay that Milbank considers the Kantian tradition overall to lie within a certain Scotist (and Ockhamist) trajectory, whereby God's relation to the world is understood in a 'fixed' and 'univocalist' fashion, and the will is given priority over the faculties of reason and understanding. Milbank is by no means the only figure to have traced such a genealogy. For example, see Muralt, "Kant, le dernier occamien."

52. Milbank's more recent appropriations of Aquinas only confirm and a further buttress the 'linguistic' and 'historicist' interpretation presented in this early essay. For more, see Milbank and Pickstock, *Truth in Aquinas*; Milbank, "The Thomistic Telescope"; Milbank, "On 'Thomistic Kabbalah.'"

Burrell, in his earlier work, sought to understand Aquinas's "grammatical" reflections on analogy in a "speculative" and "agnostic" fashion, in the sense that language of God is able to take us to the edge of finitude, without providing an intuition regarding the content of such language beyond the realms of human experience. Milbank interprets this move to be both anachronistic and proto-Kantian: "it is wholly relevant to say here that such an aesthetic was not culturally available to Aquinas," and it is "relevant to ask whether associating Aquinas with a 'speculative grammar' of this precise type is not slightly anachronistic in terms of the chronology of mediaeval thought" (13). Milbank argues that the "quasi-foundationalist" understanding of grammar, one that attempts to scientifically fix the meaning of words before they are appropriated theologically, stems from Scotism rather than Thomism. Such foundationalism (as Milbank's later work emphasizes strongly) leads to an overly epistemological and 'semantic' approach to questions of 'truth,' being predicated upon Kantian theories of correspondence.[53] As such, Milbank thinks that Burrell's interpretation of Aquinas's thought is located in a misreading of Thomas's idea of "participated perfections" (and ultimately his theology of creation), in which the "known" and "unknown" meaning of words are formed together, since (within contingency) our designations of being always remain within the tension of *esse* and *essentia*, where actualities can exceed notions of fixed "substance" and abstract "possibility." Aquinas's notion of "active potency," according to Milbank, moreover effectively "eschatologizes" reality, directing it towards the "super-addition" of divine grace (14).[54]

It follows from this that Aquinas does not give reasons why there is "being-in-general" (a Leibnizian question), nor is he interested in the Kantian question of whether being is merely a predicate or not.[55] For Aquinas,

---

53. One can compare here the comments made by Milbank in "The Grandeur of Reason and the Perversity of Rationalism," 388: "[Radical Orthodoxy] regards the linguistic turn as fundamentally correct, but does not read this in a quasi-transcendentalist way ... as confining us all the more within finite limits, but rather as rendering the Kantian basis of securing these limits as 'impossible' by undoing the Kantian 'correlation' between *a priori* categories and *a posteriori* appearances, respectively established from independent sources."

54. Also see John Milbank, "Faith, Reason and Imagination," 82, for more comments on metaphysics and historicity, and its relation to the interplay between essence and existence. For a similar reading of Aquinas's notion of *esse* and *essentia*, see Pieper, *The Silence of St. Thomas*; and Narcisse, "Thomistic Realism?"

55. Cf. "Manifestation and Procedure," 89: "Aquinas thinks that there can be no real or thought essence independent of unity or some degree of actuality. Thus he has ... shown that the merely formal distinction of being and essence (which in modern times will be exacerbated to the view that 'being is not a predicate' in Kant and Frege), by tending at once to existentialize essence and essentialise an empty existence, tends to

"being-in-general" is disclosed through particular beings, who themselves participate in God, who is a "super-ordinate trans-essentiality" (14) that gives existence to beings themselves. Being, rather than being fixed and predetermined, is open and non-finalizable, since it participates in the infinitude of God. This constitutes the ontological ground for analogical language: for Aquinas "the possibility of analogy is grounded in this reality of participation in being and goodness. Analogy is not, for him, primarily a linguistic doctrine, even if . . . it must become so for us—though not in a manner which persists in the transcendentalist illusion that a 'semantic' account of analogy can be given before an ontological account of participation" (15). A Thomistic "metaphysics of participation" implies that all generalized "grammar" lies upon a truly theological foundation (in distinction from the tradition of Scotus), and that axiological language regarding degrees of "perfections" implies analogical participation.[56]

In the second part, Milbank moves onto a discussion of how "liberal deontology" has entered into theology, here seeking to include Donald MacKinnon within this trajectory. According to Milbank, MacKinnon's work "straddles the boundary of the sublime," and "does so with more perplexity and more intensity than almost anyone else's." Milbank notes in MacKinnon's dual insistence on the category of "purgation" as merely a "descriptive" exercise in metaphysics, and the more "speculative" category of "illumination" which aims at "some sort of positive affirmation of transcendence." As such, MacKinnon attempts to articulate something like the analogy of attribution, but here through "a kenotic and tragic Christology." However, Milbank estimates that this bifurcation between "purgation" and "illumination" (like its Kantian counterpart) is problematic since "to conceive of purgation entirely as a *prelude* to illumination, or of 'description' as a task innocent of speculation, may forestall illumination altogether, or else radically determine its instance" (18). Milbank's argumentation here is aimed at placing MacKinnon within a Kantian trajectory, as seen especially in MacKinnon's program of relating ethics to metaphysics. Following Joseph Butler, MacKinnon suggests that "a deontological ethics" is ameliorated by an "attention to particular facts or particular persons regarded as embodying particular sets of values," and, moreover, that "metaphysics may have to become constitutive rather than merely regulative to the degree that our naturally-given metaphysical disposition cannot help assigning to this or

---

fantasise their prising apart. By comparison, Aquinas clearly indicates that the real distinction involves no such virtually latent sundering." Kant's own discussion of this can be found in his critique of the ontological argument; cf. Immanuel Kant, *The Critique of Pure Reason*, A592–602 = B620–30.

56. Cf. Milbank, "A Critique of the Theology of Right," 16.

that representation a better clue to ultimate reality than what is found elsewhere" (18). Butler is important for his metaphysico-ethical project because "MacKinnon effects a sort of Christological reworking of Butlerian analogy, such that the essential content of revelation tends to be reduced to a more intense affirmation of the essential 'natural' limits of human existence as providing sufficient guidance for our lives" (19).

However, Milbank thinks that this method exudes an unstable "freight of positivity," and links this heritage to the influence of the Anglican Henry Mansel,[57] whereby natural law (in a post-Suárezian manner[58]) achieves such an apex of importance that now the contents and "facts" of revelation do not tell us anything new about the criteria of moral behavior. This is not to forget the "critical" and "negative" procedure of Butlerian ethics that greatly influenced MacKinnon; however Milbank thinks that he is too quick in identifying this tradition with the *via negativa* (19).[59] Additionally problematic for Milbank is MacKinnon's version of "realist pluralism," as drawn

---

57. Of Mansel, Milbank ("A Critique of the Theology of Right," 19) writes that he "was consequently anti-mystical and clearly stressed that the positive critical determination of the 'limits of religion' and positive finite knowledge of revelation was *opposed* to any *via negativa*." This is because, as Don Cupitt has shown, Mansel equated orthodoxy with a form of "practical divinity," which he understood to be a purely "regulative" account of faith, eschewing all varieties of metaphysical "speculation." For Mansel, God is fundamentally unknowable, and therefore theology is concerned with propounding practicable verities that are to be obeyed rather than thought. Since God is eminently un-cognizable, there can be no growth or development in theological knowledge, no coherent account of analogy, or any negative theology for that matter. It is not insignificant to notice here also that Mansel, through an adoption of a Kantian epistemology and its divorce between rationality and faith, assisted in the development of Victorian and theistic agnosticism. This current, drawing from the insights of Kant and Hamilton, contributed to the religious scepticism found in thinkers such as Hebert Spencer, T. H. Huxley and Sir Leslie Stephen. On Mansel's place within the history of British agnosticism, see Lightman, "Henry Longueville Mansel and the Origins of Agnosticism." For his opposition to 'speculation,' see Cupitt, "Mansel's Theory of Regulative Truth."

58. See Milbank, "A Critique of the Theology of Right," 19. The French jurist and philosopher Michel Villey confirms this picture of Suárez: in distinction from the Aristotelian, Roman and Thomist tradition, Suárez has an *a priori*, "systematic" and "rationalist" account of legality, in which *jus* becomes convertible with *lex*, and "right" has becomes equated with the subjective and individualist rights. Cf. Villey, "Remarque sur la notion de droit chez Suarez." It is this tradition, as Villey argues, that has led to a "juridical positivism," and a rather scientistic conception of law that fails to account for the reality of prudence and flexibility as essential to any exercise of legal judgement. He makes these arguments in Villey, "Epitome of Classical Natural Law" and "Epitome of Classical Natural Law (Part II)."

59. Milbank does however think that the influence of Henry Scott Holland might make this picture a bit more complicated.

from G. E. Moore. In a passage worth quoting at length, Milbank argues that the tendency of this tradition is to insist that

> things can be adequately known and distinguished as they are in themselves without believing that their full determination awaits upon the infinity of relations they may have to everything else.... This should adequately avoid any absolute determinism, because here there can be no 'whole' distinct from the network of relationships, which are always relations of particular, distinguishable things. Certainly, to maintain this distinguishability, one needs to say that entities may be relatively discrete, relatively indifferent to certain relations in which they may fall. And yet even such indifference, such 'resistance' can help negatively to determine what they are and what they become. (19)

Milbank does grant that Aristotelian "substance" is helpful in avoiding any "totalizing" picture of sheer "process," but he suggests that "substance" should rather be understood as "a linguistic marker for certain patterns of narrative consistency in which, none the less, we can never identify any 'underlying' constant element." MacKinnon's "non-dialectical" appropriation of Aristotelian substance (here mediated through logical atomism) opens up aporias since it appears on the contrary that "things are, in fact, entirely constituted through networks of changing relationships," and that "the more one seeks to isolate them in their determinate finitude, the more their concreteness altogether escapes us, and their sheer particularity becomes paradoxically their only remaining property: a particularity about which we can say nothing." This results, through a Hegelian inversion, in an overly-formalized and empty product whereby "for all practical purposes one particular becomes the same as all other particulars," since any account of singularity will need to relationally concretized (19–20).

MacKinnon's version of sublime speculation ultimately leads to Milbank's critique of his use of tragic themes. In addition to the existential focus on the tragic found in MacKinnon's work, Milbank speculates that there are additional reasons for MacKinnon's choice of such motifs. He suggests that there are formalist reasons for his preoccupation with tragedy, and that MacKinnon's election of this genre is based on a hyper-realist "transcendence" that prioritizes metaphysics of "presence" over teleology. Such a concentration privileges a "tragic indecision which occasions a kind of *exit* from the narrative instead of remaining in the plot and seeking for resolutions." Milbank suggests that MacKinnon does not *discover* but rather *emplots* history in a tragic superstructure, hereby transforming "the categorical imperative itself into something very like the view that it is *only* in tragic perplexity that we know we are free, and at the same time are brought up against the very margins of the humanly responsible world." This imitates post-Kantian and Schillerian trends, since it implies that we only discover moral scrupulosity when we are abstracted from our "narratively instantiated characters," which for Milbank is "an extremely subtle version of the aesthetics of the sublime, of the liberal discourse of modernity" (21). Rather than placing choices within an unfolding history, MacKinnon apparently converts tragic complexity and limit into a transcendentalized mode of "presence" that defies any narrative "solution."

Rowan Williams captures Milbank's critique of MacKinnon succinctly. For Milbank, MacKinnon's moral philosophy aims to "naturalize"[60] the tragic, since it is only within "the destructively conflicting absolutes of tragic decision that we discover the nature of our human responsibility." Milbank worries that MacKinnon "lacks a theory as to how non-destructive social practices may be created and maintained, and so is trapped in a standoff between purely individual motivation, with whatever integrity it can muster, and the inescapably corrupting and lethal realities of the public world." MacKinnon, inspired by the likes of A. E. Taylor, preferred Kantian morality to Hegel's *Sittlichkeit*, in which Hegel prioritized how we come to recognize "the moral self in the other or in the communal discourse of humanity."[61] On this reading, MacKinnon's tendency to treat tragic irresolution as a mode of "presence" seems to imply "a near-Manichaean metaphysic," or even a "fundamental sickness or rupture in reality."[62] The operative mode of "tragic narration" in Mackinnon leads to a denial of "the significance of narrative itself," in which human characters are able to "genuinely grow and change with the passage of time," implying an emptying of "the very idea of plot" since it fails to account for the reality of "change" that is bound up with "a sequence of narrated events." In MacKinnon's account, it seems, "*nothing really alters*."[63] His transcendentalism avoids historical mediation, foreclosing outcomes before they have arrived.

Milbank does clarify that he is not chiding MacKinnon for his willingness to wrestle with tragic realities as such, but he does wonder whether "the ultimate Christian perspective may not be one of tragi-comic irony rather than unappeased tragedy." He thinks it might be possible "*in retrospect . . .* to determine our failure to attain the Aristotelian mean," as something due "to a lack of integration in our society, or the lack of a sufficiently encompassing

---

60. Williams, *The Tragic Imagination*, 108.
61. See Milbank, "Critique of the Theology of Right," 23–24.
62. Williams, *The Tragic Imagination*, 109.
63. Williams, *The Tragic Imagination*, 110.

social imagination"? To affirm this is to deny that evil is a necessary outcome, since "every evil is traceable to some lack, or perhaps rather to some sort of symbolic distortion, some imperfect vision" (22). But since MacKinnon appears to have problems with this move, Milbank thinks that his procedure discloses both his suspicion of the Augustinian *privatio boni* and his preference for modes of God-talk that espouse divine passibility. It seems then that a Kantian account of "radical evil" lurks in the background of MacKinnon's accounts of suffering.[64] Additionally, an affirmation of divine passibility would appear to endorse an ontological determination of divine being by evil and suffering, leaving unclear how such a God could suffer evil in order to leave evil "behind."[65] This position is ultimately entwined with a form of theodicy in which suffering is justified, and the tragic limits of the world are ontologically confirmed (23). Milbank goes as far as to say that MacKinnon's kenotic Christology, arguably, is itself a form of theodicy, insofar as it involved the "making known of limits and of evil" (23) instead of rendering evil as nothingness, something that is to be eschatologically "forgotten" rather than "known."

Summarizing what I have said thus far: Milbank's concern (like Hart's) is implicated in his adherence to a 'postmodern' retrieval of a traditioned, Christian account of metaphysics. Both see MacKinnon's penchant for tragedy as having dubious metaphysical and political outcomes. While Hart seems to emphasize, on a more general level, the negative floriations of "tragic theology" (and its entwinement with a sacrificial economy), Milbank is focused on how a 'Kantian' reception of tragedy within Christian thought leads to pessimism (i.e., 'radical evil'), and how Mackinnon's metaphysics is unable to account for historicity (due to its transcendentalist assumptions). Furthermore, it implies a minimalist account of political imagination, one that is focused largely on questions of authenticity and negative liberty, as disclosed in ethical aporias, while failing to articulate a robust account of common and distributive goods. Milbank suspects that MacKinnon's account of tragedy fails because of its ultimately "speculative" and "transcendentalist" assumptions, since it insists (in a dogmatic fashion) on tragic necessities being inserted into stories, rather than being discovered in

---

64. Milbank has stringently critiqued this Kantian tradition in a chapter entitled "Evil: Darkness and Silence," in Milbank, *Being Reconciled*, 1–25.

65. Milbank also wonders whether accounts of divine passibility are subject to Rousseau's critique of sympathy, in the sense that it can displace the subjective, first-person dimension of suffering. Milbank also thinks that accounts of 'divine passibility' can be partially deconstructed via Nietzsche's critique of Christianity's supposed glorification of sacrifice and weakness. For this, see Milbank, "Immutability/ Impassibility, Divine," 760–62.

them, a tendency which precisely *removes* such narratives from their lived historicity and openness. This is not to say that Milbank gives no space for existential tragedy within his own thinking—his comments on the South African church struggle during Apartheid in the same essay counter-act this assertion (30–31).[66] Nor does it even imply that he is fundamentally opposed to a nuanced "tragic theology."[67] He also contextualizes MacKinnon's polarization on deontology rather than on *sittlich* ethics as belonging to the fragmentation of Britain after the Second World War,[68] a concession which does soften his stringent critique somewhat.

Nevertheless, he continues to think that MacKinnon's metaphysics of "illumination" and "purgation" is unable to reconcile historicism and metaphysics, and that this is due to his rejection of the analogy of attribution and its participatory metaphysics. Such is acutely apparent in his account of the tragic, since it already claims to know in advance the limits of historical novelty, imagination and action *before* attending to the particularities of stories, and how narratives of suffering are reclaimed, re-imagined and re-worked. Again, this is due (in Milbank's view) to MacKinnon's Kantian "tragic piety," which is unable to think the historical "possibility of the ethical" since it "after all, *evades* the tragic, by hypostasizing it in a speculative fashion."[69] Such a perspective locks us (here echoing Hart's concerns) into a metaphysics of sacrifice and scarcity that is unable to account for the ontological plenitude of divine generosity.[70]

---

66. Milbank's reference to the South African context is present in his earlier version of the same essay (cf. Milbank, "Between Illumination and Purgation," 191), but has been removed in later version, due no doubt to the changed circumstances in the country since the early 1990s.

67. Cf. Milbank's comments on the economic and immanent trinity in "The Second Difference," in *The Word Made Strange,* 182. David Toole also has applied the rubric of "tragic theology" to Milbank's theology as a whole (a description I am sure Milbank would have some qualms with, or at least would like to qualify drastically). On this see, Toole, *Waiting for Godot in Sarajevo.* Also, cf. Pickstock, "Reply to David Ford and Guy Collins," 418–19. However, preeminence should fall upon Milbank's own reflections in *Being Reconciled,* 138–61, in "The Midwinter Sacrifice." Here Milbank seeks to redeem and radicalize the category of "moral luck" (echoing Bernard Williams) under the rubric of divine grace.

68. Milbank, "A Critique of the Theology of Right," 30.

69. Milbank, *Being Reconciled,* 149. He goes on to say, in the next sentence, that "Mackinnon failed to see that Speculative Idealism espoused exactly the romantic and not perhaps very Greek cult of the tragic, which he himself perpetuated—revealing thereby his own idealism despite all his explicit disavowals, rooted in his Kantianism."

70. See Milbank, "Enclaves, or Where is the Church," 349–52. For a more nuanced account of sacrifice (one that is able to retrieve its insights, while acknowledging its potential pitfalls), cf. Milbank, "Stories of Sacrifice."

Such a perspective, for Milbank, is the foundation for dubious ontologies of violence and unjust political arrangements, including liberalized capitalism (based as it is, ultimately, upon 'the myth of scarcity').

The concerns of Milbank and Hart have shown that there are several sites of contention and debate, namely (1) the relation of metaphysics to the question of history (as seen as pre-eminently in the *analogia entis*), and how this relates to (2) the reception of Kantian metaphysics within MacKinnon's work (and tragic philosophy more generally). Here the question of how the tragic operates within MacKinnon's thinking becomes pertinent, and I should hope to discover whether the suspicions that both Hart and Milbank have are warranted. Of related concern is whether (3) tragedy as such participates in a sacrificial economy and if (4) Mackinnon's appropriation of the tragic within ethics leads either to a 'liberal' or 'pessimist' mode of political reasoning. Additionally, there is the question of whether (5) MacKinnon underplays the resurrection in relation to tragic indeterminacy, and occludes the radical trans-valuation of death that Easter performs. But also important for our purposes are the cognate objections of Hart and Milbank relating to (6) theologies of divine suffering, and (7) the rejection of Platonic-Augustinian theory of evil-as-privation, and how these are connected to a post-Kantian mode of sublime speculation.

Underlying all these questions is the problem of how Christian theology narrates its specific account of God's transcendence since it relates to its analogical account of the creator-created, infinite-finite relation (1), and how this is to be distinguished from post-Kantian and postmodern theories of aesthetic sublimity (2). This classical recounting of divine transcendence, here presupposed and argued for by Hart and Milbank, also impinges upon (5), (6), and (7) since in different ways they are concerned about this fundamental question. Similarly, (3) and (4) concern the kind of transcendence here envisaged, and whether this is to be construed as malevolent or pessimistic. Such a vision underlies, according to Hart and Milbank, the sacrificial tendencies of the Greek polis, and ultimately—though with due respect to historical differences—the liberal order too.

These are the main contentions which I hope to address in what is to follow. However, a detailed response to *all* of them would be difficult. For example, it would be difficult in the space provided to engage in some detailed readings of Attic tragedy, with the aim of showing that Hart's interpretations are simplistic.[71] So since I am unable to address every issue here, I have decided to focus specifically on those critiques that relate to the research

---

71. I do hope to address some of these interpretations in other publications, presenting a slightly more nuanced picture of Attic tragedy, while not negating the difference of its vision from early Christianity.

question, namely the relationship between metaphysics and the tragic, specifically as this relates to the grammars of transcendence. Here, once more, I can restate my question: are their varieties of transcendence that make it harder for a classical metaphysics to appropriate the tragic? And if this is so, is there a systematic remedy? Can one conceptualize an orthodox account of transcendence (e.g., aseity, *analogia entis*, etc.) that is able to address the tragic in all seriousness, or is their relation strictly oppositional? There will be occasion along the way to address less pertinent objections and questions. But for the most part, the above node of concentration will serve as a guide for the way my arguments are spelled-out. My focus in the next chapter will be on MacKinnon's *The Problem of Metaphysics*, attempting here to structure its development according to that work's internal conjecture and argument, in light of the critical reception that I have just discussed.

5

Donald MacKinnon II

On Aporetics and Apophatics

In this chapter, I begin to unpack the work of Donald MacKinnon, especially as it relates to his understanding of metaphysics, and how this inquiry relates to the tragic. To gain a point of entry, I will focus pre-eminently on his revised Gifford Lectures. The structure of this text will provide a workable format in which to trace the wider contours of his rather complex and multifarious argument, spread over a diversity of published work. We cannot however avoid some detours in order to understand more fully his progression as it relates to those thinkers who informed him. In particular, I shall have to deal with the legacies of Aristotle and Kant as they impact his argument. I suggest here that MacKinnon's dependence on Aristotle's *aporetics* of substance provides an enlightening entrance into his metaphysics, firstly in that it privileges *particularity* as the starting-point for *abstraction*, and secondly in that it does not resolve the tension between these movements. Universality segues into minutiae and proceeds from them too, establishing a kind of restive duality between realism and idealism within his thought, even though his affinities lean towards the former. But this tradition is complicated by the fact that Aristotle's Prime Mover has no connection to the material particularity of things. When this is combined with an atomism of substance—after G. E. Moore—the metaphysical connectedness between things is rendered opaque, as is their relationship to the divine. Moreover, on top of this, MacKinnon adopts a Kantian *apophatics* without analogical participation. Following Aristotle and Plato's *Parmenides*, MacKinnon rejects *methexis* as a resolution to the problems of predication—of how we come to know distinct things—since it simply pushes the dilemma into a regression (the Third Man Argument). Similarly, after Kant, MacKinnon thinks that 'being' cannot be a predicate considered as something added to essence (Kant's Critique of the Ontological Argument). Like the previous argument, it says that duplication does not clarify anything. On the contrary, 'being' is simply a *positing*, that is, a judgement about concrete existence. *To be* does not add anything to essence, but just describes sheer presence or absence. For MacKinnon and Kant, to speak of 'being' as a predicate is just tautology. I suggest that this confluence within MacKinnon's thought overall tends towards a privileging of essence over relationality, and therefore has some problems with acknowledging both the constitutive historicity of things *and* their analogic-parabolic intimation of divinity.

MacKinnon initiates his discussion in *The Problem of Metaphysics* by embarking on a reading of the "descriptive metaphysics" of Aristotle and Kant. MacKinnon's estimation of them is that they "both carried out systematic enquiries aimed at laying bare the most fundamental and pervasive features of the world around us, the manner in which those features are interrelated and the identity and nature of those concepts revealed by analysis to be involved in all descriptive and referential discourse" (*PM*, 1).[1] For Kant, metaphysics is that systematic framing of any conceivable and objective world within repeatable structures, so that for *any* world to appear to us it must take place within such forms (this is Kant's 'transcendental deduction'). They cannot be *observed* but must be *presupposed* to make sense of the world, that is, they must be *a priori synthetic judgments*. These patterns are articulated as the ineradicable setting of our "recognitional capacities," which are further subdivided into the first and second order concepts of 'understanding.' The latter of these is defined as being an activity of "pure" cognition whereby the human mind or subject seeks to relate, abstractly, the various features of the world as it presents itself (*PM*, 2–4). Such structures are conceptualized by Kant within those elemental laws of constancy and constraint which are foundational for any coherent or rational understanding of the world (*PM*, 4–6). However, these consistencies need to be chastened, according to Kant, when we move from the immanent to the transcendent realm, since we cannot simply "estimate the relations of the conditioned to the unconditioned, the relative to the absolute" (*PM*, 7), that is, by applying the concepts of "substance" and "causality" beyond the phenomenal plane of perception (Kant's antinomies of pure reason are salient here). For MacKinnon, such a metaphysical reserve acts as a of *theologia negativa*, though now within the logics of transcendentalism.

---

1. *PM* is the abbreviation for *The Problem of Metaphysics*.

MacKinnon is at pains throughout to emphasize that the Kantian deduction of experience should not be understood in an anti-realist fashion, as if such structures in the world were there merely "for us" and not inherent within what-is-perceived. For Kant, "neither understanding nor imagination creates its own objects," since "to come to know what is the case is a finding, not a fashioning" (*PM*, 7). MacKinnon's predisposition here is towards the priority of 'discovery' over fabrication, and is aimed at preserving a sense of the objectivity or over-against-ness of reality. Such empiricism cannot be conceived apart from creative assimilation and conjecture, even though MacKinnon is stridently insistent that the mind does not create what it confronts. This sits in tension with Kant's general "anthropocentricism," but MacKinnon is quick to add that Kant's awareness of the inherent finitude of reason can also be commandeered for *theological* purposes, since conceptualization should not transgress the bounds of sense in its reach towards the unconditioned (*PM*, 9).

For Aristotle, the question hinges on the relation between "being" and "substance," in which "the categories of being" are considered as "a developing series" in which "substance" is "the most fundamental form of being" (*PM*, 10–11) insofar as it "transcends all other categories in that in all predication some reference to substance is presupposed" (*PM*, 94). Philosophical reflection on substantiality implies that "The whole pattern of our conceptual organization is pivoted on that which exists of itself" (*PM*, 12), that is, with the nature of things, and what they essentially are. Seeking to defend Aristotle against Collingwood (cf. *PM*, 10, 12), MacKinnon argues that "for Aristotle being is not a generic universal, but a transcendental one which manifests a peculiar sort of analogical unity," a unity which is "identified in the end with the most fundamental sorts of things there are in the world, in the peculiar dependence of lower form upon higher" (*PM*, 12–13), and in this vein, Aristotle's doctrine of categories suggests "a sort of hierarchical dependence in our concepts" (*PM*, 95). Such analogical predication implies that existence is not "univocal" since this would obfuscate the manifoldness of existing things. Metaphysical reflection on the proliferate diversity of being, in Aristotle, is understood to be a combination of "analytic" and "speculative" procedures, since the ontological foundations of experience are not enclosed within febrile certainty, but instead appear in a confusion of the "extremely elusive" and the "extremely familiar"—hence the need for analogy (*PM*, 14). But important to note is that MacKinnon's preference is ultimately for Plato and Kant's "negative theology" over Aristotelian analogy: in his eyes, anthropomorphism is the graver religious temptation when compared to aphasia. Nevertheless, there is a sort of fluctuation here, since it is shortly hereafter that MacKinnon expresses a tacit agreement with Aristotle's critique of the Platonic ideas, and his account of *methexis* (*PM*, 18), despite his worry that the Stagirite remains overconfident in his relating of "ontological analysis" and "cosmological theology" (*PM*, 14–16). So on the one hand, MacKinnon prefers the apophatic tradition of Plato over-against Aristotle, but on the other he believes that ontological participation tends to violate this principle.

The above delineation gives an outline of MacKinnon's appreciation of the descriptive metaphysics of Kant and Aristotle in *PM*. But since MacKinnon has developed these readings in more detail elsewhere, some of these texts will need to be engaged. I will begin with his treatment of Aristotle's account of substance, since this brings out the primacy within his thought on realism and particularity. I will then move onto his reception of Kantian transcendentalism, which will assume a more chronological method. This is because his treatments of Kant are spread over a much longer period, thus requiring a more nuanced account of their development, something which is not as prevalent in his reading of Aristotle.

Aristotle's Aporeticism: On Substance

For Aristotle, to know the particular is difficult since the 'whatness' of things remains elusive. To grasp concrete examples involves the persistent labour of description and re-evaluation, and it is because of this that the individual for Aristotle remains 'aporematic.' The abstraction of real entities involves establishing the essential and the universal, while not avoiding the accretions of the accidental and contingent. In the process of reflection, Aristotle argues, one intuits the intelligible Forms of nature, thereby excavating their connection to material composition, while always seeking to connect these discoveries to their ultimate reason-for-being (τὸ τί ἦν εἶναι). Such is predicated on a cosmos teleologically-orientated towards conceptualization, a movement that imitates the supreme intelligence and self-understanding of the Prime Mover itself.[2] It is this dynamic that informs the unending exploration at the basis of Aristotle's scientific inquiry into 'substance,' here within what Pierre Aubenque once described as "the gradual advent of essence" (γένεσις εἰς οὐσίαν).[3]

Aristotle recognized that 'being' had multiple instances (cf. *Metaphysics* VI.1026a34), but as MacKinnon says such diversity is unified in

---

[2]. For some accounts most relevant to our discussion, see Owens, *The Doctrine of Being in Aristotelian Metaphysics*, esp. 455–73; Perl, *Thinking Being*, 73–106; Booth, *Aristotelian Aporetic Ontology*, 1–35.

[3]. Aubenque, *Le problème de l'être chez Aristote*, 93.

accordance with an "analogous polarisation" on the idea of "substance": "The metaphysician's subject matter can be . . . properly identified with substance as the nuclear realization of being quâ being" (*ACS*, 97–98).⁴ MacKinnon understands "substance" within the divisions given in the *Categories*, a project that requires an open-ended empiricism inspired by the observation of individual things, that is, insofar as "substance" is "neither said of a subject nor in a subject" (*Categories* 2a14) but serves to indicate "a certain 'this'" (*Categories* 3b10).⁵ He articulates the contemporaneity of this project by juxtaposing it with G.E. Moore's essay on external and internal relations.⁶ This essay, as biographical details make clear,⁷ was instrumental in MacKinnon's turn towards philosophical realism, and so its appearance is not arbitrary. Encapsulating Moore's dense argumentation, one could say that Moore (and Russell) sought to critique the idealism of F.H. Bradley,⁸ and in particular the proposal that all relations are "intrinsical," in the sense that all relational propositions are "internal" to or necessary for their logical object, with the upshot being that one would be able—theoretically at least—to deduce an entire state of affairs from the knowledge of a particular relation.⁹ The problem of such universalized relations is that it disallows any excessiveness or externality within the world of objects, since every procedure of interrelation between objects or propositions is incorporated into their essential definition. Conceptually speaking, it is a closed system. On this model, a lack of a relational property (not-*p*) necessarily entails the non-deducibility

---

4. MacKinnon, "Aristotle's Conception of Substance," 97–119 (cited as *ACS* in the text). Elsewhere, MacKinnon has said that "Because substance is for Aristotle the nuclear realization of being, he alternates between characterizing the subject-matter of metaphysics as substance or being *qua* being." For this reference, see MacKinnon, "'Substance' in Christology: A Cross-Bench View (1972)," in *Philosophy and the Burden of Theological Honesty*, 239. On Aristotle's theory of substance more generally, see Aubenque, "Sur l'ambivalence du concept aristotélicien de substance," 93–106. For a critique of this idea of nuclear focality, see Berti, "Multiplicity and Unity of Being in Aristotle"; and Seifrin-Weis, "*Pros hen* and the Foundations of Aristotelian Metaphysics."

5. The translation is taken from *The Complete Works of Aristotle*.

6. Moore, "External and Internal Relations," in Moore, *Philosophical* Studies, 276–309. For a general explication, see MacBride, "Relations."

7. Cf. Muller, *Donald M. MacKinnon*. In this regard, one should also mention that MacKinnon once said that "Moore made it possible for me to be a realist . . . for the logical atomist, there *were* things with which men were coming to terms; the world was not simply an expression of their immanent rationality, but something given" (MacKinnon, "Philosophy and Christology," in *Borderlands of Theology*, 63).

8. See Griffin, "Russell and Moore's Revolt," 383–406.

9. Whether Russell and Moore fully grasped Bradley's point is another question. On this, see Manser, "Bradley and Internal Relations"; Bonino, "Bradley's Regress."

of a particular object (not-*A*).[10] In other words, any predicate or relation is metaphysically inseparable from its object. However, for Moore, deducibility is not limited to relational properties. Logically speaking, nothing prevents us from discovering realities that exceed or are non-reducible to any supposed relational predicate. Things may exist without being defined or predetermined by something else. This move assists philosophical analytics insofar as it seeks to discover what each particular thing *is*, without its connection to anything else. Butler's statement that "everything is what it is and not another thing" was a reference point for MacKinnon (and Moore) on this topic.[11] For instance, I may stop to examine a pear, but the pear is not changed through my examination of it, or (as Wallace Stevens would have it): "The pears are not viols / Nudes or bottles. / They resemble nothing else . . . The shadows of the pears / Are blobs on the green cloth. / The pears are not seen / As the observer wills."[12] On their account, without this excessiveness it is difficult to avoid monism and totalization, that is, a denial of 'externality,' since all 'external' or contingent relations become 'internal' or 'necessary' conditions. For Moore, while 'internal' relations are 'necessary' for objects, 'external' relations are simply a question of facticity.[13] One cannot presuppose in every case that one relation implies the other, since the $(f)x$ of any predication indicates an openness to temporality, and therefore cannot be comprehensively prejudged.[14] I can know certain truths without knowing others, and I can know all the propositions that make such a truth possible, without deducing the particular truth in question. Truths are the product of empirical discovery and case-by-case examination.

This reveals why MacKinnon compares logical atomism to *ousia*. Since "substance," or more specifically "primary substance," constitutes

---

10. For a summary of MacKinnon's understanding of Moore's argument, see Rowan Williams, "Trinity and Ontology," in *On Christian Theology*, 148–54.

11. MacKinnon, *A Study in Ethical Theory*, 171, 253. The quotation can be found in the preface to the *Fifteen Sermons Preached at the Rolls Chapel*. For this reference, see Butler, *The Works of Bishop Butler*, 44. This motto served as an epigraph for Moore's own *Principia Ethica*.

12. Stevens, "Study of Two Pears," in *Collected Poems*, I.2–4; VI.1–4.

13. See Moore, "External and Internal Relations," 302–3. The potential atomistic and positivistic outcomes of such a procedure should, however, also be emphasized, but they were, to a certain extent, questioned already by MacKinnon himself who spoke of "the logical mythology of 'atomic propositions' corresponding with 'atomic facts.'" He nonetheless still emphasized the core of the argument that "there are a number of propositions of whose truth in the sense of correspondence we are assured which are genuinely independent one of another" (MacKinnon, "Idealism and Realism: An Old Controversy Renewed," in *Explorations in Theology 5*, 142).

14. Cf. MacKinnon, "'Substance' in Christology," 243–44 on this point.

the first "category of being" for Aristotle (*ACS*, 100), it follows that what is "substantial exists of itself," and that "whatever else there is, whatever fundamental modes of being there are, all are relative to substance" (*ACS*, 101).[15] The addition of accidents or "secondary substance" to primary substance is essential thereafter for differentiations within the categories of knowledge. But a lingering question persists: "What is it that makes an individual thing an individual thing?" (*ACS*, 102). This remains a reoccurring node of contention within Aristotelian scholarship: according to one view "the individuating factor" is the "bare substratum" to which accidents are added (*ACS*, 102), and in another it is precisely the factor of "secondary substance" that individuates the "substratum." For MacKinnon, it is the latter perspective that is able to account for the "concrete realisations of the features of our world that in their severalty make up that world" (*ACS*, 104). MacKinnon, however, believes there is a textual indeterminacy within Aristotle regarding "individuation" that appears to say that we can have "primary substance" as bare materiality without form. But he contends that individuation, in the mature Aristotelian perspective, is concerned rather with a concrete existent, with a determinate 'this' (τόδε τι[16]) that cannot be thought apart from material instantiation and form.[17] As a result of this indeterminacy, it appears—paradoxically—that the hylomorphic compound is ontologically prior to what constitutes it (*ACS*, 104–6).[18] There remains an aporia here, as MacKinnon notes, since there is a latent tendency somewhat to assert formalization at the expense of concreteness.

The idea of substance, as MacKinnon summarizes, is "an attempt to lay the foundations of the doctrine of degrees of being at the level of the humdrum and the everyday" (*ACS*, 108), and so is the first within the categories of being. This should not lead us to confuse substance with a generic essence (*ACS*, 115), since substance is tied to particularity (*ACS*,

15. Cf. *Metaphysics* VII.1028a32–b2.

16. For Aristotle, "The doctrine of a 'this' shows that the form is individual and is identified *per se* with the singular thing as its act" (Owens, *The Doctrine of Being in Aristotelian Metaphysics*, 399).

17. However, MacKinnon went on to say a few years later ("'Substance' in Christology," 240) that "there is no part of Aristotle's ontology with which the modern reader finds himself less in sympathy than those parts in which he is exploring the principle of individuation. For the most part he seems to reduce it to a sheerly material factor, and to evacuate the uniqueness, for instance, of the individual person of the kind of significance we are tempted to attribute to it."

18. Owens on this score says that for Aristotle, "The Form must be kept as prior to and act of composite Entity and logical universal" (Owens, *The Doctrine of Being in Aristotelian Metaphysics*, 393). "Entity" is Owen's translation of the term οὐσία, usually rendered as "substance" in English.

109). Nonetheless, "substance"—not to be confused here with Locke's "substratum"[19]—is concerned with the question of what-is-the-case, and should therefore be related to facticity (as MacKinnon suggests). The 'realism' of such a position is important for him in that it serves to support the general trustworthiness of mental 'reference,' the fundamental other-directedness of human thinking (ACS, 110). Echoing the poet and theorist J. H. Prynne, one could say that Aristotle's notion of substance exhibits for MacKinnon both the qualities of "difficulty" and "resistance."[20] The world is not merely of our making but surprises us in its novelty, and therefore is not congenial to a voluntaristic ideation.

MacKinnon is aware that the relation between theology and ontology within Aristotle's *Metaphysics* remains tricky: is metaphysics primarily theological? Or are they distinct sciences? Both of these remain debated questions within scholarship (up to the present day). MacKinnon thinks that Aristotle's reflections on substance cannot be separated from his thoughts on the Unmoved Mover, and that his "ontology" is inextricably concerned with the interrelation between particularity and universality, a theme that is important for Christian theology, as can be seen in the debates regarding the ὁμοούσιος (ACS, 111–14).[21] Such sentiments seem to underscore for Aristotle, in distinction from more modern treatments, that "metaphysics" cannot be separated from "first philosophy." It is clear that the subordination of theology-as-first philosophy to the science of being *qua* being remains problematic for Christian orthodoxy.[22] But whether

---

19. MacKinnon ("Aristotle's Conception of Substance," 114) thinks that Locke's notion of the 'substratum' has led to a wide misinterpretation of Aristotle's doctrine of substance. He considers Aristotle's own teaching to be more subtle and open-ended. On the translation of οὐσία, *substantia*, and *essentia*, Joseph Owens writes "The English word 'substance' is . . . unsatisfactory as a rendition of the Greek term. . . . 'Substance' fails to express the direct relation with Being denoted by οὐσία. It can be, moreover, very misleading. Because of Locke's influence, 'substance' in English philosophical usage strongly suggests exactly what its etymology designates. It conjures up the notion of something 'standing under' something else. The background is the view of accidents ridiculed by Malebranche. Such a perspective inevitably falsifies the Aristotelian οὐσία and ends up reifying the accidents as in Locke" (Owens, *The Doctrine of Being in Aristotelian Metaphysics*, 144). Eric Perl suggests that we translate *ousia* with the word "reality" (cf. Perl, *Thinking Being*, 82–89).

20. Prynne, "Resistance and Difficulty."

21. For more on this generally, see MacKinnon, "'Substance' in Christology," 237–54.

22. For a thorough discussion of this question (viz., the relation between the metaphysics of being and theology within Aristotle's corpus), one can consult Aubenque, "The Science without a Name"; Patzig, "Theology and Ontology in Aristotle's Metaphysics," 33–49; Owens, *The Doctrine of Being in Aristotelian Metaphysics*.

Aristotle ultimately makes this onto-theological move is, however, subject to continuing speculation.[23]

The above excursion has shown that MacKinnon's reading of Aristotle aims to incorporate the latter's *aporetics* within a larger project of descriptive and realist metaphysics, insofar as it sustained the dialectic between the particular *this* and its more universal categories and concepts. Aristotle's 'particularism' had resonance for him since it proffered an empirical engagement with the world that resisted the grand narratives of idealism.[24] It also provided a fecund comparison with contemporary theories of logical atomism characteristic of early developments in British analytic philosophy. But some disquiet can be admitted regarding MacKinnon's appropriation of Aristotle. For some, the paring of Aristotle and Moore exhibits MacKinnon's "residual tenderness" towards "atomist realism," which (as Rowan Williams has suggested[25]) has trouble in accounting for the constructive element of discovery, and moreover displays an overly-modern theory of subject-object dichotomy.[26] Here MacKinnon's reliance on 'reference' remains philosophically questionable in light of post-Wittgensteinian accounts of language, developments which have questioned whether there can be any non-propositional, extra-linguistic account of the real.[27] Moreover, being a reader of Hegel should have alerted MacKinnon more to the fact that this binary is unsustainable within the phenomenology of

23. The post-Heideggerian equation of 'metaphysics' with 'ontotheology' is important to note, but Aristotle should probably be excluded from it since for him the science of being *qua* being still concerns separate or divine being and therefore does not place God within the category of 'being-in-general.' For the arguments and history of this debate, see Lefebvre, "L'image onto-théologique de la "Métaphysique" d'Aristote"; Boulnois, "Quand commence l'ontothéologie?"; Berti, "La "métaphysique" d'Aristote; Courtine, *Inventio analogiae*, 45–99.

24. Cf. Sutherland, "Donald MacKenzie MacKinnon," 388: "He constantly stressed the importance of the particular and the individual against the possibility of the grand over-arching theory. . . . He saw the individual example, assembled with others as reminders; in the end he was more in sympathy with Aristotle than Plato." Joseph Owens writes in similar terms that "Aristotle's procedure is to let *things* speak for themselves. He waits for them to reveal their own inner nature. They show themselves to be the same in some ways, to be different in others. Concepts and words simply follow and reflect as best they can the nature of things themselves" (Owens, *The Doctrine of Being in Aristotelian Metaphysics*, 131).

25. Williams, "Trinity and Ontology," in *On Christian Theology*, 154.

26. Whether Moore himself can be accused of advocating a mind-world dualism has been questioned by MacBride in *On the Genealogy of Universals*, 24–42. But he also admits that Moore remains 'realist' insofar as objects are *not* altered through our cognitive engagements with them.

27. See, for example, Davidson, "Reality without Reference," in Davidson, *Inquiries into Truth and Interpretation*, 215–25.

thought, since it tacitly works with an idea of objects existing *out there*, persisting as stable essences just waiting to be discovered. In Hegelian terms, this is a one-sided moment that requires a speculative sublation, one that transcends the dualism of cognition and material determinations.[28] MacKinnon's resistance here to a Hegelian sway is certainly traceable to his rather one-sided reading of 'idealism' as denying real externality, a misreading which he probably took over from Russell and Moore—even though they remained deeply influenced by Hegel.[29] As we will see later, MacKinnon does try somewhat to overcome such duality in a blending of *creativity* with *discovery*, but his appropriation of atomist realism at this point probably does not help his cause, which still remains too encumbered with a positivistic empiricism. His position has difficulty accounting for a stronger interrelation between the observer and the observed, between mind and world, an account which seems mandated now (amongst others) by developments such as quantum theory. In other words, MacKinnon appears to rely too much here on what analytic philosophers after Sellars have come to call "the myth of the given," which suggests that there could be any sensory or cognitive inputs extraneous to their propositional entailments.[30] It would deny the primacy of relation for the constitution of objects. Milbank similarly states, in his own critique of MacKinnon, that in order "to maintain [the] distinguishability [of things], one needs to say that entities may be relatively discrete, relatively indifferent to certain relations in which they may fall." But one must also add that "even such indifference, such 'resistance', can help negatively to determine what they are and what they become."[31] MacKinnon's objectivism, on these accounts, appears to render 'substance' as simply a continuum of stabilized objects that exist apart from linguistic description, leaving the impression that we are dealing simply with discrete items of knowledge that exist without any necessary connection to intelligent formation (even though his Kantianism would press him to avoid this). In the words of Graham Ward, the idea that "the world" (or 'substance' in our case) simply "asserts its own reality," is predicated upon an "atomism" in which "ultimate reality is found in the independence of each atom asserting its own self-enclosed being"[32]—a belief which engenders a primacy of the individual, as Ward also makes clear.

28. In particular, see Hegel's reflections on 'Absolute Knowing' in *The Phenomenology of Spirit*, §§ 788–808 / 422–34.

29. See Rockmore, "Analytic Philosophy and the Hegelian Turn." Also MacBride, *On the Genealogy of Universals*, 24–86.

30. See Sellars, "Empiricism and the Philosophy of Mind," 253–329.

31. Milbank, "A Critique of the Theology of Right," 19–20.

32. Ward, "Transcorporality," 241.

There are also lingering questions about the coherency of Aristotle's project in relation to Christian metaphysics, since Aristotle's account of individuation (as Adrian Pabst has argued[33]) denies a relation between the Prime Mover and the individuation of material being. God is understood here as having a 'final' causal relation to being, but is absolved from its 'formal,' 'material' constitution, and even (potentially) its 'efficient' causality.[34] These concerns are echoed by Philipp Rosemann who argues that Aristotle's notion of 'form' lacks an openness to historical development, and has difficulty explaining vertical causality within the cosmological hierarchy.[35] Milbank similarly states that Aristotle "thought that the *eidē* were perfectly stable within the material, temporal world, without participation in transcendence."[36] The obvious problems this makes for any analogical relating of divine to created being are clear, since particularities are *not* intrinsically related to their transcendent source. This tendency is compounded, as Pabst has also argued, by Aristotle's prioritization of 'substance' over existence, as when he writes that "being is not the substance of anything" (*Posterior Analytics* II.7.92 b13–14). It follows then that Aristotle ultimately "privileges essentiality over existentiality and drives a wedge between the science of being qua being (ontology) and the science of the divine (theology)."[37] It seems plausible to suggest then that MacKinnon's appropriation of Aristotle, when combined with his Kantianism (as I will suggest), might actually hinder him from tracing those ontological intimacies between created and uncreated being that a Catholic account of analogical participation might espouse, as well as a properly historicist account of being. To be sure, MacKinnon might have been perfectly happy with this because, as we have seen (*PM*, 14–16), he remained somewhat uncomfortable with 'analogy,' and 'ontology' in general, since it ran the risk of metaphysical domestication (a tradition which MacKinnon traced to Aristotle). But what our investigation has shown is that MacKinnon and Aristotle are in fact close in their substantial positions: both emphasize

33. Pabst, *Metaphysics*, 9–24.

34. "The derivation of plurality from unity does not appear as a problem in Aristotle. The problem is merely to reduce the plurality to a unity sufficient for a science. Nor does the series of generations and corruptions require or even allow a temporally first *efficient* cause. The series of generations is *of its nature* eternal. It requires a first and unchangeable mover to account for its eternity. But in the *Metaphysics* that immovable mover functions only as a *final* cause" (Owens, *The Doctrine of Being in Aristotelian Metaphysics*, 468).

35. Rosemann, *Omne Agens Agit Sibi Simile*, 63–67.

36. Milbank, "The Thomistic Telescope," 195.

37. Pabst, *Metaphysics*, 9.

particularity and empirical discovery, as manifest in Aristotle's thoughts on substance and the multiple modes of being, and in MacKinnon's suasion towards atomist realism and a pluralist metaphysic. Similarly, Aristotle struggles to comprehend an individuation that is relational and historical, while MacKinnon leans towards an 'objectivism' that has difficulty (at least *prima facie*) in accounting for the constructive element of perception. Both also have difficulties relating finite being to infinite being: Aristotle has no account of creation, while MacKinnon (like Aristotle[38]) denies analogical participation (as we will see shortly).

What is salient for our purposes is the way that Aristotelian ontology remains unclear in answering the question of the Prime Mover's relation to materiality. In a similar way, one could ask whether MacKinnon's suspicion of analogy creates problems as regards the ontological relation between God and created being, and moreover, how contingency might be reflective of divine infinity. Lacking a notion of analogical participation, the immanent order becomes empty of imbued metaphysical signification, while God's action comes to be viewed as an external 'intervention' in the created order. Yet by construing things so, it becomes hard to avoid the charge of theological domestication, since God is construed here as a spatialized and ontic being— ontologically greater, but still *within* the realm of finite causes, since God remains 'outside' and contrasted with finitude. MacKinnon misconstrues theological analogy as endangering transcendence, whereas the analogy of being (since Lateran IV) has been conceptualized as a *negative* theology.[39] Thus to avoid 'anthropomorphism,' it is wagered that one actually *needs* analogical participation to steer through the pitfalls of hyper-transcendence and pantheistic reduction (as Erich Przywara cogently argued[40]). Finally, MacKinnon's apparent dis-ease with Platonic *methexis* and his agreement with the Third Man Argument have their own problems. Gregory Vlastos has argued,[41] after repeating the critique of the Forms contained in *Parmenides*, that infinite regression is not applicable to Platonic metaphysics.

---

38. A significant amount of continental research into Aristotle suggests that the 'analogy of being' is *not* traceable to Aristotle but rather to the Neoplatonic School and their theory of participation. This begins with Aristotle's commentators, namely with Alexander of Aphrodisias, and Simplicius. On this see, Aubenque, "The Origins of the Doctrine of the Analogy of Being"; Aubenque, "Sur la naissance de la doctrine pseudo-aristotélicienne de l'analogie de l'être"; Libera, "Les sources gréco-arabes de la théorie médiévale de l'analogie de l'être"; Courtine, *Inventio analogiae*, 103–239; Lonfat, "Archéologie de la notion d'analogie d'Aristote à Saint Thomas d'Aquin."

39. For a standard reconstruction, see Montagnes, *The Doctrine of the Analogy of Being according to Thomas Aquinas*.

40. Przywara, *Analogia Entis*.

41. Vlastos, "The Third Man Argument in the Parmenides."

While the 'separation' (χωρισμός) between 'appearances' and their transcendent 'forms' is certainly Platonic, a thoroughgoing disjunction among the forms themselves is not supported by the mature Plato (as confirmed by Alexander Nehemas and Gail Fine),[42] nor is the copy-model of participation a particularly salient reading of Plato's metaphysics, since it implies an idea of 'external' exemplification that is at odds with the drift of Plato's thought.[43] In the end, even Plato's *Parmenides*, which is the source of the regress argument (*Parmenides* 132a–b), affirms that the reality of forms is required for the maintenance of "dialectic" (135b–c). From this, it can be suggested that while Aristotle's critique of the Platonic ideas is damaging to a certain Platonism, such criticisms were anticipated by Plato himself.

We still need to explore some other reasons why MacKinnon had reservations regarding analogical participation. He did not always have such reservations: some of his earlier texts have an explicit openness to Thomistic accounts of analogy. However, there does appear to be a progressive weakening of its hold in his thinking, for reasons that seem primarily Kantian in origin. This story needs to be traced further to make sense of this change.

Kant's Agnosticism: The De-Ontologizing of Analogy

Kant's presence in MacKinnon's corpus is widely apparent.[44] At this stage, the weight of commentary lies on those texts of MacKinnon in which Kant's metaphysics is prominent, while bearing in mind that MacKinnon viewed Kant's ethics and metaphysics as being holistically entwined (since for Kant "ethics and religion are *almost* identified"[45]). My focus now is to show that MacKinnon's digestion of Kantian scepticism played an integral role in his own project, and contributed to a gradual disinvestment in analogical metaphysics, a

---

42. Nehemas, "Participation and Predication in Plato's Later Thought"; Fine, "Separation," in *Plato on Knowledge and Forms*, 252–300.

43. See Allen, "Participation and Predication in Plato's Middle Dialogues"; De Vogel, "Was Plato a Dualist?," in *Rethinking Plato and Platonism*, 159–212.

44. MacKinnon, "Kant's Agnosticism (1947)," in *Philosophy and the Burden of Theological Honesty*, 27–34; MacKinnon, "Metaphysical and Religious Language (1954)," in *Borderlands of Theology and Other Essays*, 207–21; MacKinnon, *A Study in Ethical Theory*, 69–177; MacKinnon, "P. F. Strawson's *The Bounds of Sense*," in *Borderlands of Theology*, 249–56; MacKinnon, *The Problem of Metaphysics*, 53–72; MacKinnon, "Coleridge and Kant," 183–203; MacKinnon, "Kant's Philosophy of Religion"; MacKinnon, "Some Reflections on Time and Space," in *Themes in Theology*, 40–49; MacKinnon, "Aspects of Kant's Influence on British Theology (1990)," in *Kant and His Influence*, 348–66.

45. MacKinnon, "Metaphysical and Religious Language," 219.

process that occurs through a permeation of Kantian criticism, as well as a residual anti-Platonism that rejected 'existence' as a predicate of things. For Kant, 'being' was merely the product of a judgement that something existed, and was not a trait added onto 'essence.' Something either exists or it does not: ascribing 'being' to its 'essence' is simply pleonastic; it substitutes an 'analytic' judgement for a 'synthetic' one, and therefore constitutes a category mistake. With this assumption at hand, the idea that one could ascribe degrees of being or talk about an analogical participation in being is rendered a *non sequitur*. The so-called analogy of attribution (*analogia atrributionis*), central to Aquinas's metaphysics, is excluded outright.

In one of his *Signpost* pamphlets, MacKinnon wrote that Kant had bequeathed "relativism"[46] into Western thinking, particularly through his doctrine of categories.[47] Such a tradition seemed to occlude the awareness that our finitude might be dependent on, and answerable to, a higher order of accountability. On this score, MacKinnon said that the task of metaphysics was to indicate an "ultimate" which relativizes contingent and limited perspectives. Here MacKinnon expressed admiration for the doctrine of analogy as a "formal schematization in metaphysical terms of the creature-creator relation," and open to a "dynamical" and even "dialectical" construal of this engagement. It acknowledged that creaturely "likeness" could only be understood within a greater "unlikeness" (here echoing the *maior dissimilitudo* of Lateran IV).[48] In a piece written around the same period,[49] MacKinnon sought to recover "metaphysics" within the debates of phenomenalism and logical positivism. MacKinnon was concerned here to demonstrate the limitations of focusing only on what physical sensation alone gives us. For him, metaphysics provides us with an encompassing matrix into which physical sensations are to be placed, apart from which they lose sensibility.[50] He provided a critique of the positivist tradition, attempting to show that metaphysics cannot be written off as an 'impossible' enterprise (as A. J. Ayer

---

46. Cf. MacKinnon, *God the Living and the True*. See especially the sections entitled "The Paradox of Revelation" and "Renewal of Understanding." This specific quotation can be found in MacKinnon, *Kenotic Ecclesiology*, 57.

47. While maintaining a transcendental deduction of the categories, Kant nevertheless advanced a form of the correspondence theory of truth. Cf. Kant, *The Critique of Pure Reason*, A820-21= B848-49. MacKinnon himself held to a version of this idea (though not uncritically). On this, see MacKinnon, "The Christian Understanding of Truth," in *Philosophy and the Burden of Theological Honesty*, 35-43.

48. MacKinnon, *Kenotic Ecclesiology*, 80.

49. MacKinnon, "What is a Metaphysical Statement?"

50. MacKinnon, "What is a Metaphysical Statement," 24.

would have it[51]). Instead, metaphysics is required for the preservation of a moral and intellectual integrity.[52] MacKinnon's point here is that without some kind of metaphysical compass, moral positions have no deeper basis in reality as such, beyond the conclusion that they are just mental or conventional impositions. This idealistic deduction stands in contrast to a "pluralist metaphysics" that attends to the particular and to the irreducibly different kinds of "facts" that appear in the world. Following Aristotle again, MacKinnon stated that the "pluralist metaphysician" is concerned with conceptualizing "the self-subsistent"[53] and "the reality of the individual."[54] Such a metaphysician seeks to emulate a "healthy respect for the particularity of the individual, which continually militates against that besetting philosophical sin of reducing types of entity to terms of one another."[55] Once more, Moore's critique of Bradley lingers in the background. Especially important for MacKinnon here is how an idealist or monistic metaphysics struggles to account for the specificities of selfhood and created particularity, while a pluralist metaphysic, on the contrary, could in his mind do so. Furthermore, pluralism makes space for "analogical" thinking, in the Aristotelian sense of making comparisons between different modes of being, rather than the Thomistic account of analogical participation as such.[56] Following from this anti-idealism, MacKinnon sought to wrestle with "phenomenalism," and specifically the influence of Kant on this tradition. Kant proposed that experiences only occur within *a priori* structures,[57] apart from which any notion of "experience" becomes unintelligible, a move which has affinities to the idea of a "charmed circle," since it is precisely through transcendentally-deduced categories that "experience" is conceived.[58] The importance of these aprioristic structures is inseparably tied to subjectivity and the question of freedom.[59] For the problem of freedom is not one which can be solved

---

51. The classic text for this argument is Ayer, "Demonstration of the Impossibility of Metaphysics." The continuing importance of Ayer's criticisms of metaphysics within MacKinnon's theology can be seen in MacKinnon, "Ayer's Attack on Metaphysics."
52. MacKinnon, "What is a Metaphysical Statement," 25.
53. MacKinnon, "What is a Metaphysical Statement," 20.
54. MacKinnon, "What is a Metaphysical Statement," 18.
55. MacKinnon, "What is a Metaphysical Statement," 14.
56. MacKinnon, "What is a Metaphysical Statement," 21.
57. MacKinnon himself wrote a contribution to a symposium on *a priori* concepts. His perspective can be found in Donald MacKinnon, "Are There *A Priori* Concepts?"
58. MacKinnon, "What is a Metaphysical Statement," 22.
59. MacKinnon, "What is a Metaphysical Statement," 23. Kant himself argued for a transcendental deduction of freedom which should be adduced *a priori*, and could only operate on the very assumption of its truth, being prior to any empirical demonstration.

through an allusion to the immanent world, naturalistically conceived: at face value, one might just as well conclude that human activity was simply a link within a series of actions and reactions, which did not give any aperture for a genuine assertion of liberty. Kant's transcendentalism was a fruitful solution in this regard, so MacKinnon thought, since it suggested that there was a need for an additional imaginative element—irreducible to physical observation—that was required in order for a freely ethical agent to be born. For MacKinnon, as for Kant, material phenomena therefore required a 'synthetic' and productive composition that exceeded brute observation in order for meaning-making to occur.[60]

From this, we can see that Kant's doctrine of categories—as a mode of structuring human experience within certain limits—as well as his proclivity towards *a priori* synthetic judgements, remains important for MacKinnon. But what is interesting to note at this stage is MacKinnon's openness towards 'Catholic' modes of analogical thinking. For instance, in "The Function of Philosophy in Education (1941)," he affirms that "we are metaphysical animals, naturally curious, with minds open to comprehend the analogy of our being with that of our Creator."[61] In another essay from the same year, he has many positive things to say about this: "The process of analogical thinking whereby the human understanding schematizes to itself the dependence of all things on the sovereign will of the Creator, who called them de nihilo is complicated and subtle, yet the ultimate insight of the doctrine of that what is, depends utterly upon God for its being, but is utterly unnecessary to Him for His." He concludes that "St. Thomas was right in his insistence on the ultimacy of ontology," and that "Only if we are prepared to admit that analogy of being . . . can we hope in any sense . . . to achieve theology."[62] MacKinnon concurs that the *analogia entis* is a manifestation of "Thomist agnosticism," and he understands well that for this theology "The *via negativa* inevitably precedes the *via eminentiae* in the ordered process of our thought of God. Only thus can the worst of Kantian antinomies be avoided." But he also stresses that we "can and must

---

On this, cf. Kant, *The Critique of Pure Reason*, A532–58 = B560–86, and also, cf. Kant, *The Groundwork for the Metaphysics of Morals*, 4:446–63.

60. MacKinnon's most expansive treatment of this theme is found in "Intellect and Imagination (1991)," in *Philosophy and the Burden of Theological Honesty*, 201–7. For a more detailed treatment, see Ferrarin, "Kant's Productive Imagination and its Alleged Antecedents."

61. MacKinnon, "The Function of Philosophy in Education (1941)," in *Philosophy and the Burden of Theological Honesty*, 14.

62. MacKinnon, "Revelation and Social Justice [1941]," in *Philosophy and the Burden of Theological Honesty*, 140.

affirm a radical discontinuity between God and man"—here anticipating the Barthian critique of analogy.[63] Under the influence of Jacques Maritain, MacKinnon seeks to connect the analogical, as regards divine-human relations, to the human self-reflection of a "moral agent" in which we try to grasp the "unity" of our "nature" as a kind of "norm." For MacKinnon, to be sure, "The character of that norm may be very obscurely grasped," since "its character [is] analogical, capable of a multiplicity of diverse realizations in modes proportionate to a multiplicity of divergent historical situations." But "it is only in and through an act of specifically metaphysical (that is analogical) thought that man can thus achieve the concept of his 'nature' whether or no [sic] the impulse to perform that act be derived from acceptance of the Gospel."[64] This is part of MacKinnon's 'Catholic' (and also Butlerian) attempt to connect moral reflection to "the ethical importance of desire," and constitutes a critique of the deontological tradition which attempted to articulate an "abstract moralism"[65] apart from our created and historical constitution. Thus regarding the task of metaphysics, he says that it is not an "achievement of a theoretically satisfying system, such as certain forms of monism have claimed to provide. It was the derivation of the contingent from the necessary, but the question of why the necessary should thus have generated the contingent remained always unanswered." He goes on to say that:

> We are utterly unnecessary for [God], we cannot make our existence (unless we deny its character) a matter of any necessity whatsoever, yet we cannot deny that through revelation the character of our relation to God is profoundly illuminated by the disclosure in an act, that is necessary to its achievement, of His relation to us . . . if we refuse to allow that, in any sense, the schematization in analogical terms of the whole creature-creator relation is possible we will inevitably restrict the sphere of that relation. Unless one supposes that relation is grounded ontologically, one will put the *Anknüpfungspunkt* of creature and creator in some isolated capacity of the former, whose relation to his whole nature is not clearly definable. Students of Kantian philosophy will remember that at the last the problem of the relation of the phenomenal and noumenal self is unsolved.[66]

---

63. MacKinnon, "Revelation and Social Justice [1941]," 140.
64. MacKinnon, "Revelation and Social Justice [1941]," 141.
65. MacKinnon, "Revelation and Social Justice [1941]," 143.
66. MacKinnon, "Revelation and Social Justice [1941]," 141–42.

The last line is revealing: it appears to show that MacKinnon considers the *analogia entis*, at this juncture of his development, to be a metaphysical alternative to Kantian phenomenology. This shows that MacKinnon already here was by no means a dogmatic Kantian. But in addition to Kant, attention should also be directed to the fact that Barth already had a significant influence on MacKinnon (as the reference to the *Anknüpfungspunkt* shows). He overtly states that "I incline somewhat in a Barthian direction myself," thereby affirming the Lutheran-Reformed perspective that "nature . . . is wounded almost beyond recognition."[67] Here MacKinnon was trying to articulate a *via media* between two agnosticisms: on the one hand, the epistemological strictures of Kant and Barth,[68] and on the other the apophatics of Thomas.

A few years after this (1947), MacKinnon wrote an essay detailing the importance of Kant for theology.[69] His intention was to recover Kantian (and Thomistic) agnosticism against the "Hegelian absolutism" then making its appearance within British thought. In MacKinnon's perspective, Kant is important for his implicit *negative* mode of metaphysical inquiry, insofar as he emphasized the limits posed for sensibility as it approximated "the unconditioned."[70] This inquiry is constantly renewed in view of our time-bound consciousness[71]—a move that is a part of MacKinnon's attempt to 'historicize' Kantian transcendentalism (a lá Hegel, Dilthey, Collingwood, and Cassirer).[72] Much like we have seen elsewhere, MacKinnon sees delimitation and categorization as a central aspect of Kant's metaphysics, especially in relation to human cognition.[73] This is due to the fact that "discursive

---

67. MacKinnon, "Revelation and Social Justice [1941]," 142.

68. It goes without saying that Barth himself was heavily influenced in his theological methodology by Kantian transcendentalism as kind of negative fold to his account of divine self-revelation. On this, see McCormack, *Karl Barth's Critically Realistic Dialectical Theology*, 465–66.

69. MacKinnon, "Kant's Agnosticism (1947)," in *Philosophy and the Burden of Theological Honesty*, 27–34. This essay was originally delivered at the Oxford Aquinas Society.

70. For Kant, 'the unconditioned' can (at best) only be a regulative idea for pure reason, an ideal of which nothing concrete can be predicated, or metaphysically demonstrated. Apart from speculative theology, it can be presupposed only within the realm of practical and moral reason (cf. Kant, *The Critique of Pure Reason*, A567–704= B595–732; A795–831=B823–59).

71 See MacKinnon, "Kant's Agnosticism," 32–33.

72. I owe this point to Muller, *Donald M. MacKinnon*. George Steiner also confirms MacKinnon's historicism as having direct links to Dilthey and Collingwood; cf. Steiner, "Tribute to Donald MacKinnon," 3.

73 MacKinnon, "Kant's Agnosticism (1947)," 29.

understanding and the schematized categories are by Kant conceived as the way in which human beings make response to their world. The world must answer to their demand—that we know, for otherwise the world would not be our world as the object of our theoretical understanding."[74] For Kant, metaphysics is "primarily an extension of theoretical questioning," because human beings are continually "beset by ultimate questions. They cannot easily rest, they ask questions which cannot be settled by any mere extension of their theoretical understanding."[75]

However, the movement towards 'the unconditioned' is reflected for Kant not primarily within theoretical abstraction, but in *the claims of the ethical*.[76] This touches upon MacKinnon's metaphysics to the degree that Kant, in a manner more strident than Aquinas, placed a stronger emphasis on "the reality of morality," even though Thomas expounds a "deeper agnosticism" which Kantians should learn from.[77] But MacKinnon nonetheless says that if "Thomism, with its profound conception of analogy, is to help and illuminate the perplexities today it must take account of those whose sense of incompleteness, of duality, lies more at the level of conduct than understanding."[78] What should be marked here is that while there is still an appreciation for the doctrine of analogy, there seems to be a dampening of his earlier reception. The experience of conflict within the moral life, existing against the risks of human responsibility, seems to temper his account towards a stronger feeling for the woundedness and limits of human enterprise. And it is precisely within this claim of the ethical that transcendence enters worldly engagements, an opinion which is in accord with a Kantian conception of 'the primacy of practical reason.' Without attention to the particular, so MacKinnon thinks, the doctrine of analogy becomes abstract and formalist, unable to address moral urgency and historicity.

By the time we reach "Metaphysical and Religious Language" (1954), there is a much more critical reception of Thomism. Clearly some cleavage has opened in the years between this text and the previous ones. In this 1954 paper, MacKinnon understands Thomistic analogy as espousing an "analogically participated transcendental," as a "fundamentally ontological" concept rather than a purely logical one.[79] The influence of Kant

74. MacKinnon, "Kant's Agnosticism (1947)," 30.
75. MacKinnon, "Kant's Agnosticism (1947)," 30.
76. MacKinnon, "Kant's Agnosticism (1947)," 32.
77. MacKinnon, "Kant's Agnosticism (1947)," 34.
78. MacKinnon, "Kant's Agnosticism (1947)," 33.
79. MacKinnon, "Metaphysical and Religious Language," in *Borderlands of Theology*, 209. He also made clear, in a discussion with Anthony Flew, that he considered the "analogy of attribution" to be more "fundamental" than the "analogy of proper

here is explicit (and Barth too, though not with the same centrality[80]). He acknowledges that analogical language tries to avoid "the twin perils of anthropomorphism and agnosticism," but in a *volte-face* MacKinnon states that it relies on out-dated assumptions: "we have to admit," in relation to Thomism (and Platonism), "a kind of intuitive awareness of analogically participative being which we do not seem to have."[81] For MacKinnon, the doctrine of analogy seems untenable in a post-Enlightenment cosmos. Central to Kant's "meta-metaphysics" is his "theory of the *a priori*" and the so-called "doctrine of categories," which (following Paul Tillich) MacKinnon reads as a rendition of the "doctrine of human finitude" as this emphasized "the peculiarly limited character of human knowledge."[82] Kant was concerned not to press "the tools of ordinary empirical knowledge" towards grasping 'the unconditioned.'"[83] Therefore, Kant expressed a "confidence in discarding the scheme of analogy" since it "sprang in a way from a conviction that he was liberating the essence of religion from a false entanglement with metaphysics."[84] MacKinnon's own worry is with the problem of "intuition" since "if we claim intuitively to see things as they are, we are unwilling to give proper attention to those who bid us revise our assumptions, change our frames of reference and so on." He even speaks of "the perilous mythology of a faculty of intuition,"[85] and "the tyranny that metaphysical conviction can exert over the proper assimilation of new insights concerning the ways of human knowing," and produces a "canonizing as dogma some particular systematization of human knowledge." Such assumptions can lead to "a false acceptance as final truth of that which in its nature is inevitably impermanent and relative."[86] This seems in step with Aristotle's critique of Plato, and most certainly is integral to MacKinnon's critique of ideology more generally.[87] Overall, it is the risk of intellectual or moral absolutism that MacKinnon finds worrying in regard to the *analogia entis*, since it appears to rely on outmoded forms of metaphysical intuitionism. Nonetheless, MacKinnon does say that while

---

proportionality." For this, see "Creation: A Dialogue between Anthony Flew and D. M. MacKinnon (1955)," in *Philosophy and the Burden of Theological Honesty*, 232.

80. MacKinnon calls Barth in this same essay the "most deeply anti-metaphysical of modern theologians" (MacKinnon, "Metaphysical and Religious Language," 220).

81. MacKinnon, "Metaphysical and Religious Language," 210.

82. MacKinnon, "Metaphysical and Religious Language," 211.

83. MacKinnon, "Metaphysical and Religious Language," 212.

84. MacKinnon, "Metaphysical and Religious Language," 219.

85. MacKinnon, "Metaphysical and Religious Language," 217.

86. MacKinnon, "Metaphysical and Religious Language," 212–13.

87. Cf. Lash, "Ideology, Metaphor and Analogy," 68–94.

> Few of us find it easy to accept the principle on which the doctrine of analogy of being depends, that is the conception of being as an analogically participated transcendental; yet, we may be thankful for the statement of this doctrine as revealing something of what the problem of metaphysics is. We may even in certain moods envy those who can accept analogy as men who have at their disposal a supremely effective device for reconciling the logic of the familiar with that of the unfamiliar. The close understanding of the gulf between ordinary and transcendent description which we owe to Kant and his successors prohibits our acceptance of what scholastic analogy promises, and leaves us with the problem of the relation of settleable and unsettleable questions.[88]

In a review of P. F. Strawson's monograph of Kant (1966), MacKinnon expresses very similar views. He does not mention 'analogy' as such, but he does reiterate Kant's critique of humanity's "pretension to penetrate the secrets of the unconditioned." Here Kant appears as a metaphysician of "experience" and "an agnostic, whose delineation of the most pervasive features of the objective world is but a propaedeutic study to the definitive recognition of our ineradicable intellectual limitation."[89] In *The Problem of Metaphysics*, MacKinnon makes reference to Kant's analogies of experience as one avenue where we may discover that "the world is not of our making," not the product of "the haphazard play of our imaginings," but rather the disclosure of an "order" apart from which "no objectivity" would be forthcoming (*PM*, 167).[90] Elsewhere (in 1975), there is mention of "analogical representation" in his essay on Kant's philosophy of religion, which is here read as a form of "negative theology." But here it seems that his reference to analogy is strongly tied to Kant's phenomena-noumena division,[91] as well as his accounts of analogical predication and schematism. This text seems to show that MacKinnon's earlier disquiet regarding Kant's phenomenalism is suppressed somewhat, and that 'analogy' is being deployed as a method of relating the known to the unknown, but here within a transcendentalist division of phenomena from noumena. In Kant's 'negative theology,' we can know things only as they appear, and are unable to conceive them within themselves. At best these are known as 'a something = X' (as Kant clearly says) and cannot even be cognized, but are understood as a correlate of the

---

88. MacKinnon, "Metaphysical and Religious Language," 214–15.
89. MacKinnon, "P. F. Strawson's *The Bounds of Sense*," 253.
90. On the analogies in general, a helpful summary can be found in Melnick, *Kant's Analogies of Experience*.
91. Cf. MacKinnon, "Kant's Philosophy of Religion," 141.

postulated unity of the sensible manifold. God too can only be thought (within the sphere of pure reason) as a 'Something' of which we cannot form any positive concepts.[92] What is apparent now is that Kant's influence on MacKinnon, though not uncritically received, seems to have developed a stronger hold in his mature thinking. This conclusion stands despite even the strong influence of Catholic thinkers like Balthasar.

In an introductory essay on Balthasar (written in 1969, with a postscript dated 1974), MacKinnon speaks of the Swiss theologian's "traditionalism," namely, his Catholic "theological method which brought Christology into close, even perilously close, relation to ontological metaphysics." MacKinnon does qualify this by saying that in Balthasar "Jesus Christ, and not being as such (an analogically participated transcendental), is the *Anknüpfungspunkt* between God and man."[93] This passage does seem to imply MacKinnon had nuanced his account of analogy towards a Balthasarian appreciation of the *analogia Christi*, in which the kenotic (and even tragic) particularity of Christ's life is seen to trump any abstract, ontological analogy between God and being-as-such. This meant for MacKinnon that any ontology should be mediated by the blood-and-flesh materiality of the incarnation. But even here his reception of Balthasar's Christology has a Kantian tinge. First, he appears to read transcendental 'being' as a quantifier without qualities—a post-Scotist-Suárezian gesture in which 'being' is constructed as the pure *non-nihil*.[94] In distinction from Aquinas, Scotus and Suárez attempted to conceive God as the first object of metaphysics, including divinity within a neutral science of being qua being (*ens inquantam ens*). They were disciples of the Avicennian trend that sought to deduce the existence of God from *a priori* concepts: one begins with the most basic idea, namely that one can predicate existence to a 'something' (*aliquid*) that is not-nothing (*non-nihil*), and exhibits a *non repugnans ad esse* and an *aptitudo ad existendum*. In other words, the simplest definition of 'being' is the one that meets the minimal requirements that is the most general, non-contradictory, and intelligible. This concept should be valid for all existents, God included—which is why both Scotus and Suárez commence with a neutral and univocal concept of being into which all existents are included. It is this trend which initiates the regime of representation into which all beings are univocally conceived, a move which was a step away from the Thomistic approach which sought

---

92. Kant, *The Critique of Pure Reason*, A250–51, A355, A619, A674–75, A698, B647, B702–3, B726.

93. MacKinnon, "A Master in Israel," 7.

94. See Boulnois, *Être et représentation*, 457–515; Boulnois, *Métaphysique rebelles*, 261–311; Courtine, *Suarez et le système de la métaphysique*, 521–38; López, "Res, aliquid y nihil en Suárez y la filosofía moderna" ; Esposito, "The Hidden Influence of Suárez."

to begin metaphysical exploration of causality and the *actus essendi* of any particular thing. Moreover, it this division between *a priori* deductions from principles and *a posteriori* inductions from physics that would lay the foundation for the Suárezian rupture between general and special metaphysics, a tradition that was passed onto Kant via the *Schulmetaphysik* of Christian Wolff and Alexander Baumgarten.

Second, MacKinnon was keen to apply the concept of 'limitation' to the Trinity in a way that is distinctly Kantian. At one point he speaks of an "analogy of limits" as applicable to the triune God in a comparable manner to the *analogia personarum*. His emphasis here is to ground *ad intra* the facticity and temporality of Christ's life within the eternal life of the Trinity.[95] But as a later essay from 1986 reveals,[96] "the concept of limitation"[97] is deeply informed by Kant's "doctrine of categories," which he calls "a profound examination of the limitations of characteristically human knowledge," even suggesting that Kant's concept of free and determined 'receptivity' might have helped Balthasar's conception of the intra-trinitarian relations.[98] It is not negligible to remark here that Kant's theory of freedom and necessity is predicated on the transcendentalist division between the phenomena and noumena, and most certainly lies behind MacKinnon's idea of 'limitation' as well.

Third, we also know that by this stage that MacKinnon had accepted Kant's rejection of being-as-predicate. In an essay on Collingwood,[99] and in unison with Gilbert Ryle,[100] MacKinnon stated its crux

> to accept the ontological argument involves treating existence as a predicate, and failing to recognize that to say e.g. of tame tigers that they exist is something of a different order from saying that they growl. If we affirm that they exist, we are saying that the complex concept of tame-tiger-hood is exemplified;

---

95. MacKinnon, "The Relation of the Doctrines," 92–107, but especially 104.

96. MacKinnon, "Some Reflections on Hans Urs Von Balthasar's Christology with Special Reference to *Theodramatik* II/2 and III," in *Philosophy and the Burden of Theological Honesty*, 281–88.

97. MacKinnon, "Some Reflections on Hans Urs Von Balthasar's Christology," 285.

98. MacKinnon, "Some Reflections on Hans Urs Von Balthasar's Christology," 287. MacKinnon's meaning is that Kant was someone whose theory of autonomy sought to address the opposition between determinism and pure spontaneity or creativity (a debate inflected by his reception of Cassirer's thinking). For this, see MacKinnon, *A Study in Ethical Theory*, 69–177.

99. MacKinnon, "Collingwood on the Philosophy of Religion."

100. Ryle, "Mr Collingwood and the Ontological Argument (1937)," in *Collected Papers*, 105–19.

we are saying simply that animals of this sort are found in the world; we are not characterizing them as we are when we say that they growl. It is impossible to escape the conviction that Ryle is right and that the ontological argument is invalid inasmuch as it obliterates the distinction between characterization and affirmation of reality. *Existence is not a characteristic and must not be treated as such.* (italics mine)[101]

The central thrust of Kant's rejection of Anselm centers on predication, and concerns this dilemma: how is 'existence' distinguishable from and related to 'essence'? The 'ontological argument' (a term not used by Anselm[102]) ascribed 'existence' to God on the basis of a concept of 'perfection.' Since our imagination can postulate a most perfect being, beyond which nothing greater can be thought, it follows that 'perfection' must include 'existence,' because without 'existence' it would not be the most perfect being, since 'existence' is always more perfect than 'non-existence.' It is this logical step that Kant rejects because 'existence' is not something we add to 'essence.' It is—to use the language of G. E. Moore again—simply a question of facticity, that is, it is a 'judgement' or a 'positing' about the exemplification of certain kinds. If we say that 'being' is a predicate of 'essence,' we would be engaging in needless tautology. Kant argues thus:

> **Being** is obviously not a real predicate, i.e., a concept of something that could add to the concept of a thing. It is merely the positing of a thing or of certain determinations in themselves. In the logical use it is merely the copula of a judgment. The proposition **God is omnipotent** contains two concepts that have their objects: God and omnipotence; the little word "**is**" is not a predicate in it, but only that which posits the predicate **in relation to** the subject. Now if I take the subject (God) together with all his predicates (among which omnipotence belongs), and say **God is**, or there is a God, then I add no new predicate to the concept of God, but only posit the subject in itself with all its predicates, and indeed posit the **object** in relation to my **concept**.[103]

Jaakko Hintikka has perceptively commented that Kant's argument here "can be construed as criticizing the medieval and neo-Platonic ideas that existence *qua* existence carried with itself interesting attributes of which we can profitably theorize," a problem which goes back to "Aristotle's *aporia*

---

101. MacKinnon, "Collingwood on the Philosophy of Religion," 76.
102. Marion, "Is the Ontological Argument Ontological?"
103. Kant, *The Critique of Pure Reason*, A598–99 = B626–37.

concerning the science of being *qua* being."[104] Hintikka is referring to the question of whether metaphysics is primarily a question of 'being' (τὸ ὄν) or 'substance' (οὐσία), and certainly has in mind the Stagirite's assertion, referenced earlier, that "being is not the substance of anything" (*Posterior Analytics* II.7.92 b13–14). For our purposes, what is important to notice is that if 'being' is the product of a 'positing'—a judgement of sheer 'existence' or 'non-existence'—then *participation* (*methexis*) in transcendental 'being' is not serviceable. Ontological participation requires an axiological metaphysics in which entities are thought to exist at different levels of intensity and actuality. The analogy of attribution (and especially Aquinas's deployment of it[105]) presupposes this account, since it necessitates the predication of one thing (Being) to different entities (God and creatures), without proposing a reality that exists prior to or apart from the entities in question, as if 'being' could be an independent 'third' entity. But without participation and ontological predication, MacKinnon would have to distance himself both from Platonism and Thomism, and any account of analogy that presupposed its insights. Such a move was further buttressed by his acceptance of Aristotle's critique of *methexis*, Plato's self-critique in *Parmenides*, and his own suspicion of the Platonic intuitionism that underpinned the *analogia entis*. I have already spoken of these a bit earlier and have suggested that these ripostes are by no means decisive.

What can be gathered from the genealogy traced here is the gradual *de-ontologization* of analogy within MacKinnon's thought. Through the adoption of Kant's transcendentalism and his critique of Anselm,[106] MacKinnon chastened and ultimately departed from his earlier acceptance of analogical participation. It is this Kantian influence which explains MacKinnon's movement away from his earlier more enthusiastic reception of Aquinas. If he does have a remaining openness to analogy, it is through a post-Barthian affirmation of the *analogia Christi* without the *analogia entis*. It is surprising that MacKinnon opted for this in spite of the influence of Catholic theologians, since what is clear for Balthasar and Przywara is that Christology remains the foundation of ontological analogy. Christ as the

104. Hintikka, "Kant on Existence," 132n10.

105. This is not to say that Aquinas did not develop his views on this point, only that this appears to be his most mature position. For this development, see *De veritate* I.2.11; *De potentia dei* 7.7; *Summa contra gentiles* I.34.5–6; *Summa theologiae* I.13.5 *Compendium theologiae* I.27.

106. Now it is of course true that Aquinas was also critical of Anselm's ontological argument. Aquinas, in the wake of his real distinction between 'existence' and 'essence,' maintained the Averroist emphasis on causality over against an Avicennian preference for the primacy of *a priori* concepts found in Scotus and Suárez—and ultimately Kant. On this, see Boulnois, *Être et représentation*, 328–39.

God-Man constitutes the "concrete analogy of being" and is the paradigm for analogical participation more generally.[107]

So was this gradual rejection a necessary move on MacKinnon's part? Is there a positive appreciation of historicity and particularity within this tradition that MacKinnon has failed to discern? With perspicacity, MacKinnon did read the *analogia entis* as a participatory and ontological account of created being, and not just a semantic or logical account of language. Nevertheless, it is precisely *this* ontological version of the doctrine that he rejects. However, we cannot take his conclusion at face value, and should interrogate the reasons for it. For instance, MacKinnon (here echoing the *Schulmetaphysik*) tends to read the *analogia entis* through the scholastic prism of *metaphysica generalis* and *metaphysica specialis* (a move connected to the invention of an ontologically 'neutral' science),[108] and also through Kant's critique of being-as-predicate (which is traceable to the 'modal' and 'rational' distinctions of Scotus and Suárez).[109] Unlike the Thomistic 'real' distinction, which more coherently accounts for the actuality of being, since material and formal causality alone are not sufficient,[110] the post-Scotist and Suárezian picture continues the Aristotelian priority of the essential over existence, and tends towards a formalism at the expense of actually existing being. Because of this, 'being' is transformed into a conceptually minimalist place-holder,[111] with its prioritization on substance eventuating in an essence that was "defined solely in terms of its abstract content or intelligibility," and thereby "provided a fertile field for any metaphysics which would give primacy to *thought* over being."[112] This development lays the intellectual foundations—after its migration through Goclenius, Wolff and Baumgarten—for the later transcendental apriorism of Kant. Further aporias are unearthed here, since on the one hand, this assumption means that 'existence' does

---

107. Cf. Balthasar, *A Theology of History*, 74–75n5.

108. Cf. MacKinnon, "Finality in Metaphysics, Ethics and Theology," in *Explorations in Theology*, 99–115. On the genealogy of this division, and a sample of the scholarship that surrounds it, see Vollrath, "Die Gliederung der Metaphysik"; Lamanna, "Mathematics, Abstraction and Ontology."

109. Seigfried, "Kant's Thesis about Being Anticipated by Suárez?"; Esposito, "L'impensé de l'existence: Kant et la scolastique."

110. See Twetten, "Really Distinguishing Essence from *Esse*."

111. On the 'scientific' rationale for the metaphysical formalism of Scotus and Suárez, see Honnefelder, *Scientia transcendens*, 3–294. On Kant's Scotism, see Ludger Honnefelder, "Metaphysics as a Discipline," 53–74; Honnefelder, *Scientia transcendens*, 443–59. Also see Benoist, "Jugement et existence chez Kant"; Fichant, "L'Amphibologie des concepts de la réflexion," who argues that Kant's formalist procedure completes the destruction of ontology that began with Christian Wolff.

112. Alvira et al., *Metaphysics*, 116.

not reference anything more than the presence or absence of any particular thing, that is, anything apart from a sheer *happening*, since 'being' does not *add* anything of interest to our knowledge of particular entities. On this schema, 'being' is an undetermined X whose most transcendental structure is that it be *not nothing* and that it obeys non-contradiction. Such pliability allows for an unrestricted multiplicity of potential existents, but one in which their respective acts of being are conceptually univocal. On the other hand, the actualization within time of possible essences has no impact on their content, since 'existence' is already presupposed within their 'essence.' Within this model, 'essence' is rendered static and unchangeable, unperturbed by the accretions and advancements of history because, once more, it presupposes that being-as-such is not a predicate of real things.

It is also worth mentioning some points regarding Kant's metaphysics and *apophatics*. First, we are reminded of Milbank's comments on Kant's 'negative theology': since it is predicated on an unquestioned dogmatism regarding our access to the 'noumena,' does it in the end really avoid transgressing the boundaries it has emphatically drawn?[113] How can one survey the phenomenological borders without exceeding them at the same time? Costantino Esposito has also argued that Kant's metaphysics establishes epistemological limits which at the same time substantively determine what is projected beyond those boundaries, a move which undermines his supposed agnosticism.[114] Second, the non-realist theologian Don Cupitt is sceptical about whether Kant can be placed within the tradition of *theologia negativa*, since Kant doubts if an unknowable divine essence is philosophically tenable.[115] Kant instead chooses a regulative notion of God in which the contours of divine nature are delimited for use within practical reason. For Kant it is primarily the *existence* of God that remains unknown, *not* God's essence—a reversal of the classical position. Kant's rational theology thus moves within a different paradigm to negative theologians precisely because it undermines divine simplicity, since essence and existence are metaphysically prized apart.[116] Third, there is an irony within this radical agnosticism: since any knowledge that exceeds the bounds of pure reason is apodictically curtailed, such "anti-anthropomorphism" can only serve an "extreme anthropocentrism." For Kant, to quote Roger White, *"everything*

---

113. See Milbank, "A Critique of the Theology of Right," 7–16.

114. Costantino Esposito, "Die Schranken der Erfahrung."

115. Cupitt, "Kant and Negative Theology," 3–17. This essay was originally published in a Festschrift for MacKinnon.

116. For a general critique of this move, see Jüngel, *God as the Mystery of the World*. However, Jüngel's own theory regarding God's historicized being, as is clear, contradicts more orthodox notions of divine simplicity and aseity.

that we say about God is always to be interpreted solely in terms of the repercussions for humanity."[117] This is because, as Howard Caygill has argued, Kant ultimately oscillates between a strong anthropocentric immanence, on the one hand, and an absolute sublimity, on the other,[118] without any positive imminent deductions of divinity (as was the case with the *analogia attributionis*).[119] Such becomes especially cogent as regards the phenomena-noumena division: because there is no pre-established harmony or analogy between 'appearances' and 'things-in-themselves,' there is an indeterminacy regarding the distinct essence of beings—including God *in se*. All of this means that MacKinnon's deployment of Kantian metaphysics, especially as regards its potential ressourcement for a *theologia negativa*, might be not a finally coherent gesture, that is, in terms of MacKinnon's own desired outcome. Moreover, it leaves us with the somewhat perplexing conclusion that Kant is being used to argue for a theologically *realist* position when in fact his own critical idealism undermines the kind of objectivity MacKinnon is attempting to articulate.

Our intentions in this chapter have been to trace both the dissemination and convergence of Aristotelian and Kantian tendencies in MacKinnon's descriptive metaphysics. I argued that Aristotelian *aporetics* maintained the irresolvable tensions between *particular* substance and *universal* concepts. Such interplay was repeated in MacKinnon's reflections, and was combined with an atomist realism that advocated the primacy of *discovery* in our engagements with objects. Additionally, it was important to note the way in which Aristotle's critique of *methexis* spurred on MacKinnon's suspicions regarding ontological analogy. We also suggested Aristotle's metaphysics of causality (the Prime Mover is not involved in the material constitution of being) and his prioritization of substance over existence effectuated an ahistorical approach to the Forms (which never change, despite his emphasis on movement). Such a move did not aid MacKinnon in including historicity within metaphysics, and moreover might have hindered him from appreciating the cogency of analogical participation when combined with his Kantianism. It was also argued that MacKinnon placed a special importance on Kant's synthetic apriorism as providing a metaphysical frame into which all objectivity is to be approached. Apart from this ordering, we would be unable to meaningfully place entities in their relation and distinctions from others things. Moreover, as regards Kantian *apophatics*, I argued that his transcendentalism was read by MacKinnon as a mode of negative

---

117. White, *Talking About God*, 136.
118. Caygill, "Kant and the Kingdom," 55–59.
119. Te Velde, *Aquinas on God*, 65–93.

theology that chastened all overconfident accounts of 'intellectual intuition.' Such proclivities, as blended with Kant's critique of 'existence-as-predicate,' in sequel to Aristotle's account of substance, further repealed MacKinnon's residual endorsement of the *analogia entis* since on its assumptions any analogical metaphysics remains untenable. However, I questioned the veracity of Kant's apophatics in that it harbored a clandestine dogmatism vis-à-vis our rational access to the transcendent, and had a tenuous relation to the classical tradition of *theologia negativa*. Besides this, it remains ironically anthropocentric in its religion, and probably does not assist us in projecting a more substantive transcendence.

In the following chapter I will explicitly engage with MacKinnon's moral metaphysics, and how his Kantian prioritization on the ethical is the primary context in which his understanding of tragedy is to be understood. Like in the current chapter, I will suggest that his dependence on Kant creates problems here as well which would need to be transcended if a properly orthodox metaphysics is to be maintained.

6

Donald MacKinnon III

Between Tragedy and Metaphysics

The aim of this chapter is to show that Donald MacKinnon's metaphysico-ethical perspective informs his reception of the tragic. This is most apparent in his argument for a moral realism that mediates a truthful, albeit always approximate, disclosure of transcendent claims. In particular, MacKinnon's (Wittgensteinian) reading of Plato's *The Republic* and Kant's moral metaphysics is discussed with the purpose of displaying these connections. MacKinnon's main contention is that moral inquiry, and especially the ethical destabilization and scrutiny experienced within tragedy, constitutes a privileged area of metaphysical reflection. He claims that it is within our moral humanity that we most strongly perceive the ushering of transcendence, since it is when we encounter the questions of how we are to live morally that metaphysics is most strongly iterated. From Plato, MacKinnon draws a metaphysical realism regarding the subject matter of moral discourse, insofar as language really does have reference regarding the reality of the Good. Within a broadly Wittgensteinian therapy, MacKinnon suggests that an analysis of language-usage offers an avenue of moral scrupulosity whereby we are continually confronted by the strangeness of our speech regarding moral substance. However, Kant's prioritization of the ethical within the human experience of transcendence is the most important philosophical trajectory within his thinking at this point, and so the majority of this chapter seeks to address the nuances of this reception within *The Problem of Metaphysics*, as well as is his wider oeuvre. It is within the context of this reception that we should interpret his deployment of tragic motifs, pointing towards its possible contributions as well as its pitfalls. In particular, I will argue that MacKinnon's rejection of the *privatio boni* leads MacKinnon with little capacity to relate natural law and transcendent ends within a traditional account of the priority of the Good, and that this places his account of metaphysical "projection" within a post-Kantian regime of sublimity.

Plato the Moralist

For Donald MacKinnon, the category of "descriptive metaphysics" serves an introductory purpose in *The Problem of Metaphysics*; its deployment was aimed at showing that theological reflection must account for those limitations that chasten any over-confidence, theoretical or otherwise, that such structures could be exceeded in an uncomplicated fashion (*PM*, 1–16). But MacKinnon is not ultimately satisfied with purely descriptive accounts: he remains concerned with the "revisionary" and the "speculative" aspects of metaphysical inquiry also.[1] He is especially focused on how moral queries agitate a "thrust against the limits of language"[2] and how this pulsion in turn intimates and presupposes transcendent ends. Metaphysical method, in his terms, means being "puzzled" about how the "foundations of morality" participate in a continual "pressure" against "the familiar confines of intelligible descriptive discourse" (*PM*, 17). Such a move is placed within MacKinnon's argument for "a system of projection" that is both "descriptive and referential in intention"[3] as regards "the transcendent," without being "crudely anthropomorphic" in its scope.[4] The "system of projection" does not rely on "a *simpliste* model of correspondence,"[5] since it does not presuppose "a one-one correlation between terms of propositions and constituents

---

1. The distinction between "descriptive" and "revisionary" is drawn from Strawson, *Individuals*, 9: "Descriptive metaphysics is content to describe the actual structure of our thought about the world, revisionary metaphysics is concerned to produce a better structure." A systematic reformulation of this can be found in Glock, "Strawson's Descriptive Metaphysics."

2. This is a phrase is inspired by a lecture of Wittgenstein; cf. Wittgenstein, "A Lecture on Ethics," 12. However, the exact phrase is taken from a series of notes recorded by Waismann in discussion with Wittgenstein on the same topic. These are found in Waismann, "Notes on Talks with Wittgenstein."

3. MacKinnon, "The Problem of the 'System of Projection' appropriate to Christian Theological Statements [1969]," in *Explorations in Theology*, 70. MacKinnon draws the language of "projection" from Wittgenstein, who himself seems to have drawn it from geometry; cf. Wittgenstein, *Tractatus Logico-Philosophicus*, §§ 3.11–13; 4.0141.

4. MacKinnon, "The Problem of the 'System of Projection,'" 75–76

5. MacKinnon, "The Problem of the 'System of Projection,'" 73.

of fact."[6] Instead, it aims to articulate an "analogical unity of truth"[7] (or what he elsewhere calls a "conceptual unity" established through "focal realization"[8]). In this framework, he seeks to relate, comparatively, different modes of truth articulation such as mathematics, philosophy, or literature, etc.[9] This kind of 'truth' cannot be "described and illustrated" in "a few neat formulae."[10] On the contrary, the "complexity and many-sidedness"[11] of this means that the truth happens, as it were, on "the borderlands," at the areas of "same level criticism" between differing projections.[12] It suggests a degree of convergence, a possibility that we inhabit "similarly situated territory."[13] However, his particular interest presently is to argue that moral language has a revelatory function within its reflective structure.[14] He does this through a reading of *The Republic*, wherein MacKinnon argues for an "ethical reflection" that is always "inchoately metaphysical" (*PM*, 30). MacKinnon's thesis appears to be that the unfolding of moral language, especially when it touches on paradox and perplexity, reveals that our language has *reference*, that it is accountable to something beyond mere reflexivity. The fracture of intelligent discourse suggests that language *at this point* touches reality, opening up towards a horizon of new discovery.

MacKinnon turns to Plato's story of the perfectly just and unjust man (*Republic* II.357a–368c). Here the myth of the Ring of Gyges is used by Glaucon and Adeimantus to probe the connection between justice and happiness. The earlier cynicism of Thrasymachus lingers in the background here, who argued that people only behave "justly" when they are seen by others, and that it is rather the "unjust" who are truly honest and consistent. He also contended that "justice" could be enacted only through a hegemonic rule of the strong over the weak (*Republic* I. 336b–354c). In another thread of conversation, Glaucon and Adeimantus imagine a scenario of a perfectly unjust man who, by using the powers of invisibility granted

---

6. MacKinnon, "The Conflict Between Realism and Idealism: Remarks on the Significance for the Philosophy of Religion of a Classical Philosophical Controversy Recently Renewed," in *Explorations in Theology*, 154.

7. MacKinnon, "The Problem of the 'System of Projection,'" 75.

8. MacKinnon, "Idealism and Realism," 146.

9. MacKinnon, "The Problem of the 'System of Projection,'" 73–75.

10. MacKinnon, "Borderlands of Theology," in *Borderlands of Theology and Other Essays*, 44.

11. MacKinnon, "Borderlands of Theology," 49.

12. MacKinnon, "Borderlands of Theology," 48, 51.

13. MacKinnon, "Borderlands of Theology," 54.

14. Such a move is not dissimilar from Rowan Williams's more recent Gifford Lectures, published as *The Edge of Words: God and the Habits of Language*.

by the magic ring, was able to live a life of moral turpitude while appearing perfectly upright to others. The perfectly just man, on the other hand, would be someone who lived excellently, while sabotaging his reputation so that he might receive no recognition or reward for his achievements. It is only when we have reached these extremes that we are able to judge who, ultimately, is the happier of the two, and answer the question whether justice is necessarily bound to happiness.

MacKinnon's use of this illustration is an attempt to show that moral language can be made strange and difficult. His purpose is to illustrate how we remain "haunted" by "the system of restraints under which we live," provoking a "dream" of an alternate reality in which we could indulge ourselves without recompense (*PM*, 21). For MacKinnon, inspired here by the Socratic dialogue, it is when we question the "validity" of the assumptions that underlie our actions that we enter "the restless quest" of metaphysical inquiry (*PM*, 24), since for him it is in "the actual moral and political choice that the metaphysical problem is raised" (*PM*, 25). Such a metaphysic is pre-eminently concerned with "truth" and "what is the case," and so is not materially reductionist (*PM*, 26–29). He argues that we are concerned with the problem of how language can be truly "descriptive" and "referential" (*PM*, 27), which relates to his emphasis on the priority of "discovery" over "creation" (*PM*, 28), and with a "correspondence" between mind and world (*PM*, 29). Central to Plato's 'realism' therefore is a concern with "what is the case," a realism which aspires towards a transcendence of the Good, because it reaches for that "highest" standard of morality, that ideal which approximates, albeit incompletely, "the embodiment of the real" (*PM*, 29).

Influenced here by Wittgenstein (and John Wisdom),[15] MacKinnon offers a reading of Plato in which the enigmatic quality of moral language opens us to a perplexity that is the beginning of metaphysical inquiry.[16] The attempt to grasp and make sense of the difficulty that underlies everyday interactions alerts us to a reality of a *givenness* that exceeds ordinary perceptions. Experience reveals its strangeness, and indicates a deeper reality that defies reduction. Of course there is no infallible logic that substantiates 'transcendence,' but there is an argument which says that moral perplexity is undermined in a world without metaphysical ideals.[17] On this score,

---

15. Cf. Wisdom, *Paradox and Discovery*, 114–38. For a sample of such influence, see MacKinnon, "John Wisdom's *Paradox and Discovery*," in *Borderlands of Theology*, 222–31.

16. On the 'therapeutic' aspect of this style of philosophizing, see Bowyer, *Donald MacKinnon's Theology*, 5–43.

17. A similar argument has been recently restated by Ritchie, *From Metaphysics to Morality*.

MacKinnon, in a similar manner to Wittgenstein's *Tractatus*,[18] uses Socratic dialogue as a way of *manifesting* the transcendent, beyond what logical demonstrations can achieve alone. When we encounter in the world something that resists complete description, and becomes stranger the more we attempt to describe it, we are allowed to claim *reference* for our language, for the fact that our speaking is *about* something that transcends any uncomplicated or immediate deflation of truth to mere sense-perception. Again, there is a connection to Kant here: MacKinnon was mindful of Wittgenstein's Kantian heritage (and was appreciative of it), as seen in his appropriation of Erik Stenius. He even compared Wittgenstein's method of "manifesting" in the *Tractatus* to Kant's ethical mode of "metaphysical" projection (*PM*, 56).[19] For MacKinnon, through displaying seriousness about moral questions, by allowing its substance to work itself upon our speech, we manifest a commitment to truthfulness and realism insofar as our language shows an accountability to something more than sheer reflexivity. It is here that MacKinnon presses somewhat beyond Wittgensteinian relativism towards a more 'objective' Platonic and Kantian standard of morality.[20]

MacKinnon's concern with realist 'facticity' is clear in his ensuing argument, where he returns again to "logical atomism," and especially its assertion of a "correspondence conception of truth" (*PM*, 31), and "a thorough-going pluralistic realism" (*PM*, 32). "Pluralist realism" asserted the reality of "different sorts of facts" which cannot be reduced to one another; Moore argued that "we do know, beyond shadow of question, certain states of affairs" (*PM*, 33). This leads to a reading of empiricism, and even a chapter dedicated to its exposition in the Vienna Circle, and a critique of it given by Collingwood (*PM*, 46–52). MacKinnon does question ideas of factuality espoused by some empiricists, as when "verification" becomes equated with the merely observable. MacKinnon has internalized the contributions of Popper and Einstein on the unavoidable "speculation" and "creation" involved in any hypothetical science (*PM*, 34–36; 44–45). Nonetheless, MacKinnon would still assert that hypotheses are concerned with "what is the case," and therefore not with mere conjecture. While certain beliefs might be "self-authenticated" realities (*PM*, 37), he rejects the claims of "the thorough-going constructivists" who have precious little recourse against "a free play of undisciplined inventiveness" that dispenses with "the factuality of any world" (*PM*, 43–44). Despite idiomatic differences, MacKinnon

---

18. Cf. Wittgenstein, *Tractatus* 4.1212: "What *can* be shown, *cannot* be said." And cf. 6.522: "There are, indeed, things that cannot be put into words. They *make themselves manifest*. They are what is mystical."

19. Cf. MacKinnon, "John Wisdom's Paradox and Discovery," 231.

20. Bowyer, *Donald MacKinnon's Theology*, 151–81.

believes such conclusions are comparable to Plato's ethics, in which people are urged to live in accordance with "the way in which things are," so that "their lives *correspond* with the order of being and becoming" (*PM*, 37). Such "morality" could be described as an "ultimate seriousness concerning what is and what is not the case," and is not therefore a matter of "arbitrary choice" (*PM*, 38). However, the ethical concern with what is "the factual" should not be reduced to a "time-consuming, besetting concern with ultimate integrity," a "false scrupulosity" that "abstains from the risk of action, in the name of purity of motive" (*PM*, 39). Moral reflexivity should not be an excuse for irresponsibility. As we will see again later on, Mackinnon is critical of this kind of tragic indecisionism.

What is apparent from this discussion of Plato's ethics, as refracted through Wittgenstein and atomist realism, is a concern with 'morality' as a "system of projection" in which transcendent realities are re-presented and manifested. It is animated by a drive to establish "some kind of analogy between our commerce with the transcendent, and our commerce with the world around us," in a kind of revision of the analogy of proportionality.[21] Such predication is "the very heart of the problem of metaphysics." But such a supposed "commerce" should not give us solace for "there is no substitute for hard work, perhaps no finality of assured attainment" (*PM*, 39). In speaking about a genuine moral concern then, "we are speaking about learning facts" (*PM*, 40) in which the moral claims "press down on the stuff of human life itself" (*PM*, 41). Here literature (particularly tragedy) is able to represent processes of learning,[22] since tragedy provides a blending of "discovery" and "invention" (*PM*, 40–43). The question posed here exposes us to the precariousness of decisions risked in "a world we have not made" (to use the language of Rowan Williams).[23] Since we encounter in tragic experiences "the nature of our human responsibility,"[24] then on MacKinnon's view we cannot reduce such learning to an "ethical naturalism" (e.g., Bentham). On the contrary, to take moral dilemmas seriously, is "*one way of advancing beyond such frontiers*" (*PM*, 44), namely, beyond the "frontiers" of a purely immanent description. This linkage between ethics and metaphysics (and their connection to the tragic) is a concern that MacKinnon will return to again and again in his writings.

---

21. He makes reference to Cajetan's analogy of proper proportionality in *PM*, 80.

22. On the processes of growth-in-knowledge as found in tragic literature, see Williams, *The Tragic Imagination*, 30–55.

23. Williams, *The Tragic Imagination*, 108–15.

24. Williams, *The Tragic Imagination*, 109.

Now there are critical questions that could be raised, such as MacKinnon's acceptance of the Strawsonian distinction between "descriptive" and "speculative" metaphysics. One could deconstruct any clean separation between these methods, since "to conceive of purgation entirely as a *prelude* to illumination, or of 'description' as a task innocent of speculation, may forestall illumination altogether, or else radically determine its instance."[25] In this regard, MacKinnon does admit some sway to the 'creative' element of knowledge, but he does seem at pains to resist the excesses of a post-Kantian 'constructivism.' And while he is certainly not a positivist—nor an adherent of the fact-value distinction[26]—it is worth asking whether Mackinnon's account of 'facticity' is sufficiently sensitive to the way that facts are dependent upon historical processes.[27] This could be because MacKinnon's proclivity remains for a kind of Platonic 'presence' over Aristotelian teleology (as Milbank says).[28] Admittedly, this might not be exactly right since, as Catherine Pickstock has argued,[29] Plato's reflections on 'justice' already gave place to temporality and its impact on 'practical wisdom.' Yet despite these qualifications, one can see something of Milbank's concern here: MacKinnon appears to have abstracted Glaucon and Adeimantus's thought-experiment from the context of Socrates's *response*, which was directed to how justice is situated within the *polis*, and how our dependency on civic structures is the context in which justice should be established (Cf. *Republic* II.368d–383c). Moreover, he has neglected the "particular social practice" that formed the figure of Socrates,[30] remaining too focused on the individual philosopher and his enigmatic persona.

Much like Wittgenstein's *Zettel*, MacKinnon appears to emphasize irresolution *itself* as an answer to our dilemmas.[31] Not providing a "solution" but to "lay the texture of the problem bare"[32] is central to MacKinnon's

---

25. Milbank, "The Critique of a Theology of Right," in *The Word Made Strange*, 18. One does wonder whether Wittgenstein's Kantianism creates problems for MacKinnon as regards clarifying this relation. For a critique of Wittgenstein's Kantianism, see Cunningham, "Language," in *Radical Orthodoxy*, 64–90.

26. See Bowyer, *Donald MacKinnon's Theology*, 40–42.

27. See again Feyerabend, *Against Method*, who is pervasively critical of modern 'scientism' (Popper included).

28. Cf. Milbank, "A Critique of the Theology of Right," 21.

29. Pickstock, "Justice and Prudence."

30. Milbank, "A Critique of the Theology of Right," 20.

31. Cf. Wittgenstein, *Zettel*, §314.

32. MacKinnon, "On the Notion of the Philosophy of History," in *Borderlands of Theology*, 156. MacKinnon reference here is to St. Paul, but can be readily applied to MacKinnon himself. Also cf. MacKinnon, "The Crux of Morality."

realism. It is this emphasis on irony that makes MacKinnon wary of Platonic metaphysics, and any account of ontological participation and naïve intellectual intuition that is linked to this. Overall, MacKinnon's tendency is towards the primacy of *problem* over solution in his meta-ethics, and elsewhere more generally. MacKinnon's preference here is deontological, placing supremacy on situations where moral crises are prevalent, rather than on the ordinary virtues and institutional remedies that characterize the everyday. As Milbank suggests, and as we have this seen previously, this approach tends towards the problems of authenticity and scrupulosity rather than the development of *Sittlichkeit*, those moral institutions that remain essential for socialized justice and law-making. This is because, under the influence of A. E. Taylor and W. R. Sorley,[33] MacKinnon preferred the Kantian approach over the Hegelian one, since he believed that Kant provided a more ethically rigorous model than Hegel, who tended, on his reading, to submit moral questions to the deliverances of an already-given social order. For this reason, Kant's ethics would therefore seem more congenial to MacKinnon's desire to show that morality gives us access to a transcendental ideal to which we must show accountability.

The Irreducibility of the Ethical

Kant's theory of 'the primacy of practical' reason cannot be separated from his metaphysics, especially as this relates to his stringent limitations on the capacity of reason.[34] However, as is recognized by Kant scholars,[35] what seems unachievable within reason is essential to the ethical domain. Here a metaphysical structure is required to supplement the formalist and universal scope of ethical norms.[36] For Kant, ethical duties are not subject to contingencies or 'hypothetical' deduction; rather, they form an unequivocal claim that transgresses any particular or localized observation, and are thus "categorical."[37] As MacKinnon reiterates, in Kant's moral scheme we are claimed by something that approximates "the unconditioned,"[38] by a "peremptory authority" (*PM*, 54) that works against our parochial

---

33. Bowyer, *Donald MacKinnon's Theology*, 45–62.
34. MacKinnon is aware, however, of the ambiguities of this position (cf. *PM*, 64).
35. Cf. Kuehn, "Kant's Transcendental Deduction."
36. MacKinnon is very much aware of the risks of such formalism within the realm of ethics, as repeats he intermittently in regard to Kant; cf. MacKinnon, *A Study in Ethical Theory*, 69 and *passim;* and MacKinnon, *The Problem of Metaphysics*, 69.
37. Cf. Ameriks, "Reality, Reason, and Religion."
38. MacKinnon, *A Study in Ethical Theory*, 72.

interests. Thus we have to discipline ourselves from "trying to jump out of our cognitive skins" (*PM*, 55), since our constant temptation is to usurp our finite condition. For MacKinnon, morality is intrinsically bound up with "self-criticism,"[39] with that movement and moral therapy in which we continually test our assumptions. Such a process is essential for moral humanity, since as we are made conscious of the relative boundedness of our perspectives, we become aware of our entanglement and dependency on what is other to us. The diligence of an ethical *askesis* constitutes, for MacKinnon, a negative theology because it makes us aware of "the limits of the intelligible" against which our moral language continues to "thrust" (*PM*, 57), and awakens us to the transcendent reach of its claims.[40] Our capacity to relativize perspectives is entwined with our freedom, which for MacKinnon and Kant is our mode of "commerce with the ultimate" (*PM*, 62). For Kant (and MacKinnon it would seem), "the absolute for human beings is always realised as a *Sollen*,"[41] a willingness which establishes the ethos of self-questioning as the essence of metaphysics, a process of conscientisation whereby moral idiolects are ever-so gradually stretched towards "ultimate questions."[42]

Metaphysics according to MacKinnon is found in a "constancy" or "style" of interrogation that aims to formulate a deepened practice of questioning rather than any "positive body of achievement,"[43] which for him constitutes the only achievable "finality" within metaphysical and moral speculation.[44] Once more, the primacy of *problem* over *solution* remains paramount for MacKinnon. Within the order of ethical thinking, this questioning manifests itself in our introspective "dialogue" and "conversation" regarding moral agency,[45] a practice which forms part of the "grammar" of "transcendence,"[46] since within internalized judgements there is manifest a moral authorship that exceeds any reductive ideas of pure determinism, which are unable to account for "the quality of mystery" and "tragedy" that belongs to human freedom.[47] Our ability to question and revise our

39. MacKinnon, *A Study in Ethical Theory*, 70.
40. MacKinnon, *A Study in Ethical Theory*, 250.
41. MacKinnon, *A Study in Ethical Theory*, 88.
42. MacKinnon, "Finality in Metaphysics, Ethics and Theology," in *Explorations in Theology*, 104.
43. MacKinnon, "Finality in Metaphysics, Ethics and Theology," 105.
44. MacKinnon, "Finality in Metaphysics, Ethics and Theology," 115.
45. MacKinnon, "Moral Freedom (1969)," in *Philosophy and the Burden of Theological Honesty*, 92.
46. MacKinnon, "Moral Freedom," 93.
47. MacKinnon, "Moral Freedom," 98.

decision-making forms the essence of our freedom, but it does not imply that we can have a fully substantive account of what such freedom is. MacKinnon believes, like Kant, that "it is metaphysical agnosticism which before all else safeguards the transcendent character of morality,"[48] to the extent that "we do not know what we are saying when we say that men are free and yet we do know what we are not saying."[49] Rather than being a "dogmatic exposition,"[50] there is a kind of game-like or even "performative"[51] character to freedom, in the sense that it is only in the exercise of liberty that we "bring into being a moral universe."[52]

Once again, this is a Kantian maneuver: one only acts free on the assumption that one is free. Freedom cannot be proved: it can only be assumed—or transcendentally deduced—as a prerequisite for action. And yet the "moral universe" that is represented through action is (paradoxically) already *there*, but is not revealed apart from its performance.[53] Here again, the philosophy of the 'charmed circle' reappears. Such attains legibility within MacKinnon's attempt (after Cassirer[54]) to harmonize Kantian epistemology and autonomy through the mediation of "spontaneity,"[55] specifically as this ascribes a creative aspect to the rational and ethical faculties.[56] One could read this as a part of his attempt to alleviate the dualisms of freedom and necessity, as can be seen in his claim that the production of moral insight and freedom occurs through a experimentation in language that is at once truthful and quasi-fictional—'truthful' because we are made to recognize the impact of a world not of our making, and 'quasi-fictional' because we can imagine and create worlds that are not reducible to necessity. For MacKinnon, our freedom emerges as a kind of "game" that "matters,"[57] and

---

48. MacKinnon, *A Study in Ethical Theory*, 82–83. He says elsewhere that "Agnosticism is, in a sense, a foundation of a belief in human freedom" (MacKinnon, "Moral Freedom," 97).

49. MacKinnon, *A Study in Ethical Theory*, 104.

50. MacKinnon, "Ethical Intuition (1956)," in *Philosophy and the Burden of Theological Honesty*, 102.

51. MacKinnon, "Ethical Intuition," 108.

52. MacKinnon, "Ethical Intuition," 109.

53. MacKinnon, "Ethical Intuition," 109.

54. Cf. Cassirer, "Kant und das Problem der Metaphysik." It might be worth mentioning here that Heidegger read Kant in a proto-phenomenological manner in accordance with his own reflections on temporality, that is, as a Being-towards-death, cf. Courtine, "Kant y el Tiempo."

55. On Kant's metaphysics of spontaneity, see the summary found in Sgarbi, "The Spontaneity of Mind."

56. MacKinnon, *A Study in Ethical Theory*, 74–75.

57. MacKinnon, "Ethical Intuition," 113.

discloses for us "the irreducibility of the ethical,"[58] in which we continue to encounter "the strangeness" and "persistence" of moral debate as a sample of "the metaphysical questionings and gropings that are raised within the compass of a human life."[59]

MacKinnon chooses moral conflict and tragedy as a prime example of such "persistence," since it is here—most pre-eminently for him—that metaphysical questions impose themselves within the ordinary tracks of life. For if "conflict is a permanent element of human life" then it provides justification for thinking that we are "reckoning with the stuff of a predicament, with what is perhaps problem, or even mystery, rather than solution."[60] This discovery of what-is-the-case segues into MacKinnon's thinking around natural law in which "the way of human life" is structured according to limits and regularities.[61] Such a presence makes itself known when human beings are "pressed upon, even visited, by the eternal in the most ordinary occasion of life."[62] For MacKinnon, where "practical and theoretical perplexity meet," it is there that we encounter "the possibility of metaphysics," since it is at this juncture that we engage with the real depths of being.[63]

But the attempt to reach beyond limits has the risk attached that we might ascribe an absolutized significance to the merely local, resulting in "the denial of freedom" by sacrificing its "ultimacy in the name of a supposed vision of the world as it ultimately is."[64] MacKinnon is at pains to stress that "an advancement of our moral understanding" comes "through the banishment from the world" of "the theoretical all-embracing" (*PM*, 60). So rather than seeking for a metaphysical and visionary totality that absolutizes our fragmented perspectives, MacKinnon seems to say (following Kant) that "it is at the level of *Sollen* that we have commerce with the ultimate."[65] This seems to be because it is only within the remit of moral duty that we cannot avoid the impress of transcendent norms upon our ordinary activities.

On this point, the reason why moral freedom is considered to be the site of transcendence is because it acts, like in Kant, as a *causa noumenon*.

---

58. MacKinnon, "Ethical Intuition," 104.
59. MacKinnon, "Ethical Intuition," 111.
60. MacKinnon, "Ethical Intuition," 113.
61. MacKinnon, "Natural Law (1966)," in *Philosophy and the Burden of Theological Honesty*, 117.
62. MacKinnon, "Natural Law," 119.
63. MacKinnon, "Natural Law," 127.
64. MacKinnon, "Natural Law," 127.
65. MacKinnon, *A Study in Ethical Theory*, 89.

It resists metaphysical cognition precisely because it cannot be deduced phenomenologically, even though it has effects within the natural world.[66] We are unable to cognize the essence of freedom, but we are able to discern it effects. It is within this drive towards the actualization of freedom, and the mysteries surrounding its transcendent basis, that provides an alternative to a Catholic or Thomistic metaphysics, since for MacKinnon there is "something suspect" in finding solace within "the delineation of the modes of an analogically participated being" which purport to have glanced the wholeness of reality. For MacKinnon (and Kant), "the ultimate" is intuited through that which "engages the allegiance of our will without possibility of question or cavil."[67] As he will say in a later essay on Kant: "*We cannot represent: we achieve the sense of what we affirm in action.*"[68]

The world disclosed within the *Sollen* is discussed in a reckoning with "causality." Without a notion of 'causality'—transcendent or otherwise— moral action becomes "inconceivable" (*PM*, 62), and it becomes difficult to harmonize the realms of nature and morality. As has been mentioned already, there is a complex interplay of invention and discovery in moral reflection within MacKinnon's thinking. 'Causality' is manifest in the fact that we are both active and passive in regard to our environments, since we do not "invent our moral nature." Rather, it is something that we have received (at least partially) from without ourselves; it is something we discover. Nonetheless, through self-questioning our nature becomes something that "we disclose to ourselves" (*PM*, 66). This interplay between 'discovery' and 'creation' is a dialectic that MacKinnon returns to repeatedly in the Gifford lectures, and forms a part of his labour to articulate ways of thinking about truth beyond the reserves of mere "self-revelation" (*PM*, 73). MacKinnon is constantly concerned with the reality of that 'givenness.' To be sure, this reality cannot be represented apart from evaluative language, but MacKinnon wants to show that when we question ordinary modes of awareness, we encounter a depth-dimension to our engagements that reveals the unfamiliarity of the ordinary. The deepening of the "linguistically

---

66. Cf. Kant, *The Critique of Practical Reason*, 114: "For, one and the same acting being *as appearance* (even to his own inner sense) has a causality in the world of sense which always conforms to the mechanism of nature; but, with regard to the same event, insofar as the acting person regards himself simultaneously as *noumenon* (as pure intelligence, in his existence that is not determinable in terms of time), he can contain a determining basis—of that causality according to natural laws—which is itself free from any natural law."

67. MacKinnon, *A Study in Ethical Theory*, 89.

68. MacKinnon, "Aspects of Kant's Influence on British Theology," 364. Italics original.

or conceptually familiar" constitutes an *ars metaphysica* (*PM*, 78), and also connects to MacKinnon's penchant for the parabolic.

Parables are a mode of estranging the commonplace: they are invitations to transform our beliefs about the world (cf. *PM*, 80), disturbing the usual renderings of our environments, disclosing their "transcendent ground," though without "evacuating [the] familiar of its own proper dignity" (*PM*, 82). As such, they act as a catalyst for enlarging our perceptions of the world by de-familiarizing our normal contexts of judgement (*PM*, 83), thereby provoking us to "self-knowledge" (*PM*, 91).[69] Deceptively simple narratives can display our activities as more mysterious than we usually think, and can even be shocking in their estrangement since, to quote Roger White, "our attention becomes focused on the wholly bizarre nature of the analogy we are being asked to argue from."[70] MacKinnon states explicitly: "A parable must disturb, rather than edify."[71] And this is particularly true when one considers the parabolic use of "irony" as a mode of projecting the ultimate (*PM*, 86), since by showing that our moral actions are situated in complex and often conflicting chains of causation, we come to realize that the world is not *only* the product of human direction, but is recalcitrant, irruptive and even tragic in its fabric. This mode of expanding awareness and perception, of penetrating the metaphysics of the mundane—"the easily neglected, often unnoticed richness and diversity of the everyday" (*PM*, 109)—is also tied to MacKinnon's attempt to deepen empiricism with an account of poetic ontology. As mentioned previously, MacKinnon is resistant to the idea that 'the factual' should be equated with the observable. He questions whether the representation of reality can be reduced to a simple mirroring or 'photographic' model. Instead, here using the example of Cézanne's method of composition, MacKinnon shows that truthfulness is in some sense only gained by a process where "time and reflection, little by little, modify our vision" (*PM*, 106), a movement in which we become cognizant of "the very interior complexity of sense-perception itself" (*PM*, 109). Here there is something which needs time and patience to unfold, something that cannot be reduced to wish-fulfilment. We have to be aware of that which exists independently, of "the very externality of the natural world" as well as its "sheer objectivity."

---

69. MacKinnon's compares parables to Cajetan's 'analogy of proper proportionality' (*PM*, 80) in which two separate instances of relation are shown to have a similar proportion (e.g., A/B: C/D).

70. White, "MacKinnon on the Parables," in *Christ, Ethics and Tragedy*, 57.

71. MacKinnon, "Parable and Sacrament," in *Explorations in Theology*, 170.

> To see the scene before [our] eyes demands a tremendous effort. We may say of the world of which we take note by a cursory glance or even an elementary description, that we do not really see it, thereby suggesting a perception which transcends in the sense of lying outwith the reach of everyday concern with that with which we are in contact . . . we have to acknowledge perceptual experience which *transcends* our own, an experience which lies outwith our achieved awareness. (*PM*, 108)

This patient attention to 'the particular' also buttresses MacKinnon's critique of Plato (and Kant too). For MacKinnon, Plato seems to have "[dodged] the disciplines of close attention to the concrete and the familiar," specifically as they open us to an "enlarged awareness of realities" (*PM*, 111). This procedure is opposed to Aristotle who believed in a diversity of realizable 'goods' and resisted Plato's 'totalizing' vision of 'the Good' (*PM*, 95–103).[72] Plato's failure to attend to the particular results in a conceptualization that promotes absolute, non-negotiable claims, and leads potentially to what MacKinnon calls "the cult of the tragic" (*PM*, 105),[73] in which an individual or 'hero' sacrifices herself in the name of some all-encompassing intuition. Kant also is not immune: MacKinnon repeatedly rallies against Kant's ethical "formalism." Even though he acknowledges that Kant tried to display "the mystery of the transcendent" not from "beyond" but from within "the substance of human experience,"[74] he thinks that Kant's moral thought needs to be supplemented by using "a multiplicity of examples," so that "the austere rigour" and "paradoxes" of his thought can be tempered.[75]

We have seen how MacKinnon's reception of Kantian ethics has been used to metaphysical effect, specifically as this relates to the manner in which we as ethical subjects are able to render questionable our ordinary modes of perception. This is done with the aim of showing us how such questionability is entwined with the claim of 'the unconditioned' upon our lives. We come to realize that our entrenched habits of being are by-no-means 'natural' or unassailable, since they are finite, subject to the flux of circumstance. But if such finitude is our only point of reference, then the question as to what we are ultimately *responsible to* remains occluded from our reflection. If our moral concerns cannot be reduced to the empirical, we have to continue to probe as to what reality we *are* finally accountable to. For

---

72. On Aristotle's diversified conception of 'the good,' see Barrón, "Das Gute im Horizont der Seinsfrage."

73. Also see MacKinnon, *A Study in Ethical Theory*, 92–93, 97–98, 122.

74. MacKinnon, "Freedom Defended (1968–9)," in *Philosophy and the Burden of Theological Honesty*, 136.

75. MacKinnon, "Moral Freedom," 98.

Kant, this can only be the self-legislating moral will that is enacted 'categorically'. Any other form of responsibility implies 'heteronomy' and a denial of the voluntary agency of human actors.[76] This is arguably one of Kant's most significant insights within the field of moral philosophy, namely, that we need a procedure whereby moral claims cannot be reduced to the powers of sheer observation.[77] But it is precisely at this point also where some of Kant's most controverted claims become apparent.

Since Hegel, criticisms of Kant's ethics have centred upon its emptiness and formalism; this is because Kant appears to have separated reason from sensibility, the universal from the particular, reason from morality,[78] thereby rendering the ethical law as separate from the determined ends of moral agents, as pre-existing both good and evil.[79] Such formalism, as Gilles Deleuze suggests, corresponds to Kant's notion of the moral law as an "empty form" devoid of concrete substance (as seen in the second *Critique*), and is comparable to Kant's notion of time as "pure form" (in his first *Critique*).[80] But such formalism leaves many questions unanswered. Vittorio Hösle argues that this picture gives little sway to the operation of discernment or practical judgement in relation to competing or even conflicting duties.[81] This appears to be the case since Kant's aim to establish an abstract and autonomous ethics represses the constraints of historicity and "the intersubjective world"[82] in which agents are enmeshed. Second, as regards Kant's idea of human freedom as a *causa noumenon*, Hösle says that if the 'noumenal' self is really unknowable, we cannot know that it is really free (since we cannot exclude that it might be predetermined by another *Ding-an-Sich*). Furthermore, if there is no epistemic correspondence between the phenomenal and the noumenal self, then we cannot assert with confidence the moral integrity of *any* person, because there always remains the possibility that phenomenal 'appearance' does not cohere with the unknowable, noumenal subject of moral responsibility. Such remains the case, that is, unless one asserts that the noumenal creates the phenomenal or that God, in a Leibnizian fashion, forms a 'pre-established harmony' between these two realms. Both of these moves are ultimately rejected by Kant.[83]

76. Cf. Kant, *The Groundwork for the Metaphysics of Morals*, 4:441.
77. See Hösle, "The Greatness and Limits of Kant's Practical Philosophy."
78. See Caputo, "Metaphysics, Finitude and Kant's Illusion."
79. Cf. Wood, "The Emptiness of the Moral Will."
80. Deleuze, *Kant's Critical Philosophy*, X.
81. Hösle, "The Greatness and Limits of Kant's Practical Philosophy," 145–56.
82. Hösle, "The Greatness and Limits of Kant's Practical Philosophy," 150.
83. Hösle, "The Greatness and Limits of Kant's Practical Philosophy," 151.

This also has theological implications: for if it is through the pure formality of moral law that we have contact with the divine, then the question remains as to what kind of deity is thereby disclosed, since it is by a kind of practical "faith," rather than knowledge, that we have contact with this realm.[84] But this procedure has a difficulty, especially for theological orthodoxy, since on its assumptions it appears to include 'God' within the regime of the noumenal sublime. Kant says that freedom is a *causa noumenon*, insofar as it does not belong to 'appearance,' because to do so would apply an objective necessity to actions. Furthermore, divinity does not apply to the realm of 'appearances,' but belongs to the noumenal (or is himself a noumenon). Such a God, as Kant says,[85] can only be the creator of the noumenal self, which has no guaranteed correspondence to the sphere of phenomenality. It is difficult then to avoid the possibility that 'appearance' might be nothing more than that: *mere appearance*. And since God is not the creator of 'appearances' but is the creator of the noumenal self, and is himself a noumenon ('a Something = x'), then it becomes hard to discern whether divinity is even distinct from the noumena themselves.[86]

MacKinnon himself cannot be reduced to such tendencies: he seems to have digested, at least partially, some of the post-Hegelian critiques of Kantian ethics that have focused on its formalist character.[87] This is particularly clear in his appreciation of Butlerian ethics,[88] which sought to bring into harmony the concerns of ethics and human interest. Butler strengthened his awareness of the limitations of Kantian morality, insofar as it remained "independent" of "the contingencies and idiosyncrasies of individual character and circumstance."[89] Importantly, MacKinnon rejects "an ethics of sheer obligation" in accordance with the "arbitrary dictates of a God" that fails to take into account our created nature, since morality is bound to the fact that we are certain kinds of beings, and that our moral behavior is entwined with this reality. Desire and final happiness cannot be excluded from these considerations; however, it is only God who can

---

84. Kant, *The Critique of Pure Reason*, Bxxx.

85. Cf. Kant, *The Critique of Practical Reason*, 101–2.

86. Cunningham, *Genealogy of Nihilism*, 93.

87. In light of Hegel, MacKinnon (*A Study in Ethical Theory*, 233) said that "human freedom could and must be taken beyond Kant."

88. MacKinnon, *A Study in Ethical Theory*, 179–206.

89. MacKinnon, *A Study in Ethical Theory*, 268. Also see the comments of Milbank: "[MacKinnon] tends to suggest cautiously that a deontological ethics requires qualification in so far as our conduct may be radically guided by attention to particular facts, or particular persons regarded as embodying particular sets of values" (Milbank, "A Critique of the Theology of Right," 18).

guarantee a harmony between morality and human flourishing. Hereby, we should then be "encouraged to see ourselves as enticed by the way of obligation to tread the road of our proper humanity."[90] This is the case because MacKinnon seeks to maintain "the ethical importance of desire"[91] within the theatre of moral action. Additionally, as a theologian he does not possess the exactly same qualms as Kant does regarding a 'heteronomy' between human and divine willing, since God is the creator of reality in its totality, and not just the noumenal sphere.[92] Divine providence and omnipotence (as disclosed through the narrative of the suffering Christ[93]) applies to the whole range of created being, thereby including within its aegis human action, though without thereby implying any 'theodicy.' In short, MacKinnon thought Kant was too strident in his rejection of heteronomy, and thus created untenable dualisms.[94] Furthermore, his concern with historical embeddedness means that our moral freedom cannot be separated from the realities of tragic limit and consequence, which implies (as he makes clear) that even good-intentioned actions have unpredictable results which cannot be considered as morally neutral. This means that something like the categorical imperative cannot have the same place in MacKinnon as in Kant, even he admired its aspiration towards rigor.[95]

But such concessions do not mean that his Kantianism does not create problems. There still seems to be too much of an individualist anthropology at work within MacKinnon's account of moral deliberation, whose ideal seems to be that of a lonely agent who discovers her negative freedom through reflective abstraction and self-examination.[96] Such anthropology remains in tension with his stated opinion elsewhere that

90. MacKinnon, "Moral Objections [1963]," in *Philosophy and the Burden of Theological Honesty*, 16.

91. MacKinnon, "Revelation and Social Justice [1941]," in *Philosophy and the Burden of Theological Honesty*, 141.

92. He says explicitly, in a discussion of Genesis, that "God is the author of the world: of all things" (MacKinnon, "Creation: Dialogue with Anthony Flew and D. M. MacKinnon," in *Philosophy and the Burden of Theological Honesty*, 225.

93. Cf. MacKinnon, "Teleology and Redemption (1995)," in *Philosophy and the Burden of Theological Honesty*, 301–5.

94. "Kant's weakness that, in seeking to set morality free from any sort of heteronomous bondage through the criticism of metaphysics, he yet drew its frontiers too sharply and defended them with too impenetrable fortifications. This he did even while insisting on the dynamic quality of the form of the moral law" (*A Study in Ethical Theory*, 275–76).

95. Cf. MacKinnon, "Drama and Memory [1984]," in *Philosophy and the Burden of Theological Honesty*, 184.

96. See Milbank, "A Critique of the Theology of Right," 24.

personhood cannot be considered apart from relationality,[97] and his affirmation of Hegelian critiques of ethical abstraction. For Hegel, to remove the instance from its socio-historical circumstance is precisely to misprision the instance itself.[98] Furthermore, as Rowan Williams has suggested, MacKinnon's concern with tragedy emphasizes precisely the point that our actions are not self-enclosed but rather extend their repercussions in often unforeseen ways, binding us therefore to community.[99] These points, at least partially, rebuff an over-individualizing take on MacKinnon's ethics. And yet what Williams says does not banish completely the suspicion that MacKinnon is still too much entwined with post-idealist notions of freedom and necessity, in which there remains a "standoff" between "purely individual motivation" and the "lethal realities of the public world," a world in which the imagination of a *Sittlichkeit*, a collective ordering toward the good, remains largely absent.[100] This aporia appears to echo suggestively the Kantian distinction between phenomenality and noumenality, in the sense that we only exist as free agents when freedom is banished from material 'appearance.' This lends itself to a narrative of perpetual conflict in which the physical world as 'appearance' is considered to be the sphere of un-freedom, and the hidden world of the noumenal ego is construed as the site of liberated expression. This regime of 'sublimity' underpins what Milbank calls a "practical 'contentlessness'" that acts as a "disguised theoretical source of the insistence on a contentless infinite which goes with an exclusion of constitutive metaphysics."[101]

One can see why some have spoken of a 'gnostic' temptation within Kantian philosophy, since there is a rather pessimistic conceptualization of the physical order in it. Kant's privileging of the noumenal as the real sphere of freedom only seems to strengthen such a contention.[102] Whether MacKinnon completely bought into the Kantian division that underlies this schema remains an open question (since he was familiar with Strawson's critique of it).[103] But he does seem to have been persuaded by Kant's transcendental deduction of freedom as something to be negatively

97. See the essay entitled MacKinnon, "Things and Persons," in *Borderlands of Theology*, 131–41.

98. Cf. MacKinnon, *A Study in Ethical Theory*, 226, where MacKinnon contrasts Hegel with moral intuitionism.

99. Williams, *The Tragic Imagination*, 108–15.

100. Williams, *The Tragic Imagination*, 109.

101. Milbank, "A Critique of the Theology of Right," 24.

102. Brague, "Kant et la tentation gnostique."

103. See MacKinnon, "P. F. Strawson's *The Bounds of Sense*," in *Borderlands of Theology*, 249–56.

circumscribed but not positively stated,[104] since it remained finally "without grounds."[105] This point *does* appear to be predicated on a Kantian division, since it is only within the phenomenal-noumenal distinction that his dualism between freedom and necessity becomes intelligible. Nonetheless, while MacKinnon does take seriously Kant's determinism, he did ultimately lean towards a certain objectivity of freedom.[106] This places MacKinnon on the libertarian side of the freedom-necessity debate,[107] since when "individual responsibility" is "eroded" then "the tragic element in human life begins to disappear."[108] And yet in spite of these qualifications, MacKinnon nonetheless continued to have an appreciation for the Kantian division, as it corresponded to "the distinction between a man's unique presence to himself as agent, and his subsequent achievement of a different sort of self-knowledge through a review of his actions as a series of causally continuous events."[109] By commandeering this idea, MacKinnon desires to guard "the mystery of the individual"[110] from the sieges of metaphysical determinism and biological reductionism. But at the same time, as Milbank has provocatively suggested, this model of the 'noumenal' individual could also form a part of the "secular groundwork" within post-Kantian ethics that aims to secure "the absolute disinterestedness of ethics, and the purity of ethical freedom, by stressing agnosticism with regard to transcendence as a counterpart to an existential refusal of any materialist necessitarianism."[111]

Therefore, the Kantian influence on MacKinnon places limitations on his conceptualization of morality, and probably justifies Milbank's concern that he tacitly endorses "liberalism," that political vision which asserts private 'goods' at the expense of common beatitude. This is supplemented by the following observations: if one takes seriously his rather pessimistic

---

104. "Agnosticism is, in a sense, the foundation of a belief in human freedom" (MacKinnon, "Moral Freedom," 97).

105. MacKinnon, *A Study in Ethical Theory*, 97.

106. Cf. MacKinnon, "Ethical Intuition."

107. MacKinnon says that if we present the views of 'the libertarian' and 'the determinist' as complementary, this does not exclude the possibility "*that we incline more to the one than to the other*" (MacKinnon, "Moral Freedom," 86).

108. MacKinnon, "Moral Freedom," 88. Also cf. "No determinist could write an effective tragedy, could achieve the sort of deep exploration of responsibility, justice, guilt, that we find for instance in Electra or in Hamlet" (MacKinnon, "Atonement and Tragedy," in *Borderlands of Theology*, 101).

109. MacKinnon, "Moral Freedom," 96.

110. MacKinnon, "Moral Freedom," 94.

111. Milbank, "A Critique of the Theology of Right," 23.

account of materiality and 'evil' more generally (with its Kantian heritage),[112] it becomes harder to defend MacKinnon against the charge of a quasi-Manichaeism,[113] in which the created order is opposed to the realization of goodness, as seen especially in MacKinnon's rejection of any Augustinian theory of evil-as-privation (as we will see later). Such pessimism is not all-embracing because MacKinnon rejects such a totalizing perspective. But when one considers the fact that MacKinnon wants to assert a linkage between 'the realm of ends' and 'the realm of nature' (after Butler),[114] it becomes harder to believe in the final coherency of this project, since without the *privatio boni*, the 'natural' ordering of world towards goodness becomes unsustainable.[115] I should stress this a bit more since it touches upon themes that I have been discussing throughout and will return to again. On the one hand, MacKinnon seeks to maintain something like an intuition of moral ideals that transcend material immanence, while on the other he seeks to hold this alongside a theory of natural law that takes seriously the given limits of the physical world.[116] Here he sought to reconcile the transcendentalism of Plato and Kant with the emphasis on particularity and historicity he found in Aristotle, Butler and Collingwood. But since MacKinnon rejects the transcendental priority of the good, which since the early church has been central to the Christian account of creation, the metaphysical coherency of relating anything like transcendent realism of Good with historicism becomes problematic since now evil, in some sense, has a co-priority with goodness. And if the material world no longer has a 'natural' orientation to the Good over-against evil, then it remains difficult to see how one could "project" a metaphysical and eschatological reconciliation of desire

112. For a critical treatment of Kant's theory of "radical evil," see Milbank, "Evil: Darkness and Silence," in *Being Reconciled*, 1–25. Also cf. Milbank's comments regarding MacKinnon on the question of evil and the tragic: "The tragic gap between the political state bound to justice and the finally non-mediable wills of individuals thereby sinks into an ontological abyss, which is nevertheless a sublime opening beyond our perplexity. Evil, in this conception, seems akin to Kant's 'radical evil'—almost a necessary background for the *söllen*, the moral will towards the absolute" (Milbank, "A Critique of the Theology of Right," 22).

113. Cf. Williams, *The Tragic Imagination*, 109.

114. MacKinnon writes in the context of Kant's discussion of immortality that "If the realm of nature must be separated from that of ends in order that the peculiar dignity of the latter shall be established, we yet need sometimes to invoke the imagery of their reconciliation" (MacKinnon, *A Study in Ethical Theory*, 258).

115. In speaking this way, I am echoing figures like Maximus the Confessor who spoke of a 'natural' and 'rational' orientation towards the good, which then is elected (or not) through an exercise of the 'gnomic' will. On this, see Bradshaw, "St. Maximus the Confessor on the Will."

116. Bowyer, *Donald MacKinnon's Theology*, 173–81.

and happiness—which along with Butler and Maritain was something that MacKinnon aspired to. The specter of the post-Kantian sublime also hovers over this reading because, as I have reiterated previously, any "system of projection" regarding the transcendent is rendered formally indeterminate and the goodness of being as finally un-decidable. Being is morally ambiguous, both good and evil. And with this, the analogical edifice of ancient and medieval Christianity is problematized, since it is predicated on the participation of creation in the absolutely prior and self-donating Good whereby the goodness of the Caused reflects and imitates the Infinite Cause of all things: the Good beyond all being. Once again, it seems that MacKinnon's Kantianism might not assist him in achieving his aims.

Worth mentioning here again are Milbank's comments regarding the political implications of this vision: as we have learned from intellectual historians, the prioritization of evil has an intimate connection to the advent of liberalism, confirming the proposal that MacKinnon might not have adequate internal resources to resist this consequence, as Milbank argued.[117] Liberalism, especially in its Hobbesian assertion of private goods at the expense of collective flourishing, seems to privilege this priority of evil and violence to which the politics acts as a container. This is so because if goodness does not hold ontological priority, morality and politics become imagined as a process of *containment* and *reaction* against evil, which now is just as ontologically authentic as goodness.[118] This is not to say that he would have endorsed these tendencies, but rather that his individualist ethics, and his rejection of the *privatio boni*, make it difficult to achieve a coherent reconciliation between creation and moral teleology, between the spheres of 'nature' and of 'ends,' even though this is exactly what he wants to do.

The Transcendence of the Tragic

MacKinnon's preoccupation with tragedy is pervasive, and should not be limited to the period of the Gifford Lectures and thereafter.[119] However,

---

117. Manent, *An Intellectual History of Liberalism*, esp. 10–28. Also see the excellent analysis found in Michéa, *The Realm of Lesser Evil*; Milbank and Pabst, *The Politics of Virtue*, 13–67.

118. For a theological critique of this approach to ethics, see Milbank, "Can Morality Be Christian?" in *The Word Made Strange*, 219–32.

119. The *Signposts* tractates are filled with references to "tragedy," "the tragic" or "tragic conflict." There are also scattered allusions throughout his writings in the 1940s and 50s. For this, see MacKinnon, "Revelation and Social Justice [1941]," 147; "Ethical Intuition [1956]," 103–4; and "Prayer, Worship and Life [1953]," 61–62, in *Philosophy and the Burden of Theological Honesty*; MacKinnon, "Philosophy and Christology

MacKinnon's main discussion of tragedy within *The Problem of Metaphysics* begins with an analysis of the differences between Sophocles's *Trachiniae* and *Antigone*.[120] The particular motivation here is to query whether there is something like a continuity of tragic experience, and how this in turn inflects our own context—especially since we can no longer share the worldview that Sophocles inhabited. MacKinnon argues that while the *Trachiniae*, on the one hand, seems to inhabit a world more "remote" from ours, filled as it is with "semi-divine heroes" and "monstrous centaurs" (*PM*, 123), *Antigone* displays a series of mundane events that have a kinship to present experience. This connection becomes clear within his plangent stress on tragic "conflict" and "irony," both of which form touchstones for the larger argument regarding the relevance of tragedy for contemporary ethics and metaphysics. This is so since "irony" is an exemplary mode of showing how our moral lives are entwined with realities that exceed personal fabrication (*PM*, 86). As such, tragedy is attuned to the exigencies of living, and is "in accordance with the facts of the human situation," forming "a disclosure of what is," making apparent what is often in contradiction to "the comfortable musings of theologians and metaphysicians."[121]

Such does not imply that he is unaware of the problems related to distilling the "essence" of "the tragic." For MacKinnon, there cannot be a simplistic reduction of tragedy to a tightly-canonized, marginal mode of presentation (e.g., George Steiner), on the one hand, or an over-generalizing 'tragic sense of life' on the other (e.g., Miguel de Unamuno). MacKinnon is conscious that we need to avoid easy distillations of this kind. He was familiar with Raymond Williams,[122] and was sensitive to the opinion

---

[1956]," 55–81; and "On the Notion of a Philosophy of History [1954]," 152–68, in *Borderlands of Theology*; and MacKinnon, *A Study in Ethical Theory*, 241–42. His inaugural lecture at Cambridge (published 1961) already laid down programmatically the importance for theology to inhabit the "borderlands" of philosophy and literature. In this context, he speaks of the "revelations" of "the human condition" (MacKinnon, *The Borderlands of Theology*, 50) that can be gleaned from the writings of Shakespeare and Sophocles. On the question of tragedy and politics, see MacKinnon, "Some Notes on 'Philosophy of History,'" 171–78. Also cf. Ward, "Tragedy as Subclause," 278: "Prior to *The Problem of Metaphysics* the category of tragedy does not appear in his work, but the tragic vision hovers at the edges of articles written in the forties and fifties. . . . Tragedy emerges for MacKinnon not because of Greek literary form but because of the lives we lead and the times we have experienced." The above evidence might qualify Ward's statement somewhat.

120. The analysis to follow has been helped by the study of this theme in Waller, "Freedom, Fate and Sin," and the excellent summary in Williams, *The Tragic Imagination*, 108–15.

121. MacKinnon, "Atonement and Tragedy," 101.

122. Cf. MacKinnon, "Theology and Tragedy." The idea of the genre of tragedy as

that any taxonomy of tragedies is "inherently complex," requiring a correlation of "family resemblance."[123] This is because tragedies have a certain "open-textured quality" that defies cheaply-acquired reductions.[124] He has said that it would be "a great grave mistake to generalize about tragedy as if there were an 'essence' of the tragic that we could extract and capture in a manageable formula."[125] Yet despite these qualifications, MacKinnon assigns a privilege to the category of tragedy as a "system of projection," which can be traced to its narration of the hidden consequences of moral action, the as-of-yet undisclosed threads of connection that exceed immediate grasp. It is precisely this ironic excessiveness within the moral life that manifests the non-triviality of transcendent questions. This non-triviality of tragic disclosure requires an openness to metaphysical "presence" (cf. *PM*, 146–63), because without its admission, we would render vacuous the moral life and undermine its aporias. Without transcendence, tragedy ceases to exist, precisely because it is predicated on a moral axiology that pure immanence cannot provide.

Nevertheless, MacKinnon does not espouse a 'tragic philosophy,' or any systematic 'tragic sense of life.' Such would count as a capitulation, once more, to philosophical monism.[126] Against superficial readings of MacKinnon, one should emphasize his pervasive suspicion of any all-embracing 'tragic' or 'pessimistic' philosophy. For him, against a totalizing system, "metaphysics" must be bound to the "concretely descriptive."[127] Already in the 1940s MacKinnon had spoken (under the influence of H. A. Hodges) of tragedy as providing a mediating position between "the old-fashioned rationalism and a more nihilistic philosophy."[128] This is so because trag-

---

a question of Wittgensteinian "family resemblance" is also re-affirmed by Hamilton in *A Philosophy of Tragedy*, 82–83. Raymond Williams wrote, "Tragedy is . . . not a single and permanent kind of fact, but a series of experiences and conventions and institutions. It is not a case of interpreting this series by reference to a permanent and unchanging human nature. Rather, the varieties of tragic experience are to be interpreted by reference to the changing conventions and institutions. The universalist character of most tragic theory is then at the opposite pole from our necessary interest" (Williams, *Modern Tragedy*, 69).

123. MacKinnon, "Theology and Tragedy," 163.

124. MacKinnon, "Theology and Tragedy," 168.

125. MacKinnon, "Ethics and Tragedy [1971]," in *Explorations in Theology*, 186.

126. MacKinnon made this clear regarding the problem of evil already in his lectures on evil (1962/1963). For summary of these lectures, see the appendix in Cane, *The Place of Judas Iscariot in Christology*, 189–92.

127. MacKinnon, "Scott Holland and Contemporary Needs," in *Borderlands of Theology*, 115.

128. This statement is to be found in the unpublished minutes of the Moot

edy discloses a kind of "metaphysical ultimacy" that resists a "teleological explanation" of the comprehensive kind.[129] It provides both a realistic vision of the contingency of the world, while at the same time avoiding the trivialization of the transcendent. The "paradox" of tragedy for MacKinnon then is that it both "demands and resists metaphysics," to quote Giles Waller. For MacKinnon, "Tragedy *reveals* the necessity of metaphysics, while *regulating* the speculative metaphysics that attempts to pass 'beyond tragedy.'"[130] Tragedy proposes and presupposes a realm of values, apart from which the pathos of human circumstance is rendered trivial; but this does not imply a confident system of 'meaning' into which all suffering can be plotted. Such applies equally to accounts of natural teleology that lack tragic irony, as it does to universalized declarations that all values are without substance, as in nihilism. This is also why MacKinnon aimed to transcend philosophies that endorsed either 'pessimism' or 'optimism.' He made clear that the Christian assertion of the resurrection of the crucified surpasses these options.[131] Here MacKinnon is Johannine in his approach, reading the glory of the ascended Christ as coterminous with his crucifixion, his kenosis with his anabasis. As this implies, the Christological element has a centrality within MacKinnon's theology, and has special implications in his reception of tragic themes—a point to which I will return.

But it is important to note again that MacKinnon opposes any uncritical commitment to "the tragic sense of life" or "the cult of the tragic"[132] (or any "romantic cult of the heroic"[133]). Central to this critique is that tragic philosophy—much like Plato's politics, or Hegel's collapsing of the ideal with the actual—tends to convert the *is* of the present into an ethical *ought*. For MacKinnon, tragic philosophies are susceptible to this trend, since they imply a resignation before the seemingly unchangeable present. Treated thus, tragedy would be converted to a form of ideology, a mode of mystification in which the current order is tacitly endorsed. Additionally, it could provoke self-immolation in the name of an all-embracing totality.[134]

---

conference, at St. Julian's (17–20 December 1948). My access to this material, as elsewhere, has been granted by André Muller. For a history of this group, see Clements, *The Moot Papers*, 6–17.

129. Waller, "Freedom, Fate and Sin," 107. Also cf. MacKinnon, "Teleology and Redemption (1995)."

130. Waller, "Freedom, Fate and Sin," 108.

131. MacKinnon, "Order and Evil in the Gospel," in *Borderlands of Theology*, 90–96.

132. MacKinnon, "Prayer, Worship and Life," 61–62; MacKinnon, *A Study of Ethical Theory*, 93, 97–98, 242; MacKinnon, "On the Notion of a Philosophy of History," 156.

133. MacKinnon, *A Study of Ethical Theory*, 60, 122, 175.

134. MacKinnon, *A Study in Ethical Theory*, 90. Here he makes mention of Thomas

All of this would be a distortion of the gospel since Christianity, on the contrary, does not have a "vested interest in human failure and disaster."[135] He castigates theologians and preachers who engage in an "academically precise pessimism," who found their *métier* in the "disintegration of societies" and "the coming of despair."[136] This praxis of "despair" or tragic "pity," in his eyes, encourages a culture of moral irresponsibility that inhibits political "action."[137] MacKinnon is opposed to this move, as he makes clear: "[the] recognition of the tragic must not be allowed to inhibit action, even if it must deepen perception and, in consequence, purify the motives and intentions from which men act."[138] MacKinnon certainly acknowledges the metaphysical import of tragic awareness, but this should not imply that "the tragic is a sort of *Anknüpfungspunkt* between creature and creator." Instead, "it is to remind ourselves that it is at the level of personal self-interrogation, to which tragic perception belongs, and not at that of abstract speculation that metaphysics often finds its home. We need to revise our concept of the metaphysical, to do justice to its situation in the stream of human life," and "inevitably such a revision will enable us to take stock of its human role, and therefore of its tragic quality."[139] The only real *Anknüpfungspunkt* between God and humanity is to be found where the divine has most profoundly disclosed its nature, namely Jesus Christ.

One of MacKinnon's most trenchant Christological emphases is on "the cost of victory."[140] MacKinnon's particular inspiration is taken from the story from the Napoleonic wars: in response to a woman's adulations of his military triumph, the Duke of Wellington had replied to her by saying "Madam, a victory is the most tragic thing in the world, only excepting a defeat" (PM, 126).[141] This statement reverberates in several of MacKinnon's

---

Carlyle. Also, cf. his rather stringent remarks on the language of 'sacrifice' in MacKinnon, "Moral Objections," 21–22. These perspectives should, at the minimum, put in check the sentiments of David Bentley Hart's placing MacKinnon under the regime of a "sacrificial totality."

135. MacKinnon, "Borderlands of Theology," in *Borderlands of Theology*, 53.

136. MacKinnon, "Scott Holland and Contemporary Needs," in *Borderlands of Theology*, 119.

137. MacKinnon, "Some Notes on 'Philosophy of History,'" 177.

138. MacKinnon, "Some Reflections on Secular Diakonia (1966)," in *Philosophy and the Burden of Theological Honesty*, 70.

139. MacKinnon, "Some Reflections on Secular Diakonia (1966)," 75–76.

140. Cf. Daniels, "The Cost of Victory."

141. MacKinnon recounts this story in several places throughout his writings, thereby showing its importance for him. Cf. MacKinnon, "Some Reflections on the Concept of Rasion d'État," 44, and "Ethics and Tragedy," 192–93, in *Explorations in Theology*.

texts, but its gravitas is tied to the sense that our moral actions take place within a world "we have not made,"[142] a world which does not obey an unflinching law which guarantees that actions—even good ones—will result in desirable consequences. Even our victories can come at an unexpected cost, for ourselves and for others. To quote Rowan Williams: "If the world is our creation, or even if the world is masterable as a system of necessities, the idea of irreparable and uncontrollable *loss* ceases to make sense." In this world, "there are no tragedies."[143] Connected to this, as MacKinnon suggests, is the insight of tragic fiction in which protagonists are "frequently broken not by their faults but by their virtues,"[144] as can be seen in the examples of Deianira, Antigone, Oedipus, and Creon, to name only a sample. MacKinnon's purpose is to manifest the ever-present truth that actions, even when they are bolstered by good intentions, cannot be immunized against the moral risk that lingers over every act. To deny such would result in us becoming "frustrated" or "dangerously self-deceived"[145] in our ethical responsibility. MacKinnon's complexification of 'victory' provides an entrance to his tragic reading of the gospel. Since Christ's life cannot be abstracted from the continuum of time and space, it cannot be considered apart from its history of effects. By establishing this, MacKinnon's aim is to translate this into the sphere of Christology, countering the claim, made by some, that "where the Christian religion is concerned" we are done with, or have moved "beyond tragedy" (*PM*, 124).[146] For MacKinnon, this will not do since even at the level of scripture there are examples of 'tragic irony' that warrant comparison with tragic drama. MacKinnon mentions the story of Job, but it is the Gospel of John that becomes the central text for displaying this.

Earlier in *The Problem of Metaphysics*, MacKinnon had called the writer of this Gospel "a supreme ironist" (*PM*, 120), particularly as regards his recounting of the miracles stories (*PM*, 114–21). Apropos Lazarus (John 11:1–44), he argued that John gives an example of "omnipotence *in concreto*" (*PM*, 119) in which "a question-mark is set against the way in which we are easily to understand it," that is, the divine as an unbounded miraculous power. In his reading, John is inviting us to continue the *lectio* until we approach the end. For MacKinnon, the resuscitation of Lazarus belongs to "the world of myth" and "fairy-tale" in comparison with "[the] bitter submission to the harsh realities of the human life" (*PM*, 120) that are manifest in the

---

142. Williams, *The Tragic Imagination*, 108.
143. Williams, "Trinity and Ontology," in *On Christian Theology*, 154.
144. Waller, "Freedom, Fate and Sin," 110.
145. Williams, *The Tragic Imagination*, 113.
146. MacKinnon is probably referencing Niebuhr's *Beyond Tragedy*.

immediately subsequent section: the recounting of the Pharisees's murderous plot (John 11:45–57). This section is summarized—in a masterstroke of irony—by Caiaphas's statement "that it is better for you to have one man die for the people than to have the whole nation destroyed" (John 11:50), here understood by the writer of the Gospel as applying not just to Israel, but to "the dispersed children of God" as well (John 11:52). Their murderous scheme however is unable to resist the very thing which the Pharisees feared, namely the destruction of the city itself (John 11:48) in 70 AD. MacKinnon's purpose in using this example is to show that the gospel, through its use of "*double-intendre*" and "devastating irony," is able to display "an unmistakeable tragic quality" (*PM*, 125). In particular, it plays with ideas of recognition and misrecognition, inviting the reader to see the 'truth' that is there, but which is unrecognized by those who need it most.[147]

This reading is contrasted with the Lukan narrative which for MacKinnon (and especially the Book of Acts) evinces "a narrative of triumphal progress" (*PM*, 127) that undermines "the deep complexity of the Gospel" (*PM*, 128), and legitimates a non-tragic characterization of early Christianity. It lays the foundation for "The most devastating intellectual temptation" in Christian thinking, in which "the catastrophic course of events" becomes "expressive of the working of a traceable providential order." This leads to "the emergence of an apologetic style which seeks to make the intolerable bearable, even edifying, which seeks to eliminate the element of unfathomable mystery by the attempt to move beyond tragedy" (*PM*, 129). MacKinnon thinks that the church is constantly tempted to make history "endurable" when its task was precisely to make it "unendurable."[148] He therefore rejected all the attempts of abstract theodicies to solve 'the problem of evil' (even once describing such solvency as a "lie"[149] or "sheer nonsense"[150]). In a similar fashion, MacKinnon rejects the *privatio boni* as "the most profound spiritual error of transcendent metaphysics,"[151] since it draws upon a "metaphysical idealism" that "refuses to recognize evil as positive, and not merely a negative, force."[152] He presses his rejection by saying "that [the Platonic theory of privation] has only to be stated clearly, and worked out in terms of concrete examples, to be shown to be totally

---

147. See Rowan Williams's similar reading of this gospel in *The Tragic Imagination*, 119–27.
148. MacKinnon, "Revelation and Social Justice [1941]," 152.
149. MacKinnon, "On the Notion of the Philosophy of History," 155.
150. MacKinnon, "Order and Evil in the Gospel," 92.
151. MacKinnon, "Finality in Metaphysics, Ethics and Theology," 103.
152. MacKinnon, "Christianity and Justice," 349.

inadequate as an analysis either of moral or of physical evil."[153] MacKinnon's pluralist impulses are again at work because, in his view, any account of evil-as-privation is premised upon (what Giles Waller calls) "a totalizing order of the Good." To quote Waller more extensively: "Speaking of evil as privation in a way risks, for the metaphysical pluralist, an idolatry of our own theoretical construct of the Good at the expense of our premature reduction of suffering and evil to a mere instance of something else, in this case a lack of the Good."[154] To accept the *privatio boni* would be to miss the radical particularity of suffering, and thereby renders evil as merely an absence or lack, failing to account for its own irruptive quality. Ultimately, both theodicy and the *privatio boni*, in his opinion, are reducible to a form of metaphysical monism that is unable to recognize the refractions of the individual and the particular.

Such monistic philosophies undergird a triumphalist narration of the church that tends to ignore "the tragic element in Christianity" (*PM*, 130). It forgets that even its defining event, the death and resurrection of Christ, cannot be absolved from tragic circumstance. MacKinnon's favorite example is stark: in his mind, Christianity has to bear its share of responsibility for allowing the Holocaust to occur. He does not scold the church as such for direct responsibility, despite reprimanding (probably unfairly) the Catholic Church and Pope Pius XII for their response to the plight of Jews in Rome.[155] But beyond these details, MacKinnon's point is that the *longue durée* of the church's anti-Judaism produced "a blunting of the sensibility" (*PM*, 130) that contributed to the atrocities of Hitler's Germany. These teachings find their basis in the New Testament itself, especially (though MacKinnon does not mention this here) within John's gospel.[156] The atoning death of Christ cannot be parsed out from its historical aftermath, to which the pogroms and genocides of Europe serve as an exemplary testament.[157]

---

153. MacKinnon, "Theology and Tragedy," 165.

154. Waller, "Freedom, Fate and Sin," 107.

155. It should be said in passing that this portrayal of Pope Pius XII is probably inaccurate, as contemporary scholarship has shown. Numerous Jewish witnesses confirm that the Pope was considered a "righteous gentile" who contributed in significant ways to the anti-Nazi struggle. For a summary of the evidence, see Dalin, "Pius XII and the Jews."

156. I know it will not set this debate at rest, but it is worth mentioning here that the projection of 'anti-Semitism' onto a text like John's Gospel (or the New Testament for that matter) is anachronistic, and a stretch at best. It is better, probably, to view the reoccurring invective against 'the Jews' as form of intra-Judaic polemic (Judean *contra* Galilean, etc.). For arguments broadly supporting this approach, see Johnson, "The New Testament's Anti-Jewish Slander."

157. MacKinnon, "Atonement and Tragedy," 102–4.

As such, Christology cannot be confessed apart from particularity, as well as its historical contributions to unjust suffering.

MacKinnon's Christology at this juncture simply constitutes a deepening, in his mind, of what orthodoxy says concerning the *homoousion*. For him, to "acknowledge the supremacy of the Christology is to confess that finality belongs somehow to that which is particular and contingent."[158] This is done without trivializing, as MacKinnon thought Hegel did, "the tragic depth of human existence," in which Gethsemane is turned into a kind of "charade."[159] But just because there is "no escape from contingency,"[160] "no transcendence of the pervasive temporal, no leaping over its condition,"[161] such should not mean that Christ's particularity is refused "ontological" relevance, especially for the church which is constantly tempted to forget its own contingent polity.[162] There is a perennial tendency to convert or reduce Christ's "deed" into an "idea," rather than being drawn to "the concrete detail" that forms its specific history.[163] This explains why MacKinnon thinks that "Christian theology may be much more than it realizes the victim of the victory won in the person of Plato by the philosophers over the poets, and particular the tragedians."[164] Because Platonism has contributed to the avoidance of the particular, such an aversion to "the concrete detail" has led to a blindness around the historical limitation of Christ, and has contributed to some rather docetic renditions of Christ's humanity. Controversially, he even suggests that Christ's sinlessness cannot be divorced from contingent infractions, and even sinful outcomes. His was a "historically achieved innocence"[165] rather than a "bloodless myth" (to quote Geoffrey Hill[166]). As MacKinnon argues: "Even if we count Christ sinless . . . we still see in him one whirled to destruction by the choice he made, broken to pieces in inevitable consequence of the way he elected to follow." Therefore, to "portray him as a serene heroic figure, always the confident master of the situations which confronted him, always sure and certain of touch in his handling of them, is to trivialize his

---

158. MacKinnon, "Philosophy and Christology," 58.
159. MacKinnon, "Philosophy and Christology," 70.
160. MacKinnon, "Philosophy and Christology," 81.
161. MacKinnon, "Prolegomena to Christology," 158.
162. Cf. MacKinnon, "Philosophy and Christology," 81.
163. MacKinnon, "Atonement and Tragedy," 103.
164. MacKinnon, "Atonement and Tragedy," 101.
165. MacKinnon, "Some Notes on the Irreversibility of Time," in *Explorations in Theology*, 97.
166. Hill, "Genesis," in *Broken Hierarchies*, 3.

ordeal, and diminish his significance, to belittle his mystery, and to render inauthentic his humanity."[167] For Christ, to be human implied an element of subjection to the constraints of time, growth and limitation:

> For this element of temporality... belongs to Jesus' comings and goings. What is was for him to be human was to be subject to the sort of fragmentation of effort, curtailment of design, interruption of purpose, distraction of resolve that belongs to temporal experience. To leave one place for another is leave work undone; to give attention to one suppliant is to ignore another; to expend energy today is to leave less for tomorrow.... We have to ask ourselves how far this very conformity to the complex discipline of temporality, this acceptance of the often tragic consequences that spring from its obstinate, ineluctable truncation of human effort, belongs to the very substance of Jesus' defeat. Jesus' acceptance of this part of his burden can arguably be interpreted as a painfully realized transcription into the conditions of our existence, of the receptivity, the defined, even if frontierless, receptivity that constitutes his person.[168]

For MacKinnon, the irrepressible configurations of time and space apply to Christ, just as much as they do to us. Our natures are implicated and formed through "growth" and "estrangement,"[169] experiences that are fundamental for our advancement towards maturity. The temporality of human personhood does not imply a "facile determinism,"[170] but rather provokes an awareness that we are able "to fashion or refashion"[171] ourselves in accordance with the givens of memory and circumstance. It is through this narration that we achieve adulthood and coherency, in which we are able to let go of past identities (or fixations) in our journey towards maturity.[172] Dwelling within the constraints of time necessitates a kind of loss, but it also grants the possibility

---

167. MacKinnon, "Evidence: Preliminary Reflections," in *Explorations in Theology*, 116–28. The quote is on 127–28. Rowan Williams ("Trinity and Ontology," 157) comments on this teaching by saying that "sinlessness can only be a judgement passed on the *entirety* of a life in which the inevitable damage done by human beings to each other has not sealed up the possibility of compassionate and creative relationship (even to those most deeply injured: what could one say here of the relation between the figure of Jesus and post-Holocaust Judaism, as perceived by modern Jewish writers? Does this give a hint of what the content of 'sinlessness' would be?)."

168. MacKinnon, "The Relation of the Doctrines," 104.
169. MacKinnon, "Some Notes on the Irreversibility of Time," 96.
170. MacKinnon, "Some Notes on the Irreversibility of Time," 92.
171. MacKinnon, "Some Notes on the Irreversibility of Time," 93.
172. MacKinnon, "Some Notes on the Irreversibility of Time," 96–98.

of learning. It implies a "*ceasing* to feel and think in certain ways,"[173] a growth from childhood to adulthood. This awareness of loss and historical limitedness is intrinsic to his understanding of tragic narration. But this perspective, it should be emphasized, does not gesture towards an unavoidably 'negative' outcome. It might suggest a non-retrievable loss for some, but this does not imply an ontological 'necessity.' Rowan Williams has made some excellent comments on this aspect which deserve a hearing.

> To exist in time and its limits is to exist in a world where there is no *historical* end to risk and suffering, and thus to the likelihood of damage within any and every action. Yet this does not mean presupposing some supertemporal principle or existential curse. It is simply a matter of parsing what it means to recognize our finitude: narrative itself presupposes the irreversible passage of time and thus the omnipresence of loss. But that's the point: it is only in narrating it, 'plotting' it if your will, that it can be spoken of. What happens as result of our decisions is not an abstract and identical calamity but always the specific kind of loss that *this* unique set of temporal conditions will generate . . . the very act of narrating anything at all involves the possibility of *tragic* narration. The passage of time is a process of loss, *identified as such in the act of relating it*.[174]

This narration does not solve 'the problem of evil' or imply some soul-making theodicy. MacKinnon wholeheartedly rejects any such consolation, any "recipes for living" that insure that suffering serves "an end" by which our "endurance will be justified" (*PM*, 134). To do so would involve a blunting of the edges of tragedy, and would imply a metaphysical monism in which catastrophe is absorbed into a finalized reconciliation, obliterating the profundity of tragic deprivation (*PM*, 169). MacKinnon's provocations have been summarized by Paul Janz as offering a "system of projection" that manifests "the finality of non-resolution." Janz writes that for MacKinnon, "Orientation to the tragic—to the sheerly discontinuous in human life—allows us to project our questioning to the transcendent like no other form of discourse because it gives us *factual, tangible* examples in *real empirical* human experience, of the finality of non-resolution that we must encounter in the transcendent."[175] It is at this point that MacKinnon might be accused of adopting the "speculative closure" of the tragic sublime,[176] which—espe-

---

173. Williams, *The Tragic Imagination*, 112.
174. Williams, *The Tragic Imagination*, 113.
175. Janz, *God, the Mind's Desire*, 175.
176. Milbank, "The Programme of Radical Orthodoxy," 40.

cially in its postmodern versions—asserts the *unthinkability* of pain and prejudges its state of irresolution. However, for the moment, it is important to stress that for him it is this non-negotiable presence of the tragic that resists systematic containment, and it is Christianity which, "properly understood," that might be able to "hold steadfastly to the significance of the tragic," as this resists "that sort of synthesis which seeks to obliterate by the vision of an all-embracing order the sharper discontinuity of human existence" (*PM*, 135). The hope of the church, instructed by the crucified and resurrected Christ, is not found in consolatory visions of universal meaning or theodicy, but through a participation in the "endurance" of Jesus, as he moved through the darkness of Gethsemane towards the light of Easter.[177] This constitutes MacKinnon's own 'practical' response to the problem of evil, against the over-generalizing approaches of philosophical theology.[178]

MacKinnon appropriates this non-negotiability of the tragic as an instance of the priority of practical rationality (*PM*, 53–71).[179] As we have seen, Kantian morality is a touchstone for MacKinnon's metaphysics. Following Wittgenstein's 'intuitive' rather than 'discursive' praxis (as evidenced in the *Tractatus*),[180] MacKinnon does not construct extensive logical premises on which metaphysics is possible. Much like Kant, he thinks religion becomes most pertinent through the claims of morality than through any abstract reflection. It is through moral perplexity that questions concerning the supersensible become manifest, because without this dimension the question of transcendence is compromised and reduced to a variant of biological naturalism. And in MacKinnon's eyes, it is moral tragedy that is the best "system of projection" for manifesting such metaphysical concerns. In his words, it is "in tragedy we reach a form of representation that by the very ruthlessness of its interrogation enables us to project as does no available alternative, our ultimate questioning" (*PM*, 136). This procedure, as Milbank has said, seems to place MacKinnon within a tradition of Anglican metaphysics that aims to radicalize the impositions of natural law as a mode of revelatory disclosure through "a confirmation of the conditions of our perplexity."[181]

177. Also see MacKinnon, "Order and Evil in the Gospel," 93.

178. Cf. Surin, *Theology and the Problem of Evil*; and Williams, "Redeeming Sorrows."

179. Cf. Williams, "Trinity and Ontology," 155; Waller, "Freedom, Fate and Sin," 108. Also cf. Milbank, "A Critique of the Theology of Right," 21: "MacKinnon appears to convert the categorical imperative itself into something very like the view that it is only in tragic perplexity that we know we are free, and at the same time are brought up against the very margins of the humanly responsible world."

180. Cf. MacKinnon, "Aspects of Kant's Influence on British Theology," 361–62.

181. Milbank, "A Critique of the Theology of Right," 22. Cf. MacKinnon, "Natural Law," 117, 127.

As he emphasizes repeatedly, human beings exist in "situations that are very often not of their own making" (*PM*, 137). Our intentions, even good ones, are subject to the uncertainties of chance and "indeterminacy."[182] It is this aspect of contingency which is the kernel of MacKinnon's idea of the tragic, even though he sometimes seems to articulate "an unmistakable air of fatalism" in other contexts.[183] Such an element of 'contingency' re-appears when he returns to his discussion of the parables of Jesus.

Milbank half-jokingly described MacKinnon's "realist" interpretation of the parables "the other way round" as a form of postmodern "deconstruction"—though not in the style of Derrida but as if "done by A. C. Bradley."[184] In his opinion, MacKinnon tends to read the parables in a "Romantic" fashion, in which the "parabolic" is distinguished from the "allegorical."[185] Here the parables are taken as "woven out of a 'real life' unmediated by emplotment and carrying all the freight of a 'given' human ambiguity which can then become the symbolic vehicle of a gesture towards transcendence." And there is also "half a suggestion in MacKinnon that the element in the parables which indicates the absolute is the pointing up of some finitely irresolvable hesitation."[186] These statements, as indicated previously, are part of Milbank's critique of MacKinnon in which he charges him with reading the tragic *into* certain narratives, in which the parables (in this case) are re-narrated within an already-presupposed tragic system. MacKinnon's mistake, according to Milbank, is that he imposes 'the tragic' *onto* narratives, rather than allowing the stories to resolve *narratively*. This predisposition towards tragic narration explains, for Milbank, MacKinnon's attempt to read the parables against the grain of their texture, turning their unique construction into an illustration of moral alienation. For this reason, MacKinnon aims to shore up the presence of contingency within the parables, showing that one could read them "the other way round," instead following their extant construction. But Milbank suggests, on the contrary, that the gospel implies that "the tragic abyss" should be "*represented* rather than mutely indicated," and shown to be "*contained* in its historical occasion and final non-necessity."[187] For Milbank, we should hold out instead for the possibilities that history creates, making allowances for a narration that projects different outcomes, and it is this posture that will militate

---

182. Waller, "Freedom, Fate and Sin," 111.
183. Waller, "Freedom, Fate and Sin," 108.
184. Milbank, "A Critique of the Theology of Right," 21.
185. Milbank, "A Critique of the Theology of Right," 20.
186. Milbank, "A Critique of the Theology of Right," 21.
187. Milbank, "A Critique of the Theology of Right," 31.

against any tragic necessitarianism. By inscribing the tragic into the hinterland of the text, even where it is not present, MacKinnon cements Milbank's suspicion that he is much more concerned with a tragic and irresolvable sublime (which serves as a gesture towards transcendence) than with the *particularity* of human stories. Once more, the priority of *problem* over *solution* assumes a centrality for MacKinnon.

However, there is a qualification to this picture of MacKinnon given by Milbank himself. He admits that it is over-simplistic to characterize MacKinnon's readings simply as a whimsical re-telling "the other way round." For Milbank, this is "not quite" what MacKinnon is attempting. To encapsulate MacKinnon's exegesis so would be a failure to attend to *why* he engages in this deconstruction. It is certainly not that MacKinnon is being willful in his exegesis, or re-plotting the parables for the fun of it. On the contrary, there is as Milbank suggests a deeply *moral* rationale for his re-reading, one which places an emphasis on human contingency and finitude. Milbank admits that MacKinnon is quite right to insist "that one cannot legislate in advance the criteria for correct choices," and that his aim to undermine the "deontological schematism" (à la Kant) of ethical absolutism is certainly warranted. Seemingly then, in sequel to MacKinnon's comments on pacifism,[188] Milbank argues that "an ethics of virtue can never escape the problematic of 'moral luck', which reveals that all possibilities of good require a particular social context for their viability." This is not to castigate pacifism as such—"the way of peace, the way of exemplary persuasion and forgiveness, is always the more final way," he admits—but such a concession should not be used as a "sublime imperative." Here the parables are shown to be literary exemplars of "the partial (never complete) alienation of the very possibility of virtuous action."[189] Our actions take place within conditions of fragmentation, implying that even good-intentioned motivations can be thwarted, which is why Milbank is sympathetic to MacKinnon's exemplification of the "tragic sundering between deontology and consequentialism"[190] in the context of post-war Britain.

How do these admissions qualify his take on MacKinnon? One could hazard an answer and suggest that it is precisely through a tragic re-imagining of the parables "the other way round" that we are alerted to the finitude

---

188. MacKinnon wrote that "the pacifist, whose concern for purity of intention ... whose sense of the menace of war to personal integrity provides its own underlying justification of his policy, is easily assailed in that integrity itself, becoming not only indifferent to the claims of justice, but querulous and bigoted, sanctimonious and arrogant in his profession of pity and compassion" (MacKinnon, *A Study in Ethical Theory*, 241).

189. Milbank, "A Critique of the Theology of Right," 31.

190. Milbank, "A Critique of the Theology of Right," 30.

of all moral action. Milbank's "not quite" implies that such a re-reading of the parables is not simply arbitrary, but a way of showing that our choices are formed within a world that exceeds our making. Such exegesis, blended with an allegorical and anagogic reading, could do what Milbank describes as "the ceaseless re-narrating and 'explaining' of human history under the sign of the cross."[191] Such re-narrativisation, in which we become conscious of our historical limits, could contribute to our ethical growth as human beings, since it is by becoming aware of such limits that we are provided an opportunity for moral expansion. So the point of telling the story "the other way round" is not to somberly advocate a sublime resignation—as if we were fatalistically incapacitated by tragic facts—but to show that any actualization of ideals needs to attend to context, a context which might or might not resist the establishment of such virtue. A cognate inference of this is that if ideals are to be embodied, there must be a laboring towards a social compact in which such ideals can be incarnated. But since we are not there as of yet, one should attend to the authentic, pre-Kantian sense of 'the sublime' in which there is a constant "suspension" in our "reaching towards transcendence."[192] Having sensitivity to this perennial 'suspension' is a part of the growing and every-increasing 'estrangement' that is essential for our moral and spiritual maturation.

One can demonstrate this from MacKinnon's own reading of the parables. Take for instance his slant on the Prodigal Son (Luke 15:11–32), in which he impressionistically compares the father of the story to *King Lear*, hereby attempting to draw out the "ambiguities" of the original parables. Like the father's exuberant reception of the younger son, combined with his rather tepid response to the older one, Lear seems to adore "the flattery of Goneril and Regan in self-indulgent gratification of their hopes, and rejects the sharp but devoted honesty of Cordelia" (*PM*, 137). MacKinnon finds the expression of love and acceptance within the parable, like in King Lear, to be fraught with tragic irony. This is because the father's hyperbolic gratuity towards the prodigal are not replicated towards the more responsible older brother, whose own reception of his kin is decidedly cooler and even bitter in tone. He bemoans the fact that "For all these years I have been working like a slave for you" and yet "you have never given me even a young goat so that I might celebrate with my friends" (Luke 15:29). The father's riposte to this is undoubtedly gracious: "you are always with me, and all that is mine is yours," but "we had to celebrate and rejoice because this brother of

---

191. Milbank, "A Critique of the Theology of Right," 32.
192. Milbank, "A Critique of the Theology of Right," 31.

yours was dead and has come to life; he was lost and has been found" (Luke 15:31–32). But for MacKinnon this response is punctured with irony since:

> One wishes to ask the old man why then he had not made it plain, not merely in general terms, but with the sort of party the hard-working, dull, elder brother suggests now that he always wanted, and which might in fact have made him a more forthcoming, less unattractively puritanical human being. For if the parable affirms the power of love to recreate a life, we may well ask whether that same love should not equally avail to transform the grave, disciplined prudence of the industrious. (*PM*, 138)

What MacKinnon is saying is that the father's enthusiastic acceptance of the prodigal son had not been communicated to the elder son, and that it is precisely this paucity that has left him embittered. The brother's anger stems from a sense of inequality; it is not that the display of affection was wrong, but that it lacked parity.[193]

What is the point of such an "unduly sophisticated" reading (*PM*, 138)? It is to show "the deep, characteristic human ambiguity with which the parable is saturated" (*PM*, 138), and not simply, as Milbank suggests, to plot the parable into an *a priori* tragic edifice. This is duly expanded through examining a similar tension within the parable of the Good Samaritan (Luke 10:25–37). Here MacKinnon, at several points, raises questions concerning the supposed message of the parable. For instance, could the Priest and Levite not claim that "by passing on the other side they were exercising a proper sense of discipline, refraining from any well-intentioned but possibly disastrous attempt to do for the injured man what they could not do"? This is not to condone their action, but rather to probe as to whether such assistance, without the required "competence," is in the best interests of the suffering individual. Aid should be given—this fact is not in debate—but neighborly charity should inform genuine assistance, and not a mere "opportunity for [the Samaritan's] own gratification" (*PM*, 139). Such would *not* stem from a proper regard of the other, but rather a subtle form of "egoism" (*PM*, 140). But beyond this emphasis on personal motivation, good or bad, there are other contingent factors which are determinative.

Suppose, hypothetically, that the Samaritan upon crossing the road discovers that "his hands are infected and the oil he had used gone rancid."

---

193. Whether or not this is an adequate unfolding of the text's hidden ambiguities is not central to my efforts here, but one could further deepen this analysis by saying, in passing, that there are some comparable links, for instance, between MacKinnon's reading of the Prodigal Son and Stanley Cavell's reading of *King Lear*. For this reading, see Cavell, "The Avoidance of Love: A Reading of King Lear," in *Disowning Knowledge*, 39–123.

What would the meaning of his assistance then imply? In such a situation, his help would contribute to the injured man's suffering, rather than providing alleviation. MacKinnon's stress is that "human beings are not thrust into the sorts of situation to which they must respond as agents perfectly designed to suit the emergencies that they must meet" (*PM*, 140). Within any good intentioned response, the Samaritan included, there remains "the possibility of tragedy" (*PM*, 141). This is because even if his actions were well-intentioned and well-executed, the injured man could still be placed, so to speak, at "the mercy of his saviour." Here the potential tragic "flaw" could be activated, counter-intuitively, by that which deserves high "commendation," provoking the "sombre irony" that "in many situations it is the one who serves who, by that service, makes his beneficiary his bondslave" (*PM*, 141). His point is that we cannot predict the ripple effect that our actions will engender; they could bring about just relief, but they could also bring about other consequences in their wake. The knowledge of such possibilities, however, should not lead to debilitation, as MacKinnon clearly says, because even though "self-knowledge" is an essential part of "human maturity," this self-knowledge can potentially "inhibit action" (*PM*, 143) for those who obsessively engage in it, or who fail to yield to its insights, as MacKinnon thinks Oedipus did (*PM*, 143–45). Such knowledge is necessary to achieve a greater self-honesty, but it might lend itself to tragic outcomes.

What these last comments suggest is that MacKinnon's analyses of the parables are aimed at generating an awareness of finitude, to those instances that are not always congenial to moral action. They are directed at gaining 'knowledge' of ourselves, and the substance that forms our environment. He is not trying to be ingenious in his textual playfulness, but to show that our moral envisioning needs to be enlarged by this aspect, namely, that we do not perform our actions within an enclosed vacuum. Rather every action is contained within a *history*, and—in accordance with the heterogenesis of ends—cannot be considered apart from its effects. Our knowledge of the limits that impinge upon experiences forms an inextricable aspect of our humanness, so that a denial of them can only lead to further unwanted or tragic outcomes. By being made conscious of the often-refractory qualities of our physical and socio-historical constitutions, we are confronted with the question as to whether these indicate a non-negotiable item that cannot be suppressed, that is, without a truncation of that reality. By ignoring these factors, we fail to recognize and come to terms with 'what-is-the-case,' and therefore deny reality. For MacKinnon, it is within tragedy, and its exemplification of 'the conflict of duties,' that the problem of metaphysics becomes most tangible. Here again, we see MacKinnon's preference for *deontological* modes of ethics that centre on moral authenticity and perplexity.

In conclusion, he summarizes the impact and importance of tragedy by saying that when we are confronted by "the irreducibility of the tragic," with those experiences that restrict "ambitious metaphysical construction," we come to see that "in pondering the extremities of human life" we have to "acknowledge the transcendent as the only alternative to the kind of trivialisation" that would "empty of significance the sorts of experience with which we have been concerned," namely "the tragic." The metaphysical inquiry opened by this resilience is, indeed, not ambitious: it bespeaks of a "departure," a commencement of disclosure, rather than "arrival." The "problem of metaphysics" is not "resolved" by an attendance to those experiences that most deeply provoke such perplexities, but they might allow us "dimly to perceive the sort of aliveness to connections which will refuse facile consolation" (*PM*, 170).

Critical Evaluation

After detailing MacKinnon's account, I can now take stock of its particular contours, bearing in mind the criticisms lodged against it. A glance at the evidence catalogued seems to present a mixed picture, one that partially confirms and contests the claims of MacKinnon's detractors: does MacKinnon mistakenly transcribe the gospel into a tragic form? Does he read narratives (e.g., the parables) into a predetermined structure of perpetual deprivation and loss? I have already intimated that this is not quite the case since, as MacKinnon has shown, the gospel predisposes itself to tragic structures. I have also shown that on the question of the parables, even Milbank concedes that MacKinnon is onto something.

But beyond these easier adjudications, it is clear that Milbank and Hart's concerns touch upon wider theological problems. One has in mind here their critiques of 'sacrificial totality,' and MacKinnon's 'speculative' account of the tragic sublime. On the one hand, MacKinnon stressed the tragic as an exhibition of irresolution that in its non-triviality demonstrates metaphysical probity. He argued for moral tragedy as a 'system of projection' that is able to approximate in a more penetrating manner than others a certain "adequacy to reality" (to quote Walter Stein).[194] On the other hand, MacKinnon would be resistant to any overly-systematic account of the tragic. While he certainly deems tragedy to be a non-negotiable element of experience, this does not imply that we can construct any totalized picture from it. This is why adducing the language of "tragic theology," as Hart does vis-à-vis MacKinnon, should be approached cautiously. MacKinnon

194. Stein, *Criticism as Dialogue*, 1–31.

explicitly places himself in opposition to any 'sacrificial totality.' He opposed any metaphysical and moral totalization, as in philosophical monism (e.g., Hegel, Bradley, etc.) and Platonic 'intellectual intuition,' which all seemed to place too much confidence in our ability to perceive the spiritual 'whole.' It was for this reason that he was critical of any language of 'sacrifice' and tragic heroism that advocated holocausts in the name of any absolute. Capitulating unthinkingly would evade moral circumspection, and thus support ideological conceits. Worth mentioning, by way of contrast, is that MacKinnon did not follow the trend of other theologians interested in the tragic, who seemed to adopt a more resigned posture in relation to supposed 'inevitable' developments (e.g., nuclear armament).[195] Milbank opposes MacKinnon's realism to the "Stoicism" of Reinhold Niebuhr on exactly these kinds of questions.[196] These aspects of his thinking seem to resist, at least *prima facie,* the thesis that MacKinnon espoused a 'sacrificial totality' and any ideological conservatism.

Similar responses could be given to Hart's critiques of MacKinnon's regarding the resurrection, as well as Milbank's comments on MacKinnon's truncated historicism. It could be argued that Hart, in *The Beauty of the Infinite*, tends to underplay the kenotic elements of the gospel. Paul says that the resurrected Christ remains the crucified one (1 Cor 1:23, 2:2; Gal 3:1; 2 Cor 13:4; ἐσταυρωμένος), and is contemporaneous with us. His theology of soteriological participation in the redemptive suffering of Christ (e.g., Gal 2:19–20; Rom 6:1–14), as well as his understanding of the Lord's Supper (1 Cor 10:1–33; 11:17–34), presuppose this. The Gospel of John's identification of Christ's crucifixion with his ascendant glorification also supplements this tradition (John 3:13–14; 8:28; 12:27–33; 13:31–2; 17:1). MacKinnon's own Christology deliberately aims to bring together these dual realities.[197] He also states the resurrection is "the *prius* of my whole argument," and that it is this that constitutes "the ultimate source of that peculiar tension between optimism and pessimism" within Christianity.[198] One could say that MacKinnon does temper the clamor of Easter, and therefore is open to criticism. But he does so because he is trying to disabuse

---

195. See MacKinnon, *Borderlands of Theology*, 175–203 for his reflections on this topic.

196. Milbank, "The Poverty of Niebuhrianism," in *The Word Made Strange*, 233–54, and especially from 247 onwards. Rowan Williams also has expressed reservations about Niebuhr (echoing the critiques of Milbank and Hauerwas) regarding "the tragic perspective" being used as "a vehicle for absolution," in Williams, "The Health of the Spirit," 219.

197. MacKinnon, "Order and Evil in the Gospel," 90–96.

198. MacKinnon, "Order and Evil in the Gospel," 95.

the resurrection from any cheap optimism. "MacKinnon so resisted the reduction of the Resurrection gospel to the usual categories of happy endings—reversals of fortune, revelations, journeys ending in lovers' meetings and so on. What we are talking about is neither a comic resolution nor a simple re-presentation of the catastrophe (resurrection as the proclamation of the crucified as Lord): it is a new fact."[199] Furthermore, MacKinnon is not immune to the joy-giving aspects of Easter—even though he could have been a bit more sanguine in this regard.[200]

But if Hart castigates MacKinnon for dampening Easter, one could respond that Hart is similarly reductive in his *theologia crucis*. To say that Easter "vindicates not the cross but the Jew who died there"[201] is true enough, but it remains too minimalist. Of course one should not reduce the cross to a symbol of resignation, or abstract the crucifixion from its historical matrix as a *political* and *unjust* subjugation.[202] But one must still deal with the scriptural testimony in which Paul declares "I decided to know nothing among you except Jesus Christ, and him crucified" (1 Cor 2:2). Nor can we ignore Jesus's declaration regarding the intimate connection between discipleship and the cross (Mark 8:34; Matt 10:38; 16:24; Luke 14:27). What we should say is that the cross, as a form of repression and state-sponsored murder, has been transfigured by the resurrection into a sign of God's intention for the cosmos, that not even death can undermine the divine commitment to humanity. By our incorporation through baptism and Eucharist, we are given the promise that suffering and death are not the end, but are the birth-pains of a new life (Rom 8:18–39), one to be lived already in the present, since we have died and risen with Christ (Rom 6:1–14; Eph 2:1–10; Col 2:8–15; 3:1–4). On this model, the cross becomes a non-violent symbol of *resistance* against the operations of demonic power, and is not a sublime resignation. To avoid this would be a failure to attend to the particularity and historicity of Christ's mission.[203]

A limitation might be present in Milbank's criticism too, since he privileges a positive, Nietzschean 'forgetfulness' as regards human suffering within the eschatological climax.[204] One could raise the question as to whether Milbank's tendency to "emplot" narratives within a "tragi-comic"

---

199. Williams, "Not Cured, Not Forgetful, Not Paralysed," 280.

200. Cf. MacKinnon, "Good Friday and Easter: An Interpretation," in MacKinnon and Lampe, *The Resurrection*.

201. Hart, *The Beauty of the Infinite*, 391.

202. See the critique of MacKinnon in West, "Christology as 'Ideology.'" But also see the response given in Surin, "Christology, Tragedy and 'Ideology.'"

203. Cf. MacKinnon, "*Vexilla Regis*," 256–57.

204. Milbank, "A Critique of the Theology of Right," 27, 34n27.

structure downplays stories which *do* end horrendously. One could legitimately probe as to whether this coheres with Milbank's own historicist intentions. Rowan Williams implies as much when he says regarding Milbank's account of narrative "resolution" that

> the issue is not whether 'resolution' is ever possible but whether we can craft or imagine a resolution that embraces the narrating of what cannot be mended—rather than resolution which explains and so nullifies the tangles and injuries of what has been done or suffered. And it is clear enough that, unless you believe that resolution must mean an *unmaking* of the past (a far more serious attempt to exit from the world of narrative), it has to be thought about as a moment in which the strands of past narrative are so entwined as to mark a possible new stage in the story—not an absolute ending which obliterates the cost of what has gone before.[205]

It could be said that Milbank already pre-empts such critiques somewhat. In some later reflections on martyrdom and death, he questions as to whether mourning can be understood as "coming to terms with loss" without constituting a forgetfulness of that person's "irreplaceable" subjectivity. Such a move, in his eyes, would be both "immoral and unchristian."[206] Of note also is that he has argued that Christianity ultimately baptizes the experience of "moral luck": "the Christian construal of the total sway of moral luck is to understand fortune, as always, however disguisedly, the personal gift of grace: to believe therefore that only utter exposure constitutes the ethical."[207] However, as long as loss is "ineradicable," the possibility of "the ethical" is hindered, even impossible, because here ethics is construed as a "maximum possible minimization of loss" and therefore is bound to the givenness of death.[208]

---

205. Williams, *The Tragic Imagination*, 114–15. To quote Rowan Williams: the human 'soul' (*psychē*) is "always implicated in contingent matter, and even its final pilgrimage into God depends . . . upon the deployment and integration of bodiliness and animality," so that the particular *eidos* or *imago dei* is not cancelled by the resurrection, but rather redeems individuals in all their narrative particularity. Williams, "Macrina's Deathbed Revisited," 244–45. On the theme of resurrection and personal identity in early and medieval Christianity, see Bynum, *Fragmentation and Redemption*, 239–97.

206. Milbank, *Being Reconciled*, 145.

207. Milbank, *Being Reconciled*, 147–48.

208. Milbank, *Being Reconciled*, 148. This is why he can write, speaking of both Shakespeare and MacKinnon, that "the everyday ethical hope naturally leads to hope for resurrection. . . . After Shakespeare had written Lear, there was no possibility of him remaining with the unsurpassibility of the tragic, because this would actually be to *underestimate* the end of *Lear*. Since this play discloses a universal tragic sway (we cannot redeem our losses and misdeeds, there is no forgiveness), one cannot either mitigate

Only hope in the resurrection is able to guarantee the reality of the ethical. But the question remains as to whether an ethics that concerns the 'irreplaceability' of subjects can bypass the particular narratives that have made them to be who they are. Since the resurrection is a redemption of the temporal, can one suggest that the resurrection cancels or 'unmakes' those histories that have constituted those specific bodies? Would this not be a kind of "exit from narrative" that Milbank wants to undermine?

But what about MacKinnon's take on divine suffering? Is this not part-and-parcel with his *theologia crucis*? By affirming the passibility of God *in se*, does not MacKinnon thereby—on a more traditional account of the immanent trinity—render suffering ontologically basic? And when one combines this perspective with his Kantian positivity regarding evil, is this reading not strengthened further? I would say that these concerns are granted somewhat, but are dampened by other balances MacKinnon wanted to uphold. Under the influence of P. T. Forsyth, Hans Urs Von Balthasar and Sergei Bulgakov, MacKinnon is critical of traditional accounts of 'impassibility' as being unable to account for the revelation of God's nature in Jesus Christ.[209] He does not want to restrict the story of Christ, in his words, to a "universal pattern," but rather to allow that "career's particularity" to constitute precisely the foundational "order" of any such pattern.[210] This means that MacKinnon reads the gospel as a narrative of God's kenosis and self-limitation, which itself reveals the eternal life of the triune God to be a *coincidentia oppositorum* of omnipotence and vulnerability.[211] This particular history is where "the unity of God" is 'realized' and the "consistency of God in relation to his creation" is disclosed, providing us with "the very rationale of creation itself."[212] Of course God is absolutely "transcendent" as regards created be-

---

this circumstance nor come to terms with it; that is to say accept it, even though it is true. It is so bad, that it should be turned away from, and yet it cannot be. It *must* be turned away from because it leaves *no possibility for the ethical*. This is where 'a piety of the tragic', like that of Donald Mackinnon, simply will not do, partly because it still, after all, *evades* the tragic, by hypostasizing it in a speculative fashion. (Mackinnon failed to see that Speculative Idealism espoused exactly the romantic and not perhaps very Greek cult of the tragic, which he himself perpetuated—revealing thereby his own idealism despite all his explicit disavowals, rooted in his Kantianism.)" (Milbank, *Being Reconciled*, 149).

209. Cf. MacKinnon, "A Master in Israel: Hans Urs Von Balthasar"; MacKinnon, "The Relation of the Doctrines" (also see the appendix on Hans Küng, on 105–6); MacKinnon, "Oliver Chase Quick as a Theologian," 102, 106, 116–17; MacKinnon, "Epilogue: Kenosis and Self-Limitation," in *Themes in Theology*, 229–36.

210. MacKinnon, "Aspects of Kant's Influence on British Theology," 360.

211. Cf. MacKinnon, "Evil and the Vulnerability of God," 102.

212. MacKinnon, "The Relation of the Doctrines," 99.

ing, but the very "dependence" of the creation upon God is itself a reflection of the "eternal relatedness" of the divine life *in se*.[213] Much like Balthasar and Bulgakov, MacKinnon stresses that the divine kenosis is an expression of the unending *perichoresis* of the uncreated persons, so that temporal unveiling is not an alteration of the divine life *ad intra*.

However, MacKinnon is more reticent, than say Moltmann or even Balthasar, to speculate on the immanent trinity; he is concerned that the "aseity" and "ultimate invulnerability" of God are maintained, however "mythologized" this language remains to be. The creator and creature cannot be reversed, since there is "a genuine, if asymmetrical, reciprocity" between them.[214] However, for him, the account of transcendence presupposed by impassibility too readily supposes a "divine immunity from involvement in the affairs of the world," and thereby "securing an infinite, unaffected resourcefulness in creative design" that comes at "the cost of rendering the exercise of such resource virtually self-contradictory." For MacKinnon, it is "as if to secure the possibility of the radically self-initiated, one rendered impossible its execution." Christianity does not affirm any "abstract possibility" of the immanent triune life of God, since this would again convert the deed into an idea. Instead, it is in "Jesus of Nazareth in whom the incommensurables of God and man are found united, or in whom, and by whom the problem of the 'flow' of their union is raised by the daunting dizzying presence of its reality."[215] What these comments show, on the one hand, is that he is suspicious of 'impassibility,' but on the other hand, he does not seem to be persuaded by the more baroque speculations of Balthasar, Bulgakov, and Moltmann, which go too far in the direction of an overly-confident cataphasis.

And yet despite such qualifiers, it can be claimed that MacKinnon has not fully grasped the grammar of divine *apatheia*. As is shown by patristic scholarship,[216] *impassibilitas* or ἀπάθεια are not used to render divinity 'immune' from any or all 'passion,' as when we speak colloquially of the affection between human subjects. Rather, it says that God *ad intra* is not determined by anything 'outside' the operations of divine being, precisely because God does not exist over-against other 'beings.' God's transcendence exceeds finite being and non-being altogether. *Impassibilitas* was related to 'passions' in antiquity which were paired with 'imbalance' and

---

213. MacKinnon, "The Relation of the Doctrines," 102.
214. MacKinnon, "Prolegomena to Christology," 157.
215. MacKinnon, "Prolegomena to Christology," 155.
216. Cf. Weinandy, *Does God Suffer*; Gavrilyuk, *The Suffering of the Impassible God*.

'reaction,' and classified as 'negative' or non-temperate emotions.[217] After Nicholas of Cusa—who echoes the patristic tradition (e.g., Pseudo-Dionysius, Maximus the Confessor)—God is understood to be transcendent to such reactivity because God is the infinite source of all being and therefore *non aliud*. Since the infinite is *not* opposed to the finite—not defined over-against it—God as *actus purus* cannot be 'determined' by anything in creation, adverse or otherwise, because God would then be a merely ontic being. This becomes particularly acute when addressing evil and suffering: as we have stressed previously, if God suffers, then one appears to theorize agencies 'outside' the divine reality that determine and alter it. One could argue that this undermines the created-uncreated distinction, because the world in its limitation is seen to have a potency that works at the same 'level' as divine activity. But if this is so, then God as the infinitely creative source of everything is 'externally' determined by sinful agencies. The question then arises as to whether evil is not hereby rendered 'positive,' and therefore has as much 'reality' as beatitude.

But it should be stressed once more, to avoid misunderstanding, that 'divine impassibility' does not advocate a cold and heartless deity, unperturbed by human beings. On the contrary, precisely because God is not limited by finitude, God is able to express an intimacy to created life, as it enfolds *esse* within the unfathomable perfection of the divine persons. The undying interpenetration between the Father, Son and Spirit, undetermined by sinful degradation, provides an assurance and comfort for believers. God is not 'reactive' but infinitely active and creative, an agency at work in every creature's most intimate act of being. Precisely because God needs nothing, nor is dependent on anything, God's love towards creation is unlimited, grounded as it is only in the infinite and eternal act of the trinity, and

---

217. In this sense, divine *apatheia* did not at all imply a denial of promeity or compassion. One can show this through an example given Frances Young, a scholar of early Christianity. While speaking of caring for her son Arthur (who has a significant learning disorder), she says: "Emotions such as anger and envy remain potentially destructive, while others are easily corrupted—love itself can become damaging possessiveness and jealousy. Sometimes what passes for love is really self-centred anxiety, as I have realized when time and again distressed by Arthur's distress, finding it hard to cope when he is unsettled, unwell, or in pain, cannot express what is wrong, and the more we try to sort the problem the more frantic and furious he gets, hating to be handled, not understanding that we're trying to deal with his discomfort. Frustration mounts, creating its own distress and anger, which hardly helps his—in fact compounds it. Too easily inner demons of self-pity, a sense of failure, inadequacy and helplessness take over. So I recognize that I really need *apatheia* in order to love properly. Love requires a degree of detachment, an ability to let the other person be, to be 'other', to be what they are rather than what you want them to be" (Young, *God's Presence*, 292–93).

therefore completely gratuitous in its enactment.²¹⁸ This account does not neglect the place of Christology, or a theology of the cross. An orthodox treatment, along Cyrilline-Thomistic lines,²¹⁹ gives place for *human* suffering within divinity, because it is precisely in the unity of divine-humanity, here through the sinless offering of Christ, that suffering is endured and redeemed. Since God is transcendent and *non aliud*, God's intimacy to created being is equally infinite in scope, and not limited by tragic circumstance. Such a profound relatedness is the ground for Christ's enhypostatic union in which we, through our own participation εν χριστώ, are granted access to the divine. On this model, human suffering is re-narrated, non-identically, within Jesus's cross and resurrection: we can complete and embody in ourselves what is lacking in Christ's suffering (Col 1:24). For the church, this is enacted through our identification with Christ through baptism, the liturgy and sacraments, as well as our continuing witness, in word and deed, to the reality disclosed in these rituals. Our woundedness and trauma is united to Christ's perpetual self-offering in the Eucharist²²⁰ and in the tragedy of the Mass,²²¹ in which we continue to participate in his oblation to the Father; consequently, we are united with each other in the body of Christ, in which we are all called to bear one another's burdens (Gal 6:2).

Here tragedy is not transcribed as a 'final' necessity. Instead, suffering and tragedy are framed as a narrative of *loss*, and precisely because it is privative, because it is *a loss of some particular good*, it witnesses to the ideal of goodness, the resourcefulness of providence, and the dignity of endurance.²²² However, the question of how this process will work itself out will differ in varying circumstances. Even horrendous evils can contribute to the advancement of goodness, while still remaining deplorable.²²³ Admittedly,

---

218. Williams, "On Being Creatures," in *On Christian Theology*, 63–78 has some excellent comments in this regard.

219. See Weinandy, *Does God Suffer*, 172–213; Riches, *Ecce Homo*; Williams, *Christ the Heart of Creation*.

220. Cf. Pound, *Theology, Psychoanalysis and Trauma*, 154–70.

221. One is reminded here again of *Gemma animae* of Honorius Augustodunensis (1080–1154), who was mentioned in Chapter 2. As I mentioned there, he sought to bring Greek tragedy into an explicit relation with the Catholic Mass.

222. Cf. Augustine: "In this universe, even that which is called evil, well-ordered and kept in its place, sets the good in higher relief, so that good things are more pleasing and praiseworthy than evil ones" (Augustine, *The Augustine Catechism*, §11 [40]).

223. One could imagine ways in which past tragedies and suffering provoke us to think about how they happened, and how they might be mitigated in the future. This is a perspective that is advanced by Gillian Rose and Rowan Williams. Extreme instances may suffice to demonstrate this: the Shoah and apartheid remain monstrosities. Nothing can ameliorate that. However, one could argue that in their historical

this is never guaranteed, but what is pertinent to stress though is that without any transcendent goodness or value, we would not be able to charter the true depths of misery or joy. As Terry Eagleton has written, "there can be no tragedy without a sense of value, whether or not that value actually bears fruit. We would not call tragic the destruction of something we did not prize. If tragedy cuts deeper than pessimism, it is because its horror is laced with an enriched sense of worth."[224] Similarly Walter Stein has said that "Tragic awareness is the awareness of absolute violation of being: a confrontation with infinite meanings. This is the defining distinction between 'mere suffering' and tragic awareness. The witness of the tragic tradition—as of any authentic direct response of tragic exposure—is basically just this: that man is the locus of absolute violations of being. Tragedy occurs where we enter the timeless significance of such violations."[225]

MacKinnon, while rejecting the *privatio boni*, nonetheless desires something similar. Can one coherently grasp moral tragedy without claiming metaphysical probity? MacKinnon's answer to this is clearly no. Since we cannot evacuate the transcendent without thinning-out its texture of perplexity, we cannot avoid the metaphysical context in which our actions are placed. To reduce freedom to an illusion, or to trivialize the presence of tragedy within human affairs, would be to undermine the importance of the moral life, giving little place for what is truly valuable within human experience. It is this concern which animates his stress on "the irreducibility of the tragic," an experience which for MacKinnon—here adopting the language of Milbank—instigates both the "purgation" and "illumination" of metaphysics as such.

But this project has a weakness that deserves notice. As mentioned earlier, I suggested that MacKinnon's denial of the *privatio boni* undermines his Butlerian attempt to coherently relate 'nature' and 'ends.' This insight has pertinence here: MacKinnon hopes, apart from analogical participation, to render tragedy as a 'parabolic' gesture towards the transcendent. This presupposes, as Milbank has suggested, that MacKinnon makes use of the Anglican natural law tradition in which the preponderant 'limits' of the physical world are commandeered as a 'system of projection' for what lies beyond the material. Such a model requires an intimate connection between the creational order and those metaphysical structures that are opaquely reflected in it. However, minus an analogical metaphysics and

---

aftermath expressions of anti-Semitism and racism became more intolerable, which is something good.

224. Eagleton, *Hope without Optimism*, 115.
225. Stein, *Criticism as Dialogue*, 224.

evil-as-privation, one honestly wonders whether this project maintains coherency.[226] Besides the question of how one coherently relates the historical and metaphysical without something like the *analogia entis*, the question remains as to what kind of transcendence is implied by this system of projection. If goodness does not hold ontological primacy, then what kind of 'presence' is the subject of our practical 'intuition' of the ultimate? If the natural order has no final orientation towards the Good, then how can we trust the transcendence thereby projected is not malevolent? How do we know that the 'ends' of humanity are coherent with the operations of natural law, or that such 'ends' are aimed at the perfection of our moral nature? Without a conjecture of the primacy of the Good, it becomes difficult to articulate the 'transcendence' of tragic loss in the manner that MacKinnon so desires, since without its ontological primacy, how do we speak of loss? Would evil not then be equally an expression of the *realia* too? And would this not be a consummate theodicy since tragic deficiency could be traced to a mythic ontologization of violence? On this reading, deprivations are simply an expression of the violence of being, and thereby explained and justified. Does this not resign us to the worst of philosophical theodicies that instigate a resignation to the way things are?[227] Again, this is not MacKinnon's intention—he is diametrically opposed to such consolation—but it is, arguably at least, an outcome of its trajectory.

Summary

MacKinnon is clearly a complex thinker. The previous chapters have aimed at justice, balancing an appreciation for his achievements with an awareness of his limitations. Our larger argument, however, did not focus just on MacKinnon, but on the sources that informed him. In summary, I said that MacKinnon's metaphysics argued for a 'transcendence' that impressed itself

---

226. Graham McAleer has argued that without something like the *analogia entis* moral metaphysics tends to fluctuate between the apriorism of abstract law on the one hand or a material and biological vitalism on the other. Only the analogy of being is able to maintain the tension between our asymptotic and playful 'posture of distance' from any totalized and disembodied perspective, and the material cultures of law and establishment that are necessary for an incarnated political order. Mapping this onto our discussion of MacKinnon, we could speak of Kantianism as exhibiting an exacerbation of abstraction, while Benthamite naturalism could be seen as an example of a self-enclosed naturalism. In terms of our own argument, we could argue that MacKinnon's suspicion of the analogy of being makes it difficult for him to coherently reconcile individual ideals of freedom and what I have been calling Hegelian *Sittlichkeit*. On this, see McAleer, *Erich Przywara and Postmodern Natural Law*.

227. Cf. Tilley, *The Evils of Theodicy*, 221–56.

upon consciousness, especially within those encounters of extremity that demanded non-trivial acknowledgement. The inference to be drawn from this is that any reduction of the ontological compass of such extremities would indicate, for MacKinnon, a refusal to yield to them.

Of paramount concern here is the connection between metaphysical realism and moral responsibility. As shown throughout these chapters, MacKinnon is at pains to stress that our discernment of truth is tied to our ethical responsibility. In MacKinnon's perspective, morality is not the only site of metaphysical discovery, but it is by far the most emphatic. How ethics discloses 'the ultimate' remains for MacKinnon (as for Kant) of supreme importance. On this score, what is apparent is that his arguments do not adhere to a strictly logical or deductive approach. For him, we *"cannot* represent," but instead *"achieve the sense of what we affirm in action."*[228] What he appears to be stating is that if our image of reality lacked this dimension, namely, that morality and axiology that gives tragedy its edge, then are we really engaging the world we inhabit? Here philosophical argumentation expresses a diversity that exceeds pure analytical method. There are shades here of John Wisdom, who enacted a similar mixture of logic and poetics within his method,[229] one that focused less on sequential accumulation than on persuasion and exemplification.[230] Overall, one could say that MacKinnon's general approach implied an intermixture of argumentative styles, and so cannot be easily placed within the traditional aegis of Oxbridge analytics. MacKinnon works at the borderlands of philosophy, between the logics of Moore, the historicism of Collingwood, and the metaphysics of Aristotle and Kant, and so his arguments need to be evaluated from the perspective of this hybridity.

The focus of these chapters was MacKinnon's *The Problem of Metaphysics*, in an attempt to discern whether the critiques given by Milbank and Hart might apply to his mature thought. The prominent figures that arose were Plato, Aristotle, and Kant. My argument is that MacKinnon—here in partial agreement with Milbank—was finally unable to coherently relate the historical and the metaphysical *within his assumptions regarding analogy, the Kantian sublime, evil-as-privation and divine impassibility*. To establish this, I traced MacKinnon's reception of Aristotle and Kant.

228. MacKinnon, "Aspects of Kant's Influence on British Theology," 364.

229. Cf. MacKinnon, "Metaphysical and Religious Language," 208.

230. Martin Warner, following John Wisdom, has shown how traditional modes of induction and deduction are not philosophically exhaustive when it comes to argumentation. Philosophy is as much about rhetoric and aesthetic persuasion, which is probably even more fundamental than the usual techniques of analytic (e.g., *reductio ad absurdum*). See Warner, "Literature, Truth and Logic."

Beginning with Aristotle, I argued that his assimilation of 'substance' into atomist realism that undermined relationality, and that he tacitly endorsed a subject-object dualism which resisted the constructive elements of intelligence, hereby disconnecting historicity from metaphysics. When combined with Aristotle's disconnection between the Prime Mover and materiality, his rejections of *methexis*, and the Platonic idea of the Good, another dimension was added to MacKinnon's suspicion of analogical participation. On this point, MacKinnon adopts the approach of Kant, leading to a gradual *de-ontologization* of analogy within his thought, which complicated the problems of relating the historical to the metaphysical. In addition to this, MacKinnon's movement away from the *analogia entis* traded upon the idea that it was based on an overconfident mode of 'intellectual intuition' that failed to embrace our historical and particular situatedness, as exemplified by the Platonic intellection of Forms.

In the following chapter, I argued that MacKinnon—here following Wittgenstein—wanted to show, through a reading of *The Republic*, how ethical language might be pressed for metaphysical benefit, in the sense that it is through the intensification of moral perplexity that one might be "thrust against the limits of language." In practicing this, we manifest a moral realism, an accountability to something that exceeds the constructive habits of mind. However, it was suggested that MacKinnon tends to abstract Plato's dialogues from their drama, in accordance with his general tendency to prioritize *problem* over *solution*. Such links up with Milbank's critique that he treats moral dilemmas within a hyper-perplexity that is not always helpful. Furthermore, it was also proposed, again in agreement with Milbank, that MacKinnon's Kantianism was predicated on a individualism which, when connected to his rejection of the *privatio boni*, makes it vulnerable to a 'liberal' assimilation, which denies the mutuality of goods (the idea that my goods are bound up with yours) since liberalism accords primacy to evil and 'negative' liberty' also.

Regarding his account of the tragic, however, it appears that MacKinnon's work mounts some resistance to their critiques. Acknowledging his subtlety was important, and his concern that moral tragedy resists reductive naturalisms deserves to be taken seriously, in that sheer determinism does not accord dignity to human agency, and the tragic suffering to which it is subjected. His understanding that our experience of 'loss' can act as a form of 'estrangement' from entrenched strictures of selfhood added another dimension to this vision. This under-emphasized aspect of MacKinnon's thought shows that his sensitivity to the tragic did not occlude historical sensitivity. Growth is possible for the self and our social formations can be altered by choices. Of course these efforts are often tragically thwarted, but one should not assume that these are some kind of ontological necessity—even though MacKinnon can adopt neo-Manichaean language at moments. I did admit however that his rejection of evil-as-privation, his qualified acceptance of divine passibility, and his post-Critical phenomenalism, finally makes him susceptible to the tradition of Kantian sublimity, in which (like Schiller) it is only through the irresolution of moral tragedy that we come to know our transcendent and noumenal freedom.

In our next two chapters, I will turn to Rowan Williams, with the aim seeing whether he is able to address and critically supplement the deficits of MacKinnon's approach. This will be done, largely, through an examination of his monograph *The Tragic Imagination* (2016). But before I reach that point, I will need to unpack Williams's metaphysical assumptions, in the hope that they give a larger background to our discussion. It is also structured in this way because such an examination of these themes in Williams's writings will further assist us in addressing some questions that Hart and Milbank have regarding whether adopting the tragic within theology undermines a classical metaphysics of transcendent goodness, insofar as it denies aseity and the *privatio boni*, and thereby—tacitly or explicitly—promotes regimes of unrepresentable sublimity.

7

Rowan Williams I

On Metaphysics and Poetics

The previous chapters have led us here, where I reach some kind of conclusion regarding our central question: can one inscribe the tragic within a classical account of transcendent goodness? And if so how? In Chapter 3, I expounded this terminology as implying, on the one hand, that God cannot be reduced to an available object *within* the created universe. But on the other, the radical difference of God does not exclude an eminent description of divine nature, since everything remains caused by God, and therefore reflects God's nature, however dim and perspectival this knowledge might be. In the chapters thereafter, I addressed Donald MacKinnon, who was considered as the most preeminent figure within the dialogue between Christianity and the tragic. There I exposed his strengths and limitations, especially as regards his Kantianism. Such a heritage implicated him within a 'speculative closure' of being, since without an analogical participation and the priority of a transcendent good, MacKinnon struggled to account for *how* created being, and the materiality of language and historicity, could act as a truthful projection of divinity, one in which God is both transcendentally and infinitely *different* and *good*. Because MacKinnon rejected analogical participation, the *privatio boni*, and moreover internalized transcendentalism and the Kantian sublime, I argued that he remained conceptually hamstrung as regards his proposal of a "system of projection" that harmonizes 'the realm of nature' and 'the realm of ends.' This was the case, I argued, since once a noumenal metaphysics and 'radical evil' were accepted, as well as a denial that historical being participates within an infinite and transcendent goodness that is ontologically prior to all deprivation, then it remains hard to see how the natural order could have a more necessary linkage with moral goodness. On this model, our abstractions from 'appearance' to the invisible realm of the noumena can no longer project a transcendence that is unequivocally good as such. It remains within the indeterminacy of *the modern regime of the sublime*.

So the question lingering throughout is the following one: is there an option that is able to maintain divine transcendence and goodness, while remaining sensitive to the insights of the tragic? The assumption throughout has been "yes" but I have not expounded what such an option might be. I have hinted at a response throughout this study, but it is here that I aim to bring out this answer more fully by looking at Rowan Williams. In doing so, I will need to be alert to the way in which he develops the classical tradition, especially as this touches the topics of transcendence and ontological analogy. I have already expounded upon his thoughts on aseity and transcendence earlier on, but in light of the argument throughout it is now beneficial to expound his metaphysics of analogy, and its connection to the experience of historicity. Here I will have to unfurl the minutiae of his broader project, as this grows out of his reflections on *creativity*, *language* and *analogy*. I will also have to address a niggling lacuna, hovering throughout the discussion of MacKinnon, namely, the question of evil. If we talk about creaturely being as having an analogical existence to divine being, then what are we to say about those aspects of reality which do not reflect God's nature? As a consequence, I will need to unpack the *privatio boni*, and why we think MacKinnon (and others) misunderstand it. I will insist on seeing privation as being linked to created finitude—without identifying the two—and will also suggest, more substantively, that it implies a perversion of the gratuity of being. Evil is a *contingent* rupture and is not 'naturally' connected to existence-as-such. Such a conviction attenuates any *ontological pessimism* which propounds that createdness is fated towards non-beneficent outcomes; this is because all deviation from goodness implies a non-necessary inversion within creation. On this reading, evil is *de-natured*: it is not a 'thing' or 'substance,' but rather a perversion of rightly-ordered relations and desire.

The Metaphysical Poetics of Rowan Williams

Our previous discussion of divine transcendence in Chapter 3 has already covered some of the ground presupposed here. There I indicated the problems with a "contrastive" approach, as regards the transcendence-immanence relation, and also rejected a "conflictive" account as being dogmatically unsustainable. Since God does not occupy an ontological 'space' within the created world, we must affirm both the radical difference of divinity *and* the profound intimacy that this difference enables, since God is closer than we could ever be to ourselves. God is not a being *within* the world, but rather is the one who gives everything its reason-for-being, and in which everything persists. Consequentially, God is both infinitely different and infinitely close to the life of creatures. It is precisely this logic that underlies the affirmation of the *analogia entis*, because within its affirmation we are able to see the world as providing—however dimly—a truthful disclosure of divine truth. This means that no aspect of reality can be excluded *a priori* from revelatory potential even though such vantages cannot be absolutized, since God always remains God. It is this vision that informs Rowan Williams's constructive engagements, and is one that he seeks to develop.

Overall, Williams agrees that the reduction of 'being' to univocal or merely formalist predicates has not assisted 'metaphysics.' In his estimate, the language of 'being' has become "muddied"—to many philosophers and theologians alike.[1] However, he does not shy away from the development of such language, and is even critical of those who too quickly reject it (e.g., Jean-Luc Marion).[2] From this we can see that Williams is not opposed to the language of 'being' in relation to God, that is, when it is doctrinally qualified. Also worth noting is that Williams combines this with a proclivity for a 'realism' that accounts for the non-reducibility of truth,[3] without assuming an extra-linguistic or ahistorical "reference" for it.[4] For Williams asserts that

---

1. Williams, "God," in *Fields of Faith*, 85. Also see this: "The language of absolute being, *ipsum esse subsistens*, and so on has become problematic in the wake of the dissolution of those elements in earlier metaphysical discourse that worked against a univocity in speaking of being. When 'being' has become a more unproblematic and territorialized concept than it is in Platonic and early medieval (including Thomist) thought, the risk is of seeing God as possessor of an unlimited quantity of it—or as a synonym for the totality of what there is. God is either a supreme individual or an all-pervasive quality or force in what exists. We forget in such a context the inseparability in Aquinas of the language of pure act and the language of God's 'excess' in respect of being." He also is critical of Jean-Luc Marion—who rejects the language of God-as-being—since Marion is "at best cavalier about the *extended* social and historical processes whereby the name of God appears, concentrating instead on the luminous, timeless act of God in the eucharist; so that his focus upon love and gift as the words needed to speak of a God beyond, prior to, or other than being threatens to become abstract." But he also worries (here echoing Milbank) "whether Marion is not himself caught in the early modern misapprehension that assumes a univocal sense for being, thus missing the nuance typical of the entire Platonic tradition by accepting too uncritically the Heideggerian insistence on the ideologically malign character of ontology" (Williams, "God," in *Fields of Faith*, 85–86).

2. See his critique of Kevin Hector, in Williams, "To Speak Truly about God."

3. See Williams, "Religious Realism," in *Wrestling with Angels*, 228–54.

4. See his endorsement of "a broadly Davidsonian picture of reference" in "To Speak

'the 'real" cannot be abstracted from "the continuing processes of representation," and that apart from this it remains a "chimera." On the contrary, it is precisely through these never-ending attempts at representation that we achieve an approximation to "the real," since "realism" is shown "by 'following' what has been said and done in ways that are open to continuing scrutiny and revision." That means we "show that we are serious about the extra-mental by certain features of our linguistic behaviour" through an "exposure of our representations to response and correction or expansion, by behaving as though they were accountable to something more than their own inner logic or the convenience of the speaker."[5] Williams's realism shows a critical internalization of G. E. Moore,[6] in that he denies any "immanent comprehensiveness" or "the reduction of relationality to the necessary internal constitution of a thing."[7] Williams could, on this account, be described as an "ideal realist," since for him "materialised form is continued in another and higher . . . mode, as the form and word of thought."[8] He could even be described as "speculatively realist" (a lá Quentin Meillassoux[9]) in the way that he denies—against Kant—that "historical mediation provides a sceptical barrier to the knowledge of nature, and of essences" since for him "nature herself . . . may be seen as inherently historical" in its being.[10] For Williams, "historical mediation" is important for metaphysics: he appears

---

Truly about God," and his reference to Davidson again in his critique of MacKinnon (Williams, "Trinity and Ontology," in *On Christian Theology*, 154). Williams is drawing here upon the essay entitled "Reality without Reference," in Davidson, *Inquiries into Truth and Interpretation*, 215–25. Williams's Gifford Lectures can be fruitfully compared with the more recent essays by Hillary Putnam entitled "Corresponding with Reality," 72–79, and "How to be a Sophisticated "Naïve Realist,'" 624–39, both in Putnam, *Philosophy in an Age of Science*.

5. Williams, *The Edge of Words*, 77.
6. Williams, *The Edge of Words*, 107.
7. Pickstock, "Matter and Mattering," 611.
8. Pickstock, "Matter and Mattering," 601.
9. Meillassoux, *After Finitude*. It should be added here that Williams would reject Meillassoux's merely contingent relating of thought and world, since Meillassoux's critique of "correlation" implies a thoroughly materialistic and chaotic advent of rationality that has no "necessary" connection to the material world, except for the bare fact of its contingency. Because Meillassoux holds to a radically Humean perspective of causality, he believes intelligence is a non-necessary, chaotic upshot of sedimented habits. The appearance of consciousness literally has no explanation because to do so would imply a prior law of rational cause and effect—something Meillassoux's anti-correlationism denies. As we will see, Williams's metaphysics makes a strong argument for the necessary entanglement of materiality and intelligence. For a critique of Meillassoux on these points, see Shaviro, *The Universe of Things*, 65–83.
10. Pickstock, "Matter and Mattering," 600.

to agree with Hegel that "history is how we do our metaphysics"—not in the sense that history serves as a "record" that "delivers to us a map of the constructions of the universe, or a comprehensive account of natural kinds or a compelling thesis about the nature of reference." Instead, it is about an "engagement with history," and how this "lays bare for us the character of thinking *as* engagement, as converse, conflict, negotiation, judgement and self-judgement."[11] The reason why these processes should be described as "metaphysical" is because any thinking of "the particular" requires that we place it in a wider context of unfolding, that we move back and forth between the "law" of the universal and "the singular that eludes category."[12] Such a process renders as untenable any separation between "identity" and "difference," the particular and "the concrete universal."

Because of these tendencies, it is worthwhile to engage with his metaphysical poetics more deeply, and how it has inflected his theological output.

On Creativity

Williams has engaged with "the metaphysical or ontological dimension of poetry"[13] since the 1970s. Then already he proposed that creativity-as-such intimated something more than self-expression; for him, poetics is not reducible to manifestations of personality. He had a sense that creative practice exhibited an excessiveness that could not be reduced to the representing will of the artist.[14] Human creativity is irreducible to the particular genius or ego of the artist; rather, it forms a response to what is already *there*, a perception that somehow reality itself is expressive, that the "symmetry"[15] which is achieved in poetics represents "a hidden holding-together"[16] or "occult affinity"[17] between objects, and is not the product of an extraneous imposition, but an unfolding of their true nature.[18] Such is revealed in a ramifying process into which an artist is enfolded through an attention to her subject

---

11. Williams, "Between Politics and Metaphysics: Reflections in the Wake of Gillian Rose," in *Wrestling with Angels*, 67.

12. Williams, "'The Sadness of the King,'" 21–22.

13. Williams, "Poetic and Religious Imagination," 179.

14. Williams, "Poetic and Religious Imagination," 179.

15. Maltby, "Wordless Words," 49–70. Williams has drawn upon this work in his Clark Lectures, which will be discussed shortly.

16. Pickstock, "Matter and Mattering," 611.

17. Pickstock, "Matter and Mattering," 608.

18. John Milbank speaks of poetry as being "the apostrophic invocation of the unknown which lurks always behind the site itself," in Milbank, *The Mercurial Wood*, xiii.

matter, the product of which is not a mere sample of personal effulgence. Poetry conveys objects into relation or proportion (through rhyme, rhythm, assonance, enjambment, synesthesia, metaphor, and structure, etc.),[19] all of which is predicated on an "*analogical* vision that allows us to see one thing through another [italics mine]," where we come "to see one thing through the 'lens' of an unexpected other." This vision is not an inexplicable irruption but instead suggests that "we are always seeing 'through the other', that we never see anything in its own isolated terms, and that we cannot rule in advance which others are 'acceptable' and which [are] unacceptable in the business of extending and enlarging our perception."[20]

In order for such analogies to occur there needs to be an element of non-arbitrariness in the composition, a sense that there is an objective affinity between the layers of the composition. Within the poem, the disclosure of the total 'idea' or 'image' is only achieved through the interrelation of its active elements at the level of their arrangement. The whole is revealed through its parts and remains enfolded within them. Simultaneously, such densities of expression could not be grasped without a collective allusion to the whole,[21] without a more comprehensive spiritual invocation through material ordering.[22] In poetics there is a genuine co-operation between the forces of active collation and receptive disclosure.[23]

And it is for this reason that he denies a "poetics whose focus is the will of the artist . . . a view of poetic creation which turns away from the sense of 'coming upon' something already given."[24] This remains in tune with his Thomistic prioritization of the intellect over the will as regards the disclosure of "the basic things about ourselves-in-the-world."[25] Connected to this also is his critique of the idea that there is "a clear difference between active mind and passive stuff, between the mind and its intellectual property or acquisitions, between language and 'objects', those mysteriously self-contained or

19. Cf. Jakobson, "Poetry of Grammar and Grammar of Poetry," 36–46.

20. Williams, *The Edge of Words*, 133.

21. See the reflections of Hofstadter, "Prelude . . . Ant Fugue," 149–201. Hoftsadter's work is also influential on Williams as well, especially in the later parts of his Clark Lectures.

22. Milbank, *The Legend of Death*, 5: "poetry constantly objectifies the spiritual in order that it can exist on earth at all, while it equally spiritualizes the material in order that its meaning may be realized."

23. Cf. Prynne, "Mental Ears and Poetic Work," 138: "if the underlying textual features exist it is because poets are tuned into their language structures to an unusual degree of linguistic susceptibility. Such features are neither invented nor discovered, they are disclosed."

24. Williams, "The Standing of Poetry," 62.

25. Williams, "Between Politics and Metaphysics," 73.

self-defined things lying around waiting to be noticed and collected." Instead, the "metaphysical tradition" suggests that we "cannot think a reality in which substances exist as atomized systems." Of course there is a need to maintain the "authentic difference" that marks the multiplicity of beings; and yet, such difference should not be objectivized to the level of "discrete lumps of stuff" since there is an "everlasting 'slippage' of definition," a "pattern of self-displacement" that occurs between things. In such a schematic, "difference is *neither* (at any moment) final, a matter of mutual exclusion, *nor* simply reducible, a matter of misperception to be resolved by either a return to the same or a cancellation of one term before the Other."[26]

This needs to be clarified further: Williams argues that "'being' is apprehended primarily in the endless variety of particular forms, and it is only by attending to this *variety* of particular forms that being may be grasped as gratuitously creative—and thus as concrete fullness." For Williams—echoing Maximus the Confessor—the *logoi* of every created being pre-exists "in God as *particular* creative intentions, dependent upon the eternal *Logos* who is the divine ground of the possibility of all otherness, all differentiation." This metaphysical assumption underlies all experience since "the fundamental cognitive moment is the apprehension of *participation*, the participation of beings in being." This agitates against any "formal limitlessness"—as in the Kantian sublime—"since there is no possibility of expressing or thinking being without beings [because] Being depends upon the existence of particulars."[27] But such *difference* should not distract us from "the apprehension of being as a system of interdependent contingencies, the response to which can never be *abstraction*," and can only be enacted in "the yielding of a privatized, self-enclosed perception to an 'ekstatic' participation,"[28] or what he elsewhere calls "kenosis,"[29] that is, "a self-forgetful involvement, both active and receptive, in the world as a whole."[30]

Poetry, within Williams's Christianized vision, aims to manifest "a vision of the wholeness of the contradictory world,"[31] an "incontrovertible solidity" that intimates "God's own vision of the created order." Such serves as witness to a "grace constantly running ahead of our seeing or

---

26. Williams, "Between Politics and Metaphysics," 70–71.
27. Williams, "Balthasar, Rahner and the Apprehension of Being," in *Wrestling with Angels*, 92.
28. Williams, "Balthasar, Rahner and the Apprehension of Being," 95.
29. Williams, "Between Politics and Metaphysics," 72.
30. Williams, "Balthasar, Rahner and the Apprehension of Being," 95.
31. Williams, "Poetic and Religious Imagination," 179.

knowing, always therefore there *already* to be seen or known."[32] But it also means that there is a participatory element in our "re-creation" of things that necessitates "an entirely committed immersion in the world, a watching and listening in silences."[33] However, as one begins the perception is strengthened that there is something that exceeds the artist in her production, that there is "a tension between the life of language and its use . . . between what is meant by us as users and what is 'meant' by the elusive resource of language itself, escaping our conscious strategies."[34] "The poet *adds* to the world," but such creative impulsion should not be read as being traceable only to the genius of the artist. Rather it inchoately suggests that reality itself is "obscurely incomplete," and invites the poet to "the task of making it significant," without implying that the artist projects "an alien structure of explanation" upon the world as such.[35]

There is a peculiar kind of gratuitousness in art that goes beyond the immediately perceivable. One initiates a creative process that stems from a unique representation, and yet the creative process finally exceeds the artist's initial intention. It is as if reality exceeds itself in its repetition, and that such excessiveness is part of the substance of things. The image exceeds the original and becomes just as original.[36] It appears then, quoting Catherine Pickstock, that description remains entangled and saturated with "invocation," and that any "anterior figural process is never completed, and is matched prospectively by an accompanying sense that more has yet to be said," that "the gift of reality to us must be met by a counter-gift."[37] But in light of this, one could ask: if all "doing involves gratuitous making" (John

---

32. Williams, "The Standing of Poetry," 62.

33. Williams, "Poetic and Religious Imagination," 180. In an essay on R. S. Thomas, Williams has said that "we image/imagine/explore ourselves only by our immersion in what's other—the life the structure of which the subject is neither centre nor essence" (Williams, "Adult Geometry" 84).

34. Williams, "The Standing of Poetry," 57. It is worth consulting here the outstanding essay by Geoffrey Hill, entitled "Poetry as 'Menace' and 'Atonement.'" This can be found in Hill, *Collected Critical Writings*, 3–20.

35. Williams, "Poetic and Religious Imagination," 179–80.

36. Cf. Gadamer, *Truth and Method*, 130–38.

37. Pickstock, "Matter and Mattering," 607. She goes onto say that it "is as if a seascape naturally precipitates or demands an encomium, as naturally as it is shaped by swell and wave breaking. These poetic aspects of truth-making, it seems, covertly enter into our ordinary prosaic practices, and yet we are not attended by the sense that we are arbitrarily making things up or being dishonest as to the way things are. Do we rather feel that we are responding to the impress of reality, its imperatives?" (Pickstock, "Matter and Mattering," 607–8).

Milbank),[38] and all true poetry "adds to the stock of available reality" (R. P. Blackmur),[39] then how is one to understand this addition as being reflective of being-as-such, of what is *there* already?

To approach this, we should say initially that poetics always works within restraints, within material or medial limitations. "Absolute innovation is not possible. To add to the world, to extend the world and its possibilities, the artist has no option but to take his material from the world as it is."[40] One engages with a finite index that is *specific* and *concrete*—such as a tonal range, a unique density of words, or an ideation that emerges through the creative process. The artistic product cannot concern nothing-in-particular, nor can it accomplish everything. Creativity seeks a representation of aspects, as it has been produced within the interplay between the artist and the developing *habitus* of the artistic process. But this attempt at presentation (or re-presentation) does not render the subject matter merely self-identical or stable. The emergence of the artwork can set in motion a new chain of significance that includes a non-foreclosable range of meaning. For instance, a whole range of contingencies can alter our perception of the aesthetic object: a work produced in one context can register different overtones in another, and the movement of time can offer expanded valences. The work—especially the masterpiece—creates its own *before* and *after*; an event in which previous contributions are re-signified in light of the present addition, and sets in motion a different stage of consciousness that retrospectively alters our perception of its origins.[41] Temporality remains essential to an unfolding aesthetic, whether in relation to the production or reception of the artwork itself.[42]

But it follows that the self-identity of the specific work can only be maintained through the differences that time and context provides, that is, insofar as it remains *non-identical* to itself. It is only through temporality that the aesthetic object can achieve its "timelessness" or "contemporaneity" with our own time,[43] and it is precisely through its concreteness that the poem achieves its universality. For poetry, as for metaphysics, Being is disclosed through the specificity of beings.[44] Repetition and re-presentation implies a

---

38. Milbank, "Scholasticism, Modernism and Modernity," 668

39. Blackmur, "Statements and Idylls," 108.

40. Williams, "Poetic and Religious Imagination," 180.

41. As Pickstock says, "any poem is in excess of any poetics, and may cause us to revise our ideas as to such a poetics" (Pickstock, "Matter and Mattering," 617).

42. Cf. Williams, "Art," 25–27.

43. Gadamer, *Truth and Method*, 119–24.

44. On this point, also see Bottum, "Poetry and Metaphysics."

paradoxical difference and sameness which belongs to the objectivity of the poem. As Williams says "The poetic embrace of the concrete is something more than the repetition or reproduction of what is given; it evokes or realizes the given in a new way, it posits a new world which is the depth of the old, not by denying the particular and immediate but by seeking words for its unspoken setting, its setting within the presence of God."[45]

In the Clark Lectures, later published as *Grace and Necessity*,[46] Williams proposed an "ontology of art" that grasped "the labour of art as something rooted in the sense of an unfinishedness in 'ordinary' perception, a recognition that the objects of perception [are] not exhausted by what could be said about them in descriptive, rational and pragmatic terms" (*GN*, x). The excess within this deepening of "perception" moves against a reductive stimulus-response schematic, and rather continues to evoke and call for additional and variegated responses (*GN*, 135). Art necessitates an attunement to the way things are, to the incompleteness of the world, and is not something imposed or exerted upon it, so that one could say that art itself is in "some sense a part of nature" (*GN*, 48).

For Williams, "grace" in this register is related to the idea that beauty implies an "excess" (*GN*, 53), an "'overflow'" or "'radiance'" that addresses us, suggesting that there is a "metaphysical dimension" to creativity (*GN*, 13), that is, some kind of transcendent givenness that shows itself in-and-beyond the conscious fabrication of the artist. This is because art outstrips the instrumentality of need and the will—even though intentionality and freedom are not denied by this account (*GN*, 15, 52). This is what Williams means by "necessity" (*GN*, 124). He thus sees a connection between the tropes of grace and necessity, because "the more connections [which] appear that do not belong simply to the artist's will and decision, the more the

---

45. Williams, "Suspending the Ethical," 218. Or as Pickstock writes: "Repetition . . . is defined by non-identical variation because the universal is never sufficiently determinate as universal, and likewise, the particular never attains to sufficient determination as particular. And so it is the case that these two levels constantly interfere with one another in human discourse and have always already done so." She goes on to say that "Non-identical repetition does not serve to distinguish the way in which something is universal from the way in which it is particular, and so to deflate paradox. Rather, it reasserts a coincidence of the two to the point of apparent contradiction," and that "One can only palliate this contradiction by playing through or inhabiting the never-ending tension of such coincidence in iterative, analogical variation." For her, since we are present within "the finite world, we must be reconciled to the perplexity of the interplay of the particular and universal which is the reflex of the incomprehensible grounding of the finite in the infinite" (Pickstock, "Matter and Mattering," 612–13). She has dealt with this theme more expansively within her most recent monograph, namely *Repetition and Identity*.

46. Williams, *Grace and Necessity*. Hereafter cited in the text as *GN*.

work can embody both the freedom and necessity of the actual finite world and the material produced by the artist can communicate the excess of reality" (*GN*, 131). Art is not primarily about conscious decision or willing, but is more related to an "intelligence" that is "necessarily oriented towards being" (*GN*, 17). Poetics is develops out of an "obedience is to the integrity of the thing made," and thus "to the unfolding logic in the process of making, as the work discloses itself" (*GN*, 52).[47]

The work establishes connections and linkages that exceed the arbitrariness of choice,[48] and require the exercise of aesthetic judgment on the part of the artist (*GN*, 86).[49] Thus art seeks "to reshape the data of the world so as to make their fundamental structure and relation visible," even suggesting startlingly that "the artist *does* set out to change the world, but—if we can manage the paradox—to change the world into itself" (*GN*, 17–18). Poetics constitutes additive realism that "challenges the finality of appearance, the actual 'conditions of existence', not in order to destroy but to ground, amplify, fulfill" (*GN*, 21). Aesthetic production is not helpfully categorized as a kind of imitation (*GN*, 18) but rather implies a non-identical perception of the aesthetic object. Artistry implies a correspondence to "the whole active presence of the object" in which it is "being re-presented by the artist," and is not therefore "simply the *reproduction* of aspects of its appearance" (*GN*, 62). This is because the act of knowledge itself is already involved in a process of representation, which means that "whatever stimulus starts the

---

47. J. H. Prynne has spoken about how "the focus of poetic composition, as a text takes shape in the struggle of the poet to separate from it, projects into the textual arena an intense energy of conception and differentiation, pressed up against the limits which are discovered and invented by composition itself," in Prynne, "Poetic Thought," 596. As a side note, Agamben has made the point that the link between 'truth' and 'disclosure' (*aletheia*) and 'making' (*poeisis*) was held from early on in philosophical thinking. This is however to be distinguished from another mode of reasoning which, under the influence of certain post-Aristotelian traditions, sought to relate *poiesis* to the will, a trajectory which reached its apogee in Nietzsche's will-to-power. Cf. Agamben, "Poiesis and Praxis," in *The Man without Content*, 63–93.

48. Cf. Prynne, *Stars, Tigers and the Shape of Words*.

49. Also see the comments of Prynne: "To work with thought requires the poet to grasp at the strong and persistent ways in which understanding is put under test by imagination as a screen of poetic conscience, to coax and hurl at finesse and judgement, and to set beliefs and principles on line, self-determining but nothing for its own sake merely; all under test of how things are. Nothing taken for granted, nothing merely forced, pressure of the composing will as varied by delicacy, because these energies are dialectical and not extruded from personality or point of view. Dialectics in this sense is the working encounter with contradiction in the very substance of object-reality and the obduracy of thought; irony not as an optional tone of voice but as marker for intrinsic anomaly" (Prynne, "Poetic Thought," 597).

process off is not adequately thought of as a fixed entity requiring no more than a single identification" (*GN*, 138).

Representation progressively and literally 're-presents' and expands the object into a kind of amplifying cognition and affect, suggesting that "the initial cluster of perceptions nor any one set of responses will finally succeed in containing what is known" (*GN*, 139).[50] Such does not necessitate a post-Scotist and Kantian mode of mentalist representation,[51] a transcendentalist stricture in which there is in inscrutable *for itself* in perception that is opposed over-against the *for me* aspect. Williams's Hegelian account, on the contrary, speculates about "the inner life of a reality" as something that "unfolds in time, generating more and more symbolic structures, not a timeless and relation-free definition," whereby "the life of the object in the knowing mind is genuinely in some sense an aspect of the objects own life—not a construct by an independent thinking substance working on dead or static material presented to it as a determined set of data" (*GN*, 139–40). For Williams, the world through continuing refractions continues to "'make itself other'" (*GN*, 156).

But from whence does this otherness appear? For Williams, it is ontologically unfolds out of "the *preconscious* life of the intellect," namely, in "God's formative mental activity within our own," in a "participatory awareness" that is not expressed, at least initially, in conceptual terms (*GN*, 23–24). The divine activity within the world registers doubts for Williams about any "pristine independent subjectivity." There is always a blending of passivity and activity in our perceptions of the world, a sense of being "always already addressed, impressed, illuminated," of being "acting upon, processing and transforming raw data." Such a contention proposes a demythologization of the modernist epistemologies that have created a dualism between "the innocent receptacle of the disinterested mind and the uninterpreted data of external reality" (*GN*, 24). As Williams stresses repeatedly here and elsewhere, we need to move away from a model of there being non-intelligent stuff *out there* upon which our structures are simply added. On the contrary, there is an intelligent construction as regards things-in-themselves; materiality and significance are intimately connected, and cannot be considered independently (*GN*, 75). As is repeated throughout the monograph, aesthetic

---

50. Also see the extensive discussion on "representation" in Williams, *The Edge of Words*, 186–97.

51. Boulnois, *Être et représentation*, 505–15. One can also compare comments made by Williams on "sign-making" and his rejection of "crude representationalism," in Williams, "Christian Art and Cultural Pluralism," 40.

representation suggests that things in the world are not purely self-identical but that they *give more than they have* (*GN*, 26).[52]

This plenitude of signification is linked to the idea that art is able "to bring out relations and dimensions that ordinary rational naming and analysing fail to represent" (*GN*, 28). Such is predicated on the analogical connections or proportionalities that exist between things, "a sense of objects as it were carrying with them a charge of feeling that links them to other objects," as can be seen in music, where tonal registers coalesce and in poetry where the craft of metaphors is able to undermine our simplistic notions of "self-contained entities," making it appear that different objects are operating on a similar "'frequency.'" Here we could even speak of an interpenetration or *participation* between things (*GN*, 28–29), here intimating an "ontological depth" under "the surface of appearances" (*GN*, 76–77),[53] all within what he calls "the interconnectedness of reality" (*GN*, 89).[54] For him, there is a real sense that if "you cannot place a perception, a specific thing, in the context of its resonances and formal echoes, you cannot place it at all" (*GN*, 77).

Williams's Thomistic Hegelianism is on display here.[55] But it also reflects a historicized Platonism: materiality cannot be spoken of or known apart from a "spiral of self-extending symbolic activity" which suggests a certain kind of relationality that is "inescapably mobile, time-related." Moreover, a symbolized world articulates the idea that for us there is "no way of abstracting from the passage of time some necessary, non-revisable and exhaustive correlation between inside and outside, a set of determinate, entirely 'objective' stimuli and a 'correct' reception of and reaction to them." Truth *unfolds* itself within time, which implies "a sense of the real as active, rather

---

52. The phrase is inspired by Jacques Maritain's *Art and Scholasticism*, but Williams comes back to it repeatedly in *Grace and Necessity* to such a degree that it is difficult to pinpoint a specific reference in this regard. The whole book is in some ways a reflection on this idea.

53. "A symbol," for Williams, "is intrinsically bound up with the relations of things sensed and lodged in the subject, it is part of a system of seeing or absorbing what is there; and so it necessarily generates further symbolic connections, not merely a repeatable, generalizable response" (*GN*, 136).

54. Speaking of Flannery O'Connor, Williams writes that "the artist takes the risk of uncovering the world within the world of visible things as a way of 'doing justice', confident because of her commitment that what is uncovered will be the 'reason' in things, a consonance that is well beyond any felt sense harmony or system of explanation but is simply a coherence and connectedness always more than can be seen or expressed" (*GN*, 100).

55. Pickstock, "Matter and Mattering," 615.

than static, a mobile pattern whose best analogy is indeed musical and not mechanical." The Platonic parallels are not lost on him:

> The relation between knower and known envisaged here is remarkably similar to the 'participation' spoken of in a more traditional idiom of scholastic and Platonic thinking. There is some activity which, beginning in the object known, continues to exercise a characteristic mode of life in another medium: the material in which it is first embodied does not exhaust the formal life that is at work. The 'what' of what is known is not something that belongs to the given shape we begin with in our perception; it extends possibilities, or even, to use a question-begging word, *invites* response that will continue and reform its life, its specific energy. (GN, 137–38)

This is what Milbank is referring to when he speaks of Williams's metaphysics as proposing an "intra-finite 'horizontal' participation"[56] that reflects a "'vertical' participation in the being of the Logos." It is this that helps explicate the "analogical resonance or *convenientia* between things" as they appear and poetically represented within the world.[57] Williams, however, is more blatantly historicist and Hegelian in his approach, more so than Platonic realism would suggest. His position is a kind of transcendence of "realism" (at least in its modern variety[58]), since for Williams if the material order betokens incompleteness, while continuously intimating the virtual, then one could wager "the implication that world is not yet as it 'really' is." Williams suggestively adds—in a re-imagination of Thomistic accounts of divine causation—that all of this might indicate "the possible hidden assumption . . . that the world's reality is always asymptotically

---

56 Milbank, "Scholasticism, Modernism and Modernity," 660.

57. "Williams talks about how art most of all shows how things are 'more than themselves', so also he talks . . . about how the work of art 'participates' in its antecedents and both realises and discloses complex and hidden webs of 'participation' [so that] 'vertical' participation and analogy in his theology are echoed in horizontal structures of an ineffable *convenientia*, including those that pertain between being and knowing" (Milbank, "Scholasticism, Modernism and Modernity," 660).

58. The term 'reality' (*realitas*) was largely generated by Duns Scotus—though there are earlier precursors—and is connected to his preference for formalist 'representation' of *res* as *non-nihil*, that is, as a leveling schema that places all 'being' within the same formal plane of being as 'not-nothing.' This was predicated on the idea—developed by Scotus, Suárez and later by Wolff—that 'reality' concerned possible 'essences' which were conceived independently of their actual existence, and which were simply 'mirrored' within representation. For this genealogy, see Courtine, "Reality," in Cassin, *Dictionary of Untranslatables*, 879–87; Boulnois, "Object, Objective Being," in Cassin, *Dictionary of Untranslatables*, 723–25; Boulnois, *Être et représentation*, 88–105, 505–15; Boulnois, "L'invention de la réalité."

approaching its fullness by means of the response of imagination—the assumption of an 'ideal' fullness of perception in which things reach their destiny" (*GN*, 153–54).

But what is the nature or content of this destiny? Williams has said elsewhere regarding Hegel that "all that is *said* about [the] *telos* has a necessarily quasi-fictional character" about it, in the sense that "the *telos* is not *representable* (not present) in the structure of any given historical consciousness or set of consciousnesses, not *a* meaning which a speaker or writer could articulate as a piece of communicable information."[59] But beyond these apophatic caveats, Williams does suggest that if the "constant pattern of 'making other' that runs through the reality of artistic encounters," that if the pattern in which the world of objects are constantly changing themselves can be conceived as ontologically fundamental, then one could go further and suggest that this world-picture has a certain aptitude for a theistic, and even trinitarian account, because if we say that at "the heart of this or at the end of the tracing of it to its first principles lies an ultimate sameness, simply an endless interiority within the world"—a monistic immanence, for example—then that "ought to strike us as in some way jarring" (*GN*, 157).[60] For the Christian theologian, this continuing "making other" suggests an eternal dance of identity and difference, one that coheres with doctrine of substantial relations and of περιχορεσις.[61] The triune God expresses a "radical" and "self-dispossessing" love not only in the timeless relations of Father, Son and Spirit, but also as regards creation. Here *creatio ex nihilo* is understood as being "gratuitous" and

---

59. Williams, "Hegel and the Gods of Postmodernity," in *Wrestling with Angels*, 29.

60. Milbank dilates: "[If] we were to suppose that "making other" were confined within finite immanence, then, [Williams] suggests, being as a whole would be an inert self-identity not subject to artistic disclosure. The atheistic or pantheistic supposition might allow art within the world, but at its margins art would be as it were cancelled, revealed as a less than serious kind of play. To *remain* with the implications of art and poetry, Williams avers, we have to allow that finite reality as such can become endlessly other to itself in a kind of finality beyond finality that implies, indeed, a 'first mover'" (Milbank, "Scholasticism, Modernism and Modernity," 660).

61. "God in the intrinsic 'necessity' of the divine life itself (constrained by nothing but the character of divine love and liberty) generates the eternal other, the partner of divine action, the Word or Son, and also the bearer of the inexhaustibility of divine life who is defined neither as Father nor as Son but simply as Spirit (so that divine life is not enclosed in a simple relations of logical opposition or symmetry)" (*GN*, 159). Williams, in several other places, has sought to expand upon this kenotic and self-dispossessing reading of the trinity, in line with several thinkers. The following are a sample: Williams, "*Sapientia* and the Trinity," 317–32; Williams, "What does Love Know?"; Williams, "The Deflections of Desire," 115–35; Williams, "Balthasar and the Trinity," 37–50; Williams, *A Margin of Silence*.

"continuous," in an analogous way to "the order of the divine mind," and does not therefore imply a fundamental alteration to God's being *ad intra* (*GN*, 158–59). And this world in turn, because it is caused by and exists within God, continues to reflect this reality within its own life as a form of continuous self-othering and creative production.

The above summary of Williams's account of creativity has attempted to lay out some of the basic assumptions which will be repeated later in his reflections on language and analogy. But already, he has shown how the elementary factor of historical movement, namely change and our progressive advance through time, has significant ontological implications. We have been made aware of how ordinary perceptions are filled with a profound level of depth that exceeds our immediate grasp. Williams argued that poetics is itself an intensified form of this perception more generally, and that in order to save appearances, one needs a metaphysical supplementation that makes sense of these disclosures. That is, how is one to make sense of the paradox of difference and identity, as it appears in representation? How is it that the work of art 'exceeds' the intentions of the artist, and so takes on a life of its own? How is one to explain that apparent 'fittingness' between mind and world? And why does language give us an adequate access to reality? Might it be that reality itself remains strangely generative and intelligent in its very essence?

On Language

Williams's Gifford Lectures[62] aimed to investigate how "the very way we speak and think can be heard as raising a question about the kind of universe this is, and thus about where and how language about God comes in" (*EOW*, xi). Like *Grace and Necessity*, he explored how the import of everyday perception—which resist a simplistic model of causality (*EOW*, 53)—can be deepened more fully, finally showing that our ordinary processes of "making sense" require a metaphysical dimension in order to be comprehended (*EOW*, x).[63] What is required is "a metaphysics that thinks of matter itself as invariably and necessarily communicative" and "not as a sheer passivity moulded by our minds into an intelligible structure" (*EOW*, xi). Material reality is "'always already' language-saturated and language-bound" (*EOW*, xii), which leads Williams to therefore reject any "world beyond language"

---

62. Williams, *The Edge of Words*, cited as *EOW*.

63. Williams's argument is that our ways of "talking about God is not a marginal eccentricity in human language but something congruent with the more familiar and less noticed oddities of how we speak" (*EOW*, x).

or "word/world dualism" that "encourages us to think of language as the labelling of a passive environment" (*EOW*, 92).

Williams's own project aims to steer between those styles of natural theology in which God is simply an extra item in the universe to be discovered (*EOW*, 1), and a revelational theology (á la Barth) that holds divine disclosure to have little actual connection to the kind of cosmos we inhabit, as if revelation could be territorialized to a mythical outside—"an otherworldly agent providing otherwise inaccessible information," as Williams puts it (*EOW*, 176). Rather, a practicable natural theology should be focused on "taking into account of whatever pressures [move] us to respond to our environment by gesturing towards a *context* for the description we have been engaged in," as this appears through "a cluster of models and idioms and practices working quite differently from the discourse we have so far been operating [in], and without which our 'normal' repertoire of practice would not finally make sense" (*EOW*, 8).[64] And if such a pressure yields to "the horizon of further questioning"—which is "unlimited in prospect"—then we could conceive this unconstrained expanse, this "indeterminate diversity of representational possibility," as evoking "a shadow of the image of an infinite flow of activity" that could be conceptualized as "generosity" (*EOW*, 32, 170) and "intelligence," since such is "literally the only phenomenon in the universe that makes sense of the overall direction of material existence towards coherent, sustainable, innovative, adaptable forms" (*EOW*, 102).

This again does not involve an extraneous impulse on our part, a willful imposition upon the disarray, but rather indicates a continuing "participation" between objects themselves, as well as the knowing subject who represents them. Such "representation," again, does not imply a simple mirroring "reproduction" but rather displays that inherent amenability of the world to be carried into "another medium," one that does not require an exact likeness (since repetition, as we emphasized earlier, does not necessitate tautology).[65] This means that what-is-thought is related to, but not identical to, the object perceived. It can take on another "form" in which some "aspect of what is perceived" can "be read into another moment in our seeing and speaking." We are not simply dealing with "a set of wholly discrete monads" or "mutually oppositional moments," but instead "a continuum of 'analogical' relations in which we can speak of one thing in terms of another," that is, "of participation

---

64. Williams goes on to show how this project has a kinship with Aquinas's own *quinque viae* (*EOW*, 10–14).

65. For more on this non-dualistic matrix of representation, and it connections to the dynamics of allegory, see Ward, "Transcendence and Representation," 127–47. The essay is relevant insofar as it situates the 'representation' within a genealogy of the sublime.

existing between not only object and object in the world but between object and representing subject." On such a model, any one object can "come to be" *differently*, and is not blandly self-identical (*EOW*, 20). We thus continually, through the simple act of knowing and representing, "*make things other than themselves*" (*EOW*, 60).[66] The continuities between *Grace and Necessity* and *The Edge of Words* are clearly evident here.

Representation is mistakenly construed as an activity that comes *between* subject and the object, as in the tradition of Descartes and Locke. One should instead understand it as something like the *thereness* of the object within perception (*EOW*, 191), as an activity which "*performs* what it refers to," and "enacts the mutual investment of subject and object," (*EOW*, 194), disclosing the fact that reality in itself includes and anticipates "*its life in speaking and thinking*" (*EOW*, 194–95). By adopting the language of representation, Williams is rejecting a "pure postmodern dualism . . . of compromised speech and silent, formless, non-historical interiority" and a "pre-critical revival" of "representation without mediation" (*EOW*, 193). The act of representing should not be confused with sheer imitation or exchangeability, since mediation is that which "enables us to recognize our act in the other, and the other's act in us, and the need to understand truth as more than the correspondence of formal elements in a structure" (*EOW*, 196–97). Representation does not imply a mirror effect, a direct imaging of the world without linguistic and affective mediation, but is always a non-identical repetition of our perceptions in a different form, perceptions which are never neutral or value-free, but always a *seeing-as*, a seeing of something in particular.[67] This means that our attempts at reference are always over-determined by a historical and linguistic density that defies an unmediated perspective.

But it should be added that this ever-increasing "density of reference" does not mean that communication is without limits. There is a sense in which material limitation affects our language-usage—our physical capabilities and language-mastery included. But there is an additional valence given in the fact that the continuing accretion of historico-linguistic deposits means that we cannot just signify whatever we please. To say anything, is "to set it in the context of the echoes and resonances that come with utterance" (*EOW*, 54). Such implies a continuing interpenetration between "freedom" and "determination"—again alluding to terminology

---

66. Also see his reflections on *EOW*, 121–25 which repeat some of the insights contained *Grace and Necessity*, though now with a distinctly Milbankian tone (in light of his reading of "Scholasticism, Modernism and Modernity").

67. For some reflections on this phenomenological *sine qua non*, see Ward, *Unbelievable*. Further commentary can be found in Delport, "Why Faith Makes Sense."

found in *Grace and Necessity*.⁶⁸ We are thus always placed in a context that is "irreducibly charged with intelligence" in which there is a "mutual adjustment and readjustment of meaningful communications and intelligence receptors" (*EOW*, 64). This basic over-determination within our linguistic engagements is visible even at an elementary level, since we cannot repeat the same words twice with exactly the same meaning and denotation (*EOW*, 67). Here the movement and irreversibility of time augments our perception so that past activity ultimately "becomes 'material' to the next utterance and performance, so that this latter cannot be in any very interesting sense the same" (*EOW*, 68). As such, "what has been said cannot be unsaid, and what is now to be said has to reckon not only with the environment as such but with the speech of others which makes the environment we encounter always already *represented*." We discover our context as something as already saturated with meaningful resonance, as a "symbolized world," that is always-already being "taken up into a process of speaking and making sense together" (*EOW*, 69).

This is exemplified by Margaret Masterman's essay on metaphysics and ideographs,⁶⁹ which Williams draws heavily on.⁷⁰ In the construction of ideographical signs, one begins for example with a simple word or sign, like "Play"; this word, while evidencing at the outset a "basic indeterminacy,"⁷¹ can then be subject to a form of "Progressive Definition" through repeated usage. One repeats the word "Play," within temporal gaps, and eventually one infers an "indexical" reference, so that we can talk of "*that* Play," since "past performance contributes to present meaning."⁷² Using language that echoes Hegel's *Phenomenology*, Masterman argues that metaphysical and ideographical language abstracts from particularity, from a focus on *this*, *here* and *now* towards more "universal" forms of designation,⁷³ from unitary "statements" towards "clusters" of implication that set this specificity within an ever-widening context of meaning. The generalized context abstracted from particulars is then condensed into words that are "the simplest possible, the most compact, the simplest, the

---

68. More expansively stated, this idiom speaks to the "unceasing effort to re-work perceptions as our means of exploring what it is for something to be 'there' for us is both free, in the sense that it is never accounted for by an energy-impulse exchange model, and deeply constrained, in the sense that we are always trying to allow what is there to show itself" (Williams, *The Edge of Words*, 60).

69. Masterman, "Metaphysical and Ideographic Language," 283–357.

70. Williams, *The Edge of Words*, 105–8.

71. Masterman, "Metaphysical and Ideographic Language," 333.

72. Masterman, "Metaphysical and Ideographic Language," 334.

73. Masterman, "Metaphysical and Ideographic Language," 314–15.

most stark."[74] Metaphysics and ideographs thus *extend* the scope of statements, and *reduce* them so that "sufficiently specific meaning is attained."[75] Within this remit, the word "Play" may come to refer to a universal activity extracted from a horizon of complexity and implication.

For Williams, this continual building-up of historical meaning implies that we can never be isolated speakers, but are always socialized in our interactions, being subject to the constraints and plenitudes of human exchange (*EOW*, 81–86). Linguistic objects present themselves in a "three-dimensional" manner that implies a certain level of "resistance" which assumes "a convergence of different possible points of view and points where resistance is met" (*EOW*, 98). On this reading, any "coherent material object" comes to be "through a fairly intricate interplay of processes," so that such an object is "always already 'saturated' with the workings of mind" (*EOW*, 101). Materiality is therefore "inherently 'symbolic,'" implying a "cosmos of interacting signals" implying that we are "engaged with and [are] in a shared situation." Truthfulness is maintained insofar as we attempt to "find a way of speaking that does maximal justice to the diversity and plurality of a situation" (*EOW*, 117). But it also implies that we take seriously the assertion that the universe is "an intelligible *whole*," that is, we should read it as a *world*. As Williams goes on to suggest, this intelligible whole might reflect to us the fact that there is an intelligent mind that gives rationality to this order, even though he knows this is not a conclusive deduction (*EOW*, 118).

Williams's reflections on the inherently additive nature of language leads him to conclude that excessiveness or extremity are revelatory regarding the workings of language itself (*EOW*, 130). If our very speaking concerns an attunement to the material world, then this tells us that the world is always in excess to itself, that there is a "complexity we are always catching up" to. Our attempts at comprehensiveness will continually fall short of their ideal, since it is herein that we encounter *difficulty*, the world in all "its complex resistance to exhaustive description" (*EOW*, 143). What does this excessiveness tell us about this reality in itself? As reiterated previously, it means that if we can speak of "intelligence" as being radically pervasive and that there is no such thing as materiality without the workings of mind, then we are able to propose that we are "an important sense 'addressed' by what we encounter." The semantic and linguistic exploration of extremity, as in religious hyperbole and paradox, is done with the aim of ever-so gradually acquiring a kind of *precision* since it is "only then do we see what it actually means for some agency within our experience to

---

74. Masterman, "Metaphysical and Ideographic Language," 342.
75. Masterman, "Metaphysical and Ideographic Language," 316.

come into speech," especially when that agency cannot be described in the language appropriate for finite actors (*EOW*, 147).[76] This requires a certain "*faith in language*" (*EOW*, 146), a trust that our continued speaking contains "resources beyond its immediate referential vocabulary," thereby "disclosing futures we had not consciously imagined" (*EOW*, 152). And if such language is inherently social and produced through a multiplicity of perceptions, then one could suggest that it appears "as if 'Being' itself were in effect the irreducible otherness of speakers, the complex of inexhaustible potential for relatedness" (*EOW*, 155). The trinitarian implications of this should be open to the careful reader.

But what happens when words stop? What are we left with? Williams suggests that no silence is "pure absence" since we "cannot imagine an 'unframed' or pure silence," but only a "silence in which *we* are not hearing anything, not hearing what we might expect to hear" (*EOW*, 156–57). Silence is never value-free, so that the assumption that silence communicates nothing in itself is not a valid inference. There is always a context in which non-speech occurs, which further implies that not all silence is innocent. We have to look at where this stoppage occurs and the kind of language it "interrupts or refuses." Silences appears when we have to deal with "difficulty" (*EOW*, 162) that is, where language reaches an aporia, where it begins to "break down" (*EOW*, 179). When this "incompleteness" or "difficulty" is stressed, this does not necessarily imply "a failure exactly," but rather shows "that *this* is one way in which language copes with *this* sort of difficulty, by naming the bare fact that it is difficult" (*EOW*, 163–64). This interrelation between speech and silence leads Williams to question any privileging of silence over speech as regards "truth-telling," since "speech points into silence and is itself altered by it" (*EOW*, 162–63). For Christian and mystical speech, this has traditionally be associated with the naming of God, with the fact that God does not exist as a definitive 'object' within history—since he is both *innominabile* or *omninominabile*—a fact which reveals the "time-and-matter-bound nature" of language more generally (*EOW*, 165).

The significance of this incapacity on the part of language does not mean that communication itself is inherently or fatalistically a distorting medium. It is temporal and therefore has an "unfinished character"—a sense of "what has not *yet* been said"—but it should not be conceived as

---

76. In Williams, *The Edge of Words*, 148, he writes that this "means in practice that when we invoke a God's eye perspective as our final horizon on the world, we are, in that very act, acknowledging the always receding horizon of our knowing; we are recognizing that representation for us has no end, because we cannot occupy the entire range of possible perspectives from something can be seen. And, whatever God knows, it is not the ensemble of finite perspectives but something of another order."

"intrinsically corrupt" (*EOW*, 167–68). Speech about what is difficult is continually primed to be towards *paradox* and the *suspension* of our ordinary ways of speaking (*EOW*, 169). Williams draws on the moral aspects of this habit of language, since it also speaks to "the existence and survival of a certain kind of *humanity*." Williams adds this because he believes that there are contemporary accounts that are "hostile to that account of humanity which sees it as basically *accountable*, engaged in growth, risk, love," and in a practice of "shaping itself in relation to what is given," (*EOW*, 183). Such might also hold in check those "shapeless ideas of liberty and autonomy" (*EOW*, 197) that are predominant in neoliberal constructions of selfhood.

Williams's argument has served to show that the material practices of language-usage and language-creation are not irruptions into an otherwise non-intelligent matrix. For him, materiality itself is imbued with symbolic resonance and capability that defies any reductively immanent account. To say or think anything involves us in a deeply profound undercurrent of meaning that is only rarely brought to the surface consciously, but is present nonetheless. There is an ever-expanding range of significance implicated and enacted in every act of speaking and thinking we engage in. There is no dualism for Williams between the material and the metaphysical, the immanent and the transcendent, the temporal and non-temporal: we are rather given a framework in which the symbolic excess of being is reflective of the nature of the cosmos, and therefore of the divine life in which all things participate and have their being. With this participatory structure in place, we are ready to approach Williams's account of analogy.

On Analogy

Throughout the previous two sections, there have been various hints at a more substantive account of analogy that underlies Williams's tangential commentary. In various places, there have been allusions to analogy as providing insights regarding the real proportion between mind and world, or the affinity between objects that implies an intersection between vertical and horizontal modes of participation. However, it is worth expanding Williams's own take on analogy, and its impingements on metaphysics. Here it can be said that one will not find a text where Williams expounds his own systematic account of analogy as such. The closest one comes to this are "Balthasar and Difference,"⁷⁷ "Dialectic and Analogy,"⁷⁸ and in the concluding section to his recent monograph on Christology.⁷⁹

In "Balthasar and Difference," like other texts in *Wrestling with Angels*, Williams aims to counteract a postmodern disavowal of representation, here understood by critical theorists as a drive towards "identity and totality."⁸⁰ Here Williams is thinking specifically of Derridean *différance* which drifts towards finally non-presentable and "the unsayable."⁸¹ He reckons that Derrida and other poststructuralists (e.g., Lyotard) have not successfully articulated a defensible account of ontological difference; instead, in their "refusal of a relation between same and other," they have produced "another kind of reduction to the same," a postmodern sublimity of the unpresentable.⁸² In distinction from the post-phenomenological appraisals of embodiedness, Williams believes the Derridean prioritization of writing implies a "curiously disincarnate" imaginary in its denial of the human speaking-situation and "the temporal conflicts and resistances of 'ordinary' interpersonal exchange."⁸³ In contrast, he thinks we need to conceptualize "a difference that is both simultaneous and interactive, a difference that allows temporal change, reciprocity of action," and which avoids all "varieties of totalization."⁸⁴ It is here that the *analogia entis* comes to its own, especially as mediated through Balthasar and Nicholas of Cusa's *non aliud*.⁸⁵

But how does Williams understand the *analogia entis* more substantively? He begins with a qualification: analogy is "emphatically *not* a correspondence between two or more things exhibiting in varying degrees the same features, as if God had a very great deal of good and creatures

---

77. Williams, "Balthasar and Difference," 77–85.
78. Williams, "Dialectic and Analogy: A Theological Legacy," 274–92.
79. Williams, *Christ the Heart of Creation*, 219–54.
80. Williams, "Balthasar and Difference," 77.
81. For Derrida, "If there is speech, there is the unsayable, simply because speech cannot be everything, cannot escape its mobile, anarchic temporality, cannot do other than reflect itself and rework itself. But what is unsayable is strictly unsayable, not to be gestured towards in a timidly religious way. There is no relation between the same and the other, the said the unsayable. The one is not even the 'opposite' of the other, as it cannot belong in one frame with it at any point" (Williams, "Balthasar and Difference," 78).
82. For on the way that the *analogia entis* resists the post-Kantian, post-Lyotardian sublime, see Betz, "Beyond the Sublime (Part One)," and "Beyond the Sublime (Part Two)."
83. Williams, "Balthasar and Difference," 78–79. The argument that Derridean ontology leads to the elision of ontological difference has been put forward in more detail by Pickstock, *After Writing*, 1–46.
84. Williams, "Balthasar and Difference," 79.
85. Williams, "Balthasar and Difference," 80.

steadily diminishing qualities of the same." God and creatures cannot be participants on the same plane of reality, two "moments in one story." Incorporating God and finite being within the same ontological narrative would violate the dogmatic ordering of aseity, as I have previously emphasized elsewhere. The creator-creature distinction remains fundamental for Williams. He denies that the *analogia entis* implies an ontotheology—in the sense implied by Heidegger[86]—as if the participatory relation between God and creatures were simply an amplification of common traits. On the contrary, the analogy of being is predicated on a radical *difference* between Being and beings, which cannot be occluded without undermining the unfathomable interval between created and uncreated. To put it in terms he has more recently formulated, the logic of analogy implies an unfolding of "the non-dual, non-identical grammar of divine relation and thus of divine relatedness to what is not divine, infinite relation to the finite."[87] In a more Balthasarian inflection:

> It is the active presence of the divine liberty, love and beauty precisely within the various and finite reality of material/temporal reality. 'The divine' is not present in creation in the form of 'hints of transcendence', points in the created order where finitude and creatureliness appear to thin out or open to a mysterious infinity, but in creation being itself—which includes, paradigmatically, creation being itself in unfinishedness, time-taking, pain and death. The crucified Jesus is, in this context, the ground and manifestation of what analogy means.[88]

The material processes whereby language concerning God is produced are not about "denying undialectically the realities of time." Rather it is by "working with the modalities of talk about time" that "the timeless ... reality of reciprocal differentiations of trinitarian life is brought to view." For Williams, temporality and historicity are not excluded from metaphysics and the doctrine of analogy. In distinction from the contrastive account of transcendence (which we have earlier encountered), Williams repeats that "God is not to be spoken of by denying contingency," since—in consonance with the Cusan accent on divine non-otherness—he maintains that the "mysterious difference of God is never an abstract otherness defined simply by the negation of predicates of contingent being." To think God's transcendence

---

86. On the Heidegger, ontotheology and the *analogia entis*, see Betz, "Translator's Introduction," in Przywara, *Analogia Entis*, 76–83. Also see Courtine, *Inventio analogiae*, 45–107.
87. Williams, *Christ the Heart of Creation*, 245.
88. Williams, "Balthasar and Difference," 80.

in this way would actually imply a subtle renouncement of it: for to speak as if the difference of God was simply a matter of "the negation of all finite predicates," then we would be speaking of a divinity conceived as "the other belonging to a discourse about the finite world," that is, "the antithesis of the world's thesis."[89] Once again, the implication here is that any account which makes God's self-definition dependent upon finitude, even if it is imagined via a negative polarization of distinguishing attributes, ends up transgressing the difference between creator and creation. To quote Herbert McCabe's pithy formulation: "God cannot be a thing, an existent among others. It is not possible that God and the universe should add up to make two."[90] The same goes for any negative arithmetic.

Similar trajectories are present in "Dialectic and Analogy"; however, rather than focusing on postmodern aversions to representation, "Dialectic and Analogy" is penned against the background of post-Kantian and Romantic ideas of subjectivity. These are particularly related to Barthian worries about how the ego has served as the "pre-existing constant" over-against which God's being is contrasted.[91] If one's starting point, already at the outset, subordinates God to a finite measure of proportion, then that decision taints any outcome, no matter how far one extends the chain of measuring, even unto infinity.[92] For Barth, the God conceived along these lines could be hardly less than "a fantastically deferred and re-routed vision of a human form of mental life" that is supposedly "reconciled with its own unlimited possibilities."[93] Barth's concern is that the knowledge of truthful language about God should stem from "a process or activity that is not generated by the finite subject, whether in terms of ideas or 'experiences.'"[94] It is for this

---

89. Williams, "Balthasar and Difference," 83. A longer and more dense study on the relation between the question of historicity and analogical metaphysics can be found in Puntel, *Analogie und Geschichtlichkeit*. For some historical background for this argument in this monograph, see the historical treatment given in Holzer, "Les thomismes de langue allemande au xxe siècle." Holzer makes the point that many German Catholics, especially those who rely heavily on Kant and Heidegger, to a lesser or greater degree, are unconsciously influenced in their reading of Aquinas by a kind of crypto-Suárezian ontology in which the study of general being is separated from particular being itself (e.g., God-as-Being), a tendency that operates in accordance with the distinction between *metaphysica generalis* and *metaphysica specialis*.

90. McCabe, "Creation," in *God Matters*, 6.

91. Williams, "Dialectic and Analogy," 274.

92. This argument has deep similarities with Aquinas's rejection of an analogy of proportion as a legitimate option for Christian metaphysics, as we saw in a previous chapter.

93. Williams, "Dialectic and Analogy," 276.

94. Williams, "Dialectic and Analogy," 277.

reason that Barth emphasizes the importance of God's self-revelation as being the only basis for a theology worthy of its name.

In this regard, Barth's negative antipode is Hegel, who exemplifies this trajectory which he desires to counter. Williams contemporizes this debate through an interpretation of Hegel offered by Conor Cunningham, which proposes that Hegel collapses all difference into a univocal grammar, in that each distinct thing is defined in relation to *what it is not*.[95] If this reading of Hegel is correct, then it implies that everything is determined by its shadowy and non-existent opposite, an alternate reality of sublime vacuity—which is the highest instance of univocal predication.[96] Williams suggests that these concerns are centered on the problem of analogy, in that Hegel's metaphysics (as read by Cunningham and others) cannot sustain a vision of ontological difference. Williams contests this, asserting, here and elsewhere,[97] that Hegel's philosophy as a form of *thinking* does not necessitate that any object be determined in contrast to what it is not, but that it always is thought in its particular or "determinate" location.[98] Furthermore, the act of thinking itself implies an objectivity that can never be reduced to the machinations of the ego, and therefore indicates a never-to-be-completed process of *dispossession* by the thinking subject (a point I will return to later).

However, Williams's main focus in this essay is not primarily on which of these readings of Hegel is more correct. Instead the central protagonist in this text is Barth's theological *bête noire*, Erich Przywara. It is well-known that Barth had a profound distaste for the *analogia entis*,[99] and was particularly critical of Przywara (even though he probably did not read his *magnum opus*[100]). But Williams argues that Barth's rejection of the analogy of being leaves in place "a stark dilemma as to the relation of God to creation," leading to ultimately to an unhelpful oppositional construal of creature and creator, "a picture that entails a univocal understanding of finite and infinite being, two modes of action that are in competition for one logical space."[101] In Williams's estimate, it is analogy—against a decadent Hegelianism and Barthianism—that "moves us on from a dialectic that threatens to collapse into an

---

95. Williams, "Dialectic and Analogy," 279.

96. Williams, "Dialectic and Analogy," 277–78; also see Cunningham, *Genealogy of Nihilism*, 100–30.

97. Williams, "Hegel and the Gods of Postmodernity," 25–34; "Logic and Spirit in Hegel," 35–52; and "Politics and Metaphysics," 53–76; all in *Wrestling with Angels*.

98. Williams, "Dialectic and Analogy," 278.

99. For on Barth and the analogy of being, see Betz, "Translator's Introduction," in Przywara, *Analogia Entis*, 83–115.

100. Williams, "Dialectic and Analogy," 292n50.

101. Williams, "Dialectic and Analogy," 280.

ultimate self-identity."[102] It proposes "a non-rivalrous difference," a difference that is *not* understood in "binary terms."[103] Substantively, this is fleshed out in Przywara's proposal for "creaturely metaphysic,"[104] or more specifically, a dual emphasis on a "meta-noetics" and "meta-ontics."[105] These respectively relate to *the act of knowing* and *the object of knowing*, and constitute "the irreducible duality" in our relation to the world.[106] Within this analogical duality, as Williams writes in *Christ the Heart of Creation*, "Every particular . . . is more than its own particularity" and "every vehicle of formal understanding allows particulars to be seen in relation to other particulars and to a connecting rhythm within all of them."[107] In other words, things are seen and conceived *through* the mediation of other things, so that everything becomes "more than a single and containable phenomenon but something opening out to an unlimited horizon of connection."[108] Particularities are always exceeding themselves within the act of perception and knowing, never being merely self-identical or self-contained, existing within the flux between *Dasein* and *Sosein*, "meta-noetics" and "meta-ontics."

Within Przywara's Heideggerian language, "meta-noetics" is related to *Dasein* ("being-there") while "meta-ontics" is connected to *Sosein* ("being-thus").[109] The former speaks to "the givenness of a certain process

102. Williams, "Dialectic and Analogy," 287.
103. Williams, "Dialectic and Analogy," 288.
104. Williams, "Dialectic and Analogy," 286.
105. See Przywara, *Analogia Entis*, 119–24.
106. Williams, "Dialectic and Analogy," 285.
107. Williams, *Christ the Heart of Creation*, 240.
108. Williams, *Christ the Heart of Creation*, 247.
109. In *Analogia Entis*, Przywara's purpose is to reflect upon 'metaphysics "as such,"' as found in the outworking and development of its "formal principle" (Przywara, *Analogia Entis*, 117). This comes into focus within his bipolarity between "meta-ontics" and "meta-noetics," the articulation of being-as-such and the historical phenomenology of consciousness, "the act of knowledge and the act of being, understood as the object of the act of knowledge" (Przywara, *Analogia Entis*, 120). For Przywara both sides of the polarity express themselves *within* human consciousness: on the one side, "The meta-noetic transcends itself in a forward intentionality, towards the meta-ontic," and on the other, "The meta-ontic moves backward in self-critique, reflexively, towards the meta-noetic" (*Analogia Entis*, 121). The duality that characterizes the structure of a *creaturely metaphysics* is then a marker of the *Spannungs-Schwebe* within being-as-such, our existence *in fieri*, in becoming. It is this finite and "creaturely" dynamic which illuminates "the suspended tension," within metaphysics, "of the correlation (in its object) and upon the becoming proper to the back-and-forth relation (in its method)." This interplay is grounded upon the Thomistic distinction between essence and existence, on an "essence-in-and-beyond existence" [*Sosein in-über Dasein*] (Przywara, *Analogia Entis*, 124). In Heideggerian language, "meta-noetics" is directed towards knowledge-as-such, its primary object is the problem of "existence" [*Dasein*], while "meta-ontics"

of becoming" while the latter says that there is "no engagement with the historical givenness without recognising the continuity-in-change."[110] Within this framework, the *analogia entis* is aimed at bringing-out the "balance of tension" that occurs between these two polarizations, between "what is being thought" and "the temporal or process-related dimension in our knowing."[111] Such *balance* aims to counteract "a 'pure' Idealist construction of the subject" and a "crude realism" found in some variations of neo-scholastic thought.[112] It does so by emphasizing the consistent interplay between *Sosein* and *Dasein*, whereby this "unity-in-tension" moves thinking onto "the analogical plane," since it is through the temporalized becoming of *Dasein* that we realize that *Sosein* is "not identical with any moment of our perception."[113] Expressed theologically, this means that "God is never exhaustively the other of creation. God is God, the identity of essence and existence, of *Da* and *So*." This is not so for finite beings since, in accordance with the Thomistic distinction, they will always experience an irreducible non-coincidence between *esse* and *essentia*. For Przywara, God remains "outside any process of measurement or proportion, but through "the sheer gift simultaneously of existence and intelligible form to the finite, God establishes a world in which tension is inbuilt in our apprehension and thus 'analogical' thinking becomes of central importance."[114] Once more, we can see that the radical difference of God makes analogy possible, and precisely in a way that gives time-bounded existence its due regard.

This section concludes the previous three sections. Its aim was to deepen our earlier expansions on Williams's account of divine transcendence, attempting to show that his non-conflictive approach is deepened through his reflections on creativity, language and analogy. Williams's metaphysics dilated these trajectories by examining the material practices of poetics and language, displaying that the interstices between time and matter disclose a

---

focuses on being-as-such, that is, on "essence" [*Sosein*]. As Przywara says: "truth is the region of the pure "thus"—*So*; history, the region of the "there"—*Da*" (Przywara, *Analogia Entis*, 152).

110. Williams, "Dialectic and Analogy," 286.
111. Williams, "Dialectic and Analogy," 285.
112. Williams, "Dialectic and Analogy," 285.
113. Williams, "Dialectic and Analogy," 287.
114. Williams, "Dialectic and Analogy," 288. Williams's reflections here on analogy as having an intrinsic relation to the act of knowing and thinking connect to our earlier discussion of "representation," which implied that there is no simple mirroring process implied in our acts of cognition. Using the language of Przywara, there is a "tension" that exists in "our capacity to *think* ('noetics') [that] is neither separable from nor identical with the judgement that it is in fact there ('ontics')." This quotation can found in Williams, *The Edge of Words*, 20.

world that is inherently symbolic and meaningful. Such contentions transgress the dualisms between mind and matter, nature and super-nature, time and eternity, the vertical and the horizontal. Connecting this to our previous allusions to 'the sublime,' this argument further substantiates the idea that the infinite can be mediated, however imperfectly, through creaturely ideation. We are not dealing here with a sheer negativity of the postmodern sublime, but a positive infinity of transcendent form.

But all of this raises a question: what about evil? One can anticipate a response, given by thinkers like MacKinnon, namely that our argument here fails to take into account the tragic seriousness of our lot, the deeply troubling factor that evil continues to characterize our being-in-the-world. It cannot be erased or papered over. It must be engaged.

Without Substance: Augustine and the Problem of Evil

One of the critiques lodged by Hart and Milbank at Donald MacKinnon's plea for the tragic was its clearly stated aversion to the *privatio boni*.[115] We can recall his statement that the Platonic-Augustinian theory of evil-as-privation[116] was "the most profound spiritual error of transcendent metaphysics,"[117] and further "that it has only to be stated clearly, and worked out in terms of concrete examples, to be shown to be totally inadequate as an analysis either of moral or of physical evil."[118] MacKinnon's concern appears to be that we fail to conceive evil if we consider it primarily as a lack, or as simply a deviation from an ideal. There is a real sense in which evil cannot be described as simple negation, that is, as an absence of the good. According to him, evil has a devastating positivism that resists this.

Williams's major treatment of this theme is his essay "Insubstantial Evil."[119] Expounding Augustine's *grammar* of evil, Williams argues that the language of evil and sin is not "about what makes the constituents of the world the sorts of things they are," but is instead about a temporal and ontological *process*, "about something that happens to the things that there are in

---

115. For a discussion of Augustine's theology of evil more generally, see Evans, *Augustine on Evil*; Cress, "Augustine's Privation"; Brachtendorf, "The Goodness of Creation and the Reality of Evil."

116. For the Neoplatonic tendencies that underlay Augustine's own account, see Cherniss, "The Sources of Evil According to Plato"; Rist, "Plotinus on Matter and Evil"; Narbonne, "Aristote et la mal"; Steel and Opsomer, "Evil Without a Cause."

117. MacKinnon, "Finality in Metaphysics, Ethics and Theology," in *Explorations in Theology*, 103.

118. MacKinnon, "Theology and Tragedy," 165.

119. Williams, "Insubstantial Evil," 105–23. Cited as *IE*.

the universe." For Augustine, evil is not a hypostatized "object" that we encounter in the world, but rather names "that process in which good is lost" (*IE*, 105). This temporal devolution is connected to Augustine's orthodox account of creation: God creates the world as a contingent and interrelated totality, as one shaped by *forma* and *pondus*—form and balance—in a way that constitutes the metaphysical rationale for created goodness-as-such. Created beings are placed and shaped within a hierarchy of relation that determines their particularity. Without this *forma* and *pondus* there would be no way to register what change might actually mean, because in total formlessness and contingency, change and process are meaningless.[120] It is within this context that evil-as-privation and evil-as-process finds its possibility. One of the golden threads running through this essay is Williams's argument that Augustine's account of evil is deeply connected to the doctrine of God and creation. Being and goodness are convertible. On Williams's perspective, these two things are so intimately related that if we reject the one, the other is put in question as well (*IE*, 105).

As Williams knows, this teaching has been questioned in recent times. In this text, his interlocutors are John Hick and Kathleen Sands, and not MacKinnon explicitly (though it is certainly conceivable that MacKinnon remains a latent subtext in the discussion). For his part, Williams thinks the non-substantiality of evil is not a negligible aspect of Christian metaphysics, since it concerns "the question of what it is to speak of 'a' world at all, with all that this implies about the universe's relation to a maker" (*IE*, 106). But in talking about non-substantiality, what are we saying? Does evil really not 'exist'? Williams suggests that we cannot see this clearly unless we see that for Augustine there is no concept of "sheer thereness," since "to be at all is to have a particular place in the interlocking order of things," that "to exist is necessarily to exemplify certain 'goods', to be, in a certain way, actively exercising the ordered and interdependent life that belongs to the creatures of a good God." Augustine's "axiological" account of being does mean that existents can be subjected to various levels of ontological *gradation*, that is, we can speak of differing levels of deficiency and actuality among distinct things. This should not be read as implying grades of *thereness* as such but

---

120. Williams, "Good for Nothing?," 17–18. Elsewhere, he writes that creation (for Augustine) is "the setting in being of a living system destined to grow toward beauty and order, even if this beauty and order is not at any given moment fully apparent. Thus . . . the *temporal* character of the world is axiomatic: it is a world in motion, a set of processes in which potential is realized.' He goes on to say "The story of creation as a whole . . . is . . . a *story*, a process. Its goal is certainly something beyond time, though not exactly an eternal stasis: there is still the movement of love, the steady pressure towards God, the *pondus* drawing and holding things in God-centred harmony." Williams, "Creation," 252–53.

rather that "the exercise of the goods that go with existing may be more or less constrained in its environment, more or less capable of modification," which indicates that there is an "overall notion of interdependence" in which "some realities are more dependent than others" (*IE*, 106). Augustine continues here the tradition of ontological 'intensiveness' found in the Neoplatonic tradition, one that would be carried on in the likes of Aquinas.

Addressing Hick, Williams disputes whether Augustine's *privatio boni* should be read as an 'aesthetic' theodicy in which evil does not exist, because, from the divine perspective of the whole, evil is cancelled by the balancing of good, much like the way dark blotches on a painting are absorbed into the product's completion.[121] Williams thinks Augustine's proposal is more radical than this: if there is no 'evil' from the divine perspective this is because evil is not a *thing* or *substance* that literally stands-out on its own terms (*IE*, 107). Evil is a perversion; it is parasitic—a *parhypostasis*, to quote Proclus—and, for Augustine, is preeminently manifest in the distortedness of desire (*IE*, 109). Our very perspective on reality is so warped that even our acknowledgement of evil is tainted, so that we cannot speak dispassionately about it. Only God remains untainted (*IE*, 108).

An additional argument in favour of rejecting the 'aesthetic' reading of evil is that God—for Augustine and classical theology more generally—does *not* need anything outside of the sufficiency of God's own life. Therefore, any claim that God 'uses' us to achieve some aesthetic balance that exceeds the particular goods of created things is theologically questionable: since God requires no further fulfillment, creation can *only* be there for the good of creatures: "The creature's perspective simply is defined by God's creative purpose . . . but that divine purpose is to maximize all possible fulfilment for the creature, since the good, the joy, the flourishing of the creature could never be in any way a threat to the divine bliss" (*IE*, 108).[122] Such a conclusion intimates that the co-ordination of divinity and humanity needs to be thoroughly *despatialized*, as being non-conflictive, since we are not talking about different agencies vying for the same ontological territory (*IE*, 110). A consequence of this is that evil can have no "space" ontologically at all (*IE*, 109); evil is a question of contingency and not metaphysical necessity. It is a question of *time* and *process*, and the inherent limits that these impose on us. To use some remarks given elsewhere, "an authentically contingent world is one in which you cannot guarantee the compatibility of goods. That's what it

---

121. A critique of this style of 'aesthetic' theodicy can be found in Williams, "Redeeming Sorrows: Marilyn McCord Adams and the Defeat of Evil," in *Wrestling with Angels*, 255–74.

122. See also Williams, "On Being Creatures," in *On Christian Theology*, 63–78.

is to be created."[123] Evil is not a question of timeless essences or hypostatized entities engaged in eternal and bellicose opposition, as in Manichaeism, but are the historical consequence between finite actors.

Hick's further criticisms however bring us into an explicit relation with something near to MacKinnon's concerns: for Hick there is a necessary distinction between *metaphysical* and *empirical* accounts of evil: according to him, "whatever the accuracy of the metaphysical definition of evil as privation, it cannot be accurate to speak of evil *as experienced* in such terms." For instance, to say that an evil 'will' implies no volition or that evil acts are simple negations or privations of existing states of affairs would not be correct. Because of this, and now against Augustine, Hick thinks we need to maintain that "Evil activity has a power and 'integrity' of its own," and is not reducible to the absence of certain qualities, like when "pain" is understood as just an "absence of pleasure"—which of course, as Williams readily admits, is a "grossly inadequate account" of how evil "manifestly *impresses* itself upon the subject" (*IE*, 110). Nonetheless, Williams thinks this is not, overall, an accurate reading of the matter: rather, as Augustine argues, one can coherently sustain what Hick calls the "terrifying quality and power" of metaphysical evil without implying that it has some kind of ontological solidity of its own. One can maintain by saying evil is a perversion of "those elements, in whatever reality we are talking about, that are most alive and active." The particular malignity of evil is that distorts and undermines "the kind of world this is, a world in which the active, joyful goodness of God is mirrored or shared by creatures," and evil is terrifying precisely because our existence is pervaded by an "intensity of action," and this is why "the diversion or distortion of worldly reality is appalling." Hick's language of the "impress" of evil indicates a field of intelligent action, and is connected to volition, which for Augustine as such—even as it is maimed by sin—cannot mean that it lacks power or agency, that is, as long as it possesses those "excellences" that characterize human and angelic freedom. The implication to be drawn is that sin or evil are not necessarily the result of an anemic will. On the contrary, Williams thinks that "[what] makes . . . evil terrible are those excellences [and] nothing else." Evil-as-privation does not necessitate the absence or removal of something that was there previously (temporally-speaking), or as simply an exercise in negation (remove this or that quality and suddenly you have something evil). It is precisely by taking that which is good, energetic and excellent and distorting it that its beneficent qualities are morphed into something destructive (think of the example of the evil genius). Here there is a causative nexus of action and willing which brings

---

123. Williams, "Saving Time," 322.

about evil occurrences, but it is precisely *what* is distorted that makes its effects so awful (*IE*, 110–11).

So even though evil should be understood as privative—defined as a loss or perversion of the good—this should not imply that the consequences of evil can be categorized merely as a lack of some characteristic. What makes evil truly devastating is that it corrupts the agencies of intellectual will, and that it is precisely this factor that makes evil heinous and destructive (*IE*, 111). So while evil is ontologically inexistent—it does not stand out as an independent 'thing'—the consequences it has on active agents is certainly not just privative: it has a "terrifying quality and power" that is irreducible to the sheer absence of particular qualities, because, as is certainly the case, our particular *experience* of evil cannot be summarized as simply one of "void" or "lack." One could say that it is "the effect of a lack, the displacement of true by untrue perception," even though "its effects within a system of forces may be powerful" (*IE*, 113).

This might sound paradoxical and strange, or at least counter-intuitive, but Williams thinks the alternatives are even more stark and dire: if evil has "a power of initiative, a capacity to set intelligible goals and to advance those goals in a lastingly coherent manner," this would mean, firstly, that 'evil' is analogous to other finite actors, and secondly that 'evil' could be pursued as a teleologically *rational* enterprise. On this model, if evil acts at the same level as other beings, and exhibits its own distinctive *ratio*, then it follows that goodness and evil can be said to possess 'being' univocally, which (as a result) places being-as-such into a formally sublime indeterminacy. Williams goes on to say that the first position is Manichaeism pure and simple, since it proposes a mythical picture of evil as external or "invasive" power *outside* "the moral responsibility of the finite person, so that the victory of evil is the victory of a subject, or substance, distinct from the finite person."[124] The second position suggests, even more problematically, that "what is good for one subject is not necessarily good for any other," or "that there is a plurality of intelligible goods, goals that may be pursued without absurdity by reasoning subjects" (*IE*, 111–12).

This view stands in contrast to the traditional account of transcendent goodness given by Augustine, in which the "good of all persons is both unified and interdependent," insofar as "I can not specify what is good for me without including what is good for you in the same calculation." For Augustine, "cause or agency are bound up with a conviction about the location of evil in the malfunctioning of relations between subjects, not in the relation

---

124. Williams calls this view "a mythological conception of something outside that agency displacing the person's own responsibility" (Williams, "Insubstantial Evil," 112).

of this or that subject to some other *thing* called 'evil.'" So an account undermines "the very idea of intelligibility as something relating the individual's mental/verbal life to a system or order transcending the individual frame," because "if the Good is in some sense one, evil cannot be allowed a place of its own, outside the system of balancing and interweaving relations that actualise the Good for particular beings, and which, in a contingent world, are vulnerable to malfunction and distortion" (*IE*, 112).[125]

Hick's final criticism of evil-as-privation is linked to the Neoplatonic roots of Augustine's metaphysics, which could be read as offering that the world develops in accordance with a principle of plenitude that has little connection to a divine choosing or willing. That is, there is a process of necessary "emanation" from the One which undermines a traditional account of divine freedom (as in Plotinus). Williams contests whether Augustine can be read like this: the diversity and the relative hierarchies of finite being, as we have seen previously, are linked to a temporal process of generation and dependence, in which lack or deficiency are not merely there to serve some 'aesthetic' purpose for a detached observer, or impersonal principle; moreover, deficiency as such does not designate something evil per se (as Williams has reiterated above).[126] For Augustine, the universe does not maturate in accordance with some independent principle of harmony that has little connection to a personal God. Rather God elects a world that is "both temporal and interdependent," and it is this that underpins the self-determination of beings whereby "agents act upon each other, never at any one point attaining perfect balance within the world's history" (*IE*, 115).

Nonetheless, this Neoplatonic trajectory is subjected to an even fiercer attack, this time by Kathleen Sands. According to her, Augustine's theology of evil effectively denies "the tragic" since on the "rationalist" and "dualist" model proposed by him there is no event or act of evil which is ultimately "beyond comprehension or rehabilitation" (*IE*, 116). As such, it fails to deal with the radical contingency of the world, and consequently divides the world up into hard categories of good and bad agents, without taking into

125. Williams goes on to use an analogy to describe this: "A discord on a musical instrument is not the result of the instrument being interfered with by an external agency *called* discord, it is a function of the workings of what is there, of what constitutes the instrument itself" (Williams, "Insubstantial Evil," 112).

126. In Williams, "Insubstantial Evil," 115, we read: "Without sin, the hierarchy of the universe would have been a steady flow of interaction in which what is conventionally called the 'corruption', the disintegration, of elements is only a moment in their proper temporal unfolding and mutation, which is, in itself, good. It is only with the corruption of will and intelligence that change and passivity become problematic, infecting the whole of the world's order. Hence, Augustine's conviction that the Fall has *physical* consequences (human death)."

account the complexity and tragic interpenetration between virtue and vice. In creating these kind of divisions, Augustine lays the groundwork for an oppositional mentality—an "us-versus-them" ethic—that (at its worst) legitimates the oppression of those who do not conform to *my* conception of goodness (*IE*, 117), as in Augustine's repression of the Donatists.[127] It serves an "anxiety to secure moral fixity" through "the adversarial definition of evil in the present, and the negative account of it in the distant metaphysical horizon," "an anxiety about the maintenance of the threatened dominant position of the male, reasonable will." Evil-as-privation, for Sands, presupposes a metaphysics of "closure," one that "constantly slip[s] into polarisations of 'the Good' and 'the not-Good,'" "polarisations that encourage the identification of actual agents here and now with the Good and the not-Good, and the projection of failure and lack on to certain classes and categories of existence," such materiality, the body, women, minorities, and so on (*IE*, 117). It ultimately denies a tragic perspective which displays that even good actions can be entwined with negative outcomes, and that we cannot fully anticipate the historical shape of our decisions.

Here following Martha Nussbaum's proposal in *The Fragility of Goodness*, Sands wants to propose an account of "the good" that is "various, mobile, vulnerable, rather than unified and stable," (*IE*, 116) against an account of transcendent beatitude that denies historicity. Yet it is on precisely this point that Sands, according to Williams, misreads Augustine: on the contrary, the Bishop of Hippo readily affirms that "there is no timeless and stable goodness," "no incarnation of evil," since every "creaturely good is realised in *time*," even as "the perfection of goodness exists not as something that issues from a process, but as the eternal standard and direction of creaturely good" (*IE*, 117–18). Now it is precisely this latter move that Sands wants to reject, namely, any "transcendent measure of good." She distinguishes her account of the good as that which "emerges as a possible, a 'viable', wholeness and balance in the life of moral communities" (*IE*, 118). This serves to counteract the ahistorical and dualistic metaphysics of evil which Sands traces to Augustine.

But Williams wonders whether this denial has the desired effect Sands wants from it. Because if this is so, then it would imply an oppositional account of the good, whereby my good could be theoretically opposed to

---

127. Williams does contest this reading of the Donatist controversy: "Part of Augustine's gravamen against both Pelagians and Donatists is to do with their identification of possible states within history as bearers of a goodness that is somehow complete or adequate. The Donatist absolutises the purity of the empirical church; the Pelagian affirms the possibility of keeping the commandments of God. Both take the church out of time, in their different ways. The church which continues to pray 'forgive us our trespasses', is a church whose purity and integrity are inseparable from continuing self-questioning and penitence" (Williams, "Insubstantial Evil," 118).

yours, without mediation, or it could be conceived as so radically contingent, so alternating and diverging that no "'grammar' of continuity" can be found between different situations. Moreover, he goes on, it can also read as implying "that the Good of or for certain subjects might simply and finally fail or prove impossible of realisation." If this is the logical outgrowth of her position, then there are some stark conclusions to consider:

> The first reading implies that there are genuine (truthfully conceived) creaturely goods that can be realised only at the expense of the genuine goods of others [which is] a view [that is] hard to reconcile with any properly emancipatory ethic, since it is the argument ... of the slave-master. The second suggests that particular developments might render good what once was not, that torture or racial discrimination might be *made* good by historical changes. The third suggests that there are worldly subjects 'predestined' to final and irredeemable frustration. To appeal to the notion of a viable balance in a community's life as a way of avoiding the Hobbesian consequences of these possible readings (the war of all against all, the *inevitable* nonconvergence of creaturely good) will not really meet the case. It assumes that the reconciliation of partial and competing goods is itself a good to *be* pursued, without qualification, it seems. There is no argument to establish why this good should be exempt from the general prohibition against general goods. An absolutist assumption is being smuggled in under the guise of pragmatism. (*IE*, 119)

Augustine's theodicy is not averse to the inescapability of the tragic *within* time: he might say that the "world is tragic, in the sense that our fallen perceptions of the world are so flawed that we are constantly, and inevitably (since the Fall), involved in mistaken and conflictual accounts of our true interests." He does suggest that the after Fall our collective pursuance of the good, within the conflict of time and mutual limitation, means that we might need some level of coerciveness, as a matter of tragic necessity. But this only reaffirms that "*loss* is always bound up with creaturely virtue, [and] even sanctity." Moreover, because "there is no coercion that can ultimately overcome the perverse will, there are creaturely subjects whose good *is* eternally frustrated," even though these destinies are "contingent on a history," and therefore "not intrinsic to the nature of their good." What Augustine would reject is "a definition of tragic conflict as a *necessary* feature of created order," because it is precisely *that* which will provoke a "return to naked dualism," since there is no unity of the Good which we are able to progressively access. The metaphysical and eschatological upshot of this dualism intimates that there is "no convergence of goods," resulting in an "irreconcilable cosmic struggle, with no ontological priority accorded to either side" (*IE*, 119).

In contrast to Sands, Augustine proposes something that is simultaneously more radical and (arguably) more hopeful: because evil has been despatialized and temporalized, we can come to discern certain "processes" which we "identify as loss or corruption," those in which "we identify more clearly and truthfully . . . the whole interlocking pattern of the world's activity." Augustine's reflections on time, and the self's implication in it, means that "talking about God is always talking about the temporal processes of clarification, reconciliation, self-discovery in love, the processes that lead us beyond rivalry and self-protection" (*IE*, 120). Once more, Augustine's vision provides resources for engaging horrendous evils, without collapsing this recognition into ontological despair or radical indeterminacy. Returning again to the central plea posed at the beginning of the essay, Williams argues that Augustine's reflections on evil and the transcendence of the Good cannot be considered apart from his wider acceptance of a specifically Christian metaphysic: if evil is not deontologized and despatialized, in something like the manner described above, then can we follow Augustine in his portrayal of "God as subsistent and overflowing fullness," as 'the non-competitive other whose freedom makes us free" (*IE*, 121)?

What the above exposition has shown is that the question of evil is intrinsically related to one's vision of God. The Platonic-Augustinian assertion of evil-as-privation is based on the assumption of transcendent goodness, and that the world has a necessary relation to this truth, beauty, and goodness. Evil, on the other hand, comes about as a result of a historical process that is contingent and non-necessary. This is primarily evidenced in the distortion of intelligent agencies that have a greater capacity for creating harm and destruction than non-mental ones ('*corruptio optimi pessima*'). This explains why evil, despite being ontologically privative in nature, has effects in the world that are not privative, and also expands why it can exhibit a horrific positivity. Such does not, however, necessitate metaphysical pessimism: since goodness holds a transcendent sway over reality, and is more 'substantially' connected to its material and historical development,[128] this militates against any created part of reality as predestined to disaster—in the sense of being eternally fated, without any contingent involvement.[129] This Christian metaphysics helps to explain why we can coherently claim that materiality contributes positively to our knowledge of God, since creation participates in God's goodness as its cause. But we can also see why evil is explicable in

---

128. Cf. Burt, "Courageous Optimism."

129. This admittedly might sit in tension with Augustine's own later reflections on double predestination, but one can see how later—in Eriugena, for example—this Augustinian trajectory of privation leads to a revisioning of the doctrine of predestination itself.

this context: evil has no space in being, and therefore is not a thing which 'exists' in the way everything else does.[130] It comes as a result of a process, a privation within temporal being. Sinfulness means that our knowledge of God is always partially distorted by finite or perverted desires, but it does not mean that no truthful knowledge of God is possible. Because all of creation flows from goodness, and is providentially-directed to its respective goods, this means that our attempts to know the truth of being are never completely amorphous or eternally alienated. Our reflections on the world, on its repleteness of beauty and form, can give us truthful access to the transcendent, to that ordering reality that gives shape and unity to all things.

This background helps us as we move to the final chapter, where I place our discussion of tragedy within Williams's expansions on the self. Apart from this wider context, the distention and fragmentation of the soul could imply an unremitting hemorrhaging of the subject, a never-ending rupturing that destroys any coherency of self, and which glorifies pain and woundedness as an end in itself.[131] But as we will see, Williams's reflections on selfhood are placed within an eschatological context that refuses pessimism, or any final dissolution of the subject. Instead, it is placed in a frame in which the self's dispossessive and kenotic release of old identities are *not* opposed to the subject's good. Our continual self-transcendence and estrangement involves us, to be sure, in risk and difficulty for sure, but it is by-no-means a hopeless progression. It certainly does not imply a sublime elevation of sacrificial abjection-without-return, or a nebulous infinite opposed to human intellection. For Christianity, this self-transcendence is 'shaped,' primarily by the character of God, who is the *summum bonum* of all creatures, and by the crucified and risen Christ who gives meaning to our rhythms of surrender and reception. Such patterning implies that self-sacrifice and kenosis is held open to the gift of a *novum*, and the unending plerosis of God's vitality. It speaks of a tragedy held within grace of an excess that cannot be foreclosed by reward or merit. We cannot predict the circumstances of every decision, nor fully predict their ultimate outcomes. For the Christian, this means we live without certitude, but not without a certain kind of trust. Such emphasis means that we need an "eschatology" that is able to address tragedy "without diminishing its seriousness."[132] And it is these themes to which we now turn.

---

130. As Williams writes elsewhere, Augustine effectively "demythologizes" the concept of evil, since for Augustine evil is "not a *thing* in the universe" but rather a distortion of reality itself. See Williams, "Review of *Augustine on Evil*," 96.

131. For a critique of postmodern approaches to the topic of pain, see Ward, "Suffering and Incarnation."

132. Williams, "Christian Art and Cultural Pluralism," 42.

8

Rowan Williams II

The Tragic within Grace, or On the Politics of Estrangement[1]

In this penultimate chapter, I will try to disentangle Williams's reflections on the tragic. The argument is made that Williams reads tragedy through the heuristic of *estrangement*, specifically as this is polarized on the trope of *learning*, that is, on the processes in which the self becomes distanced from self within time. Connected to this Augustinian doctrine of the soul's distention is Williams's affirmation that our existence as finite agents implies a fragile subjectivity that is always labile to the risk of tragic irreversibility. But for Williams, such loss does not necessitate a closure of being, as if loss could be read as a kind of transcendental limitation (in the manner of a Kantian *a priori*). This is because deprivation always happens within the regime of history, and in the complex systems of meaning-making that form a part of human enculturation. Such implies that we cannot preclude that our knowledge of loss *as* loss can open us to other ways of being-in-the-world, a sense of avenues closing, and different paths widening, while being apprised that consolatory visions do not save us from difficulty. We cannot know beforehand whether this or that tragedy will occasion a disastrous climax, or whether it will destroy any possibility of integration, or something else. This constitutes our tragic state of uncertainty.

But to assume that this necessitates, in every instance, an irremediable devastation is precisely to claim too much, because for Williams it is precisely that we *know* such loss, and are able to *speak* and *mourn* it, that allows

---

1. The phrase "the tragic within grace" is drawn from Williams, *Grace and Necessity*, 114.

such events to be included within sign-making, which is basic for our sense of 'world.' Furthermore, since all of this occurs within a process governed by God's loving care, no distention, however fragmented, can finally separate us from this providential direction. Because God is transcendent, and therefore not subjected to the chances of history, we can trust that there is a final order that gives unity to existence, without the implication of a cheaply-acquired theodicy. Pertinent for Williams is that language implicates us in a community of language-bearers: we cannot communicate without placing ourselves in a socio-political context. The self does not evolve in isolation, and so the reverberations of tragedy are felt by others, since its material consequences happen in a nexus of causation that includes communities within its expansion of effects. This means that the tragic cannot be reduced to an individualist struggle of actors who are discharged with a private fate. Because tragedies influence communities, this means that its occurrence cannot be removed from the context of political mediation, and how such changes are re-worked by the societies it affects.

On Learning[2]

It is clear that Rowan Williams's theology has had a persistent focus on the exigencies and disciplines of *learning*, on how the practices of patient observance—or *attente*[3]—can contribute to the moral growth of human personality.[4] As a philosophical theologian he is concerned to account for how we, as finite beings, are educated and formed in our language-usage,[5] that is, with how we are to negotiate the claims of 'otherness,' and that communality given within the dynamics of speech. He is focused particularly here on how this process becomes a necessary element in our discovery and dilation of truth, since there can be no privatized or punctiliar 'meaning' discerned by lone agents. There is no sublimely-rendered 'otherness' beyond the reaches of intelligent communication, since how could we even cognize 'what-is-other' without the adjudications of language itself? But even more

---

2. This section is expanded and heavily edited version of another essay of mine. For this, see Delport, "Of Danger and Difficulty."

3. The reference here is to Simone Weil, who has had a significant influence on Williams's thinking from early on. This can be seen in Williams, "Simone Weil and the Necessary Non-Existence of God," in *Wrestling with Angels*, 203–27.

4. Williams, *Lost Icons*, 13–63. Also see Higton, *Difficult Gospel*, 89–111; and Myers, *Christ the Stranger*, 51–58, for a summary of this aspect of his thinking.

5. Williams, "Trinity and Revelation," in *On Christian Theology*, 131: "Theology . . . is perennially liable to be seduced by the prospect of bypassing how it *learns* its own language."

profoundly, and from a metaphysical vantage, this certainly cannot be the case since for Williams *all* of reality is teleologically-directed towards intellection; the world is always-already saturated with an excess of significance[6] that participates, and is consummated in, the Father's creative and loving contemplation of the world itself within the Logos and the Spirit.[7] 'Difference' and 'difficulty,' within this theological (and Hegelian) model, are not then amorphous generalities, devoid of description or human 'recognition,' but are precisely *thinkable* entities since they are continually discovered through the dialectic of linguistic and interpersonal mediation.[8] These realities are thinkable just because they can be brought into speech and articulated amongst fellow language-bearers. But such a process implies that meaning can never be an individual project undertaken, but is irreducibly relational, entrenched within the interactions and communication of human agents. We are always-already placed within a context that exceeds our grasp, which implies that there can be no 'private' articulations of 'the self' apart from the negotiations of language,[9] and that there is always a larger context in which our attempts at communication are to be placed, so that the significance thereof continually awaits a further social and metaphysical accretion. There is a perennial openness towards learning, and there is always a potentially deeper perspective from which something can be engaged ("Humility is endless" as T. S. Eliot once said.[10]).

This means that the subject's engagement with 'difficulty' should not be seen as an 'indulgent' exercise in problems for their own sake, as if "one's moral being [were] somehow heightened by the mere fact of having become problematic"[11] (recalling here again Cornelius Ernst apropos Donald MacKinnon). Rather, for Williams 'difficulty' is always tied to a moral framework of "dispossession," which in his usage implies a refusal to halt "the process of exchange"[12] that constitutes us in our humanness. Any attempt to extricate ourselves from this continuing conversation would imply a mythological picture in which we could establish for ourselves a *locus standi* apart from the unfolding drama of history, claiming thereby for ourselves a 'divine'

---

6. See our previous discussion of *The Edge of Words*.

7. Cf. Williams, "What Does Love Know?"

8. Williams, "Hegel and the Gods of Postmodernity," 25–34; "Logic and Spirit in Hegel," 35–52; and "Politics and Metaphysics," 53–76; all in *Wrestling with Angels*. Also cf. *The Edge of Words*, 186–97.

9. Williams, "The Suspicion of Suspicion: Wittgenstein and Bonhoeffer," in *Wrestling with Angels*, 186–202.

10. T. S. Eliot, "East Coker II," in *Collected Poems*, 187.

11. Ernst, "Ethics and the Play of Intelligence," 326.

12. Williams, "Politics and Metaphysics," 53.

perspective above the fray of temporal strictures.[13] A conscious and willing avoidance of 'difficulty'—here repeating Cora Diamond once more—would connote a "deflection," a refusal to accept our finite "bodies."[14] It would imply a refusal to appreciate "the apparent resistance by reality to one's ordinary modes of life, including one's ordinary modes of thinking," and could be read as a failure to acknowledge "the difficulty" of being "shouldered out of how one thinks, or how one is supposed to think."[15] These words by Diamond summarize justly Williams's thoughts (as they did MacKinnon's), showing how for him the acknowledgement of 'difficulty' or 'actuality' has a deep moral and political register within his thinking, and cannot be reduced to a love of the 'problematic' for its own sake. Instead, his concern with 'difficulty' is tied to a vision of spiritual transformation that refuses to understand such moral growth as a reductive or privatized 'technology,'[16] as if such development was exclusively about self-expression, self-management, or any kind of egoism for that matter. Spiritual growth cannot be a solitary accomplishment, apart from a 'world' of interaction; and so the denial of 'difficulty' and limited perception, within the sphere of interpersonal engagement and spirituality, can only imply a furtive 'ideological' bid towards a conclusive power, a 'totalized' knowledge that claims metaphysical comprehensiveness for febrile parochialisms.[17] This aspect of moral expansion is essential for his understanding of the self, and its place within the order of the world, and requires that we tease out this theme a bit further, since it remains important for the discussion that is to follow.

The Self in Fragments: On Tragicomic Augustinianism[18]

Williams's dilations on the self, overall, place an emphasis on "the inescapable significance of time as a correlate of bodiliness."[19] Personhood cannot

13. Cf. Williams, "Theological Integrity," in *On Christian Theology*, 6: "[R]eligious and theological integrity is possible as and when discourse about God *declines the attempt to take God's point of view* (i.e., a 'total perspective')."
14. Diamond, "The Difficulty of Reality," 59.
15. Diamond, "The Difficulty of Reality," 58.
16. Cf. Foucault, "Technologies of the Self," 16–49.
17. Cf. Williams's remarks in "Theological Integrity."
18. In what follows, I have been greatly helped by Ryan Green's "Kenosis and Ascent." I have addressed this topic elsewhere in Delport, "*Interior intimo meo*." That essay did not give significant space to Williams's Hegelianism. My presentation here aims to supplement that account somewhat.
19. Williams, "Author's Introduction," in *Wrestling with Angels*, xvi.

be prized from its materiality and relational connectedness, especially as its physicality and temporal placement contribute to meaning. For Williams, there is no *matter* without *mattering,* no objectivity apart from an intellectual investiture: "the body is never helpfully described as an object like other material objects," since it is through "that curious material transaction called language" that "we continue to recognize that the oddity of this material reality that is *my* body is an oddity shared by other materially recognizable bodies."[20] As becomes clear, Williams's phenomenology is resourced by Aquinas and Merleau-Ponty: the body *is* the form of the soul and therefore is "a *meaning* portion of matter."[21] The en-mattered body is inseparable from the limits of communicative and relational exchange; it is temporal and therefore cannot exceed its material circumscription, since "what we are *are* our limits."[22] Our embeddedness means that we are finite, but it is precisely through these strictures (here adapting Heideggerian terms) that we are opened to "the being-at-hand of love."[23] This is radically *incarnational* because what we are concerned with here is not "some mysterious inner core, but my body." He thinks that if we do not come to love "our mortal vulnerability," then our care of others will be stripped of its pedagogical basis, namely in the love of God and the love of self.[24] This is because "we encounter God truly only when we accept our mortal fragility for what it is, do not seek to escape it, but put our trust in a God who speaks and relates to us through flesh."[25]

Consequently, Christians should not aspire to an untrammelled existence separate from embodiment; ours is not a gnostic escape from the bodily but an incarnated discipline "to be perfected in grace."[26] It is within our temporal fragility that sanctity is received and discovered, where we come to "the recognition of the holy within the contingent order," even though this progression is punctuated by the "disruptive and 'discontinuous'" features of everyday life, by the continuing threat of "exile and alienation, loss and death."[27] Such means that our subjectivity remains exposed to the stochastic

20. Williams, "On Being a Human Body," 406.

21. Williams, "On Being a Human Body," 406. For more on this account of the soul, see Williams, *Lost Icons,* 171–228. Also see Williams, "Macrina's Deathbed Revisited," 227–46, for a discussion on the relation between reason, animality, the body as well as the passions.

22. Williams, "The Suspicion of Suspicion," in *Wrestling with Angels,* 186.

23. Williams, "On Being a Human Body," 408.

24. Williams, *A Ray of Darkness,* 35.

25. Williams, "Good for Nothing?," 18.

26. Williams, *The Wound of Knowledge,* 61.

27. Williams, "Troubled Breasts," 77.

flux of "unstable circumstances," and it is this that serves as the ontological foundation for the persistence of tragedy within the world. However, what is important to stress is that for the Christian an existence within time's unfolding compass is about how these indeterminacies "bring to light who and what we actually are," and so consequently requires a discipline without repression or a retreat from bodiliness, but a therapeutic transformation of physical desire: "what Christ delivers us from is not bodily circumstance, contingency, or instability," but instead "the habits of mind and heart that make of this environment only a theatre for our private obsessions to be staged and our lust for control to be exercised."[28]

This emphasis on our rapacious drive towards mastery, or the *libido dominandi*, transitions us now to Augustine. A discussion of this figure is apt now since he is considered by some as being the foundational theorist of Western subjectivity, a proto-Cartesian thinker who anticipates the self-reflexivity of modernity.[29] Williams takes a serious departure from this perspective: in his estimate, Augustine resists the suasions to ground self-knowledge within the ego. He does so by placing the soul within an *epektasis* of desire, in an active movement towards God in a continuing self-displacement and de-centering. In his estimate, the Augustinian self is at its profoundest recesses one formed through a "radical incompleteness and other-directedness."[30] Augustine's understanding of the soul is *relational*, and is ontologically analogous to "the self-relatedness of the divine essence,"[31] so that rather than being "proto-Cartesian or proto-Kantian,"[32] Augustine aims "to 'demythologise' the solitary ego by establishing the life of the mind firmly in relation to God," a God understood as "self-gift, as movement to otherness and distance in self-imparting love."[33]

For Augustine, our identity is hidden within the relations of the Trinity, in the divine *memoria*, and therefore is not self-constituting. This differentiates Augustine from the Platonic account of *anamnesis*—or so Williams thinks—since Augustine is not talking about the soul as "a non-temporal thing." The self is in "some sense *made*, by the infinitely painstaking attention to the contingent strangeness of remembered experience in conscious reference to

28. Williams, "'Tempted As We Are,'" 400–1.
29. Taylor, *Sources of the Self*, 127–42.
30. Williams, "The Paradoxes of Self-knowledge," 127.
31. Williams, "Sapientia and the Trinity," 317.
32. Williams, "Sapientia and the Trinity," 318.
33. Williams, "Sapientia and the Trinity," 331. Williams considers the trinity itself to involve a movement of desirous relation within the immanent relations of triune being, which is in turn the ontological foundation of our own created longing towards God and other-directed desire. For this, see Williams, "The Deflections of Desire," 115–35.

God."[34] The soul grows within time, dilating out of a specific biography which comes to fruition "now in a new set of particular options, responses and determinations, providing a resource of given past-ness out of which the next decision and action can flow."[35] Augustine's emphasis on *memoria* implies the inevitability of self-fabrication in time, and a denial of any notion of the soul's timelessness.[36] This sense of contingency and constructedness is linked to the imagery of the soul as a wandering pilgrim, existing without a final home in time. Its movement is continual, everlastingly drawn towards its final cause. However, the counterpart to this ascent is that the soul continues to be 'wounded' by divinity (here referencing the imagery of Gregory of Nyssa[37] and John of the Cross[38]), and so is fragmented within its *distentio*, and in its inability to reach an achieved unity within time.[39]

This coheres with the Pauline concept of *kenosis*, and its cruciform pattern, which requires that we leave behind identities which hinder us from inhabiting Christ's identity. Precisely because we are not God, and therefore limited, personal integrity cannot be achieved apart from self-dispossession, an acknowledgement that our true identity is 'ungraspable' (to reference Philippians 2). Of course, such an unhanding of self is always contextualized by resurrection, by the plenitude of the divine *memoria*, and therefore is not an emptying-without-reserve. The Bishop of Hippo suggests that despite the fragmentary nature of the soul, there is still the hope that God "can make a story, a continuous reality, out of the chaos of unhappiness, 'homeless' wandering, hurt and sin."[40] So there is a double-sidedness to desire here: on the one hand, it is what continually draws us to our final beatitude in the life of God, however, on the other, this attraction implies a perpetual non-satisfaction

---

34. Williams, *The Wound of Knowledge*, 71.

35. Williams, *Resurrection*, 23.

36. Williams, *Resurrection*, 24.

37. In his homilies on the Canticles, Gregory reflects several times on the 'wound of love.' For instance in his sermon on Song 1:15—2:7, he says, "See, then, the soul that has been exalted through the divine ascents sees in herself the | sweet arrow of love by which she is wounded and makes boast of such a blow by saying, *I have been wounded by love*" (Gregory of Nyssa, *Homilies on the Song of Songs*, 141).

38. The poetry of John of the Cross is replete with this imagery: in his own rendition of the Canticles he says, "In solitude she bided, / And in solitude her nest she made: In solitude he guided / His loved-one through the shade / Whose solitude the wound of love has made (*También en soledad de amor herido*)." The translation is taken from one of the *Canciones* in *The Poems of St. John of the Cross*, 27.

39. For some reflections on the connections between *distentio* and 'woundedness,' see Ward, "Suffering and Incarnation," 203.

40. Williams, *The Wound of Knowledge*, 72.

this side of the eschatological veil, a "questing" that remains vigilant against becoming "glued to any object of satisfaction."[41]

This dynamic is most clearly explicated in an essay on Augustine's *De doctrina*. Here Williams unpacks Augustine's distinction between *frui* and *uti* ("enjoyment" and "use") in parallel to the pair of *res* and *signum* ("thing" and "sign").[42] For Augustine, we can approach any particular *res* in two distinct ways: either we treat it as an end in itself, or as a sign towards something else. Since God for Augustine is supremely *res*—the one who forms the context in which all things are to be meaningfully positioned—Augustine argues that created reality should be read as *signum*, since it does not have its existence within itself. Therefore "no worldly *res* is securely settled as a fixed object 'meaning' itself, or tied in a fixed designation." Such implies that "no worldly state of affairs can be allowed to terminate human desire ... all that is present to us in and as language is potentially *signum* in respect of the unrepresentable God."[43] Hereby the self is moved by *dilectio* towards God, who as the *telos* of human desire is the only one who can be enjoyed for his own sake, being the *res* itself. But since this is the case, and it is only within God's life that *res* and *signum*—or essence and existence—coincide, it follows that created reality can only be 'used' towards 'enjoyment,' since it is only God who is self-existing.

Language like this is easily open to misinterpretation, since as post-Kantians we are suspicious of categorizing people as 'means' rather than 'ends.' But in Williams's opinion, Augustine's language of *uti* avoids such a conclusion, since he orientates the final end of *dilectio* towards God. Precisely because God is the end of desiring, human beings should not be treated as an 'end' but rather as a *signum* towards our ultimate source: as he says "the language of *uti* is designed to warn against an attitude towards any finite person or object that terminates their meaning in their capacity to satisfy my desire, that treats them as the end of desire, conceiving my meaning in terms of them and theirs in terms of me."[44] Augustine's deployment of the *uti-frui* distinction does not justify an instrumentalization of human persons for the sake of some transcendent goal—completion or self-satisfaction—at the expense of another's given dignity. One could even suggest that it is precisely the opposite: it is to affirm that *no human object* can be reduced to a mere tool precisely because it remains a *signum*—an *imago dei*. Since desire is infinite, no worldly object can bring it to completion: only God can do

---

41. Williams, "The Paradoxes of Self-knowledge," 131.
42. Williams, "Language, Reality and Desire," 138–50.
43. Williams, "Language, Reality and Desire," 145.
44. Williams, "Language, Reality and Desire," 140.

that. Therefore, to speculatively project any person as the 'end' of my desire would be to indulge in a toxic form of self-alienation. It would idolatrously claim that a finite entity could act as 'God' for me. This would be the supreme instance of the *libido dominandi*, in which "the subject distorts its self-perception into fixity," into a form of ontological closure whereby selfhood is reduced to "the meeting of needs in the determinate form in which they are mediated to [me] in the perception of the Other."[45] If we become stuck within this restriction, according to Williams, then we hinder spiritual growth, thinking that our good finds completion within time.

Moreover, Augustine's account of desiring is linked to his idea that the self is "bound up with the desire for the Good," for *iustitia*. Such means that "the self in construction is a self whose good is understood in terms of a universally shareable good." For Williams, there is no true understanding of the self apart from a wider ordering of just relations between human subjects, and therefore necessitates "the dissolution of any fantasy that the good can be definitively possessed in history by any individual or any determinate group in isolation."[46] But this refusal implies that we accept a certain level of dispossessive negotiation, in which one must explain oneself and make oneself accessible to another.[47] My own interiority is therefore mediated: there is no immediate 'access' to the self, no bypassing of the deposits of language and history, and the various strategies we may adopt to make ourselves understood by another, and vice versa. In Williams's mind, this negates any uncomplicated "transparency" or "authenticity" one might have, since "I do not cease to be *vulnerable* to other accounts of myself, to the pressure to revise what I say of myself."[48] To quote Jean-Luc Nancy, one could say that for Williams "The absoluteness . . . of [the body's] sense, and the absoluteness of sense 'in general' . . . is not kept 'within' [the body], since it is itself nothing but the being-exposed, the being-touched of this 'inside.' As body, the absolute is common, it is the community of bodies."[49]

Similarly for Augustine and Williams, such vulnerability implies a *kenosis*, an imitation of the *infirma divinitas* as this paradoxically betokens an "emptiness of meaning and power" which simultaneously, and paradoxically, makes him a *signum* of the divine.[50] For Williams, the story of Christ's

---

45. Williams, "Know Thyself," 223–24.
46. Williams, "Know Thyself," 222.
47. See Williams, "Interiority and Epiphany," in *On Christian Theology*, 240.
48. Williams, "Interiority and Epiphany," 241.
49. Nancy, *The Birth to Presence*, 204.
50. Williams, "Language, Reality and Desire," 144.

resurrection and crucifixion—here in a quasi-Derridean fashion[51]—"represents the absence and deferral that is basic to *signum* as such," and is also the means "whereby God engages our desire so that it is freed from its own pull towards finishing, towards presence and possession."[52] So rather than affirming a desire to control, Augustine's theology implies that we surrender identities which place the ego at its magnetic centre, and come to find our deepest interiority in the exteriority of kenotic self-giving, thereby blurring any uncomplicated boundary between 'inside' and 'outside.'

The general trend of this take on Augustine is analogous to my earlier comments on Donald MacKinnon, who as we mentioned tends to conceptualize temporal categories in terms of loss, and particularly our tragic deficiencies. The reoccurring motifs of misdirection, fragmentation, sacrificial suffering, and a pervasive regard for ontological woundedness certainly invites these comparisons. Williams in other places has drawn explicit connections between the Augustinian vision and tragic limitation, as when he says that for Augustine "an authentically contingent world is one in which you cannot guarantee the compatibility of goods,"[53] or when he deduces that for Augustine the "world is tragic, in the sense that our fallen perceptions of the world are so flawed that we are constantly, and inevitably (since the Fall), involved in mistaken and conflictual accounts of our true interests," and therefore that "*loss* is always bound up with creaturely virtue, [and] even sanctity."[54] The connections on this score, therefore, are quite apparent, even though it should be added that this picture does not imply a fatalistic or pessimistic resignation: as Williams shows in *The Tragic Imagination*, moral augmentation is indeed a potential outcome of tragic fiction and experience (something that MacKinnon, in his own way, also gestures towards). It is therefore to be distinguished from pure 'stoicism.'

But in saying this, I am not implying that Williams is in unanimity with MacKinnon on every point. Brett Gray has argued that Williams's Augustinianism privileges a metaphysics more congenial to the claims of orthodoxy. MacKinnon was dogmatically more unstable in this regard, and tended to leave open the question of an eschatological redress of the tragic, due to his aversion towards theodicy. However, Williams is somewhat more open to this option, since his fundamentally Augustinian position "transposes" human finitude into "an almost eudaemonic register." Hereby the *distentio* of the self is placed within an eschatology in which the finality of the goodness

---

51. See McCurry, "Towards a Poetics of Theological Creativity."
52. Williams, "Language, Reality and Desire," 148.
53. Williams, "Saving Time," 322.
54. Williams, "Insubstantial Evil," 119.

is paramount—here in accordance with Augustine's Platonic equation of the good with the highest principle of being. Moreover, this vision is mediated through a specific "social manifold," namely the church, which assists the believer's own gradual and incremental approach "towards repair."[55] In Gray's phrasing, this constitutes Williams's own attempt to put forward "an amelioration of the tragic."[56] Even though this should be distinguished from a final cancelation or erasure of history, it does imply that tragedy as such "does not persist as an intractable fate" since new futures and options may be opened by God's providence.[57] Williams does not at all deny that healing and reparation can take place within time,[58] nor does he deny that the "work of grace" and "victory" is "never produced by history itself."[59] Williams does not oppose revelational history to history-as-such - as if there could a purely secular recounting of time—and yet he would still insist on an eschatological reserve insofar as there is "no *temporal* mending of the drama."[60] Redemption always comes as a supernatural augmentation of nature, and therefore is not resourced from within human agency. To assert otherwise would be to deny the gospel and our radical dependency as creatures. As such, the soteriological tension will continue to persist throughout the interregnum of the ages; there is neither a perfect balancing of relations nor a comprehensive healing this side of the eschaton. As Williams imagines Christ saying in one of his poems: "here is / not innocence but absolution, for / your scars are true but I (always) / will bleed in them."[61]

But one could ask (as others have): if the MacKinnon-trajectory within his thinking predisposes Williams to 'tragic' sensibilities more generally, and his reading of Augustine in particular, then could one not assert that this amounts to a one-sided presentation? One could raise this question with legitimacy. However, I have hopefully already shown that these affinities within Williams's thought are not absolutized, and that there are qualifications that counter its over-emphasis. Nevertheless, it is worthwhile developing these themes a bit further, especially as they reveal that more explicit 'comic' register which remains active in his contribution. It is for this reason that we turn to the influence of Hegel and Gillian Rose, in the hope of recovering some of these other trajectories.

55. Gray, *Jesus in the Theology of Rowan Williams*, 127–28.
56. Gray, *Jesus in the Theology of Rowan Williams*, 134.
57. Gray, *Jesus in the Theology of Rowan Williams*, 136.
58. Williams, "Saving Time," 321–22.
59. Williams, "Insubstantial Evil," 118–19.
60. Gray, *Jesus in the Theology of Rowan Williams*, 140.
61. Williams, "Twelfth Night," in *The Poems of Rowan Williams*, 25.

Overall, Williams's approach to Hegel is to be found in the primacy that he places on *thinking*, that is, how is it possible to conceptualize anything in particular. In "Hegel and the Gods of Postmodernity,"[62] Williams situates Hegel in opposition to a postmodern emphasis on sheer negativity (or *différance*) in which "the sacred" is equated with pure "absence" and "rupture"[63]—a move that has strong affinities for the post-Kantian sublime of unknowable transcendence. Williams takes issue with the anti-representational strand of this tradition, which in its allergy to any invocation of 'presence' ends up privileging a realm always-already *beyond* the interpersonal field of human interaction and speaking. The practical upshot of this is a perpetual ironizing and relativizing of perspectives, with little resource for a social mediation of viewpoints in the here and now, because the staking of a particular representation means, on this view, that I am already compromised from the outset. For one thing, if I attempt to represent I have claimed an uncomplicated access to the representational object, and if I attempt to interpret and understand the presentation of another speaker, I risk reducing them to my own co-ordinates. It is for this reason that Hegel is often paraded within critical theory as the prime example of that "totalizing dialectic" that reduces otherness to "*my* other," to "a resolvable, confrontable difference."[64] Or to use the standard lingo, it implies a return to sameness. But Williams thinks that Hegel's speculative philosophy, on the contrary, constitutes an attempt "to challenge the all-sufficiency of the polarity of simple identity and simple difference." This is because what is "thinkable is so precisely because thinking is not content with the abstraction of mutual exclusiveness, but struggles to conceive a structured wholeness nuanced enough to contain what appeared to be contradictories."[65] To adopt Hegel's own language, thinking requires a transition from the immediacy of something like sense-certainty, with its particularities of the *here*, *this* and *now*, towards a more universal account of perception that will be able to accrue a multiplicity of properties to the object-in-question.[66] In this way, it achieves a universality of concepts in an oscillating and unending concreteness of phenomenological description, whereby consciousness achieves an understanding of the object within "the

---

62. Williams, "Hegel and the Gods of Postmodernity," in *Wrestling with Angels*, 25–34.
63. Williams, "Hegel and the Gods of Postmodernity," 27.
64. Williams, "Hegel and the Gods of Postmodernity," 27.
65. Williams, "Hegel and the Gods of Postmodernity," 29–30.
66. This is the argument that can be found in Hegel's reflections on 'consciousness.' For this, see Hegel, *The Phenomenology of Spirit*, §§90–165/63–102.

totality of its determinations."[67] It is in this light that Williams argues that, for Hegel, metaphysical language in its general thrust is "bound up with the making of sense," a move which distinguishes Hegelian thought from any "voluntarist play."[68] This kind of negativity does not emphasize the transcendent as an unspeakable rupture; rather, it requires a kind of "moral and spiritual dispossession and recreation" on our part.[69] This mediating dispossession here militates against a "depoliticized" extraction from the human speaking-situation in which "there is a subtle suggestion that social and linguistic order (as opposed to this or that particular and questionable order) is what we need to be delivered from."[70]

In "Logic and Spirit in Hegel,"[71] Williams argues that for Hegel thoughts and ideas cannot be engaged abstractly since they are always placed within the environment of their arrival, what he calls "their concrete, time-taking actuality."[72] There is no thinking of any particularity without *mediation*, a term which he defines as something that is "realised and maintained by something other than itself alone." For Hegel, *otherness is always potentially thinkable*, which means that any claim of "absolute otherness is fundamentally confused."[73] But because this context is never circumscribable, this means that thought takes place *within* a horizon of "an infinite relatedness, a comprehensive intelligibility," a reality which we ultimately call God.[74] Much like Augustine, Williams's Hegel understands that there is no "timeless subjectivity." Consciousness, since it is mediated, is tied to "the recognition of the self in the other," in what is truly *different* to the ego.[75] It should be registered that the language of 'recognition' has a deep resonance for Hegel, insofar as it plays a salient role in the continual re-discovery of rationality and selfhood. "Self-consciousness is *in* and *for itself* while and as a result of its being in and for itself for an other," which means that being-as-such, for

---

67. Hegel, *The Phenomenology of Spirit*, §788/422. Or as Hegel says in §789/423, where he says that "the object" is to be conceived as "in part a shape of consciousness per se and in part a number of such shapes that we gather together, in which the totality of the moments of the object and of the conduct of consciousness can be pointed out only as having been dissolved in the totality's moments."
68. Williams, "Hegel and the Gods of Postmodernity," 30.
69. Williams, "Hegel and the Gods of Postmodernity," 31.
70. Williams, "Hegel and the Gods of Postmodernity," 31.
71. Williams, "Logic and Spirit in Hegel," in *Wrestling with Angels*, 35–50.
72. Williams, "Logic and Spirit in Hegel," 35.
73. Williams, "Logic and Spirit in Hegel," 36.
74. Williams, "Logic and Spirit in Hegel," 38.
75. Williams, "Logic and Spirit in Hegel," 41.

Hegel, is perceived and understood "only as a recognized being."[76] This is not a conflictual model that supposes a necessary repression or reduction of one pole of the relation to another. Rather, we achieve a concretized freedom that is drawn out of "the otherness of what is given,"[77] in which individuality is not conceived *over-against* or in *competition with* some kind of "passive externality."[78] To do so would make one guilty of the *one-sidedness* (*Einseitigkeit*) that Hegel's speculative philosophy is at pains to oppose. For Williams, this means that the development of Spirit (or consciousness) is thus both *ecstatic* and *kenotic*, a self-augmenting and self-renouncing movement of "the self's being-in-the-other"—a move which (according to Williams) is simply a contemporization of the Christian notion of love.[79]

More could be added but enough has been said to lay the groundwork for his reception of Gillian Rose (who lies heavily in the background of the Hegel essays). The most explicit indications of this influence are found in two texts in particular: in his earlier text ("Between Politics and Metaphysics"), Williams attempts to outline a metaphysical register that takes historicity seriously, one that does not halt that "process of exchange" as this discloses the world as *difficult*.[80] The trope of 'difficulty' is a reoccurring theme in Williams's corpus, and carries with it overtones of attending and waiting, to use the language of Simone Weil,[81] of being committed to a re-description of phenomena, without reducing them to an easily digestible index that simply serves wish-fulfilment. One part of this intractability is that our speech takes place within a historical and temporal continuum, a sense of having recognized that collective meaning is not limited to my selfhood. Since we are sign-making creatures, we are concerned with that which "sustains intelligibility in the exchanges and negotiations that constitute our actuality," and not therefore with inexplicable and rhapsodic articulations of the ego. I can only work and communicate what I want to say within "a distinct accumulation of past negotiation" in which all unique vantages are made "accessible,"[82] so that our attempts at meaning-making are able to be "followed" by others.[83] This is essential to the process of coming-to-understand, since apart from being able to follow and repeat argumentation, we are not yet in a position

---

76. Hegel, *The Phenomenology of Spirit*, §178/109.
77. Williams, "Logic and Spirit in Hegel," 43–44.
78. Williams, "Logic and Spirit in Hegel," 45.
79. Williams, "Logic and Spirit in Hegel," 48.
80. Williams, "Between Politics and Metaphysics," 53.
81. See Weil, *Waiting on God*.
82. Williams, "Between Politics and Metaphysics," 54.
83. Williams, "Between Politics and Metaphysics," 57.

to grasp what is being represented, and so would be unable to chart "how error arises,"[84] since without an intelligible basis for political arguments we would be unable to recognize our *mistakes*. Rose suggests that every claim for meaning is socially implicated, and is not created by *me* alone: it is, to use her staple terminology, "the taking of a *position*," and yet such positioning cannot be abstracted from "the entirety of the path" which is yet to be undertaken, and therefore should not be foreclosed.[85]

This emphasis on staking a position does not imply a hopelessly antagonistic model, because it is through our discovery of the-self-in-the-other—albeit within "scarcity"—that we come to an awareness of shareable goods, a context of "potential abundance,"[86] "a common life" that exceeds exclusionary competition.[87] On the speculative level, this wager on the shareability of goods—that my goods are bound up with yours, that our interests are connected—suggests an "intelligible structure" that is not the product of "arbitrary willed options,"[88] since for Williams (as for Thomas Aquinas) knowledge about 'being' is primarily about the deepening of intellection, and not the imposition of will.[89] From this metaphysical perspective, the discovery of a non-conflictive account of the good implies, on the one hand, a universalizing abstraction from particular experiences towards concepts that are comprehensive and simple enough to grasp multiplicity, and on the other hand, it suggests an ethical posture of "dispossession" (or "collaboration"), a coming to an awareness that *my* good exceeds "any individual decision or project,"[90] since (once more) there is no personal good that is opposed to the good of others. On the contrary, our understanding of what is truly good is expanded through differing examples of goodness.

For Williams, our intellection of the good is achieved in an engagement with particular standpoints as they continue to unfold within time; but this does not mean that the Good-as-such, the transcendent Good in the Platonic sense, is produced through these contingencies. The Good can be represented in negotiation, and yet it cannot be reduced to any individual representation. On this reading, Hegel is distinguishable from what Williams calls "the pathos of perpetual negation,"[91] as exemplified in

---

84. Williams, "Between Politics and Metaphysics," 57.
85. Williams, "Between Politics and Metaphysics," 61.
86. Williams, "Between Politics and Metaphysics," 55.
87. Williams, "Between Politics and Metaphysics," 56.
88. Williams, "Between Politics and Metaphysics," 57.
89. Williams, "Between Politics and Metaphysics," 73.
90. Williams, "Between Politics and Metaphysics," 59.
91. Williams, "Between Politics and Metaphysics," 69.

the post-Kantian sublimities of postmodernity (e.g., Jean-François Lyotard, Jacques Derrida). Of course, Williams and Rose admit that there is both a surplus and entropy in the cultural bids for meaning—since reconciliation does not dissolve otherness—but this does not imply that a "labour of analogy" between "processes of production" is unachievable.[92] Conflicting paradigms may be agonistic, and yet there remains a hope that through a commitment to negotiation, we can charter avenues of commonality.

Williams's recent essay on Rose could, however, be read as an attempt to provide a balance to the more austere vision given in his previous readings of Hegel. Here he emphasizes that Hegel's dialectic can be described in comedic rather than tragic terms, a specific distinction which he explicitly takes from Rose.[93] As far as definitions go, Williams follows Hegel, arguing that "Comedy arises from the gap between what we think we are and what in fact we are," in which "the more developed the apparent mastery of the environment by the subject, the more developed are the comic possibilities."[94] This is simply a reflection of the Hegelian idea that comedies at their height (e.g., Aristophanes, Cervantes) are dramatizations of the subject's *failure* to recognize their projected aims and goals as being basically insubstantial, and therefore dissolvable before the claim of the Absolute.[95] But unlike tragedies, which depict the dire consequences of one-sided passions, comedies do not lead to the destruction of the actor, but to the awareness that one has *misrecognized* the true workings of history. This opens us to the possibility of a "comic resolution," that suggests that we "move decisively away from fear and bewilderment in the face of the other." If we are to follow this Hegelian trajectory, as Rose and Williams argue, then it is "only recognition that liberates us, the recognition of the other as, like me, engaged, whether knowingly or not, in 'comic' self-discovery."[96] Comic self-recognition thus occurs when we become conscious of the fissure between our various intentions and their actualizations, and it is this distinction or "gap" which is amusing, thereby becoming a basis for a "holy" laughter which is neither cynical nor

---

92. Williams, "Between Politics and Metaphysics," 59.

93. Rose, *Mourning Becomes Law*, 63–76. In distinction from 'comedy,' Hegel understood 'tragedy' (especially in its Attic variety) to be concerned with the dramatization of conflict between agents of "fixed character" who assert their "one-sidedness" in destructive ways. For his discussion of this distinction, see Hegel, *Aesthetics*, 2:1192–237.

94. Williams, "The Sadness of the King," 22.

95. See Hegel's claim in *Aesthetics*, 1:607, that "the Divine is the absolute subject-matter of art," but the way in which divinity becomes manifest through its "cancelling" of resolute individuality "by [a] humour which could make every determinacy waver and dissolve."

96. Williams, "The Sadness of the King," 22.

despairing.[97] This is why Williams has appreciation for a novel like Vodolazkin's *Laurus* since it is able to imagine a repetitive displacement of personal identity without self-destruction.[98] It does not exhibit the lacerating or harmful irony that Hegel himself dismissed.[99] Instead, the laughing of Hegelian comedy is emblematic of an ontological "humour" that elevates "characters away above themselves and their crude, restricted, and false aims."[100] For Hegel, that which is destroyed in comedy is ultimately non-substantial, while what survives are the characters themselves. Therefore to laugh-at-oneself does not necessitate postmodern melancholy or unremitting irony, but on the contrary a distancing from parochial visions that hinder human flourishing. It implies a relativization of the ego and an acknowledgement that what is active in history exceeds my own representations of ultimacy, and thereby opens me to a renewed discovery of self within the continuing dialectic of recognition and otherness.

This seeing of my own self within the other, as we have hinted at already, is intrinsically connected to the discovery of *reason*, a sense of coherency within "the risky activity of assuming recognizability."[101] Because every agent is comically distanced from aims incommensurate with the Absolute, this means they are able to recognize their own misdirected behavior in the lives of others. And if their mutual discoveries are truly analogous, then there is an order that exceeds idiosyncrasies, and makes allowance for a comparison through a transcending medium of relation. For Williams and Rose, such mediation is the very essence of "reason." This does not however abolish uncertainty, since reason according to Rose "has to act with a confidence not in its final justification but in the possibility of truthfulness"—hence its riskiness.[102] But without an assumption of this basic *truthfulness*, so Williams argues, we end up baptizing the violence of exclusionary confrontation.

He does admit, however, that a complete avoidance of violent confrontation is not always possible, since engagement occasionally requires coercion in order to move forward. But it is also critical to emphasize that such violence should not be equated with evil-as-such, or assumed to be

---

97. Williams, "The Sadness of the King," 28.

98. Vodolazkin, *Laurus*. For more, see Williams, "A Curious Novel." For more on the figure of the *iurodstvo* and *salotes*, and Vodolazkin's novel, see Williams, "Holy Folly."

99. See Hegel's distinction between 'the comic' and 'the ironic,' see Hegel, *Aesthetics*, 1:67–68.

100. Hegel, *Aesthetics*, 1:592.

101. Williams, "The Sadness of the King," 23.

102. Williams, "The Sadness of the King," 33.

always necessary.[103] It is rather a sign of tragic limitation or incapacity. The important distinction to be made here is that even though conflict may be unavoidable in some contexts, this does not mean it always has to be like this. If conflict arises, then reason unpacks *how* this conflict has arisen *here*, at this specific juncture. "Reason serves by exposing contradiction, showing the incomplete nature of this inhabiting and declaring that this need not be."[104] It is about thinking *why* certain errors have occurred rather than declaring that they have developed from some necessary logic.[105] We should be wary of any position that underwrites prophecies of "foredoomed failure" that assert "the impossibility of public virtue."[106] Both of these are fatal for a truly transformative politics. To avoid this gloomy picture, we need to re-think political progress not in "tragic" terms—that is, in terms of inevitable defeat (to adopt Rose's lexicon), but rather as a "comedy" in which the self is able to recognize its mistakes, without self-laceration or what she calls "aberrated" mourning.[107] Our diagnosis of error involves us in thinking more comprehensively about how structures have contributed to disorder, and also invites us "To know and think the complicity in and by which my agency is formed."[108]

The picture of the self that has emerged in the above discussion is one that is time-bound and relational, one formed through interpersonal and historical development. For Williams, the self emerges through temporal growth, as it is pulled, knowingly or unknowingly, by its desire for the Good—that is, by God. On this model of selfhood, because it is de-centered, the constitution of the self is kenotic, in the sense of having an identity that is primordially given, and therefore not to be grasped. The temporal aspect of the self's development is bound up with potential loss, and therefore has a certain tragic quality about it. However, this must be placed alongside Williams's assertion that Augustine's metaphysics of the self implies a being-ness

---

103. This point has been emphasized well by Gray in *Jesus in the Theology of Rowan Williams*, 136–44.

104. Williams, "The Sadness of the King," 25. Raymond Williams, in a comparable manner to Rose, has also spoken about how "by selecting the facts and by subtly reducing the pressures," we can "go over to propaganda or to advertising." A genuinely historical and tragic position, on the contrary, suggests that we are "committed to an actual process, and to seeing not only this movement but also that, so that not only this but also that must be said. We have to see not only that suffering is avoidable, but that it is not avoided. And not only that suffering breaks us, but that it need not break us" (Williams, *Modern Tragedy*, 240).

105. Williams, "The Sadness of the King," 27.

106. Williams, "The Sadness of the King," 31.

107. Rose, *Mourning Becomes Law*, 65.

108. Williams, "The Sadness of the King," 32.

discovered as gift, and therefore received in gratitude. Against some readings of Augustine, the self is not a proto-Cartesian *cogito*, but is discovered in movements and displacements of desire, in the unhanding of carapaced identities that restrict the agency of Christ in our lives.

But while *kenosis* is an essential part of our moral growth, it is balanced by the continuing advent of desire and the *plerosis* of our participation in the triune life of God. This means that a surrendering of the ego does not necessitate a wounding without relief or healing; on the contrary, it predicates a trust that self-forgetfulness does not betoken complete loss; it works within a hope of plenitude beyond scarcity. Additionally important to note is that since the self is both social and *ek-static*, this implies a certain political vision as well. Following Augustine, Hegel and Rose, Williams argues that there is no concept of the self and one's private goods that can be thought apart from the discovery of shareable goods. The speculative counterpart to this is an account of transcendence and universal goodness that is non-reducible to the local. If such were the case, then there could be no rational mediation of differing accounts of goodness; instead, we would have a Hobbesian picture of scrambling individuals within zero-sum conflicts. It is Williams's position that such a conclusion implies a denial of a common good, and the baptism of a metaphysical and cultural pessimism. One can say in summary then that Williams's Hegelian Augustinianism aims to balance the kenotic and 'tragic' aspects of temporal *distentio* (after Donald MacKinnon) with a 'comic' reading of self-discovery (after Gillian Rose). These clarifications will assist as we move forward in this chapter.

Tragedy and Estrangement

The above summaries regarding language, the self and the pedagogics of time might seem to be an overly-laborious and oblique introduction to our current preoccupation. But it is the contention of this chapter that Williams's recent monograph on the tragic genre should be engaged from this perspective, as we will see shortly. *The Tragic Imagination* constitutes Williams's most significant contribution to date on the question of the tragic, and therefore deserves engagement, since it also forms one of the most subtle and tightly-argued attempts to bring Christian theology into dialogue with the heritage of tragic drama. However, it has to be mentioned that its appearance brings to fruition an almost career-long interest with ideas related to this topic, and so it is worth tracing genealogically its working within his thinking up to the present time. There are relatively few extensive engagements with

Williams on this theme, especially before this book was published,[109] and so this essay aims at once show its history within his thinking, as well as expositing its most full-bodied treatment.

The tragic imagination, particularly *King Lear*, had already grasped Williams from a young age and so antedates his tertiary studies.[110] But it is widely perceived, and admitted by Williams himself,[111] that Donald MacKinnon's influence on him was decisive in this regard. What is important to note again is that MacKinnon's attention regarding the tragic occurred within an over-arching moral awareness that resisted, through a contemplation of its refractory qualities, any attempt to claim a finalized human authorship for the world we inhabit. As we have seen in earlier chapters, MacKinnon's precise targets here were idealistic philosophies[112] and Benthamite versions of 'naturalism'.[113] But more generally-speaking, these criticisms would apply to any egoistic project that adhered to the fantasy that we can circumscribe our reality, bringing it thereby under our teleological mastery. Reality does not strictly adhere to how we conceptualize it, and any claim we could fully grasp it is an exercise in tragic hubris. For MacKinnon, our perception of truth is something that continues to unfold: there is an unflinching and recalcitrant 'objectivity' within our correspondence to reality. And yet, such 'objectivity' is not immediately graspable: much like an artistic craft—here remembering MacKinnon's reference to Cézanne—it takes time for the *realia* to disclose themselves.[114] These tendencies, as we will see, are present within Williams's own work, but it will take several decades until they reach mature amplification in *The Tragic Imagination*.

109. See Myers, *Christ the Stranger*, 21–27; Gray, *Jesus in the Theology of Rowan Williams*, 119–44. There is also some critical comments on Williams's use of the tragic in Milbank, "Enclaves, or Where is the Church," 349–52, and Milbank, "The Archbishop of Canterbury," 50–53. After this book was published, *Modern Theology* (2018) also published a symposium on *The Tragic Imagination*. The contributions are listed as follows: Hart, "The Gospel According to Melpomene"; Ward, "Extremities"; Waller, "Felix Culpa?"; Eagleton, "Tragedy and Liberalism"; Quash, "*The Tragic Imagination* and the Ascesis of the Eye"; Wallace, "Tragic Remembrance in the Era of Fake News"; Schwartz, "The Ethics of the Tragic Imagination"; Williams, "'Not Cured, Not Forgetful, Not Paralysed.'"

110. Cf. Breyfogle, "Time and Transformation," 295; Williams, *The Tragic Imagination*, 1.

111. Cf. Williams, "Obituary," 31. See also, Williams, *The Tragic Imagination*, 1.

112. MacKinnon, "Idealism and Realism: An Old Controversy Renewed," 138–50; and "The Conflict Between Realism and Idealism: Remarks on the Significance for the Philosophy of Religion of a Classical Philosophical Controversy Recently Renewed," 151–65; both in *Explorations in Theology*.

113. MacKinnon, *The Problem of Metaphysics*, 44–45, 145.

114. MacKinnon, *The Problem of Metaphysics*, 104–13.

What is particularly noticeable in the early work of Williams is a tragically-imbued sense of *historicity*. Much like MacKinnon, Williams's sensitivity towards "the complex discipline of temporality"[115] was distinctly present even in his more youthful forays. In one of his first essays published, entitled "The Spirit of the Age to Come" (1974),[116] he speaks of "an awareness of present reality as divided, fragmented, liable to internal struggle and frustration, an awareness, in fact of the *tragic*."[117] It is within this context that the Spirit works to cultivate practices of hope and redemptive longing that are precisely *not* extractions from lived history, that is, they are not a "negation or abolition of what has gone before."[118] If they were abstractions, they would imply a denial of the goodness of creation, and also it would reduce the Spirit's futurity as working on the same plane as other historical events.[119] But even more strikingly, these contentions are grounded Christologically, in a Johannine and quasi-Lutheran fashion, through his ontological identification of the crucified and risen Christ.[120] Within this model, the church itself can be strikingly read as "a communion in horror and in glory." This is because we are still "in history, that history where tragedy occurs," in which "the gift of the Spirit is a gift that increases our vulnerability to a terrifying degree," and "are left exposed and humanly defenseless before the universal weight of tragedy," since the Spirit into which we are incorporated is a "Spirit of kenosis" that translates, into our varying contexts, the experience of the cross and resurrection.[121] These revelations betray a starkness of vision from early on that is simultaneously realist and non-pessimistic in character, a kind of traversal of the optimism-pessimism binary altogether. This opinion is further weighted upon the consideration that, for Williams, classical tragedy already understood itself as a literary-dramatic mode of protest, which in its aesthetic constitution denied passivity and silence.[122]

But it is also substantiated by the Christian belief that the presence of the Spirit in the here-and-now constitutes an anticipation of a future hidden within the present. This contemporaneity of the Spirit gives believers the "power and confidence to *act*" because of the expectancy put before

---

115. MacKinnon, "The Relation of the Doctrines," 104.
116. Williams, "The Spirit of the Age to Come," 613–26.
117. Williams, "The Spirit of the Age to Come," 616.
118. Williams, "The Spirit of the Age to Come," 614.
119. Williams, "The Spirit of the Age to Come," 614–15.
120. Williams, "The Spirit of the Age to Come," 619.
121. Williams, "The Spirit of the Age to Come," 622–23.
122. Williams, "The Spirit of the Age to Come," 624.

them.[123] Many of these thoughts remain with Williams up to the present, but it is worth mentioning one area where there is a marked difference, namely, his reading of Hegel. In this early text, Williams still read Hegel as putting forward the notion that tragedy was about a conflict between rival goods—as in Sophocles's *Antigone*—provoking situations where "the good is divided against itself."[124] Such a reading is hardly reconcilable with his later view that conflicting goods should not be seen as absolute. Instead, the *agon* of ethical difference should be submitted to a dispossessive negotiation, with the aim of discovering where the node of conflict truly lies. As regards tragedy, Williams would come to see Hegel's reading of *Antigone* as focused less on the question of mutually exclusive goods, and rather on the problem of *one-sidedness* (*Einseitigkeit*) in our understanding of the good. But since this problematic will be discussed in more detail below, we will hold off further discussion until then.

Returning to the genealogy, I should emphasize again that this vision of a redemption not bypassing 'the historical' remains an assumption throughout Williams's theology up until the present day, as we will see. It is particularly apparent in his (as yet) unpublished lectures on Eliot's *Four Quartets* (delivered twice during 1974–1975),[125] which could be read (if one could summarize them) as an expanded commentary on Eliot's line in *Burnt Norton* that "Only through time time is conquered."[126] This central motif of Eliot's was, for Williams, simply an outworking of the poet's adherence to the "gospel" as a form of "incarnational religion."[127] He argued that Eliot's own poetic practice of writing displayed a process of learning in which, through the labour of composition, he discovered that the original conclusions of *Burnt Norton* could not be the final word on the matter. This insight explains the oppositional voices displayed in the remaining poems which often place a question mark next to Eliot's initial statements regarding "the immutable present."[128] In Williams's estimation, this vision failed to account for the diachronic, and reduced the present into a 'timeless' abstraction.[129] This shows that Williams already at this point had a deep sense of the pedagogics of time and irony, of how our temporal endurance implies

---

123. Williams, "The Spirit of the Age to Come," 624–25.
124. Williams, "The Spirit of the Age to Come," 616.
125. See Delport, "Towards a Visionary and Historical Consciousness."
126. Eliot, "Burnt Norton II," in *Collected Poems*, 180.
127. Williams, "The Four Quartets (1975)," lecture 1, 1. Brett Gray has characterized these lectures as being examples of Williams's *incarnational historicism* (cf. *Jesus in the Theology of Rowan Williams*, 44–49).
128. Williams, "The Four Quartets (1975)," lecture 1, 2.
129. Williams, "The Four Quartets (1975)," lecture 1, 5–8.

a continuing movement of moral education that can only be avoided through a collapse into the fantasies of the ego, or what Eliot calls "a world of speculation."[130] This history to which we are subjected, to be sure, is a history of wreckage and disaster, one that could even be read as "Godless"—as is made clear in Eliot's *The Dry Salvages*.[131]

The Christian faith, Williams stresses, cannot be an attempt to mitigate these refractory aspects of the world; on the contrary, he says that the incarnation both "validates" and "condemns" us to the "unresolved tensions" of history.[132] However, we should not read this insight as implying an unreconstructed pessimism, since particularities are still able to formulate themselves into "a pattern of unified beauty."[133] The vision of *Little Gidding*'s fulgurating and pentecostal dynamism shows, on the one hand, that our moments are able to be redeemed in the "crowned knot of fire,"[134] without, on the other, ceding their concrete individuality. Already apparent here, in these early lectures, is a deep sense of how for us "the complex discipline of temporality" is an unavoidable element for human growth. Our redemption cannot be understood as an "escape" from the strictures of time and embodiedness without resulting in a denial of our humanity and, for Christians, the truths of incarnation. For Williams, as for the church fathers, the unassumed is the unhealed.[135] But the stringent application of this antique dogma needs to hold even for those most difficult, tragic aspects of reality that refuse easy consolation, even those experiences, as Williams readily admits, which invite conclusions of historical 'godlessness.'

Such hyperbolic and vertiginous language re-appears in several texts written shortly after he delivered his lectures on the *Four Quartets*, as for instance where he starkly admonishes believers of the fact that God will not wipe the tears away from our eyes until "we have learned to weep."[136] There are also comments (found in a review essay) that reiterate the vision exposited in his lectures on *The Dry Salvages*: "God is revealed in the death of Jesus, revealed in his cry of dereliction, revealed in Gethsemane [and] all this is straining

---

130. Williams, "The Four Quartets (1975)," lecture 2, 2. The quote is taken from Eliot, "Burnt Norton I," in *Collected Poems*, 177.

131. Williams, "The Four Quartets (1975)," lecture 3, 7.

132. Williams, "The Four Quartets (1975)," lecture 4, 5.

133. Williams, "The Four Quartets (1975)," lecture 4, 4.

134. Eliot, "Little Gidding V," in *Collected Poems*, 209.

135. Gregory of Nazianzus, "Letter 101," in *On God and Christ*, 155–66. This aspect of temporality remains important for Williams, as can be seen in his reading of the figure of Prince Myshkin; cf. *Dostoevsky: Language, Faith, and Fiction*, 47–57. Also see Williams, "Augustine's Christology," 176–89.

136. Williams, "To Give and Not to Count the Cost," 403.

language to the breaking point," that is, "because what we are affirming is that God is revealed by his *absence*, revealed in the condition of 'Godlessness' . . . a world of chaos, anguish and senselessness."[137] Similar motifs of extremity are noticeable in a sermon on T. S. Eliot (given in 1984, but published in 1995) that shows the longevity of this vision within his thinking.[138]

But cognate disclosures can also be discovered in a longer essay, penned within the same general period, called "Poetic and Religious Imagination (1977)."[139] He spoke there of finding "a place" within "the disordered flux"—which is a good definition of "personal maturity," he adds. It is about finding a "position," a "direction" that orientates us amongst the world's seemingly disparate constituency. In language that anticipates Gillian Rose's work, he speaks of making and taking forward "an *option* about reality,"[140] one that forms an aesthetic protest against meaninglessness, and opposes political postures that seek to close-down the range of human language. This curtailing of creative reference can only imply a foreclosure of the claims of history and its continued opening up of human conversation and meaning. "Significance is a function of communication," which means that establishing meaning cannot be reduced to "an individual matter," because the artist does not offer us a moment of self-expression, but rather an "incomplete" picture of his or her "world" which is then offered to us as something "not yet fully realized or grasped," and to which we are invited to respond.[141] This struggle with incompleteness, the experience of "irony," the sense that every attempt at creative re-description is a falling short of the whole picture, is an intrinsic part of the poet's growth in maturity.[142] At this point, we are beginning to see an argument that anticipates the emphasis on tragic irony and one-sidedness to be found in his later work.

In his contribution to Donald MacKinnon's *Festschrift* (delivered in 1986 and published in 1989), he adumbrates many of the themes which will

---

137. Williams, "'Person' and 'Personality' in Christology," 259. Also compare another contemporary statement regarding divine absence: "Life in the polis is life in the world from which God has withdrawn for the sake of its liberty. It is thus life charged with ambiguity, vulnerable to the tragic. There are no final solutions—the very words have appalling connotations. History and the polis are where God is condemned to death." For this quotation, see Williams, "Mankind, Nation, State," 124. The underlining is in the original.

138. Cf. See his sermon "Lazarus: In Memory of T.S. Eliot," in *A Ray of Darkness*, 186–91.

139. Williams, "Poetic and Religious Imagination."

140. Williams, "Poetic and Religious Imagination." 179.

141. Williams, "Poetic and Religious Imagination." 180.

142. Williams, "Poetic and Religious Imagination." 183.

recur in his most recent volume on this topic.[143] There he said that if "the world is our creation, or even if the world is masterable as a system of necessities, the idea of irreparable and uncontrollable *loss* ceases to make sense: there are no tragedies."[144] A further expansion reads thus:

> All explanation of suffering is an attempt to forget it as suffering, and so a quest for untruthfulness. . . . The resolution of the sheer resistant particularity of suffering, past and present, into comfortable teleological patterns is bound to blunt the edge of particularity, and so to lie; and this lying resolution contains that kind of failure in attention that is itself a moral deficiency, a fearful self-protection. It is just this that fuels the fantasy that we can choose how the world and myself shall be.[145]

The moral register that I have mentioned previously reoccurs here: the invocation of an irrepressible tragic element within the human and natural world serves to highlight our contingent location and boundaries, with the purpose of showing how such an awareness of human limitation can provide imaginative resources for "transformative *action*."[146] This is because "the tragic *by definition* deals with human limit," with "what is not to be changed, with a pain that is 'non-negotiable.'"[147] In itself, this might suggest a model of "acceptance" that is "ideological" in its conceits.[148] However, Williams suggests on the contrary that "it is *one's own* appropriation of the limits of possibility" that serves as a "protest against a polity and culture that lure us to sink our truthful perceptions" into "a collective, mythologized identity that can shut its eyes to limits."[149] But "the possible world of truthful perception" does not fall to us from the sky but is "*made* possible, however precariously and impermanently, for actual persons in communication with each other." In a sentence that summarizes a position he will expand on later, he writes that "Tragedy is capable of being lived with and articulated because . . . of the particular, the narratively specific, out of which certain kinds of new language grow."[150] What is apparent again here is how an awareness of the temporal limits of human action can serve as a truly creative source for human transformation. This is not to imply that

---

143. Williams, "Trinity and Ontology," in *On Christian Theology*, 148–66.
144. Williams, "Trinity and Ontology," 154–55.
145. Williams, "Trinity and Ontology," 155.
146. Williams, "Trinity and Ontology," 162.
147. Williams, "Trinity and Ontology," 162.
148. Williams, "Trinity and Ontology," 162.
149. Williams, "Trinity and Ontology," 163.
150. Williams, "Trinity and Ontology," 164.

suffering as such is invested with a transcendent significance, because this would imply again an attempt to access a *locus standi* apart from the fray of contingency,[151] a supra-temporal position from which such deprivation could be aesthetically plotted.[152] It would be a denial of that truth to which tragedy is an exemplary disclosure. This emphasis on the 'always-already,' non-extricable aspect of our involvement in history (and its often-tragic implications) is often reiterated in his friendly, but critical, engagements with John Milbank on the question of tragedy,[153] and is also apparent in his writings on Gillian Rose.[154]

Responding to a rather critical review of *The Tragic Imagination* (written by the classicist Edith Hall), Williams encapsulated his monograph on tragedy within this problematic: rather than "attempting to force Greek tragedy into a Christian mould," Williams said that he wanted "to grant the full weight of its negativity" and probe further as to whether "Christian discourse" would be able to "sustain" such "negativity."[155] Williams does not expand here upon his sense of "negativity," but what we have read up to this point provides some indication: it is a short-hand for "what is utterly unresolved in the human experience" (*TI*, 1).[156] For Williams, tragedy is concerned with how "language" is able to accommodate "unwelcome truth" and its "own failure to master extreme experience" (*TI*, 1). But such accommodation is entwined with the production of "new knowledge," since "we are not simply passive in the face of terror and suffering, because we can *imagine* it, narrate it, make pictures of it that make it an agenda for others and for ourselves" (*TI*, 1–2). When "ordered community" is "shaken'" we look for words even in "extremity" to make sense of the "challenge" or "pressure" before us (*TI*, 2). So rather than indicating a sense of inescapable doom, one could argue that tragic drama simply "assumes that practically unspeakable things happen" and that our various

---

151. Williams, "Trinity and Ontology," 155–56.

152. See Williams's comments on theodicy in "Redeeming Sorrows: Marilyn McCord Adams and the Defeat of Evil," in *Wrestling with Angels*, 255–74. Williams's criticisms of Adams are centrally focused on her attempt to aesthetically resolve the problem of evil via the notion of 'proportion.' Williams thinks this theory fails to account for the complexity of how diverse stories of suffering are appropriated by *human* agents. It also, unfortunately, seems to adopt a model of divine action that is rather onto-theological and metaphysically unsophisticated, treating God's activity as a kind of human form of intervention, with the exception being that is on a transcendentally superior scale.

153. Cf. Williams, "Saving Time."

154. See the discussion of Hegel and Rose in our previous section.

155. Williams, "Tragedy and Redemption."

156. The pagination for *The Tragic Imagination* is cited in parentheses as *TI*.

"concordats with reality are as fragile as could be" (*TI*, 2). But this is not the same as sheer passivity, since "language" which takes tragedy seriously sits uncomfortably with certain visions of the world ("an instrumentalizing and managerial spirit, an anxious shrinking of language into cliché and formula, a nervousness around emotional risk and exposure," etc.). It is not supinely *laissez-faire* in posture, or simply reducible to a Nietzschean *amor fati*. We could rather say that it is concerned with how we "speak without false consolation in a world like this," hopeful of the fact that language (and "religious language" in particular) is able to account for the reality of "non-resolution" within our experience; not out of a sense of "pessimism," but in a rather "odd confidence" that our language is "not so easily exhausted or defeated" by these realities (*TI*, 3).

By way of clarifying our treatment, one could summarize Williams's harmonization of Christianity and the tragic in the following way. The first thing to say is that tragedy avoids pessimism by showing that "suffering can be narrated" and therefore "communicatively or imaginatively shared," becoming thereby "a *cultural* fact." Reading tragedy in this way means that "existential guilt," or understanding "identity as burden and trap, would have to be modified as soon as this becomes a matter of language and representation," because as he states, "identity is reconfigured in exchange and recognition." As a result of this, we become *strange* to ourselves. The adoption of such a posture would instigate, as a consequence, both "a critique of fatalism" and "an affirmation of value," a refusal of any proposal that we are damned to meaninglessness (*TI*, 132).[157]

The second point to mention is the centrality of "irony" for tragedy, which in its own way stifles the totalization of pessimism. For him, "if tragedy is the sheer burden of existence, that would leave us with another non-ironic model." Tragic drama specifically—and implicitly, "the tragic" as such—is concerned with "the unbearable nature of finitude." Such is reflected within the performativity of tragic drama itself since "There is no generative gap between what the dramatic agent knows and what we know," because there is a shared "awareness of ignorance in both the dramatic characters and the observing audience." The reason why this resists metaphysical pessimism is because irony shows that since we do not know the outcome, we cannot know how "the mere fact of narration, the *following*

---

157. Williams is probably drawing somewhat on Raymond Williams's work on tragedy, who has written about how "[a] particular evil, in a tragic action, can be at once experienced and lived through. In the process of living through it, and in a real action seeing its moving relations with other capacities and other men, we come not so much to the recognition of evil as transcendent but to its recognition as actual and indeed negotiable" (Williams, *Modern Tragedy*, 83).

on from the record of horror and failure" will change the meaning of the unfolding circumstance (*TI*, 132). Things could get worse, even when we think they cannot sink any lower. The bottom could fall even more, revealing new tonalities of horror (e.g., *Agamemnon, Choephori, Antigone, The Women of Trachis, Oedipus the King, Medea, The Bacchae*). But the opposite could be true as well: circumstances can take a surprising turn towards happier outcomes (e.g., *The Eumenides, Oedipus at Colonnus, Alcestis*). And it should be stressed again: even if things get worse, the very fact that they are able to be communicated shows that meaningful engagement with suffering is not finally excluded. These two points regarding 'narration' and 'irony' give us orientation for what is to follow.

In a remarkably distilled treatment of "the political roots of tragedy," Williams speaks of the origins of Attic tragedy within the staging of the City Dionysia of Athens,[158] in which the citizens are invited "to contemplate disaster and suffering, chains of events unleashed by rash action . . . engulfing guilty and innocent alike." This occurs within "the context of a celebration both of the city's solid identity and the god associated with the dangerous realm of excess," namely Dionysos. It is this theme of *danger* that becomes prevalent within Greek drama (*TI*, 5), the sense that reality is unstable and requires some kind of containment. But in order for these narratives to be brought home, such a presentation of danger requires familiarity (*TI*, 6), which is why tragedies draw upon the stock of common fable and legend. And yet, the risk is that a mere repetition of ancient and familiar tales might not appear to give a sense of "continuing threat or risk."

But as Williams insightfully suggests, "the fact of repetition itself declares that we have not yet-*never* yet-grasped the nature of the danger being represented. We tell the familiar story because we know that we do not yet know it," because "we don't know yet what the scale of the danger is" (*TI*, 7). Stories, as they are re-told, become "readable" in more than one way, and as "the dramatic complexity increases, so does the danger experienced by the audience, despite the familiarity of the story being represented" (*TI*, 7). They teach us that "we cannot be certain of what is past" (*TI*, 9). This tendency of increasing danger, this intensification of "risk," seems to be further nuanced and increased, not only in the transition from story to dramatic retelling, but even *within* the development of the tragic genre from Aeschylus to Euripides (*TI*, 8). But Williams also wants to stress that since tragedy occurred within the context of "ritual" and "liturgy," this assumes that, to a certain extent, "it can in some degree manage, if not control the Dionysian,"

---

158. See Goldhill, "The Great Dionysia and Civic Ideology."

but only if it is willing "to be rediscovered again and again by posing new challenges to it, testing it to destruction" (*TI*, 9). To quote further:

> 'the tragic' is originally a function of how a verbal and visual representation works in the mind of a community gathered to celebrate or affirm its resilience and legitimacy in full awareness of the fragility that always pervades its life. It exists in the disturbing gap between that affirmation and a complementary recognition: the acknowledgement that we do not have a *final* point of view about the crises or catastrophes which both haunt and justify the existence of the political order. (*TI*, 10)

One of the precipitous occupations of tragedy is its portrayal of "the different pressures and impulses that are at work on actual agents in the world." Tragedy "obliges us to pay attention to sheer *circumstance*," to the fact that we live in a world in which "the fantasy of a virtue that has no cost" is constantly being undermined (*TI*, 11). The city's self-description, as found within Greek drama, is concerned to show "a divinely ordered balance of different obligations running in different directions" that requires "law as the institutionalized means of recognizing these multiple interdependencies." It is within this context that "the individual agent" is presented as "always *implicated*," as "always defined by unchosen connections and the obligations that come with them." This is because "Human action is not a simple assertion of the individual will but a *thinking-through* of the diverse sorts of connection that we inhabit," with the purpose of discerning "courses of action that are as truthful as possible and as little harmful as possible" (*TI*, 13).

Williams, here drawing on the work of Martha Nussbaum, argues that tragedy aims to "handle danger by challenging the idea that obligations can be so ordered that we will never collide" (*TI*, 15). There is no social space in which we are completely safe, in which our actions are immune to asseverations of conflict and loss. But it is precisely through narration that tragic drama acts as "a vehicle for managing loss." As long as these events "can be spoken of," we are not "reduced to absolute silence or paralysis" (*TI*, 15–16). Adopting the language of Nussbaum again,[159] Williams says tragedy is a mode of representation that provides healing without giving a "cure" for what ails us (*TI*, 16). Tragedies do not necessarily give us a "happy ending" in which all deprivations have been resolved, but rather provoke us to an "urgency" regarding the containment of such repercussions, without "softening the atrocity or making more bearable what should be terrible to us" (*TI*, 17). An avoidance of seeing or speaking about such things would imply that "the self and the city" would become "less secure," since the

---

159. Nussbaum, *The Fragility of Goodness*, 82.

refusal to know leaves intact "the very mechanisms from which the drama is supposed to deliver us" (*TI*, 17).

Williams is also concerned to distinguish his account from some pervasive understandings of tragedy which reduce the question of "conflict" to one of "duties," since this seems to stem from a rather "modern argument" that "demands a central figure who is distinguished by 'nobility' of spirit, a figure who is morally sophisticated enough to grasp the seriousness of rival imperatives"—as seen in post-Kantian accounts of the tragic. On the contrary, as should be clear from tragic drama and our experiences, "tragedy does not affect only the morally sophisticated" (*TI*, 25). Rather its more basic impulse lies in the fact that our social relations are "breakable" (*TI*, 25), and that we are herein confronted with "the utterly unpredictable dissolutions of human solidarity and humanist stability," in which we become aware of "the *fact* of our not-knowing," the fact that we might have "*never* really known," where the danger truly resides (*TI*, 27). Here echoing Gillian Rose, Williams provides us with a call to recognize our precarity, to acknowledge our complicity within these dynamics, and therefore to convert from habits that continue to entrench such structures. This should not take the form of self-laceration or mere self-edification, but rather should focus on the question of "law": how is it that certain *institutions* continue to reinforce or allow the existence of historical tragedy or "atrocity"? It is an invitation to *think* about why these realities continue to exist (TI, 26–27).

This problem of knowledge is deepened in Williams's appropriation of Cavellian ideas regarding skepticism and Shakespearean drama.[160] For Cavell, tragedy is about "what we *know* and do not acknowledge"; or more specifically, it concerns "the failure to *acknowledge what we know*." In this universe, we "seek a complete and unmediated transparency and fail to tolerate the ordinary uncertainty that attends the ordinary certainties we know" (*TI*, 31). It is what happens when "the human is denied," in the sense of being "engaged, invested, a participant in language and so in interdependence" (*TI*, 32). It involves "*refusing* to be conscious of its own urge to resolve tension in favour of a fantasized freedom" (*TI*, 34). For Williams, and Cavell, our attendance to tragic drama provokes a sense that time is needed for the drama to unfold, that our learning is temporally bound to the mediation of plot and development. This is exposed when reflecting on the physicality of such attendance: Williams says that if "we watch a tragic drama, we are deliberately immobilized; we cannot respond as we should do to human suffering in other circumstances." This experience "reinforces the recognition of *separateness*," that we have "*to allow to happen what the tragic agents*

---

160. Cf. Cavell, *Disowning Knowledge*.

on stage are struggling not to allow" (*TI*, 35). Here Williams is underscoring the contemplative dimension of tragedy, which involves our attention to the "inexhaustible dense 'solidity' of the other" (*TI*, 36). It allows "difference" to unfold, to not promote a premature closure of the narrative. As he says in his commentary on *King Lear* (referencing the statement in Act IV.1 that "The worst is not/ So long as we can say 'This is the worst'"):

> No reconciliation on this personal scale will be adequate to the unreconciled reality that prevails all around and that may once again intrude into the lives of the reconciled. 'This is the worst' is a statement that seeks to close down the history of suffering; now we know how bad it can be. But the drama declares that we do not know how bad it can be, and that this is one of those things we must *know* that we don't know. (*TI*, 41)

And yet, this 'it-could-be-worse' attitude does not necessitate pessimism: "The business of tragedy is neither to tell us that the world is more bearable that it is nor to insist that it is 'absolutely' unbearable." On the contrary, tragedy transcends such binaries by showing "how *some* pain can be spoken of and understood, 'humanized', and some cannot, because the words are not yet there" (*TI*, 41). It does not exclude the various agencies of suffering subjects who are able to grasp suffering precisely as *human* suffering, that is, a pain that can be thought and shared beyond sheer passivity (*TI*, 42–45). But even at this level of sharing and communication (here drawing upon the figure of Iago from Shakespeare's *Othello*), Williams says that there are potential ironies and ambiguities, since the possibility remains that the suffering of others can be co-opted in a narrative which serves *our own* ideological interests, rather than giving space to their unique deprivations (*TI*, 45–51). Our re-telling and exaptation of 'the pain of others' (Sontag) might be liable to miss the particular contours of such stories, and constitutes a moral failure since it implies, once again, a return to a form of narration that colonizes these extremities for our own purposes. It implies, at the level of practice, a denial of *difference*.

This concern with difference, as has been hinted at earlier, is central to Williams's reading of Hegel. And since Hegel has proved, like Aristotle, to be a central figure within the philosophical reception of tragedy, Williams devotes an entire chapter to Hegel (one that draws on the work of Gillian Rose[161] and Stephen Houlgate[162]). As Houlgate argues, for Hegel "The problem in Greek tragic drama is that each individual is so absorbed by [their own] governing 'pathos,'" and that they fail "to respect (or even

---

161. Cf. Rose, *Mourning Becomes Law*, 63–76.
162. Houlgate, "Hegel's Theory of Tragedy," 146–78.

recognize) the justified pathos that moves another individual."[163] Tragedy is produced through an adherence to one's pathos in a "*one-sided way*"[164], in a fashion that is "*unyielding*"[165] in the face of the claims of other agents. For this reason, it is tragic and self-destructive since it fails to internalize the truth within opposing perspectives. However, Hegel's argument should not be misunderstood (as it often is): such ethical contradiction is not an unavoidable metaphysical datum, but is rather the consequence of intransigent human actors who fail to acknowledge a judicious balance of concerns.[166] Tragic conflict is aimed then at "reconciliation" and harmonization, since it desires to produce in the audience a sense of "justice" by displaying the catastrophic outcome for agents who are one-sidedly and individualistically committed to their own stake on things.[167] In Williams's own words, tragedy for Hegel is about a *misrecognition* in which the subject understands themselves as "already unified," fully identified with "an embodied ethical value" and a "particular imperative" that denies "another subject's equally misrecognized self-identification" (*TI*, 57). It implies a failure to *learn*, to see the other has having a claim that deserves attention and respectful engagement. And it is this, rather than "fate," that explains the disaster of the *dramatis personae*, as exemplified in Sophocles's *Antigone* (*TI*, 58–66).

In this drama, both Creon and Antigone articulate truths that are good in themselves: as regards Creon, "we owe respect and the ritual acknowledgement of dignity to those who have not broken the basic contract of human community," and for Antigone it is the case that "we owe respect to any and all, because nothing is more universal than the death we all confront" (*TI*, 61). The problem of Creon and Antigone is that they have "made themselves fixed objects of self-contemplation. Their identities and value are as solid and externalized as the principles they uphold." But for Williams, any self so constructed is "*a fiction*" since no self can be understood as "an atomized external object" (*TI*, 63). More specifically, "Creon's problem is that he wants to absolve himself of obligation in a particular and extreme case; while Antigone's problem is that she treats obligation has having no specific content beyond the recognition of a general claim that is based on the universal fact of mortality" (*TI*, 62). Such exemplifies the dilemma of "law" itself, as Williams has said elsewhere, namely that "law by its very nature must be forgetful of the particular," and that "if it is recaptured or

---

163. Houlgate, "Hegel's Theory of Tragedy," 149.
164. Houlgate, "Hegel's Theory of Tragedy," 149.
165. Houlgate, "Hegel's Theory of Tragedy," 155.
166. Houlgate, "Hegel's Theory of Tragedy," 166.
167. Houlgate, "Hegel's Theory of Tragedy," 158–61.

restructured by the particular, it risks returning to the level of violence and contest, and so to the level of what cannot be thought." But this is not all that needs to be said, since "to maintain law at the expense of the particular is potentially to unleash the same unthought violence" upon human society. Thus there is a constantly shifting perspective, or even a "metaphysics," that is required here to account for "the singular that eludes category and the universal without which we cannot think past "coercive" definition."[168] Here again, we encounter the Aristotelian aporia between the individual and the universal, between the τόδε τι and the τί ἐστιν.[169]

This concept of lawfulness also forms for Hegel the intrinsic source of "conflict" within modern tragic drama, with the difference here that law is no longer tied "essentially to an 'externalized pressure', a 'set of imperatives 'out there' with which the agent is driven to identify." Rather, it is about "an ultimately self-contained model of integrity and authenticity" (*TI*, 64), a tragic "necessity" that is bound-up with "certain kinds of misrecognition" that is "bound to destroy human agents," and is, therefore, *not* about the "mechanically inevitable" (*TI*, 71). Tragic drama consequently is able to provoke within us reasoned reflection, but not in the sense that rationality will simply produce "triumphant order." Instead, we are invited to sympathize with the characters in their misrecognition, and therefore are made aware of "what we must search out and change in ourselves" (*TI*, 72). This "comic" reading of Hegel, which Williams draws from Rose, undermines the conclusion that "existence is tragic," or any "fully tragic worldview" (Nietzsche is presumably the target here), since that would mean that "there is no continuity in thought," no "perspective from which we can see what it is for humans to live unreal, deluded, and profoundly pain-ridden lives." The "comedy" of Hegel here is that "there is nothing that cannot be looked at truthfully" (*TI*, 74); and such an acknowledgement already militates against a conception of tragedy as inherently pessimistic, because herein we are made aware of "the *sources* of particular kinds of error and suffering" (*TI*, 76), and how they might be avoided. Here again we are made aware of how a conflictive account of exclusionary goods is unable to underwrite a transformative politics, and rather promotes an ontology of unremitting violence.

It is for this reason, amidst others, that Williams distances himself from George Steiner's reading of tragic "extremity." Steiner has spent a significant portion of his career making the argument that tragedy is a very limited and specific category of artistic presentation, one that is no longer

---

168. Williams, "The Sadness of the King," 21–22.
169. Cf. Rose, *Mourning Becomes Law*, 56.

attainable within a strictly *modern* consciousness.[170] Steiner, to be sure, does not celebrate this loss, but simply points us to the fact that the cultural imaginary that once nourished tragic drama is longer an assumed index of reference. This is not because "modern suffering is not interesting enough" but rather that "our representation of suffering has become thinner" (*TI*, 83). Steiner's import is that within modern technological and scientific framing, the erstwhile givens of divine "grace"—that which exceeds the merely human—are no longer taken as given. Therefore suffering is rendered simply as an "environmental malfunction" rather than an "irredeemable loss." In this perspective, "no tragic vision" is possible any longer (*TI*, 83). Without any sense of "presence"[171] or "the sacred," meanings are always going to be "disposable and exchangeable, never crushingly difficult." There will no longer be any true depth to our engagement, or any "words for what we are *bound* to wrestle with" (*TI*, 84). For a "culture in which all signs are exchangeable, or in which no signs have a value that cannot be renegotiated," it is doubtful that such a culture will be able to deal with "the idea of inescapable *cost*" (*TI*, 100–1), since any language which celebrates the "entirely fluid would be inimical to tragedy" because "it would treat loss as an invitation to compensation, not as an invitation to mourning" (*TI*, 101). Here Williams appears to be echoing the sentiments of MacKinnon as regards the interplay between "transcendence" and "the tragic," since (as he has said elsewhere) "Without the evocation . . . of God in [tragic] narratives, the scope of human actuality would be denied or reduced."[172]

Up to this point at least, Williams seems to support Steiner's concerns; where he differs is in regards to his theory of "absolute tragedy." Herein, Steiner attempts to articulate a rather narrow canon of tragic drama that reduces it to the finally and utterly disastrous, in which human beings, so to speak, are placed before the yawning, unspeakable horror

---

170. In a not-so-hidden jab at Steiner, Raymond Williams summarized this kind of reading in the following way: "The whole tradition of tragic drama is then defined around a single meaning, and other kinds of drama or theory are seen as 'not really' tragic, or as at best 'mixed'" (Williams, *Modern Tragedy*, 67). Also pertinent here is Raymond Williams's commentary on how modernity transformed the category of *accident* into a generalized *contingency*, to such an extent that ancient ideas of divine providence and fate no longer have the same cultural purchase that they once had. This is one of Steiner's main points in *The Death of Tragedy*: because such meaning is no longer generally available—since Steiner buys into the secularization thesis—"tragedy, is pushed back in time to periods when fully connecting meanings were available, and contemporary tragedy is seen as impossible because there are now no such meanings. The living tragedies of our own world can then not be negotiated at all" (Williams, *Modern Tragedy*, 75).

171. Cf. Steiner, *Real Presences*.

172. Williams, *Grace and Necessity*, 120.

of being itself.[173] It is this conceptualization which most coheres with Steiner's attempt to relate the essence of tragic consciousness to the post-Shoah milieu. But Williams's central gravamen is that Steiner, ultimately, reads tragedy as "a *text*" rather than a "shared event" (*TI*, 85): he fails, in Williams's mind, to account for tragedy precisely as *drama* (*TI*, 86). Here the dedication to find a "pure and definitive literary form is always shadowed by the passion to *ignore* something in the actual material work" (*TI*, 86). This continuing risk of misprision is inherent within all generalizing accounts of the tragic, as Simon Goldhill has already argued.[174] But beyond Steiner's hyper-reduction of the tragic, Williams seems especially concerned to show how Steiner's reading of tragedy, in fact (against his own stated affinity for renewed notions of 'presence'), is very much attuned with postmodern and Derridean suspicions of embodied communication, tendencies that privilege 'writing' over the human speaking-situation. For Williams, "the perception of suffering as capable of being spoken about" is excluded by "Steinerian tragedy," because it is "compromised as soon as it opens its mouth, because it is committed to representation, and so to an undetermined future exchange of words" (*TI*, 86).

For Steiner, the paradigm of tragedy is the silence of *Timon of Athens* rather than the "Never, never, never, never, never!" of *King Lear*. This model appears to refuse dialogue, and therefore seems to be undermined, in its focus on textuality, by the actual experience of tragic drama, which assumes that pain can be represented and spoken. Against Steiner's contentions, Williams shows that this is the case even for the most brutalizing and extreme versions of modern drama, like that of Sarah Kane (*TI*, 89–96). Even within

---

173. The most extreme sample of this tendency can be found in Steiner, "A Note on Absolute Tragedy." In his words, "absolute tragedy" asserts that "human life is a fatality," and "proclaims axiomatically that it is best not to be born or, failing that, to die young." It portrays "men and women as unwanted intruders on creation, as beings destined to undergo unmerited, incomprehensible, arbitrary suffering and defeat." It proposes "a negative ontology," which does not "admit of the rationale or therapy of discourse, be it philosophic or aesthetic," or any "pragmatic amelioration" for that matter. Absolute tragedy imposes a phenomenology of utter abjection ("Clarity of perception entails a stringent nihilism. Only nothingness is acquitted of the fault, of the error of being"). The conclusions are unremitting: "The man or woman possessed of the certitude of existential, ontological unwantedness seeks silence and death" (147). Its projections are of "unequivocal doom," a "zero-point" that "gathers all blackness to it" (148). In our modern world—especially within that "carnival of bestiality" that marks our epoch—we have been subjected to "the sheer dimensions of the inhuman," in ways that simply "impose silence" upon us, negating our attempts at representation (151). Metaphysically, this vision is "heretical," since "absolute tragedy" proposes an "innate evil," a "manichean dialectic," a *"performative mode of despair"* (155).

174. Goldhill, "Generalizing About Tragedy."

these admittedly horrendous narratives, the potential for ethical provocation remains: it gives the opportunity to learn and expand our moral sensibility by showing that our refusal to acknowledge certain truths about ourselves leads to catastrophe. We are again aware here of how tragedy cannot be equated with a pessimistic or capitulatory vision, precisely because it does not leave us with silence and passivity, but rather a form of narration in which pain is "integrated," even if "not consoled" (*TI*, 105).

It is worth pausing here for a moment to touch on tragedy and the sublime, as this is revealed in the interplay between suffering and its representation. Steiner's proclivities are exemplary of an intellectual proclivity (e.g., Adorno) that theorizes the non-representablity of tragic suffering (especially within the post-Shoah epoch). As Brett Gray has argued, such a "dark ineffability," which is ultimately "destructive of representation," is traceable to "the aesthetics of the sublime." This trajectory bothered Milbank vis-à-vis MacKinnon,[175] and Williams too—particularly as regards certain postmodernists (e.g., Derrida, Lyotard, etc.) who have privileged a "pathos of perpetual negation."[176] Williams has concerns that this tradition of the "sublime" tends to emphasize "the intense feelings of moral awe and emotional pathos" without a corresponding focus on its intellectual content (*TI*, 150–51).[177]

One problem derivable from this unsayablity is that it hypostasizes evil (e.g., Auschwitz) into an unspeakable or even deified reality: Giorgio Agamben has compared it to a perverse religiosity: an "adoring in silence, as one does with a god."[178] Gillian Rose also spoke about a "Holocaust piety" present within thinkers such as Adorno and Lyotard, who—in her estimate—conceptualized the Shoah as a manifestation of "the ineffable." Such "non-representablity" animates the drive "*to mystify something we dare not understand*, because we fear that it may be all too understandable, all too

---

175. Gray, *Jesus in the Theology of Rowan Williams*, 142.

176. Williams, "Between Politics and Metaphysics," 69.

177. Even though he is important for Williams's account (see *TI*, 52–53; 77–79), this would probably be his concern with Walter Davis's attempt to revive the kernel of the Kantian theory of the sublime—though without its rationalizing bent. Davis's plea for a dialectical and re-dramatized inwardness that seeks to take the tragic seriously is something that has much in common with MacKinnon and Williams's contribution. However, his push-back against "transcendence" and "rationality" as simply one more egoistic attempt to secure existential "guarantees" over-against tragic "affect" would be contested by MacKinnon and Williams. Moreover, Davis's preference for the noumenal sublime, subtracted from the Kantian *ratio*, has significant continuities with the poststructuralist tradition he is contesting throughout his text. For his admittedly controversial reading of the Kantian sublime, see Davis, *Deracination*, 47–97.

178. Agamben, *Remnants of Auschwitz*, 33.

continuous with what we are – human, all too human."[179] It transcendentalizes evil into a substantial entity and converts "*the positivity of evil*" into "*the evil of the positive*."[180] It demonizes the affirmatory and is finally *logophobic*.[181] This is connected to Rose's critique of "aberrated mourning" as a form of lament that "*cannot work*" because it remains entrenched in "melancholia."[182] Such a refusal of "inaugurated mourning," as Rose argues in the case of Walter Benjamin,[183] implies a denial of "mediation" and "negotiation" (or "law," to use her recurring term) which leaves us with a stark dualism between the violence of law-making and the "divine violence" of law-abolition. Here we are denied representation, judgement or mutual recognition, being entrenched in a "stasis of desertion,"[184] waiting on God for the anarchic destruction of every law. Here again, we are dealing with a subtle vision of the Kantian sublime that involves a denial of the mediation of Being through the particularities of beings. It also suggests a canonization of melancholia and pessimism at the expense of an emancipatory ethic.

In its postmodern iteration (e.g., Lyotard), sublimity is associated, as Jacques Rancière puts it, with "the immemorial law of alienation," a sacrificial economy in which we are to submit ourselves either to "the disaster of the sublime," that is, "the recognition of the immemorial dependence of the human mind on the immemorial law of the Other inside it," or we give sway to the greater or lesser forms of "totalitarianism" that have characterized our century.[185] For Lyotard, there is no *mediation*, no option beyond self-abjection and sacrifice—against a totalizing culture—or an ideological subjugation to ahistorical mythologies. For all their supposed anti-Hegelianism, those like Lyotard who seek to invoke the Shoah as *the* event of the unpresentable merely continue the unfolding of "dialectical reason," which "makes it possible to identify the existence of a people with an original determination of thought and to identify the professed unthinkability of the extermination with a tendency constitutive of Western reason." This

179. Rose, *Mourning Becomes Law*, 43.
180. Rose, *Mourning Becomes Law*, 56.
181. Rose, *Mourning Becomes Law*, 70, where she speaks of "the *logophobic* ethos of Derrida's thinking."
182. Rose, *Mourning Becomes Law*, 63.
183. Rose, "Walter Benjamin—Out of the Sources of Modern Judaism," in *Judaism and Modernity*, 175–210. Benjamin's adoption of melancholic themes are linked to his affinities for baroque drama. See Benjamin, *The Origin of German Tragic Drama*. A confirmation of Rose's reading of Benjamin can be found in Bielik-Robson, "Walter Benjamin (1892–1940)."
184. Rose, "Walter Benjamin," 209.
185. Rancière, "The Sublime from Lyotard to Schiller," 14–15.

"radicalizes" this dialectic "by rooting it in the laws of the unconscious and transforming the 'impossibility' of art after Auschwitz into an art of the unpresentable. But this perfecting is ultimately a perfecting of the dialectic," and *not* its dissolution.[186] Lyotardian sublimity is a post-factum rationalization of the rupture of "Western Reason," but rather than tracing these ruptures to the moral debasement of legal institutions, which need re-thinking and progressive alteration, this stream of post-Kantian sublimity tends to enclose suffering within a pious silence, beneath "the sign of holy terror."[187] If we are unable to think-through the systematic reasons for such terrors, we resign ourselves to their unintelligibility, and so transcendentalize its evil without investigating *why* catastrophes happen. In the end, the reasons might be all-too-prosaic, all-too-ordinary.

Here an anti-representational aesthetic imitates metaphysics: to allude to a discussion in an earlier chapter, as Being is rendered unspeakable and unthinkable, since it presents *nothing-in-particular* to the mind, so do extreme instances of suffering approach the threshold of inexpressibility.[188] As Lyotard says, inspired by Barnett Newman, the sublime is like the *makom*: the Unnameable, the unfathomable essence of YHWH.[189] But if these are conceived as sublimely indeterminate, such presentations become univocal, or at least practically indistinguishable. Being and Evil converge in their apophasis, in a strange reversal of the Platonic goodness-beyond-being.[190] Here ontological un-concealment and suffering reveal the nothingness of Being, thus demonstrating their convertibility, or to use Heideggerian terms, their equiprimordial status. Once more, evil is mythologized and de-historicized, since being and violence are rendered exchangeable. Violence is no longer traceable to some malfunction within history, but rather is a metaphysical dilation of Being itself. Similarly, the postmodern sublime—in its assertion of the *unthinkability* and *unspeakability* of some tragedies—already states *in advance* that such events remain unrepresentable, and has already augured the borders of its possibilities. But it remains perfectly reasonable to interrogate whether this does not merely repeat the separation of Being's un-concealment from historicity. Does it not trace a transcendental limit on the representability of tragedies in advance of their rhetorical or existential performance, forming an abstract 'universalism' shorn of particularity?

186. Rancière, *The Future of the Image*, 134.

187. Rancière, *The Future of the Image*, 137.

188. On the convergence between the unspeakabilities of evil and divinity within the postmodern sublime (Kristeva, Lyotard, Žižek, etc.), see Kearney, *Strangers, Gods, and Monsters*, 88–100.

189. Lyotard, *The Inhuman*, 89–90.

190. Kearney, *Strangers, Gods, and Monsters*, 187.

Leaving this discussion for now, and returning to *The Tragic Imagination*, we can see how this theme of ontological pessimism comes forward in the chapter on religious language and tragedy. It is here that Donald MacKinnon re-appears, refracted again through the critiques of 'tragic theology' given by David Bentley Hart and John Milbank, of which we have discussed at length. Overall, it seems that Williams considers Milbank's critique to be the more serious and nuanced of the two, as can be seen in the space he gives to his arguments. Hart seems to reduce Greek tragedy to "a single theme which has to do with the sovereignty of unfriendly fate and the unavoidability of appeasing a violent sacred order" (*TI*, 111).[191] But it is a reading that sits rather lightly on detail, and fails to account for how tragedy interrogates notions of "lawfulness," and how even some tragedies (e.g., *Antigone*) display "the destructive effect of setting the sacred against itself" (*TI*, 111). Williams does not go into much detail regarding Hart's critique here[192]—even though it appears to lie in the background of his chapter on Hegel. At this point, his preference is to engage Milbank more extensively.

As I have noted previously, Milbank argues that MacKinnon's moral philosophy aims to "naturalize" (*TI*, 108) tragic occurrence, since (as he sees it) it is only within "the destructively conflicting absolutes of tragic decision that we discover the nature of our human responsibility" (*TI*, 109). Milbank worries that MacKinnon "lacks a theory as to how non-destructive social practices may be created and maintained, and so is trapped in a standoff between purely individual motivation, with whatever integrity it can muster, and the inescapably corrupting and lethal realities of the public world." Being Kantian, MacKinnon shied away from a more Hegelian *Sittlichkeit*, in which we come to recognize "the moral self in the other or in the communal discourse of humanity." Rather, MacKinnon's treatment of tragic irresolution seems to imply "a near-Manichaean metaphysic," or even a "fundamental sickness or rupture in reality" (*TI*, 109), that ultimately achieves a non-negotiable and ontological status. For Milbank, the operative mode of "tragic narration" in Mackinnon's thinking leads to a denial of "the significance of narrative itself," in which human characters are able to "genuinely grow and change with the passage of time," implying an emptying of "the very idea of plot," since it fails to account for the reality of "change" that is

---

191. Hart's more recent contribution in the *Modern Theology* symposium has not significantly changed Williams's judgements. In his reading, Hart remains committed to the same essentialism that characterized his earlier reflections in *The Beauty of the Infinite*. Once more, Hart makes little reference to the classical scholarship that many of Williams's conclusions are predicated on.

192. He does engage Hart to a greater degree in Williams, "Not Cured, Not Forgetful, Not Paralysed." This essay will be referenced in our conclusion to this study.

bound up with "a sequence of narrated events." In MacKinnon's account then, it seems, *"nothing really alters"* (*TI*, 110). Where Hart and Milbank's critiques converge is in their rejection of any ontological violence, and in their disavowal of all abstracted accounts of human suffering. For them, this metaphysic would constitute "the very opposite of a discipline of specific attention to pain and loss." Against MacKinnon's stated concern with particularity and a pluralist realism then, his actual practice is "universalizing" and appears to buttress "violence and conflict as the omnipresent conditions of human existence." In their reading, his tragic vision ultimately "mystifies and glamorizes violence" itself (*TI*, 110).

But Williams does not think the issue is quite so simple: rather than giving-in to a form of politics that privileges personal authenticity, he thinks that for MacKinnon tragedy is not simply about self-discovery in the moment of tragic indecision, where one is confronted with that "conflict of duties" on which one's personhood is staked. MacKinnon's more primary concern, rather, is to show how "horrors" can be the result of "good intentions" that are "as much personal and relational as they are public or social" (*TI*, 112). For MacKinnon, "ignorance of the effects of our actions" is the manner in which we experience our finitude and "limitedness," and that it is precisely through internalizing this that we become human beings who "*cease* to think and feel in certain ways," enduring our existential "estrangement" as a part of human "growth" (*TI*, 112). This is another way of saying that our actions cannot avoid precariousness since there is "no *historical* end to risk and suffering," even though we should not imply by this some kind of "supertemporal principle or existential curse" (*TI*, 113). On the contrary:

> It is simply a matter of parsing what it means to recognize our finitude: narrative itself presupposes the irreversible passage of time and thus the omnipresence of loss.... What happens as result of our decisions is not an abstract and identical calamity but always the specific kind of loss that *this* unique set of temporal conditions will generate ... the very act of narrating anything at all involves the possibility of *tragic* narration. The passage of time is a process of loss, *identified as such in the act of relating it*. Telling the story of the past is a representation of what both is and is not 'here'... Yet to recognize this element of loss or absence is not necessarily to be committed to a picture of finite existence as a struggle between fate and the noble but helpless subject. There are no subjects independent of awareness in time, and so to be a human subject is to be involved in understanding that growth, movement in time, [and] entails a letting-go of past identities. (*TI*, 113–14)

So our finitude and contingency, our *estrangement* from fixed identities, does not stem from "a form of pessimism," an insuperable woundedness, because "if acts and events are uncontrollable in their effect, if we do not know what may flow from this or that happening," then we cannot exclude the possibility that "anguish and atrocity do not make a future impossible," even if such a future may be "incurably damaged for at least some." It does not deny the openness inherent within historical action, nor does it imply that such tragedies "stop things happening" and "things being spoken of." For Williams, tragedy would be "incompatible" with the "Christian narrative" only if it advocated "a form of Stoicism," "[a] reconciliation with the unbearable as inevitable" (*TI*, 115). All that Williams has said thus far should question such a conclusion.

All this is not to say that Williams is in complete unison with MacKinnon's perspective. Since Williams presupposes that the human self is "fundamentally desirous, motivated by its foundational lack of God as its ultimate good,"[193] this means that tragedy as such "does not persist as an intractable fate" since, for Williams, a "future is always being opened up" by the God who providentially orders it.[194] Thus we are enjoined not to place hope not in some primordial harmony, but in the Creator, who has made a world in which the "good will take time to realise."[195] Such a reading does not exclude that "healing or mending" can take place,[196] even though this "healing" should not bypass or simply cancel those histories that constitute personhood, because that would precisely imply an "exit from the narrative" (as was noted in Williams's critique of Milbank). So while it must be emphasized that Williams expands and continues MacKinnon's thinking into the present, we should not assume that they are of one accord at every juncture.

As I bring the discussion of this monograph to a close, it could be said Williams's focus on tragic drama is open to the misunderstanding that it is only through *this* kind of narration that we are provoked to "the unwelcome and subversive knowledge of our flawed self-picturing" (*TI*, 151). Such a reading might indicate an overly narrow or even Westernized and elitist conclusion—only the privileged are granted such knowledge—a conclusion that is certainly at odds with the spirit of his text. This non-elitism is presupposed in the place he gives to Raymond Williams, who disputed the conclusion that tragedy could not be about "ordinary" people and events (*TI*, 96–101), and is also implied in Williams's, admittedly

---

193. Gray, *Jesus in the Theology of Rowan Williams*, 126.
194. Gray, *Jesus in the Theology of Rowan Williams*, 136.
195. Williams, "Saving Time," 323.
196. Williams, "Saving Time," 321–22.

brief, discussion of African and non-Western drama (TI, 137–42). But on a further note, he clearly distances himself from this conclusion by arguing that tragic drama is simply *one* instance of "dispossession" (a recurrent word in his lexicon, as we have seen) that makes us conscious of "the world of bodily limit" and "mutual negotiation" (*TI*, 151). It is not through tragedy *alone* that we are given access to such insights; rather, tragedy forms an intense and acute example of those processes of learning and conversion to which we are constantly enjoined. This leaves open the possibility (though Williams does not explicitly discuss this) of relating his insights on tragic drama to 'narration' more generally, especially in its relation to the communication of trauma.[197] Such an emphasis on narrative might then provide an analogical link between drama and 'ordinary' experiences of suffering, while being fully aware of Williams's caveat that we should not simply reduce "tragedy" to "*accidental* misfortune" (*TI*, 97–98). But this might also imply that Williams's criticisms of treating tragedy as a "text" rather than "drama" (in regard to Steiner) might have to be nuanced further, since there is intriguing evidence that suggests the collective *reading* of tragic texts has produced healing results amongst PTSD sufferers, for instance.[198] But these are all rather minor quibbles, which do not undermine his concern to show that tragedy is concerned with how we learn through time and human engagement, and about how, consequently, it cannot be equated *tout court* with metaphysical pessimism.

A synthesis of what I have been trying to say as regards Williams can be attempted now: in the previous chapter, I attempted to show why for Williams the very materiality of creating and speaking has metaphysical significance; this is because 'matter' and 'mattering' are profoundly connected for Williams. The process of creating form, of giving shape to the world is *not* a willful imposition on an otherwise non-intelligent environment, but rather a discovery of something excessive within reality itself. Similarly, language

---

197. Herman, *Trauma and Recovery*. However, in Williams, *The Edge of Words*, 137, Williams writes that "there is . . . a dimension of fictional narrative which imagines possibilities of positive change that our 'normal' perceptions routinely encourage us to ignore, hope that cannot simply be brought out of the simply given. If ultimate convergence, healing, consolation, is apparently impossible to imagine, that's why it is necessary to imagine it. Or, to avoid merely annoying paradox: if we cannot rationally predict or organize or guarantee some sort of reconciliation and healing, we have no choice but to approach it through fiction—not as a means of evading or denying an unpalatable present but as a form of acknowledging resources that are there in or for our present world, but to which we do not yet have straightforward access."

198. See the two interpretive essays in Meagher, *Herakles Gone Mad*, 3–67. Such has some surprising connections with Aristotle's own reflections in this regard (cf. *Poetics* 1453b1–11).

and representation always involves us in a super-addition of meaning, because we can never say exactly the *same* thing twice, since representation does not involve a simplistic mirroring procedure. Because of our placement within time, and in a community of language-users, our meaning is never defined by individuals alone, but in conjunction with the wider context in which it is placed. This means that the self-identity of any item or person can only be maintained through difference, through a non-identical repetition within time. Such impresses, in contemporary terms, the intuition (that has been suggested since Aristotle) of a perennial interplay between the particular and universal. For his part, Williams's own register leans more on Hegel's historicism, and specifically focuses on the way Hegel sought to overcome the dichotomies between sameness and difference. This rejection of dualism, that is, between particular and its abstraction, between the transcendent and the immanent, gives credence to the analogical metaphysic I have been stressing throughout, namely, that there is an intimate—albeit infinite qualitative distinction—between the *being-there* and the *being-thus* (to use Przywara's lexicon), between temporal being and Being-as-such. In order to think particulars then, we have to place them within the context of their unfolding, which stretches into the infinite.

The same can be said in regard to selfhood: we cannot think of ourselves apart from the regimes of language and community, and especially, for Augustine, in the way that we are related desirously to God in an unending pilgrimage. We exist as embodied and temporal beings, and therefore we cannot come to a self-understanding apart from embracing our limited existence, our sense of createdness. Again, as in the case of language, our material bodies have a significance that is not simply imposed arbitrarily, but is something that is discovered as gift, as something received in trust. This means that the self does not have to assert itself at all costs, or hang onto strict identities for the sake of survival. For Williams, one of the elements of our moral pilgrimage is that we learn to let go of identities that hinder expansion. Such dilation might imply loss, but precisely because this forfeiture can be spoken and historically communicated, we cannot foreclose the meaning such loss might accrue. And because matter matters, we should not assume prematurely that 'meaning' is a product of self-deception or fantasy. Certainly, 'meaning' can be credulous or delusory, but that is something which can only be tested relationally, through the way that narratives display their "adequacy to reality" (Walter Stein). Through reflections on narratives of loss, and in having the courage to speak them, we may chance upon disclosures which we did not expect. We might encounter another self on the other side of death.

But because the self exists within relations, this also implies a political order that does not privilege atomized individuals or privatized goods. To say that I discover myself in another is to imply that I am not defined in opposition to other agents. If I can know or recognize myself in someone different, this means that I am not a self-constituting subject, but rather am re-discovered in the other. But if this is the case, then it means that my interests are not exclusively mine alone, but are found within the encounters and negotiations I have with others. And this suggests that what is good for my well-being does not have to come at the expense of others, in the sense that their goods are opposed to mine. The alternative option, which assumes that my good is opposed to yours, would seem to be predicated on an inherently conflictive account of bilateral exclusion—an ontology of violence that fates us to a lugubrious social compact. This is the conclusion that follows if we think of the Good as being purely contingent or hopelessly pluralistic. It is this metaphysic that underlies the Hobbesian *bellum omnium contra omnes*, and the liberal order that denies a deeper commonality beyond sectional interests. The alternative to this picture is the assumption that the Good is transcendent and universal, and finally convertible with infinite Being-as-such. The Good cannot be grasped in its plenitude within time, but only slowly and progressively inched towards—with plenty of setbacks and misconceptions along the way. But to say that the Good is historically mediated *for us* does not mean that the Good is a product of history itself. To assume this would reduce the Good to a purely immanent site of production, without any ontological ground for intersectional interest. Such a vision, if true, would mean that I could not engage with others on the assumption that we might recognize a common good; rather, it presupposes an endless rivalry and exclusionary politics.

In a text entitled "Resurrection and Peace,"[199] Williams speaks about the "error" of seeing "the reality and inevitability of conflict" as a "kind of metaphysical statement about the inevitability of mutual exclusion and strife." Instead, we should trace them to "the ways in which we are formed in the hard tasks of responding to resistance [and] the otherness of the world," in "the accepting of our inability to guarantee ourselves or anyone an untroubled passage through it."[200] It is into these tensions that we are placed: neither pessimism nor optimism, but a sober acknowledgement of where we are at, how we got here, and how this might assist us in imagining alternate futures.

---

199. Williams, "Resurrection and Peace," in *On Christian Theology*, 265–75.
200. Williams, "Resurrection and Peace," 273.

9

Conclusion

Our study has focused on a single question: can a classical account of transcendence reckon with the tragic? And if so, how might it do this? Behind this question was the assumption (as suggested in Chapter 3) that the regime of the tragic, especially within the modern period, carried residual imports that a classically-orthodox theology would struggle to accept. I did not suggest these were the *only* problems, but that they were some of the most pressing for a traditional metaphysic. In other words, I was not so much focused on the relation between Christianity and the tragic *in general*. I was not primarily concerned whether other varieties of Christian thought and practice would have greater (or less) ease in appropriating the negativity of the tragic. Though I certainly think that a classical theology has something important to say, I do not presume it provides the only viable Christian response to the tragic. Instead my intention was narrower, insofar as I have been trying throughout to ask whether there are specific grammars of transcendence—especially within their contemporary reception—that hinder a more 'systematic' correlation between orthodox Christianity and tragedy. Are there ways of construing transcendence which alleviate this juxtaposition, or are we resigned to opposition?

In first two chapters I unpacked some of my presuppositions regarding theological method, and situated our discussion of tragedy within the debate between the poets and philosophers, with a concentration on the writings of Plato. Our goal here was to find out where some of these tensions might have begun, that is, between ancient philosophical metaphysics and the tragic. We noticed that the Platonic rejection of theatre was ambiguous, and therefore could not be decisive for the contemporary debate. I subsequently moved on to the interconnections between Christianity and the tragic, there once more emphasizing its more traditional incarnations within the patristic and medieval periods. Here we encountered a significant diversity of responses, which were difficult to schematize into a single strategy. There was a suspicion of the genre and its broader thematic within influential quarters (e.g., Tertullian and Augustine), but an acceptance and deployment of its structures by others. What this means is that we cannot assume a permanent antagonism between Christianity and the tragic *as such*, and therefore should not situate the conceptual abrasiveness at this point at least. Instead, I suggested that the supposed tension between Christianity and the tragic was a more recent phenomenon, and had more to do with a specific generalization of the tragic and Christianity *in toto*. Thereafter, I introduced the figures of David Bentley Hart, Donald MacKinnon, John Milbank, and Rowan Williams as modern theologians who were representative within this debate.

Within Chapter 3 there was a treatment of the grammar of aseity, and how transcendence and the tragic were reconfigured in modernity. This was done specifically in relation to *the modern regime of the sublime, the idea of a suffering Absolute,* and *the rejection of evil-as-privation,* developments which ultimately have created tensions for a classical reading of transcendence, specifically as regards *analogy, aseity* and *the ontological priority of the Good.* In Chapter 4 I introduced Donald MacKinnon more substantially, before engaging in a detailed reading of his critics, namely Hart and Milbank. It was argued by Hart that MacKinnon's adoption of tragedy implicated him in a sacrificial totalitarianism that was unable to account for the irruption of the resurrection gospel. Hart also castigated 'tragic theology' as being entwined with a rejection of divine impassibility and evil-as-privation, and therefore remained problematic for an orthodox theology. Milbank for his part argued that MacKinnon's use of the tragic was interlaced with an acceptance of the Kantian sublime, and a failure to appreciate an analogical metaphysics as providing an avenue for reconciling transcendence and historicity.

In Chapters 5 and 6, I entered into a detailed reading of MacKinnon, with the aim of seeing whether these critiques hit their mark. Our answer was a qualified yes with some dissensions. Chapter 5 argued, through an examination of his reception of Aristotelian philosophy, atomist realism and Kantian metaphysics, that MacKinnon was unable, in our opinion, to sufficiently account for the interrelation between historicity, constructionism and transcendence within *The Problem of Metaphysics*, and his wider corpus. I suggested that this was connected to his rejection of analogical participation, a decision based upon his suspicion of Platonic intellectual intuition, and also his Kantian rejection of the idea that being is a predicate of particular things.

The following chapter turned to his account of ethics, metaphysics and the tragic. Here I discussed MacKinnon's desire to construct a "system of projection" that deduced transcendence through a focus on moral perplexity and the tragic. MacKinnon's argumentation supposed that these realities required something more than a purely immanent description could give, because without this transcendent supplementation, these realities would be rendered trivial, and therefore the tragic would cease to be about anything truly difficult. Biological naturalism displaces metaphysics, and with it tragedy ceases to be a problem. However, I nonetheless suggested, as a result of his acceptance of Kantian transcendentalism and radical evil, that he remained captured within the modern regime of sublimity, insofar as he lacked a coherent model of projection regarding the relation of created finitude to infinite beatitude. Insofar as he rejected the *privatio boni*, and accepted divine passibility and a noumenal sublime, he rendered indeterminate the quality of the unconditioned. Therefore, it remained difficult for him to establish an intimate connection between the realm of nature and the realm of ends, between nature and its transcendent good, and thereby escape the critiques of Milbank. I did *not* argue that this was his explicit intention, but rather that it was an implication of his conceptual instability. However, I did suggest that Hart's comments regarding sacrificial totality could not be applied to the substance of MacKinnon's thought. Moreover, Milbank's accusations that the "speculative closure" of the tragic avoids historicity, while having some validity did not address everything that needed to be said regarding MacKinnon vis-à-vis tragedy. I also argued that Milbank's own approach, at points, might not be historicist enough.

It was the intention of Chapters 7 and 8 to provide a critical supplementation to MacKinnon's insights through an intensive reading of Rowan Williams. This was done with the aim of showing that a classical account of transcendent goodness can be coherently related to the negativity of the tragic. In view of the previous argumentation, Williams's contribution would need to traverse the conceptual problems which I associated with MacKinnon's approach. It would need to espouse an orthodox metaphysic of the creator-creature relation, via the doctrines of aseity and analogy, and would also have to address questions of historicity. Also, his position would need to advance an account of the *privatio boni* that was able to endure the critiques lodged at it by MacKinnon and others, and would moreover have to transcend what I have been calling the Kantian and postmodern sublime. I suggested that Williams meets these requirements: I examined his metaphysical writings to show that he was able to bring-together a traditional account of analogical transcendence within a modernist and Romantic theory of poetics. This was seen in his various writings on *creativity*, *language* and *analogy*, insofar as it attempted to reconcile a metaphysical realism with a robust historicity. Thereafter I discussed Williams's interpretation of Augustine as regards the question of evil, and its deep interconnection with his idea of God as transcendent goodness. We saw him argue that the rejection of evil-as-privation is a by-no-means trivial choice, and has implications as regards our conceptualizations of metaphysics, politics and ethics. If the Good is not convertible with the transcendent and infinite One, and not anterior to any ontological perversion, then evil is rendered transcendental, and our respective 'goods' can no longer be implemented on the assumption that they are reconcilable within the higher order of the Good. Both of these outgrowths tacitly imply either an *ontological violence* or *ontological pessimism*—neither of which gives us much assistance with regard to a truly emancipatory politics.

Chapter 8 provided a capstone to the argument of this book, as far as it sought to exposit Williams's *The Tragic Imagination*, a monograph which constitutes his most significant testament on the question of tragedy. In a comparable manner to our discussion of MacKinnon, I prefaced our take on Williams with a discussion of 'difficulty' and its relation to moral maturation. I then moved to a discussion of his reception of Augustinian concepts of selfhood through Hegel and Gillian Rose. It was argued that Williams's appropriation of the self proposes a kenotic restatement of the Augustinian path, specifically as this connects to the displacement of the ego through desire and the unhanding of self. We could say that this is the 'tragic' aspect of his reading. However, Williams's predilection for rupture and dispossession is complemented by a Hegelian 'comic' iteration in which human failure and error was bracketed by laughter. Moral growth is not about self-laceration or simply ego-bashing, but about a letting-go of those assertions that restrict and distort—in other words, those identities that are taken *too* seriously. After that, I turned to *The Tragic Imagination*, placing its content within the background that led up to it. In this part, I argued that Williams's approach was centered on the claim that 'the tragic' characterized events that could be carried in *language*: they are communicable and subject to relational engagement between agents. Pain is not locked within a silent abjection of the sublime, but incorporated into narratives, stories that can be re-told, engaged and enlarged. Therefore, tragic suffering does not mean we are isolated into any transcendental restrictions of unthinkability or unspeakability, as if we could not imagine *that* pain within a larger story, or that we could not think about *how* and *why* certain tragic errors might have arisen in the past, or that any sense-making is *a priori* excluded. Rather, it is to say that we never quite know whether *this* word will be the *last* word. This insight brings us to the next major theme, namely the problem of *irony*. It says that history places indeterminacy over actions, which (because they happen within a finite causal nexus) can irrupt into conflict and suffering; to exist within time means that we never quite know the outcomes of our decisions and actions, or whether these outgrowths are final or not. History has a way of overturning expectations, for better or for worse. The import of tragic experience is that we can never quite know what this outcome will be. And one could say that this is intrinsic to what we have been calling *the negativity of the tragic*.

Reflecting on these last chapters, it is worth remarking upon some ways in which Williams sustains this negativity, because they are not always spelled out in detail within *The Tragic Imagination* and the other texts I have discussed. One of the things that should be brought out here is that Williams's acceptance of the *privatio boni* means not only that the Good is granted priority, but also that evil has *no meaning in itself*. If this is the case, then it resists *any* theodicy that presupposes that we can ascribe depth or order to evil. Such is excluded at the outset by the Platonic-Augustinian perspective. On this reading, evil does not have any 'being,' nor is it a distinct 'thing' within the world, nor does it have any persistence apart from the reality it corrupts. Evil is devoid of rationality: it is the black hole of meaning.[1] What this means is while we cannot equate *all* suffering with evil, it certainly means that we cannot ascribe meaning to suffering as such. Williams's criticisms elsewhere of philosophical theodicies as "an attempt to forget [suffering] as suffering" and therefore as entwined with "untruthfulness"[2] remain in force, as does his rejection of more subtle theodicies (e.g., Marilyn McCord Adams).[3] However, this necessary qualification does not exclude the possibility that human beings are able to create

---

1. To quote Milbank: "evil for the Christian tradition was radically without cause—indeed it was not even self-caused, but was rather the (impossible) refusal of cause. In this way privation theory offers not an 'explanation' of evil, but instead rigorously remains with its inexplicability, for 'explanation' can pertain only to existence, and here evil is not seen as something in existence. Indeed it is regarded for this reason as not even explicable *in principle*, not even explicable for God. Since evil is in this way so problematic that it falls outside the range of *problema*, there has never been for theologians any 'problem of evil'. The idea that there is such a problem has only arisen since, roughly, the time of Leibniz. As inherited evil was held to have already impaired our finitude, there was, indeed, for the authentic tradition, in us a causal bias to evil; yet since grace renews our will, our evil decision to refuse grace is as groundless and causeless as Adam's original sin" (Milbank, *Being Reconciled*, 18).

2 Williams, "Trinity and Ontology," in *On Christian Theology*, 155.

3. Williams, "Redeeming Sorrows," 255–74. Her own project is summarized in Adams, *Horrendous Evils and the Goodness of God*.

meaning *within* suffering. Williams's major contribution to our discussion is that tragic experience is not excluded from communication, which means that suffering can be narrated in such a way that it is included (potentially) within a larger scope of meaning. We cannot predetermine the scope this or that event will generate, and the context into which it will be ultimately placed. Because of this, we do well to hold onto a healthy dose of irony, in the knowledge that it is possible that "there are unpredictable, unsystematisable integrations of suffering into a biography in the experience of some,"[4] while for others this may be lacking. This aspect of narrative touches upon one of the other ways Williams attempts to incorporate tragic loss within his system: one can recall here how he criticized Milbank regarding the question of "resolution" within narrative, and whether Milbank himself could be accused of an account that was implicated in "an *unmaking* of the past," one that conjectured "an exit from the world of narrative," and "an absolute ending which obliterates the cost of what has gone before."[5]

One conclusion to be drawn from this is that Williams's attachment to the negativity of the tragic cautions him against any eschatological cancellation of the tragic. Our gospels appear to confirm this: *Christ's wounds are not erased but raised with him* (John 20:24–29). The resurrection does not obliterate human history but redeems it. This is a continuing motif within Williams's oeuvre ever since his lectures on Eliot's *Four Quartets*. For Williams, as Benjamin Myers says, "Whatever Christian eschatology might mean, it cannot posit any final triumph over human imperfection and limitation. To eliminate tragedy would be to do away with the difference that makes us human."[6] Moreover, "Christian hope does not invalidate [a] tragic vision, but reaffirms it—just as Christ's resurrection does not cancel out the crucifixion, but transfigures it and discloses its inner significance."[7] This eschatological vision is able to sustain MacKinnon's phraseology of 'the transcendence of the tragic' insofar as it does not attempt "to eliminate the element of unfathomable mystery by the attempt to move beyond tragedy,"[8] nor does it deny what Paul Janz called "the finality of non-resolution."[9] This does not negate what Brett Gray has said, namely that Williams's eschatology has "an almost eudaemonic register"[10] that proposes a final "amelioration of the tragic" within its

---

4. Williams, "Redeeming Sorrows," 272.
5. Williams, *The Tragic Imagination*, 114–15.
6. Myers, *Christ the Stranger*, 56.
7. Myers, *Christ the Stranger*, 94.
8. MacKinnon, *The Problem of Metaphysics*, 129.
9. Janz, *God, the Mind's Desire*, 175.
10. Gray, *Jesus in the Theology of Rowan Williams*, 127.

scope.[11] But it does mean that redemption does not necessitate the erasure of any past, but rather implies its transformation.

Another thing needs to be remarked upon before we transition to some critical commentary on Williams's work. One of the running strains throughout this book is the impact of the Kantian sublime on the reception of the tragic. We saw this already in Chapter 3 and it has persisted throughout this study, as seen in the debate between Milbank and MacKinnon that was unfurled in Chapters 4–6. However, it should be said that Williams (except for a rather brief reference) scarcely addresses this trope explicitly within *The Tragic Imagination*, or in his other writings for that matter, nor does he engage much with MacKinnon's Kantianism (at least in this work[12]), and how it featured prominently within Milbank's critique of MacKinnon. It is this paucity that has inspired my own study. So in the previous argument, I have suggested that Williams's metaphysics is incompatible with a Kantian transcendentalism or an abstract negativity of postmodernity. Williams's questions anti-representationalism, or any wager that privileges an ontological excess which remains absolutely non-thinkable and unspeakable, one entrenched within the "pathos of perpetual negation."[13] Moreover, his proposal that "suffering can be narrated," "communicatively or imaginatively shared" and therefore made into "a *cultural* fact,"[14] implicitly counteracts a tragic sublimity that would baptize silence as being the *only* response to traumatic anguish. Such is seen in his interactions with George Steiner, but within the space of his monograph these connections are not unfurled as much as they could have been. This is not a negligible point, since (as I already indicated in earlier chapters) the post-Kantian sublime has had a seminal impact on continental readings of the tragic, running from Schiller, through Nietzsche, up to postmodernity. My own study has been written within this background, suggesting that Williams contributes a particular lucidity to the debate around the modern sublime, even though he does not always explicitly address it in those terms.

That being said, Williams's account is not immune to critique or opacity. David Bentley Hart, in his response to *The Tragic Imagination*, remains largely unrepentant—despite Williams's countervailing. Hart complains about how Williams's Hegelian reading of tragedy proposes "an unhistorical imposition of post-Christian notions on a society to which they are

---

11. Gray, *Jesus in the Theology of Rowan Williams*, 134.

12. However, see Williams, "Trinity and Ontology" for some supplements on this point.

13. Williams, "Between Politics and Metaphysics," 69.

14. Williams, *The Tragic Imagination*, 132.

irrelevant."[15] Hart repeats his previous critiques that tragedy "beautifies" suffering,[16] and narcotizes us into submission, implying that "all these terrible truths could somehow, by the application of sufficient art, be made beautiful, hypnotic, gorgeously grave, and stupefying."[17] In a lapidary remark, he argues that rather than instigating critical reflection, "the infallible mark of the tragic is that it helps one sleep well."[18] Here Hart is echoing his earlier contention that tragedy does not provoke a clear-eyed wisdom regarding the nature of reality, but rather consoles us into inaction. He qualifies perceptions of his previous work (e.g., *The Beauty of the Infinite*) by saying that his problem with tragedy is not that it proposes a "pessimistic" outlook, but that "it is not yet terrible enough to account for what the gospel brings into human reflection."[19] For Hart, tragedy does not diagnose the depth of our alienation and loss, nor does it provide remedy. On the contrary, it is only the "logic" of resurrection faith, with its "mad and quite imprudent vision of divine truth," which establishes that "the only horizon of hope is that of the humanly impossible." In his estimate, Christianity is more child-like in in its hope, having greater affinity to fairy-tales than the tragic.[20] Moreover, Hart assumes within these interventions the idea that a narrative-dramatic representation of pain as a mode of "healing without cure," however beneficial, is not yet the gospel.

Williams concedes that the eschatological dimension of Christianity says that "'happy endings' are not earned by the logic of a narrative, nor do they cancel what has happened in the story so far," but have "the nature of a startling novelty, a gratuitous plot-twist."[21] For Hart and Williams, the resurrection does not succeed the crucifixion like a simple alteration in the *mise-en-scène*. Surely the gospel is more radical and apocalyptic than that. Nevertheless, Williams does write that:

> The discourse, the imaginative labour, which we call 'tragic' is an act of faith that what in its intensity of pain or emptiness defies language may not after all be a final victory for chaos. Perhaps it is not inappropriate to say that in this sense

15. Hart, "The Gospel According to Melpomene," 223. For his critique of Hegel (and Williams's) reading of *Antigone*, see 228–29.

16. Hart, "The Gospel According to Melpomene," 231.

17. Hart, "The Gospel According to Melpomene," 225.

18. Hart, "The Gospel According to Melpomene," 221.

19. Hart, "The Gospel According to Melpomene," 230.

20. Hart, "The Gospel According to Melpomene," 233.

21. Williams, "Not Cured, Not Forgetful, Not Paralysed," 280. One is reminded at this point of J. R. R. Tolkien's *eucatastrophe*.

tragic representation is *analogous* to theological proclamation. It states that something remains possible in the wake of atrocity. And how to make such a statement without doing less than justice to the weight of what has been seen or felt is precisely what makes this kind of discourse difficult and laden with ambiguities and possible failures.[22]

In addition to this qualification, one could advance several other points of reply: firstly, Hart once more displays a rather entrenched concept of Attic tragedy that is advanced without any references to contemporary classical scholarship (e.g., Vernant, Goldhill, etc.), even as he accuses Williams of "a literary interpretation" of tragedy, a "treatment principally of texts, abstracted from the historically concrete realities of both the aesthetic form and the religious context of the plays."[23] Williams remains perturbed by this: he is worried by "a continuing essentialism" within Hart's critique, and argues that if Hart's characterizations of tragic art are serious, then "my disagreement is fundamental (to a degree that surprises me)." While Hart "appears to reduce tragic representation to a stratagem to *avoid* seeing," Williams makes the opposing argument "that it is one of those disciplines that *enables* some kinds of seeing."[24] The contradiction could not be clearer than this.

Secondly, Hart makes some rather confusing remarks regarding beauty which stand in contrast to some of his earlier proposals. There are moments in Hart's text (scattered at various moments[25]) where he appears to suggest that beauty itself is "automatically elided with a manifest form that veils rather than reveals," which appears to contradict his earlier contentions that "the beauty embodied in the form of what we actually see or hear or touch is precisely its aptness to the truth, not an embellishment."[26] What Williams is suggesting is that Hart rather strangely appears to succumb, at moments, to a quasi-Kantian sublimity that proposes the negligibility of form to the communication of the beautiful. This is despite his metaphysical conceits expressed elsewhere, in *The Beauty of the Infinite*, that the triune God is the coincidence of both infinite beauty and perfect form. These apparent tensions would need to be addressed by Hart, who seems to have muddled things a bit in this particular response.

Thirdly, one could query Hart's *prima facie* dualism between the tragic and the fairy-tale, inasmuch as fairy-tales—especially in their earlier

---

22. Williams, "Not Cured, Not Forgetful, Not Paralysed," 280–81.
23. Hart, "The Gospel According to Melpomene," 223.
24. Williams, "Not Cured, Not Forgetful, Not Paralysed," 281.
25. Hart, "The Gospel According to Melpomene," 221, 222, 225.
26. Williams, "Not Cured, Not Forgetful, Not Paralysed," 281–82.

recordings—often resist the simplistic resolutions found within their expurgated versions. Fairy-tales can display a moral complexity and tragic irresolution that deconstructs hard and fast distinctions.[27] As even a cursory knowledge will tell, *faerie* is a tenebrous and ambiguous realm within the folkloric tradition, more disturbing than Disney films will let on. By way of example, drawing from pop culture, one only has to watch Guillermo Del Toro's *Pan's Labyrinth* (2006) or Matteo Garrone's *Tale of Tales* (2015) to notice that these divisions are not absolute. Also important to recognize is that some tragedies themselves have been compared to the structures of fairy-tales (like Euripides's *Alcestis*).[28] Hart might respond that these samples are not really tragedies, but then we are back at Steinerian essentialism. So in relation to Hart and the tragic, it appears that not much has changed.

Graham Ward has also penned a largely appreciative critique of Williams's book.[29] His responses are centered on the question of liminality, on the thresholds between the human and non-human. Ward's recent excursions into evolutionary psychology most certainly occupy a hinterland, as seen in the way that he shows how the tragedians themselves toyed with the interplay between the human and non-human in their imagery. The central thread of this text is that the tragic touches upon something deeper, more traumatic, than intellectual resources can capacitate. He worries that Williams rushes too quickly towards "eloquence."[30] Ward desires to linger, to tarry with the negative. Or to use Lacanian terminology, he wants to more greatly emphasize the traumatic Real vis-à-vis the Symbolic. For Ward, the tragic or traumatic reaches towards the animality we share with the non-human, exposing us to the threat of a "nothing" (as in *King Lear*) that is "ontological, even meontological," and "not epistemological."[31] Ward's language here projects tragic risk onto a cosmological landscape, a risk he takes, despite refusing the fatalisms of "absolute tragedy." One imagines that this would be something Walter Davis might also say in riposte to Williams: Davis has spoken forcefully and repeatedly, particularly in *Deracination*, about the concept of the *crypt* as applying to that "psychic register defined by desires, disorders, and conflicts that cannot be subsumed in a triumphant march toward reason and morality."[32]

27. Cf. Williams, "No More Happy Endings."
28. Burnett, *Catastrophe Survived*, 22–46.
29. Ward, "Extremities," 235–42.
30. Ward, "Extremities," 236.
31. Ward, "Extremities," 239.
32. Davis, *Deracination*, 55.

Williams takes on Ward's concern insofar as "to observe that tragedy is always already something *said* is not to flatten it into a matter of verbal bromide and quick consolation. It isn't so much that a tragic drama wins through to a conclusion that is thinkable and therefore consolatory in some illegitimate way." In his perspective, the "imagination" is always-already implicated in representation, so that we should be weary of proposing a traumatic Real that is non-representable (in the manner of postmodern theorists like Lyotard and Nancy).[33] In reference to Davis's concept of the "crypt," Williams acknowledges that "internal chaos" is "the raw substance of any tragic imagining," and moreover that "the roots of outrageous pain and atrocity in a damaged cosmic order should indeed be drawn into any thinking about tragedy."[34] But he is worried that Ward's de-centering of humanity within the tragic imagination is not sufficiently lucid: how does one speak of the cosmically tragic without advancing the "absolute tragedy" or the "ontological violence" he clearly desires to traverse? Additionally, Ward opens himself to the misinterpretation of relativizing human agony within a cosmological and evolutionary glance—which is certainly not his intention. Williams thinks, on the contrary, that "to speak about trauma is to speak from *where we actually are*; never mind the black holes and the deep evolutionary history."[35] There is also the not uncontroversial suggestion, given by Ward, that the "nothing" of *King Lear* and the *creatio ex nihilo* are identified *ex profundis*. This relation might need to be clarified further in the future.

Nevertheless, Ward's critique of "eloquence" is well-taken: his interventions have been echoed by trauma theorists and metaphysicians such as William Desmond.[36] Cathy Caruth argues that traumatic occurrences fall into a category that resists comprehension within normal symbolic registers, as so far as trauma disrupts the relative homeostasis we habituate. As such, precisely because it is unexpected and comes without warning, trauma comes too "early" for the mind to conceptualize and resists simplistic incorporation into what Bessel Van der Kolk calls "implicit" memory.[37] Desmond also theorizes that the tragic reveals our "being at a loss," a particularity of suffering that is manifest in "the Once" or "the Howl" (to echo King Lear). These experiences demand attention, and problematize any cozy metaphysics. However, we should register the ambiguity of trauma too, somewhat more than Ward himself does in this admittedly short text. Desmond admits there is "no

---

33. Williams, "Not Cured, Not Forgetful, Not Paralysed," 282.
34. Williams, "Not Cured, Not Forgetful, Not Paralysed," 282–83.
35. Williams, "Not Cured, Not Forgetful, Not Paralysed," 283.
36. Desmond, "Being at a Loss," 154–86.
37. Caruth, *Unclaimed Experience*, 57–72; Van Der Kolk "Trauma and Memory."

geometry of the tragic"[38]—no doubt a swipe against the Spinozist perspective that would cancel the tragic within the mirror of eternity. But Desmond also proposes a concept of "the posthumous mind," which imagines trauma as a "thinking of being as if from beyond death, being in the worthiness of present joy," of a "Tragic insight [which] crosses over from life to death, and looks back on life, crosses back and lives life otherwise."[39] On this reading, tragic events, and their post-traumatic narration,[40] exhibit an openness which cannot simply be predetermined.[41] Traumas are radically life-altering events, for better or worse, and it is this that makes it ambiguous and liminal. For those who have gone through traumatic experiences, the intermingling of "death" and "life" involves the problem of "survival," a living after death—an ambiguous "middle," to reference Shelly Rambo.[42] Kirby Farrell says something apt to similar effect: "trauma destabilizes the ground of experience, and therefore is always supercharged with significance and always profoundly equivocal in its interpretative possibilities. Like a traditional religious conversion experience, it can signify rebirth and promise transcendence, or it can open into an abyss."[43] One could also reference Jacques Lacan when he says that "when the traumatic elements—grounded in an image which has never been integrated—draw near . . . holes, points of fracture appear in the unification, the synthesis, of the subject's history." But he goes on to say "how it is in starting from these holes that the subject can realign himself within the different symbolic determinations which make him a subject with a history."[44] In light of these comments, the re-alignment of the subject within language should certainly not be glossed over or treated as negligible; and so Ward's criticisms

38. Desmond, "Being at a Loss," 168.

39. Desmond, "Being at a Loss," 183. In a critique of Camus and Sartre, Raymond Williams—no doubt echoing Arendtian ideas of natality and her criticisms of the Heideggerian priority of *Sein-zum-Tode*—has spoken about how "Life is not only negated by death, but is also renewed by birth. The reasoning mind is only contradicted by the universe when the supposed irrationality is not merely indifferent but hostile—an assumption about nature (in fact, a late bourgeois version of evolution) that is very near the creative roots of all this writing. The life-death contradiction is limited, in fact, to the kind of individual consciousness especially characteristic of bourgeois philosophy" (Williams, *Modern Tragedy*, 224).

40. On this, see Wigren, "Narrative Completion in the Treatment of Trauma"; Herman, *Trauma and Recovery*; Laub, "From Speechlessness to Narrative."

41. Caruth has said that "speaking and listening *from the site of trauma* . . . does not rely . . . on what we simply know of each other, but on what we don't yet know of our own traumatic pasts" (Caruth, *Trauma*, 11).

42. Rambo, "Spirit and Trauma."

43. Farrell, *Post-traumatic Culture*, 18.

44. Lacan, *The Seminar of Jacques Lacan*, 197.

of "eloquence" should not undermine the importance of narrative integration. The stakes are just too high.[45] However, his concern about proceeding too quickly towards epistemological categories is important.

Terry Eagleton's comments about the book are addressed within a more political vein: he wonders whether "to regard tragedy from Aeschylus to Arthur Miller as being essentially concerned with a recognition of otherness is to project a modern (even, one might add, fashionable) liberal motif into spuriously universal terms."[46] He opines that "Williams is a man of profound convictions who like many a liberal is rather wary of conviction," since it is "too close for comfort to the zealous and doctrinaire." Here Eagleton disagrees: on the one side, "Not all certainties . . . are dangerously narrowing. On the contrary, there are assured truths that can be liberating." On the other side, "Being exploratory, self-questioning and open-ended about the latter fact is to put yourself on the wrong side," at least in some circumstances.[47] These critiques appear to center on the question of commitment, or lack thereof, and the degree to which Williams's tragic mindset tends to baptize an overly-hesitant approach to political action (a point echoed by Milbank[48]). Such is related to Eagleton's suspicions of Williams's Hegelian dramatic criticism, especially as regards the *Antigone*.[49] As Eagleton says, "the solution to tragic conflict is not some Arnoldian flexibility of mind. You can be as pliable and unself-deceived as you like, as open to otherness and difference as the most dedicated Derridean, and still get it in the neck. Williams is too quick to endorse the Hegelian case that tragedy springs from the collision of two equally justified but lopsided positions."[50]

But Williams is not convinced by this critique (which seems to echo Hart's).[51] While he is fully aware that "it will not do to suspend action in

45. See Fuchs, "Fragmented Selves"; Fuchs, "Existential Vulnerability."
46. Eagleton, "Tragedy and Liberalism," 254.
47. Eagleton, "Tragedy and Liberalism," 255.
48. See Milbank, "The Archbishop of Canterbury," 50–53.
49. Eagleton, "Tragedy and Liberalism," 256.
50. Eagleton, "Tragedy and Liberalism," 256.
51. In relation to this and Hart criticisms of Williams's Hegelian reading, Williams gives three responses: "First, the conflict in the play is not about 'family' versus 'state': it is, as I argued, about two kinds of sacred solidarity, with immensely serious claims, and it is something of a shortcut to conclude that Antigone has to die so that the polis is conserved. The disaster that overtakes Creon is clearly to do with the offence that he offers to the solidarity of the dead; it is *not* that his version of sacrality triumphs. Second, this does rather reinforce Simon Goldhill's point about how Attic tragedy reminds its audience that the polis is more fragile than they would like to believe, and that its continuing coherence depends on the intensely difficult, near-impossible attempt to do justice to a diversity of sacral claims. But thirdly, to recognise that doing such justice

order to honour moral complexity," and is generally persuaded by Eagleton's comments regarding the importance of commitments, he still thinks that Eagleton has not recognized the nuance of his position. He emphasized (along with MacKinnon) that "the need for action does not guarantee absolution." Additionally, "There is indeed nothing much to be said for a view that simply identifies the virtues of contending positions and shrugs its shoulders or wrings its hands over the difficulty." But he does qualify this, since "to say there is a serious case to be made for two contending positions is not the same as saying that there is no informed choice to be made between them." As he has stressed, "what the tragic imagination insists upon is the recognition that even a choice believed and undertaken in thoughtful, responsible moral conviction may carry a cost for the agent and the agent's world. Recognizing this should not paralyse, but it should inform."[52] MacKinnon would agree. So it is not that a tragic perspective condones perpetual hesitancy or refrainment from action, but that we count the *cost* of our actions, with the realization that even good intentions can occasion unpredictable outcomes. Our awareness of this should not morally debilitate us, but rather chasten our resolve.

To conclude this book on the note of "action" is probably appropriate. If anything our plea for a non-contingent goodness and oneness, which we can gesture towards but never grasp, might lay the ground for an ethic that is at once hopeful but not hubristic. It wagers a foundation for a politics that acknowledges the persistence of conflict, but denies that this is necessary, that my goods are at their depth opposed to yours. Moreover, it says that if the Good is primordial, then this supports that basic trust required for transformative action, so that we may let-go and thereby "clear a space for the new," for a hope that "even in these desolate conditions you can't give up on your faith or love, however little it can be realized or rewarded." And it is precisely this conviction that might "just transform [a] barrier into a horizon."[53] Or to adapt a phrase taken from Paul Ricoeur, it may stimulate within us the affirmation of "the Joy of Yes in the sadness of the finite."[54]

If tragedy, as Williams says, is conceived as an event of "the particular, the narratively specific, out of which certain kinds of new language grow,"[55]

---

is difficult and fraught with the possibility of blasphemous offence should not imply that we are immobilized, only that we must act with fuller awareness than we might otherwise do of the risks attending our acts" (Williams, "Not Cured, Not Forgetful, Not Paralysed," 284–85).

52. Williams, "Not Cured, Not Forgetful, Not Paralysed," 285.
53. Eagleton, "Introduction," 5–6.
54. Ricoeur, *Fallible Man*, 140
55. Williams, "Trinity and Ontology," 164.

and, moreover, constitutes a "protest against a polity and culture that lure us to sink our truthful perceptions" into "a collective, mythologized identity that can shut its eyes to limits,"[56] then Wallace Stevens's invocation in the "Esthéthique du Mal" that "The tragedy ... may have begun, / Again, in the imagination's new beginning" is rather apt.[57] Tragedy was birthed within an *imagination*, at the cusp of the Aegean, in that "tremulous cadence slow" where the "eternal note of sadness" was ushered in.[58] At this shore, the poets invented a representation of the city, a *mimesis* of provocation which ran "counter to the tendency of the city and the law to reify its horizon and cast itself as wholly self-sufficient."[59] It is this self-sufficiency that MacKinnon, imperfectly as we have seen, tried to counter-act, and it was this tradition that Williams non-identically repeated in his own work. Neither of their contributions is beyond criticism. However, our study has *not* been an attempt to resolve this debate, but rather to address tensions with the aim of moving the conversation forward.

In closing, there is a thinker who has not been featured very prominently in this book, at least as much as his reputation in this whole debate would warrant. Friedrich Nietzsche is not someone Williams or MacKinnon reference that often. His absence in *The Tragic Imagination* is especially surprising (something that Williams acknowledges[60]). And when one considers Nietzsche's repeated commentary on the "aesthetic" justification of the world, one wonders if there could not have been more fruitful interaction than was presented up till now. Towards the end of his rather extraordinary (and now infamous) text *The Birth of Tragedy*, Nietzsche writes some rather provocative things regarding the "origins" of tragedy that are pertinent as we conclude. Despite being a classical philologist, Nietzsche does not follow the usual historicist trajectory of speculating about the beginnings of Attic theatre—a fact that invited the scorn of someone like Wilamowitz-Moellendorff. While speaking on whether events of suffering themselves are the source of the tragic imagination, Nietzsche writes:

> For the fact that such tragic things really do happen in life would in no way explain the origins of a form of art, unless art did not simply imitate the reality of nature but rather supplied *a metaphysical supplement to the reality of nature*, and was set

---

56. Williams, "Trinity and Ontology," 163.
57. Stevens, "Esthéthique du Mal VIII," in *Collected Poems*, 320.
58. Arnold, "Dover Beach," in *Poetry and Criticism*, 161.
59. Janssens, "Locus Tragicus. The Problem of Place in Greek Tragedy," in *The Locus of Tragedy*, 27.
60. Williams, "Not Cure, Not Forgetful, Not Paralysed," 288.

alongside the latter as a way of overcoming it. Inasmuch as it belongs to art at all, the tragic myth participates fully in the aim of all art, which is to effect a metaphysical transfiguration; but what does it transfigure when it presents the world of appearances in the image of the suffering hero? Certainly not the 'reality' of this world of appearances, for it says to us: 'Take a look! Take a close look! This is your life! This is the hour-hand on the clock of your existence!'[61]

There is much here that finds echoes in Rowan Williams (one thinks of *Grace and Necessity* and *The Edge of Words*). The idea that the tragic imagination cannot be simply abstracted from "reality" but constitutes "a metaphysical supplement to the reality of nature," suggests that even though tragic drama is imitative, in the Aristotelian sense of the word, a tragic aesthetic cannot be reduced to a purely naturalized deduction. Some kind of transcendent influx is required—something like, dare I say it, a "Dionysian" excess. Here the epigraph for Jean-Luc Godard's film *Adieu au Langage* (2014) might be appropriate, in regards to both art and politics: *tous ceux manquet d'imagination se réfugient dans la réalité* ("those who lack imagination take refuge in reality"). I wonder if the tragic poets, within the pomp and bacchanals of the City Dionysia, conceived something similar: against a "reality" that had become complacent and self-congratulatory, they instituted a vision that nudged us into consciousness, a renewed distance in which we might know ourselves once more—theologians included.

---

61. Nietzsche, *The Birth of Tragedy*, 113. Italics mine.

Bibliography

Adams, Marilyn McCord. *Horrendous Evils and the Goodness of God.* Cornell Studies in the Philosophy of Religion. Ithaca: Cornell University Press, 1999.
Adorno, Theodor W. *Negative Dialectics.* Translated by E. B. Ashton. London: Routledge, 1973.
Aeschylus. *The Oresteian Trilogy: Agamemnon, The Choephori, The Eumenides.* Translated by Philip Vellacott. London: Penguin, 1956.
―――. *Prometheus Bound, The Suppliants, Seven Against Thebes, The Persians.* Translated by Philip Vellacott. London: Penguin, 1961.
Agamben, Giorgio. *Homo Sacer: Sovereign Power and Bare Life.* Translated by Daniel Heller-Roazen. Stanford: Stanford University Press, 1998.
―――. *The Man without Content.* Translated by Georgia Albert. Stanford: Stanford University Press, 1999.
―――. *Remnants of Auschwitz: The Witness and the Archive.* Translated by Daniel Heller-Roazen. New York: Zone, 2002.
Ameriks, Karl. "Reality, Reason, and Religion in the Development of Kant's Ethics." In *Kant's Moral Metaphysics: God, Freedom, and Immortality,* edited by Benjamin J. Bruxvoort Lipscomb and James Krueger, 23–47. Berlin: de Gruyter, 2010.
Aquinas, Thomas. *Summa Theologiae.* http://dhspriory.org/thomas/.
Aristotle. *The Complete Works of Aristotle: The Revised Oxford Translation.* Vol. 1. Edited by Jonathan Barnes. Princeton: Princeton University Press, 1984.
Arnold, Matthew. *Poetry and Criticism of Matthew Arnold.* Edited by A. Dwight Culler. Boston: Houghton Mifflin, 1961.
Aubenque, Pierre. "The Origins of the Doctrine of the Analogy of Being: On the History of a Misunderstanding." *Graduate Faculty Philosophy Journal* 11 (1986) 35–46.
―――. "The Science without a Name." *Graduate Faculty Philosophy Journal* 29 (2008) 5–50.
―――. "Sur la naissance de la doctrine pseudo-aristotélicienne de l'analogie de l'être." *Les Études philosophiques* 3–4 (1989) 291–304.
―――. "Sur l'ambivalence du concept aristotélicien de substance." In *Ontologie et Dialogue: Mélange en Hommage à Pierre Aubenque,* edited by Nestor L. Cordero, 93–106. Paris: Vrin, 2000.

Augustine of Hippo. *The Augustine Catechism: The Enchiridion on Faith, Hope and Charity.* Translated by Bruce Harbert. New York: New City, 1999.

Alvira, Tomas, et al. *Metaphysics.* Translated by Luis Supan. Manila: Sinag-Tala, 1991.

Ayer, A. J. "Demonstration of the Impossibility of Metaphysics." *Mind* 43 (1934) 335–45.

Balfour, Ian. "Paradoxen: On the Sublimity of Tragedy in Hölderlin and Some Contemporaries." In *Tragedy and the Idea of Modernity*, edited by Joshua Billings and Miriam Leonard, 59–87. Oxford: Oxford University Press, 2015.

Balthasar, Hans Urs von. *Explorations in Theology, Volume III: Creator Spirit.* Translated by Brian McNeill. San Francisco: Ignatius, 1993.

———. *The Glory of the Lord: A Theological Aesthetics IV: The Realm of Metaphysics in Antiquity.* Translated by Brian McNeil et al. San Francisco: Ignatius, 1989.

———. *Theology of History.* New York: Sheed and Ward, 1963.

Barish, Jonas A. "The Antitheatrical Prejudice." *Critical Quarterly* 8 (1966) 329–48.

Barnes, Timothy. "Christians and the Theater." In *Beyond the Fifth Century: Interactions with Greek Tragedy from the Fourth Century BCE until the Middle Ages*, edited by Ingo Gildenhard and Martin Revermann, 315–34. Berlin: de Gruyter, 2010.

Barrón, Jorge Uscatescu. "Das Gute im Horizont der Seinsfrage: Zur Bedeutungsmannigfaltigkeit des Guten bei Aristoteles." *Perspektiven der Philosophie* 28 (2002) 47–83.

Beiser, Frederick. *Schiller as Philosopher: A Re-examination.* Oxford: Oxford University Press, 2005.

Bengston, Josef. *Explorations in Post-Secular Metaphysics.* London: Palgrave Macmillan, 2015.

Benjamin, Walter. "Left-Wing Melancholy [1931]." In *Walter Benjamin: Selected Writings, Volume 2: Part 2, 1931–1934*, edited Michael Jennings et al., 423–27. Cambridge: Belknap, 1999.

———. *The Origin of German Tragic Drama.* Translated by John Osbourne. London: Verso, 1998.

Benoist, Jocelyn. "Jugement et existence chez Kant: Comment des jugements d'existence sont-ils possibles?" *Quaestio: Journal of the History of Metaphysics* 3 (2003) 207–28.

Berlant, Lauren. *Cruel Optimism.* Durham: Duke University Press, 2011.

Berlin, Isaiah. *Liberty: Incorporating Four Essays on Liberty.* Edited by Henry Hardy. Oxford: Oxford University Press, 1969.

Bernhardt, Reinhold. "Die Erfahrung des Tragischen als Herausforderung für Theologie. Versuch zur Theodizee." *Theologische Zeitschrift* 59 (2003) 248–70.

Bernstein, J. M. *The Fate of Art: Aesthetic Alienation from Kant to Derrida and Adorno.* Pennsylvania: Pennsylvania State University Press, 1992.

Berti, Enrico. "La 'métaphysique' d'Aristote: 'onto-théologie' ou 'philosophie première'?" *Revue de Philosophie Ancienne* 14 (1996) 61–85.

———. "Multiplicity and Unity of Being in Aristotle." *Proceedings of the Aristotelian Society* 101 (2001) 185–207.

Betz, John R. "Beyond the Sublime: The Aesthetics of the Analogy of Being (Part One)." *Modern Theology* 21 (2005) 367–41.

———. "Beyond the Sublime: The Aesthetics of the Analogy of Being (Part Two)." *Modern Theology* 22 (2006) 1–50.

Bielik-Robson, Agatha. "Walter Benjamin (1892–1940)." In *Religion and European Philosophy: Key Thinkers from Kant to Žižek*, edited by Philip Goodchild and Hollis Phelps, 115–26. London: Routledge, 2017.

Billings, Joshua. *Genealogy of the Tragic: Greek Tragedy and German Philosophy*. Princeton: Princeton University Press, 2014.

Billings, Joshua, and Miriam Leonard, eds. *Tragedy and the Idea of Modernity*. Oxford: Oxford University Press, 2015.

Blackmur, R. P. "Statements and Idylls." *Poetry* 46 (1935) 108–112.

Blanchette, Oliva. *Philosophy of Being: A Reconstructive Essay in Metaphysics*. Washington, DC: Catholic University of America Press, 2003.

———. "Suárez and the Latent Essentialism of Heidegger's Fundamental Ontology." *The Review of Metaphysics* 53 (1999) 3–19.

Blowers, Paul M. "Augustine's Tragic Vision." *Journal of Religion & Society Supplement Series* 15 (2018) 157–69.

———. *Visions and Faces of the Tragic: The Mimesis of Tragedy and the Folly of Salvation in Early Christian Literature*. Oxford Early Christian Studies. Oxford: Oxford University Press, 2020.

Bohrer, Karl Heinz. "The Tragic: A Question of Art, Not Philosophy of History." *New Literary History* 41 (2010) 35–51.

Bonino, Guido. "Bradley's Regress: Relations, Exemplification, Unity." *Axiomathes* 23 (2013) 189–200.

Booth, Edward. *Aristotelian Aporetic Ontology in Islamic and Christian Thinkers*. Cambridge, Cambridge University Press, 1983.

Bornemark, Jonna. "Limit-situation: Antinomies and Transcendence in Karl Jaspers' Philosophy." *Sats – Nordic Journal of Philosophy* 7 (2006) 51–73.

Bottum, Joseph. "Poetry and Metaphysics." *Philosophy and Literature* 19 (1995) 214–25.

Bouchard, Larry D. *Tragic Method and Tragic Theology: Evil in Cotemporary Drama and Religious Thought*. Pennsylvania: Pennsylvania State University Press, 1989.

Boulnois, Olivier. *Être et représentation: Une généalogie de la métaphysique moderne a l'époque de Duns Scot (XIIIe–XIVe siècle)*. Épiméthée. Paris: Presses Universitaires de France, 1999.

———. "L'invention de la réalité." *Quaestio: Journal of the History of Metaphysics* 17 (2017) 133–54.

———. *Métaphysique rebelles: genèse et structures d'une science au Moyen Age*. Épiméthée. Paris: Presses Universitaires de France, 2013.

———. "Quand commence l'ontothéologie? Aristote, Thomas d'Aquin et Duns Scot." *Revue Thomiste* 95 (1995) 85–108.

Bourdieu, Pierre. *The Field of Production: Essays on Art and Literature*. Edited by Randal Johnson. New York: Columbia University Press, 1993.

Bradshaw, David. "St. Maximus the Confessor on the Will." In *Knowing the Purpose of Creation through Resurrection: Proceedings of the Symposium on St. Maximus the Confessor, Belgrade October 18–21, 2012*, edited by Maxim Vasiljević, 143–57. Belgrade: Sebastian, 2013.

Bowyer, Andrew. *Donald MacKinnon's Theology: To Perceive Tragedy Without the Loss of Hope*. London: T&T Clark, 2019.

Brand, Gerrit. *Speaking of a Fabulous Ghost: In Search of Theological Criteria with Special Reference to the Debate on Salvation in African Christian Theology*. Contributions to Philosophical Theology Vol. 7. Frankfurt: Lang, 2002.

Brague, Rémi. "Kant et la tentation gnostique." In *Kant und die Philosophie in weltbürgerlicher Absicht: Akten des XI. Internationalen Kant-Kongresses*, Band 1, edited by Stefano Bacin et al., 93–105. Berlin: de Gruyter, 2013.

Breyfogle, Todd. "Time and Transformation: A Conversation with Rowan Williams." *Cross Currents* 45 (1995) 293–311.

Brown, David. *Tradition and Imagination: Revelation and Change*. Oxford: Oxford University Press, 1999.

Brümmer, Vincent. *Brümmer on Meaning and the Christian Faith: Collected Writings of Vincent Brümmer*. Aldershot: Ashgate, 2006.

———. "Spirituality and the Hermeneutics of Faith." *HTS Teologiese Studies* 66 (2010) 1–5.

Burke, Edmund. *A Philosophical Enquiry into the Origins of Our Ideas of the Sublime and the Beautiful*. Oxford: Oxford University Press, 1990.

Burkert, Walter. *Kleine Schriften VII: Tragica et Historica*. Göttingen: Vandenhoeck & Ruprecht, 2007.

Burnett, Anne Pippin. *Catastrophe Survived: Euripides' Plays of Mixed Reversal*. Oxford: Clarendon, 1971.

Burt, Donald X. "Courageous Optimism: Augustine on the Good of Creation." *Augustinian Studies* 21 (1990) 55–66.

Butler, Joseph. *The Works of Bishop Butler*. Edited by David E. White. New York: University of Rochester Press, 2006.

Bynum, Carolyn. *Fragmentation and Redemption*. New York: Zone, 1991.

Cane, Anthony. *The Place of Judas Iscariot in Christology*. London: Routledge, 2005.

Caputo, John D. "Metaphysics, Finitude and Kant's Illusion of Pure Practical Reason." *Proceedings of the American Catholic Philosophical Association* 56 (1982) 87–94.

Carr, David. "On Historicity." *Graduate Faculty Philosophy Journal* 37 (2016) 273–88.

Caruth, Cathy, ed. *Trauma: Explorations in Memory*. Baltimore: Johns Hopkins University Press, 1995.

———. *Unclaimed Experience: Trauma, Narrative, and History*. Baltimore: Johns Hopkins University Press, 1996.

Cassin, Barbara, ed. *Dictionary of Untranslatables*. Princeton: Princeton University Press, 2014.

Cassirer, Ernst. "Kant und das Problem der Metaphysik: Bemerkungen zu Martin Heideggers Kant-Interpretation." *Kant Studien* 36 (1931) 1–26.

Cavell, Stanley. *Disowning Knowledge in Six Plays of Shakespeare*. Cambridge: Cambridge University Press, 1987.

Caygill, Howard. "Kant and the Kingdom." In *Post-Secular Philosophy: Between Philosophy and Theology*, edited by Phillip Blond, 55–59. London: Routledge, 1998.

Certeau, Michel de. *The Writing of History*. Translated by Tom Conley. New York: Columbia University Press, 1980.

Charlesworth, James. *Old Testament Pseudepigrapha: Volume 2*. New York: Doubleday, 1985.

Cherniss, Harold. "The Sources of Evil According to Plato." *Proceedings of the American Philosophical Society* 98 (1954) 23–30.

Clements, Keith, ed. *The Moot Papers: Faith, Freedom and Society in 1938–1944*. London: Bloomsbury, 2010.

Clery, E. J. "The Pleasure of Terror: Paradox in Edmund Burke's Theory of the Sublime." In *Pleasure in the Eighteenth Century*, edited by Roy Porter and Marie Mulvey Roberts, 164–81. Hampshire: Macmillan, 1996.

Coakley, Sarah. *God, Sexuality, and the Self: An Essay 'On the Trinity.'* Cambridge: Cambridge University Press, 2013.

Connor, Timothy G. "From Galilee to Jerusalem to Galilee: The Kenotic Trajectory of the Church in Donald Mackinnon's Theology." PhD diss., University of Toronto, 2003.

Courtine, Jean-François. "Différence ontologique et analogie de l'être." In *Historia Philosophiae Medii Aevi: Studien zur Geschichte der Philosophie des Mittelalters*, Band 1, edited by Burkhard Mojsisch and Olaf Pluta, 163–79. Amsterdam: Grüner, 1991.

———. *Inventio analogiae: Métaphysique et ontothéologie.* Paris: Vrin, 2005.

———. "Kant y el Tiempo." *Universitas Philosophica* 24 (2007) 55–77.

———. "Of Tragic Metaphor." In *Philosophy and Tragedy*, edited by Michel de Beistegui and Simon Sparks, 57–75. London: Routledge, 2000.

———. *Suarez et le système de la métaphysique.* Épiméthée. Paris: Presses Universitaires de France, 1990.

———. "Tragedy and Sublimity: The Speculative Interpretation of Oedipus Rex on the Threshold of German Idealism." In *Of the Sublime: Presence in Question*, edited by Jean-Francois Courtine et al., translated by Jeffrey S. Librett, 157–76. New York: State University of New York Press, 1993.

Cress, Donald A. "Augustine's Privation Account of Evil: A Defense." *Augustinian Studies* 20 (1989) 109–28.

Critchley, Simon. *Tragedy, the Greeks and Us.* London: Profile, 2019.

———. "The Tragical Sublime." In *The Sublime and Its Teleology: Kant—German Idealism—Phenomenology*, edited by Donald Loose, 169–85. Leiden: Brill, 2011.

Cunningham, Conor. *Genealogy of Nihilism: Philosophies of Nothing and the Difference of Theology.* London: Routledge, 2003.

———. "Language: Theology after Wittgenstein." In *Radical Orthodoxy: A New Theology*, edited by John Milbank et al., 64–90. London: Routledge, 1999.

Cupitt, Don. "Kant and Negative Theology." In *Is Nothing Sacred? The Non-Realist Philosophy of Religion: Selected Essays*, 3–17. Fordham: Fordham University Press, 2002.

———. "Mansel's Theory of Regulative Truth." *Journal of Theological Studies* 18 (1967) 104–26.

Dalferth, Ingolf. "Ereignis und Transzendenz." *Zeitschrift für Theologie und Kirche* 110 (2013) 475–500.

———. "The Idea of Transcendence." In *The Axial Age and Its Consequences*, edited Robert Bellah and Hans Joas, 146–88. Cambridge: Belknap, 2012.

———. *Malum: Theologische Hermeneutik des Bösen.* Tübingen: Mohr Siebeck, 2008.

Dalin, David G. "Pius XII and the Jews." *Rivista di Studi Politici Internazionali* 69 (2002) 614–28.

Daniels, Joel. "The Cost of Victory." *Anglican Theological Review* 95 (2013) 155–67.

Dante. *The Divine Comedy: Inferno, Purgatorio, Paradiso.* Translated by Robin Kirkpatrick. London: Penguin, 2012.

Davidson, Donald. *Inquiries into Truth and Interpretation.* Oxford: Clarendon, 1984.

Davies, Rachel Bryant. "Reading Ezekiel's *Exagoge*: Tragedy, Sacrificial Ritual, and the Midrashic Tradition." *Greek, Roman, and Byzantine Studies* 48 (2008) 393–415.
Davis, Walter A. *Deracination: Historicity, Hiroshima, and the Tragic Imperative.* New York: State University of New York Press, 2001.
Dawe, R. D. "Some Reflections on *Ate* and *Hamartia*." *Harvard Studies in Classical Philology* 72 (1968) 89–123.
Deguy, Michel. "The Discourse of Exaltation (Μεγαληφορειν): Contribution to a Rereading of Pseudo-Longinus." In *Of the Sublime: Presence in Question*, edited by Jean-Francois Courtine et al., translated by Jeffrey S. Librett, 5–24. New York: State University of New York Press, 1993.
Dehart, Paul J. *The Trial of the Witnesses: The Rise and Decline of Postliberal Theology.* Oxford: Wiley-Blackwell, 2006.
Deleuze, Gilles. *Kant's Critical Philosophy: The Doctrine of the Faculties.* Translated by Hugh Tomlinson and Barbara Habberjam. London: Athlone, 1984.
Delport, Khegan. "*Interior intimo meo*: Rowan Williams on the Self." *Stellenbosch Theological Journal* 4 (2018) 471–504.
———. "Of Danger and Difficulty: Rowan Williams and the Tragic Imagination." *The Heythrop Journal* 61 (2020) 505–20.
———. "Towards a Visionary and Historical Consciousness: Rowan Williams's *Four Quartets* Lectures (1974–1975)." *Studia Historia Ecclesiasticae* 43 (2017) 1–26.
———. "Why Faith Makes Sense: On Graham Ward's *Unbelievable*." *Stellenbosch Theological Journal* 3 (2017) 515–45.
Desmond, William. "Being at a Loss: Reflections on Philosophy and the Tragic." In *Tragedy and Philosophy*, edited N. Georgopoulos, 154–86. New York: Palgrave MacMillan, 1993.
———. "Maybe, Maybe Not: Richard Kearney and God." In *After God: Richard Kearney and the Religious Turn In Continental Philosophy*, edited John Panteleimon Manoussakis, 55–77. New York: Fordham University Press, 2006.
De Libera, Alain. "Genèse et structure des métaphysique médiévales." In *La métaphyisque: son histoire, sa critique, ses enjeux*, edited Jean-Marc Narbonne and Luc Langlois, 159–81. Paris: Vrin, 1999.
———. "Les sources gréco-arabes de la théorie médiévale de l'analogie de l'être." *Les Études philosophiques* 3–4 (1989) 319–45.
De Muralt, André. "Kant, le dernier occamien: une nouvelle définition de la philosophie moderne." *Revue de Métaphysique et de Morale* 80 (1975) 32–53.
De Vogel, C. J. *Rethinking Plato and Platonism*. Leiden: Brill, 1986.
Diamond, Cora. "The Difficulty of Reality and the Difficulty of Philosophy." In *Philosophy and Animal Life*, edited by Stanley Cavell et al., 43–89. New York: Columbia University Press, 2008.
Dominik, W. J. "Reception of Greek Tragedy in (Sub- Saharan) African Literature." In *The Encyclopedia of Greek Tragedy*, edited by H. M. Roisman. Oxford: Wiley & Sons, 2014.
Donini, Pierluigi. "*Mimesis* tragique et apprentissage de la *phronesis*." In *Commentary and Tradition: Aristotelianism, Platonism, and Post-Hellenistic Philosophy*, edited by Mauro Bonazzi, 38–51. Berlin: de Gruyter, 2011.
DuBois, Page. "Toppling the Hero: Polyphony in the Tragic City." *New Literary History* 35 (2004) 63–81.

Eagleton, Terry. *Hope without Optimism*. Charlottesville: University of Virginia Press, 2015.

———. "Introduction: Tragedy and Hope." In *The Locus of Tragedy*, edited by Arthur Cools et al., 1–6. Studies in Contemporary Phenomenology 1. Leiden: Brill, 2008.

———. *Sweet Violence: The Idea of the Tragic*. Oxford: Blackwell, 2003.

———. "Tragedy and Liberalism." *Modern Theology* 34 (2018) 252–57.

———. *The Trouble with Strangers: A Study of Ethics*. Oxford: Wiley-Blackwell, 2009.

Eliot, T. S. *Collected Poems: 1909–1962*. London: Faber and Faber, 1963.

Else, Gerald F. *The Origin and Early Form of Greek Tragedy*. Martin Classical Lectures 20. Cambridge: Harvard University Press, 1965.

Ernst, Cornelius. "Ethics and the Play of Intelligence." *New Blackfriars* 39 (1958) 324–26.

Euben, J. Peter. *The Tragedy of Political Theory: The Road Not Taken*. Princeton: Princeton University Press, 1990.

Exum, J. Cheryl. *Tragedy and Biblical Narrative: Arrows of the Almighty*. Cambridge: Cambridge University Press, 1992.

Esposito, Costantino. "L'impensé de l'existence: Kant et la scolastique." *Quaestio: Journal of the History of Metaphysics* 17 (2017) 259–76.

———. "Heidegger, Suárez e la storia dell'ontologia." *Quaestio: Journal of the History of Metaphysics* 1 (2001) 407–30.

———. "The Hidden Influence of Suárez on Kant's Transcendental Conception of 'Being,' 'Essence' and 'Existence.'" In *Suárez's Metaphysics in Its Historical and Systematic Context*, edited by Lukás Novák, 117–34. Berlin: de Gruyter, 2014.

———. "Die Schranken der Erfahrung und die Grenzen der Vernunft: Kants Moraltheologie." *Aufklärung* 21 (2009) 117–45.

———. "Suárez and the Baroque Matrix of Modern Thought." In *A Companion to Francisco Suárez*, edited Victor Salas and Robert Fastiggi, 124–47. Leiden: Brill, 2014.

Evans, G. R. *Augustine on Evil*. Cambridge: Cambridge University Press, 1982.

Farley, Wendy. *Tragic Vision and Divine Compassion*. Louisville: Westminster John Knox, 1990.

Farrell, Kirby. *Post-traumatic Culture: Injury and Interpretation*. Baltimore: John Hopkins University Press, 1998.

Felski, Rita. "Introduction." In *Rethinking Tragedy*, edited by Rita Felski, 1–25. Baltimore: Johns Hopkins University Press, 2008.

Feyerabend, Paul. *Against Method*. 3rd ed. London: Verso, 1993.

Fichant, Michel. "*L'Amphibologie des concepts de la réflexion*: la fin de l'ontologie." In *Recht und Frieden in der Philosophie Kants: Akten des X. Internationalen Kant-Kongresses*, Band 1, edited by Valerio Rohden et al., 71–93. Berlin: de Gruyter, 2008.

Fine, Gail. *Plato on Knowledge and Forms: Selected Essays*. Oxford: Clarendon, 2003.

Foucault, Michel. *The Archaeology of Knowledge*. Translated by A. M. Sheridan-Smith. London: Routledge, 1989.

———. "Technologies of the Self." In *Technologies of the Self: A Seminar with Michel Foucault*, edited by Luther H. Martin et al., 16–49. Amherst: University of Massachusetts Press, 1988.

Fuchs, Thomas. "Existential Vulnerability: Toward a Psychopathology of Limit Situations." *Psychopathology* 46 (2013) 301–8.

———. "Fragmented Selves: Temporality and Identity in Borderline Personality Disorder." *Psychopathology* 40 (2007) 379–87.
Gadamer, Hans-Georg. *Dialogue and Dialectic: Eight Hermeneutical Studies on Plato.* Translated by P. Christopher Smith. New Haven: Yale University Press, 1983.
———. *Truth and Method.* Translated by J. Weinsheimer and D. G. Marshall. 2nd rev. ed. London: Continuum, 1989.
Gasché, Rodolphe. ". . . And the Beautiful? Revisiting Edmund Burke's 'Double Aesthetics.'" In *The Sublime: From Antiquity to the Present*, edited by Timothy M. Costelloe, 24–36. Cambridge: Cambridge University Press, 2012.
———. "The Sublime, Ontologically Speaking." *Yale French Studies* 99 (2001) 117–28.
Gavrilyuk, Paul L. *The Suffering of the Impassible God: The Dialectics of Patristic Thought.* Oxford: Oxford University Press, 2004.
Gellrich, Michelle. *Tragedy and Theory: The Problem of Conflict since Aristotle.* Princeton: Princeton University Press, 1988.
Glock, Hans-Johann. "Strawson's Descriptive Metaphysics." In *Categories of Being: Essays on Metaphysics and Logic*, edited by Leila Haaparanta and Heikki J. Koskinen, 391–419. Oxford: Oxford University Press, 2012.
Goff, Barbara, and Michael Simpson. *Crossroads in the Black Aegean: Oedipus, Antigone, and Dramas of the African Diaspora.* Oxford: Oxford University Press, 2007.
Goldhill, Simon. "Collectivity and Otherness—The Authority of the Tragic Chorus: Response to Gould." In *Tragedy and the Tragic*, edited by M. S. Silk, 244–56. Oxford: Oxford University Press, 1995.
———. "Generalizing About Tragedy." In *Rethinking Tragedy*, edited Rita Felski, 45–65. Baltimore: Johns Hopkins University Press, 2008.
———. "The Great Dionysia and Civic Ideology." *The Journal of Hellenic Studies* 107 (1987) 58–76.
———. *Sophocles and the Language of Tragedy.* Oxford: Oxford University Press, 2012.
Goosen, Danie, and Jaco Kruger. "Radical Orthodoxy – Panel Discussion between Profs Graham Ward, John Milbank, Danie Goosen and Dr Jaco Kruger." *Acta Theologica* 37, supplementum 25 (2017) 1–28.
Gould, John. "Tragedy and Collective Experience." In *Tragedy and the Tragic*, edited by M. S. Silk, 217–43. Oxford: Oxford University Press, 1995.
Green, Ryan. "Kenosis and Ascent: The Trajectory of the Self in the Writings of John Milbank and Rowan Williams." PhD diss., Charles Sturt University, 2017.
Gregory of Nazianzus. *On God and Christ: The Five Theological Orations and Two Letters to Cledonius.* Translated by Frederick Williams and Lionel Wickham. New York: St. Vladimir's Seminary Press, 2002.
Gregory of Nyssa. *Homilies on the Song of Songs.* Translated by R. A. Norris Jr. Atlanta: Society of Biblical Literature, 2012.
Griffin, Nicholas. "Russell and Moore's Revolt against British Idealism." In *The Oxford Handbook of the History of Analytic Philosophy*, edited by Michael Beaney, 383–406. Oxford: Oxford University Press, 2013.
Grondin, Jean. *Introduction to Metaphysics: From Parmenides to Levinas.* Translated by Lukas Soderstrom. New York: Columbia University Press, 2012.
Gray, Brett. *Jesus in the Theology of Rowan Williams.* London: Bloomsbury, 2016.
Guyer, Paul. "Kant's Distinction between the Beautiful and the Sublime." *The Review of Metaphysics* 35 (1982) 753–83.

———. "The German Sublime after Kant." In *The Sublime: From Antiquity to the Present*, edited by Timothy M. Costelloe, 102–17. Cambridge: Cambridge University Press, 2012.

Hall, Edith. "Is There a *Polis* in Aristotle's Poetics?" In *Tragedy and the Tragic*, edited by M. S. Silk, 294–309. Oxford: Oxford University Press, 1995.

Halliwell, Stephen. "Human Limits and the Religion of Greek Tragedy." *Literature & Theology* 4 (1990) 169–80.

———. "Plato's Repudiation of the Tragic." In *Tragedy and the Tragic*, edited by M. S. Silk, 332–49. Oxford: Oxford University Press, 1995.

Hamilton, Christopher. *A Philosophy of Tragedy*. London: Reaktion, 2016.

Harman, John D. "The Unhappy Philosopher: Plato's 'Republic' as Tragedy." *Polity* 18 (1986) 577–94.

Hart, David Bentley. *Atheist Delusions: The Christian Revolution and Its Fashionable Enemies*. New Haven: Yale University Press, 2009.

———. "Baptism and Cosmic Allegiance: A Brief Observation." *Journal of Early Christian Studies* 20 (2012) 457–65.

———. *The Beauty of the Infinite: The Aesthetics of Christian Truth*. Grand Rapids: Eerdmans, 2003.

———. *The Devil and Pierre Gernet: Stories*. Grand Rapids: Eerdmans, 2012.

———. *The Doors of the Sea: Where Was God in the Tsunami?* Grand Rapids: Eerdmans, 2005.

———. *The Experience of God: Being, Consciousness, Bliss*. New Haven: Yale University Press, 2013.

———. "God, Creation, and Evil: The Moral Meaning of *creatio ex nihilo*." *Radical Orthodoxy: Theology, Philosophy, Politics* 3 (2015) 1–17.

———. "God or Nothingness." In *I Am the Lord Your God: Reflections on the Ten Commandments*, edited by Carl E. Braaten and Christopher R. Seitz, 55–76. Grand Rapids: Eerdmans, 2005.

———. "The Gospel According to Melpomene: Reflections on Rowan Williams's *The Tragic Imagination*." *Modern Theology* 34 (2018) 220–34.

———. *The Hidden and the Manifest: Essays in Theology and Metaphysics*. Grand Rapids: Eerdmans, 2017.

———. "Notes on the Concept of the Infinite in the History of Western Metaphysics." In *Infinity: New Research Frontiers*, edited by Michael Heller and W. Hugh Woodin, 255–74. Cambridge: Cambridge University Press, 2011.

———. "Response to James K. A. Smith, Lois Malcolm and Gerard Loughlin." *New Blackfriars* 88 (2007) 610–23.

———. "Response from David Bentley Hart to McGuckin and Murphy." *Scottish Journal of Theology* 60 (2007) 95–101.

———. *That All Shall Be Saved: Heaven, Hell and Universal Salvation*. New Haven: Yale University Press, 2019.

Hartog, François. *Regimes of Historicity: Presentism and the Experiences of Time*. Translated by Saskia Brown. New York: Columbia University Press, 2015.

Hauerwas, Stanley. "Bearing Reality: A Christian Meditation." *Journal of the Society of Christian Ethics* 33 (2013) 3–20.

Hebblethwaite, Brian. "Donald MacKinnon (1913–94)." In *The Student's Companion to the Theologians*, edited by Ian Markham, 454–57. Oxford: Wiley-Blackwell, 2013.

Hegel, G. W. F. *Aesthetics: Lectures on Fine Arts.* 2 vols. Translated by T. M. Knox. Oxford: Clarendon, 1975.
———. *The Phenomenology of Spirit.* Translated by Terry Pinkard. Cambridge: Cambridge University Press, 2018.
Heidegger, Martin. *Identity and Difference.* Translated by Joan Staumbach. New York: Harper & Row, 1969.
Herman, Judith. *Trauma and Recovery: The Aftermath or Violence – From Domestic Abuse to Political Terror.* New York: Basic, 1997.
Higton, Mike. *Difficult Gospel: The Theology of Rowan Williams.* New York: Church Publishing, 2004.
Hill, Geoffrey. *Broken Hierarchies: Poems 1952-2012.* Edited by Kenneth Haynes. Oxford: Oxford University Press, 2013.
———. *Collected Critical Writings.* Edited by Kenneth Haynes. Oxford: Oxford University Press, 2008.
Hintikka, Jaakko. "Kant on Existence, Predication, and the Ontological Argument." *Dialectica* 35 (1981) 127-46.
Hofstadter, Douglas R. "Prelude... Ant Fugue." In *The Mind's I: Fantasies and Reflections on Self and Soul,* edited by Daniel Dennett and Douglas R. Hofstadter, 149-201. New York: Bantam, 1981.
Holzer, Vincent. "Les thomismes de langue allemande au xxe siècle: science de l'être et métamorphoses du transcendantal." *Revue des sciences philosophiques et théologiques* 97 (2013) 37-58.
Honnefelder, Ludger. *Scientia transcendens. Die formale Bestimmung der Seiendheit und Realitat in der Metaphysik des Mittelalters und der Neuzeit (Duns Scotus - Suarez -Wolff - Kant - Peirce).* Paradeigmata 9. Hamburg: Meiner, 1990.
———. "Metaphysics as a Discipline: From the 'Transcendental Philosophy of the Ancients' to Kant's Notion of Transcendental Philosophy." In *The Medieval Heritage in Early Modern Metaphysics and Modal Theory 1400-1700,* edited by R. L. Friedman and L. O. Nielsen, 53-74. The New Synthese Historical Library 53. Dordrecht: Kluwer Academic, 2003.
———. "Der zweite Anfang der Metaphysik. Voraussetzungen, Ansatze und Folgen der Wiederbegründung der Metaphysik im 13./14. Jahrhundert." In *Philosophie im Mittelalter. Entwicklungslinien und Paradigmen,* edited by J. P. Beckmann et al., 165-86. Hamburg: Meiner, 1987.
Hösle, Vittorio. "The Greatness and Limits of Kant's Practical Philosophy." *Graduate Faculty Philosophy Journal* 13 (1990) 133-57.
Houlgate, Stephen. "Hegel's Theory of Tragedy." In *Hegel and the Arts,* edited by Stephen Houlgate, 146-78. Evanston: Northwestern University Press, 2007.
Hughes, Samuel. "Schiller on the Pleasure of Tragedy." *British Journal of Aesthetics* 55 (2015) 417-32.
Hütter, Reinhard. "Attending to the Wisdom of God – from Effect to Cause, from Creation to God: A Relecture of the Analogy of Being according to Thomas Aquinas." In *The Analogy of Being: Invention of the Antichrist or the Wisdom of God?,* edited Thomas Joseph White, 209-45. Grand Rapids: Eerdmans, 2011.
Hyland, Drew A. "Philosophy and Tragedy in the Platonic Dialogues." In *Tragedy and Philosophy,* edited by N. Georgopoulos, 123-38. New York: Palgrave MacMillan, 1993.

Jakobson, Roman. "Poetry of Grammar and Grammar of Poetry." In *Verbal Art, Verbal Sign, Verbal Time*, edited by Krystyna Pomorska and Stephen Rudy, 36–46. Minneapolis: University of Minnesota Press, 1985.

Janssens, David. "Locus Tragicus: The Problem of Place in Greek Tragedy." In *The Locus of Tragedy*, edited by Arthur Cools et al., 9–27. Studies in Contemporary Phenomenology 1. Leiden: Brill, 2008.

Janz, Paul D. *God, the Mind's Desire: Reference, Reason and Christian Thinking*. Cambridge: Cambridge University Press, 2004.

Jaspers, Karl. *Über das Tragische*. München: Piper & Vo, 1952.

John of the Cross. *The Poems of St. John of the Cross*. Translated by R. Campbell. New York: Grosset & Dunlap, 1967.

Johnson, David B. "The Postmodern Sublime: Presentation and its Limits." In *The Sublime: From Antiquity to the Present*, edited by Timothy M. Costelloe, 118–31. Cambridge: Cambridge University Press, 2012.

Johnson, Luke Timothy. "The New Testament's Anti-Jewish Slander and the Conventions of Ancient Polemic." *Journal of Biblical Literature* 108 (1989) 419–41.

Jüngel, Eberhard. *God as the Mystery of the World: On the Foundation of the Theology of the Crucified One in the Dispute between Theism and Atheism*. Translated by Darrell L. Guder. Grand Rapids: Eerdmans, 1983.

Kamerbeek, J. M. *The Plays of Sophocles, Part IV: The Oedipus Tyrannus*. Leiden: Brill, 1967.

Kant, Immanuel. *The Critique of the Power of Judgement*. Translated by Paul Guyer and Eric Matthews. Cambridge: Cambridge University Press, 2000.

———. *The Critique of Pure Reason*. Translated by Paul Guyer and Allen Wood. Cambridge: Cambridge University Press, 1998.

———. *The Critique of Practical Reason*. Translated by Werner S. Pluhar. Indianapolis: Hackett, 2002.

———. *The Groundwork for the Metaphysics of Morals*. Translated by Mary Gregor. Cambridge: Cambridge University Press, 1997.

Kelly, Henry Ansgar. *Ideas and Forms of Tragedy from Aristotle to the Middle Ages*. Cambridge Studies in Medieval Literature 18. Cambridge: Cambridge University Press, 1993.

Kearney, Richard. *Strangers, Gods and Monsters: Interpreting Otherness*. London: Routledge, 2003.

Kerr, Fergus. "Comment: Remembering Donald MacKinnon." *New Blackfriars* 85 (2004) 265–69.

———. Review of *Reimagining the Sacred: Richard Kearney Debates God*, edited by Richard Kearney and Jens Zimmermann. *Modern Theology* 33 (2017) 325–27.

Keshgegian, Flora A. *Time for Hope: Practices for Living in Today's World*. New York: Continuum, 2006.

Koselleck, Reinhart. *Futures Past: On the Semantics of Historical Time*. Translated by Keith Tribe. New York: Columbia University Press, 2004.

Krell, David Farrell. *The Tragic Absolute: German Idealism and the Languishing of God*. Bloomington: Indiana University Press, 2005.

Kuhn, Helmut. "The True Tragedy: On the Relationship between Greek Tragedy and Plato, I." *Harvard Studies in Classical Philology* 52 (1941) 1–40.

———. "The True Tragedy: On the Relationship between Greek Tragedy and Plato, II." *Harvard Studies in Classical Philology* 53 (1942) 37–88.

Kuehn, Manfred. "Kant's Transcendental Deduction of God's Existence as a Postulate of Pure Practical Reason." *Kant-Studien* 76 (1985) 152–69.
Lacan, Jacques. "Kant with Sade." In *Écrits: The First Complete Edition in English*. Translated by Bruce Fink et al., 645–68. New York: Norton, 2006.
———. *The Seminar of Jacques Lacan, Book 1: Freud's Papers on Technique 1953–1954*. Edited by Jacques Alain-Miller. Translated by John Forrester. New York: Norton, 1991.
Lacoue-Labarthe, Philippe. "Sublime Truth (Part 1)." *Cultural Critique* 18 (1991) 5–31.
———. "Sublime Truth (Part 2)." *Cultural Critique* 20 (1991–1992) 207–29.
———. *Typography: Mimesis, Philosophy, Politics*. Edited by Christopher Fynsk. Cambridge: Harvard University Press, 1989.
Lash, Nicholas. "Ideology, Metaphor and Analogy." In *The Philosophical Frontiers of Christian Theology: Essays Presented to D. M. MacKinnon*, edited by Brian Heblethwaite and Stewart Sutherland, 68–94. Cambridge: Cambridge University Press, 1982.
———. *Theology on the Way to Emmaus*. London: SCM, 1986.
Lamanna, Marco. "Mathematics, Abstraction and Ontology: Benet Perera and the Impossibility of a Neutral Science of Reality." *Quaestio: Journal of the History of Metaphysics* 14 (2014) 69–89.
———. "Ontology between Goclenius and Suárez." In *Suárez's Metaphysics in Its Historical and Systematic Context*, edited by Lukás Novák, 135–52. Berlin: de Gruyter, 2014.
Landry, Bernard. "L'analogie de proportion chez saint Thomas d'Aquin." *Revue néoscolastique de philosophie* 24 (1922) 257–80.
———. "L'analogie de proportionnalité chez saint Thomas d'Aquin." *Revue néoscolastique de philosophie* 24 (1922) 454–64.
Laub, Dori. "From Speechlessness to Narrative: The Cases of Holocaust Historians and of Psychiatrically Hospitalized Survivors." *Literature and Medicine* 24 (2005) 253–65.
Lear, Jonathan. "Katharsis." *Phronesis* 33 (1988) 297–326.
Lefebvre, René. "L'image onto-théologique de la 'Métaphysique' d'Aristote." *Revue de Philosophie Ancienne* 8 (1990) 123–72.
Leonard, Miriam. *Tragic Modernities*. Cambridge: Harvard University Press, 2015.
Lesky, Albin. "Decision and Responsibility in the Tragedy of Aeschylus." *The Journal of Hellenic Studies* 86 (1966) 78–85.
Lightman, Bernard. "Henry Longueville Mansel and the Origins of Agnosticism." *History of European Ideas* 5 (1984) 45–64.
Lonfat, Joël. "Archéologie de la notion d'analogie d'Aristote à Saint Thomas d'Aquin." *Archives d'histoire doctrinale et littéraire du Moyen Âge* 72 (2004) 35–107.
Longinus. "On the Sublime." In *Poetics, On the Sublime, On Style*, translated by W. Hamilton Fyfe and Donald Russell. Loeb Classical Library 199. Cambridge: Harvard University Press, 1995.
Longo, Oddone. "The Theater and the Polis." In *Nothing to Do with Dionysos? Athenian Drama in Its Social Context*, edited J. J. Winkler and F. I. Zeitlin, 12–19. Princeton: Princeton University Press, 1990.
López, Leopoldo Prieto. "*Res, aliquid* y *nihil* en Suárez y la filosofía moderna." *Anales del Seminario de Historia de la Filosofía* 30 (2013) 49–69.

Lurie, Michael. "Facing Up to Tragedy: Toward an Intellectual History of Sophocles in Europe from Camerarius to Nietzsche." In *A Companion to Sophocles*, edited by Kirk Ormand, 440–61. Oxford: Wiley-Blackwell, 2012.

Lyotard, Jean-François. *The Inhuman: Reflections on Time*. Translated by Geoffrey Bennington and Rachel Bowlby. Stanford: Stanford University Press, 1991.

MacBride, Fraser. *On the Genealogy of Universals: The Metaphysical Origins of Analytic Philosophy*. Oxford: Oxford University Press, 2018.

———. "Relations." In *The Stanford Encyclopedia of Philosophy* (Winter 2016 Edition), edited by Edward N. Zalta. https://plato.stanford.edu/archives/win2016/entries/relations.

MacKinnon, Donald M. "Are There A Priori Concepts?" *Proceedings of the Aristotelian Society, Supplementary Volumes* 18 (1939) 49–54.

———. "Aristotle's Conception of Substance." In *New Essays on Plato and Aristotle*, edited by R. Bambrough, 97–119. London: Routledge, 1965.

———. "Aspects of Kant's Influence on British Theology (1990)." In *Kant and His Influence*, edited by George Macdonald Ross and Tony McWalter, 348–66. London: Continuum, 2005.

———. "Ayer's Attack on Metaphysics." In *A. J. Ayer: Memorial Essays*, edited A. Phillips Griffiths, 49–61. New York: Cambridge University Press, 1991.

———. *Borderlands of Theology and Other Essays*. Edited by George W. Roberts and Donovan E. Smucker, 1968. Reprint, Eugene: Wipf & Stock, 2011.

———. "Christianity and Justice." *Theology* 42 (1941) 348–54.

———. *The Church of God*. London: Dacre, 1940.

———. "Coleridge and Kant." In *Coleridge's Variety: Bicentenary Studies*, edited by John B. Beer, 183–203. London: Macmillan, 1974.

———. "Collingwood on the Philosophy of Religion." *Scottish Journal of Religious Studies* 13 (1992) 73–83.

———. "The Crux of Morality." *The Listener* 40 (1948) 926–27.

———. "The Euthyphro Dilemma." *Proceedings of the Aristotelian Society, Supplementary Volumes* 46 (1972) 211–21.

———. "Evil and Personal Responsibility." *The Listener* 39 (1948) 457–59.

———. "Evil and the Vulnerability of God." *Philosophy* 62 (1987) 102.

———. *Explorations in Theology 5*. London: SCM, 1979.

———. *God the Living and the True*. London: Dacre, 1940.

———. "Kant's Philosophy of Religion." *Philosophy* 50 (1975) 131–44.

———. *Kenotic Ecclesiology: Select Writings of Donald M. MacKinnon*. Edited by John C. McDowell and Scott Kirkland. Minneapolis: Fortress, 2016.

———. "A Master in Israel: Hans Urs von Balthasar." In *Hans Urs von Balthasar: Engagement with God*, translated by J. Halliburton, 1–16. London: SPCK, 1975.

———. "Oliver Chase Quick as a Theologian." *Theology* 96 (1993) 101–17.

———. *Philosophy and the Burden of Theological Honesty: A Donald MacKinnon Reader*. Edited by John McDowell. London: T&T Clark, 2011.

———. *The Problem of Metaphysics*. Cambridge: Cambridge University Press, 1974.

———. "Prolegomena to Christology." *The Journal of Theological Studies* 33 (1982) 146–60.

———. "The Relation of the Doctrines of the Incarnation and the Trinity." In *Christ, Creation and Culture: Essays in Honour of T. F. Torrance*, edited Richard W. A. McKinney, 92–107. Edinburgh: T&T Clark, 1976.

———. "Some Notes on 'Philosophy of History' and the Problems of Human Society." In *The Logic of Personal Knowledge: Essays Presented to Michael Polanyi on His Seventieth Birthday, 11 March 1961*, 171–78. London: Routledge, 1961.

———. *A Study in Ethical Theory*. New York: Collier, 1957.

———. "Theology and Tragedy." *Religious Studies* 2 (1967) 163–69.

———. *Themes in Theology: The Threefold Cord: Essays in Philosophy, Politics and Theology*. Edinburgh: T&T Clark, 1987.

———. "Vexilla Regis: Some Reflections for Passiontide, 1939." *Theology* 38 (1939) 254–59.

———. "What is a Metaphysical Statement?" *Proceedings of the Aristotelian Society* 41 (1940–1941) 1–26.

MacKinnon, D. M., and G. W. H. Lampe. *The Resurrection: A Dialogue Arising from Broadcasts by G. W. H. Lampe and D. M. MacKinnon*, edited by William Purcell. London: Mowbray, 1966.

Maltby, Michael. "Wordless Words: Poetry and the Symmetry of Being." In *Acquainted with the Night: Psychoanalysis and the Poetic Imagination*, edited by Hamish Canham and Carole Satyamurti, 49–70. London: Karnac, 2003.

Manent, Pierre. *An Intellectual History of Liberalism*. Translated by Rebecca Balinski. Princeton: Princeton University Press, 1995.

Manser, A. R. "Bradley and Internal Relations." *Royal Institute of Philosophy Supplements* 13 (1982) 181–95.

Marion, Jean-Luc. "Is the Ontological Argument Ontological? The Argument According to Anselm and Its Metaphysical Interpretation According to Kant." *Journal of the History of Philosophy* 30 (1992) 201–18.

———. "Thomas Aquinas and Onto-theo-logy." In *The Essential Writings*, 288–311. New York: Fordham University Press, 2013.

Marx, William. "La véritable catharsis aristotélicienne: Pour une lecture philologique et physiologique de la Poétique." *Poétique* 166 (2011–2012) 131–54.

McAleer, Graham James. *Erich Przywara and Postmodern Natural Law: A History of the Metaphysics of Morals*. Notre Dame: University of Notre Dame Press, 2019.

McCabe, Herbert. *God Matters*. London: Chapman, 1987.

McCormack, Bruce. *Karl Barth's Critically Realistic Dialectical Theology: Its Genesis and Development 1909–1936*. Oxford: Clarendon, 1997.

McCurry, Jeffrey. "Towards a Poetics of Theological Creativity: Rowan Williams Reads Augustine *De Doctrina* after Derrida." *Modern Theology* 23 (2007) 415–33.

———. *Traditioned Creativity: On Rowan Williams and the Grammars of Theological Practice*. PhD diss., Duke University, 2006.

McDowell, John C. "Silenus' Wisdom and the 'Crime Of Being': The Problem of Hope in George Steiner's Tragic Vision." *Literature & Theology* 14 (2000) 385–98.

Meagher, Robert Emmett. *Herakles Gone Mad: Rethinking Heroism in an Age of Endless War*. Northampton: Olive Branch, 2006.

Meillassoux, Quentin. *After Finitude: An Essay on the Necessity of Contingency*. Translated by Ray Brassier. London: Continuum, 2008.

Melnick, Arthur. *Kant's Analogies of Experience*. Chicago: University of Chicago Press, 1973.

Metz, Johann Baptist. "Suffering unto God." *Critical Inquiry* 20 (1994) 611–22.

Michéa, Jean-Claude. *The Realm of Lesser Evil: An Essay on Liberal Civilization*. Translated by David Fernbach. Cambridge: Polity, 2009.

Michel, Laurence. "The Possibility of a Christian Tragedy." *Thought* 31 (1956) 403–28.
Milbank, John. "Against Human Rights: Liberty in the Western Tradition." *Oxford Journal of Law and Religion* 1 (2012) 1–32.
———. "The Archbishop of Canterbury: The Man and the Theology Behind the Shari'a Lecture." In *Shari'a in the West*, edited by Rex J. Adhar and Nicholas Aroney, 43–58. Oxford: Oxford University Press, 2010.
———. "Beauty and the Soul." In John Milbank et al., *Theological Perspectives on God and Beauty*, 1–34. Harrisburg: Trinity, 2003.
———. *Being Reconciled: Ontology and Pardon.* London: Routledge, 2003.
———. *Beyond Secular Order: The Representation of Being and the Representation of the People.* Oxford: Wiley & Sons, 2013.
———. "Between Purgation and Illumination: A Critique of the Theology of Right." In *Christ, Ethics and Tragedy: Essays in Honour of Donald MacKinnon*, edited by Kenneth Surin, 161–96. Cambridge, Cambridge University Press, 1989.
———. "Dignity Rather than Right." *Open Insight* 5 (2013) 77–124.
———. "The Double Glory, or Paradox Versus Dialectic: On Not Quite Agreeing with Slavoj Žižek." In Slavoj Žižek and John Milbank, *The Monstrosity of Christ: Paradox or Dialectic?*, edited by Creston Davis, 110–233. Cambridge: MIT Press, 2009.
———. "Enclaves, or Where is the Church?" *New Blackfriars* 73 (1992) 341–52.
———. "Faith, Reason and Imagination: The Study of Theology and Philosophy in the 21st Century." *Transversalités: Revue de l'Institut Catholique de Paris* 101 (2007) 69–86.
———. *The Future of Love: Essays in Political Theology.* Eugene: Cascade, 2008.
———. "The Grandeur of Reason and the Perversity of Rationalism: Radical Orthodoxy's First Decade." In *The Radical Orthodoxy Reader*, edited by Simon Oliver and John Milbank, 367–405. London: Routledge, 2009.
———. "Hume Versus Kant: Faith, Reason and Feeling." *Modern Theology* 27 (2011) 276–97.
———. "Immutability/Impassibility, Divine." In *Encyclopedia of Christian Theology: Volume 2*, edited by Jean-Yves Lacoste, 760–62. London: Routledge, 2005.
———. "The Invocation of Clio: A Response." *Journal of Religious Ethics* 33 (2005) 3–44.
———. "Knowledge: The Theological Critique of Philosophy in Hamann and Jacobi." In *Radical Orthodoxy: A New Theology*, edited by John Milbank et al., 21–37. London: Routledge, 1999.
———. *The Legend of Death: Two Poetic Sequences.* Eugene: Cascade, 2008.
———. "Manifestation and Procedure: Trinitarian Metaphysics after Albert the Great and Thomas Aquinas." In *Tomismo Creativo*, edited by Marco Salvioili, 41–117. Bologna: Edizioni Studio Domenicano, 2015.
———. *The Mercurial Wood: Sites, Tales, Qualities.* Salzburg: University of Salzburg, 1997.
———. "Only Theology Saves Metaphysics: On the Modalities of Terror." In *Belief and Metaphysics*, edited by Conor Cunningham and Peter M. Candler Jr., 452–500. London: SCM, 2007.
———. "The Politics of the Soul." *Open Insight* 6 (2015) 91–108.
———. "The Programme of Radical Orthodoxy." In *Radical Orthodoxy?–A Catholic Enquiry*, edited by Laurence Paul Hemming, 33–45. Aldershot: Ashgate, 2000.

———. "Scholasticism, Modernism and Modernity." *Modern Theology* 22 (2006) 651–71.

———. "The Sublime in Kierkegaard." In *Post-Secular Philosophy: Between Philosophy and Theology*, edited by Phillip Blond, 68–81. London: Routledge, 1998.

———. "The Soul of Reciprocity, Part One: Reciprocity Refused." *Modern Theology* 17 (2001) 336–91.

———. "Stories of Sacrifice." *Modern Theology* 12 (1996) 27–56.

———. "Sublimity: The Modern Transcendent." In *Transcendence: Philosophy, Literature, and Theology Approach the Beyond*, edited by Regina Schwartz, 211–34. London: Routledge, 2004.

———. *Theology and Social Theory: Beyond Secular Reason*. 2nd ed. Oxford: Blackwell, 2006.

———. "The Thing That is Given." *Archivio di Filosofia* 74 (2006) 503–39.

———. "On 'Thomistic Kabbalah.'" *Modern Theology* 27 (2011) 147–85.

———. "The Thomistic Telescope: Truth and Identity." *American Catholic Philosophical Quarterly* 80 (2006) 193–226.

———. *The Word Made Strange: Theology, Language, Culture*. Oxford: Blackwell, 1997.

Milbank, John, and Adrian Pabst. *The Politics of Virtue: Post-Liberalism and the Human Future*. London: Rowman & Littlefield, 2016.

Milbank, John, and Catherine Pickstock. *Truth in Aquinas*. London: Routledge, 2001.

Millet, Louis. "Analogie et participation chez Saint Thomas d'Aquin." *Les Études philosophiques* 3–4 (1989) 371–83.

Moltmann, Jürgen. *The Crucified God: The Cross of Christ as the Foundation and Criticism of Christian Theology*. Translated by R. A. Wilson and John Bowden. Minneapolis: Fortress, 1974.

———. *God in Creation: An Ecological Doctrine of Creation – The Gifford Lectures 1984–1985*. Translated by Margaret Kohl. London: SCM, 1985.

———. *The Trinity and the Kingdom: The Doctrine of God*. Translated by Margaret Kohl. Minneapolis: Fortress, 1981.

Montagnes, Bernard. *The Doctrine of the Analogy of Being according to Thomas Aquinas*. Translated by E. M. Macierowski and Pol Vandevelde. Milwaukee: Marquette University Press, 2004.

Moore, G. E. *Philosophical Studies*. London: Routledge, 1922.

Mulhall, Stephen. *The Wounded Animal: J. M. Coetzee and the Difficulty of Reality in Literature and Philosophy*. Princeton: Princeton University Press, 2009.

Muller, André. *Donald M. MacKinnon (1913–94): An Intellectual Biography*. Forthcoming.

Murrmann-Kahl, Michael. "*Mysterium Trinitatis?*" *Fallstudien zur Trinitätslehre in der evangelischten Dogamtik des 20. Jahrhunderts*. Berlin: de Gruyter, 1997.

Murray, Paul D. "Theology in the Borderlands: Donald Mackinnon and Contemporary Theology." *Modern Theology* 14 (1998) 355–76.

Myers, Benjamin. *Christ the Stranger: The Theology of Rowan Williams*. London: T&T Clark, 2012.

———. "Disruptive History: Rowan Williams on Heresy and Orthodoxy." In *On Rowan Williams: Critical Essays*, edited by Matheson Russell, 47–67. Eugene: Cascade, 2009.

Nancy, Jean-Luc. *The Birth to Presence*. Translated by B. Holmes et al. Stanford: Stanford University Press, 1993.

———. "The Sublime Offering." In *Of the Sublime: Presence in Question*, edited Jean-Francois Courtine et al., translated by Jeffrey S. Librett, 25–53. New York: State University of New York Press, 1993.
Narbonne, Jean-Marc. "Aristote et la mal." *Documenti E Studi Sulla Tradizione Filosofica Medievale* 8 (1997) 87–103.
Narcisse, Gilbert. "Thomistic Realism?" *Nova et Vetera, English Edition* 8 (2010) 783–98.
Nehemas, Alexander. "Participation and Predication in Plato's Later Thought." *The Review of Metaphysics* 36 (1982) 343–74.
Niebuhr, Reinhold. *Beyond Tragedy: Essays on the Christian Interpretation of History*. London: Nisbet, 1938.
Nietzsche, Friedrich. *The Birth of Tragedy and Other Writings*. Edited by Raymond Geuss and Ronald Speirs. Translated by Ronald Speirs. Cambridge: Cambridge University Press, 1999.
Nussbaum, Martha. *The Fragility of Goodness Luck and Ethics in Greek Tragedy and Philosophy*. Rev. ed. Cambridge: Cambridge University Press, 2001.
Ochieng, Omedi. *The Intellectual Imagination: Knowledge and Aesthetics in North Atlantic and African Philosophy*. Notre Dame: University of Notre Dame Press, 2018.
Owens, Joseph. *The Doctrine of Being in Aristotelian Metaphysics: A Study in the Greek Background of Mediaeval Thought*. 3rd ed. Toronto: Pontifical Institute of Mediaeval Studies, 1978.
Pabst, Adrian. *Metaphysics: The Creation of Hierarchy*. Grand Rapids: Eerdmans, 2012.
Patzig, Günther. "Theology and Ontology in Aristotle's Metaphysics." In *Articles on Aristotle*, vol. 3, edited by Jonathan Barnes et al., 33–49. London: Duckworth, 1979.
Peperstraten, Frans van. "The Sublime and the Limits of Metaphysics." In *The Sublime and Its Teleology: Kant—German Idealism—Phenomenology*, edited by Donald Loose, 187–203. Leiden: Brill, 2011.
Perl, Eric D. *Thinking Being: Introduction to Metaphysics in the Classical Tradition*. Leiden: Brill, 2014.
Pieper, Josef. *The Silence of St. Thomas: Three Essays*. London: Faber and Faber, 1957.
Pietropaolo, Domenico. "Whipping Jesus Devoutly: The Dramaturgy of Catharsis and the Christian Idea of Tragic Form." In *Beyond the Fifth Century: Interactions with Greek Tragedy from the Fourth Century BCE until the Middle Ages*, edited by Ingo Gildenhard and Martin Revermann, 397–424. Berlin: de Gruyter, 2010.
Pickstock, Catherine. *After Writing: On the Liturgical Consummation of Philosophy*. Oxford: Blackwell, 1998.
———. "Justice and Prudence: Principles of Order in the Platonic City." *Heythrop Journal* 42 (2001) 269–82.
———. "Matter and Mattering: The Metaphysics of Rowan Williams." *Modern Theology* 31 (2015) 599–617.
———. *Repetition and Identity*. The Literary Agenda. Oxford: Oxford University Press, 2013.
———. "Reply to David Ford and Guy Collins." *Scottish Journal of Theology* 54 (2001) 405–22.
Plato. *Complete Works*. Edited by John Cooper. Indianapolis: Hackett, 1997.

Poole, Adrian. *Tragedy: A Very Short Introduction*. Oxford: Oxford University Press, 2005.
Pound, Marcus. *Theology, Psychoanalysis and Trauma*. London: SCM, 2007.
Prynne, J. H. "Mental Ears and Poetic Work." *Chicago Review* 55 (2010) 126–57.
———. "Poetic Thought." *Textual Practice* 24 (2010) 595–606.
———. "Resistance and Difficulty." *Prospect* 5 (1961) 26–30.
———. *Stars, Tigers and the Shape of Words*. London: Birkbeck, 1993.
Przywara, Erich. *Analogia Entis. Metaphysics: Original Structure and Universal Rhythm*. Translated by John R. Betz and David Bentley Hart. Grand Rapids, Eerdmans, 2013.
Puntel, Lorenz. *Analogie und Geschichtlichkeit I: Philosophiegeschichtlich-Kritischer Versuch über das Grundproblem der Metaphysik*. Freiburg: Herder, 1969.
Putnam, Hilary. *Philosophy in an Age of Science: Physics, Mathematics, and Skepticism*. Edited by Mario de Caro and David Macarthur. Cambridge: Harvard University Press, 2012.
Quash, Ben. "Christianity as Hyper-Tragic." In *Facing Tragedies*, edited by Christopher Hamilton et al., 77–88. Perspectives on Social Ethics 2. Berlin: LIT, 2009.
———. *Theology and the Drama of History*. Cambridge: Cambridge University, 2005.
———. "*The Tragic Imagination* and the Ascesis of the Eye." *Modern Theology* 34 (2018) 258–66.
Rambo, Shelly. "Spirit and Trauma." *Interpretation: A Journal of Bible and Theology* 69 (2015) 7–19.
Rancière, Jacques. *The Future of the Image*. Translated by Gregory Elliott. New York: Verso, 2007.
———. "The Sublime from Lyotard to Schiller: Two Readings of Kant and Their Political Significance." *Radical Philosophy* 126 (2004) 8–15.
Raphael, D. D. *The Paradox of Tragedy*. Bloomington: University of Indiana Press, 1960.
Rasche Michael. "Das Phänomen des Tragischen und die tragische Dimension des Christentums." *Theologie und Philosophie* 89 (2014) 515–33.
Richards, I. A. *Principles of Literary Criticism*. London: Routledge, 1924.
Riches, Aaron. *Ecce Homo: On the Divine Unity of Christ*. Grand Rapids: Eerdmans, 2016.
Ritchie, Angus. *From Metaphysics to Morality: The Theistic Implications of Our Ethical Commitments*. Oxford: Oxford University Press, 2012.
Ricoeur, Paul. *Fallible Man*. Translated by Charles A. Kelbley. New York: Fordham University Press, 1986.
Rigby, Paul. *The Theology of Augustine's Confessions*. Cambridge: Cambridge University Press, 2015.
Rist, John M. "Plotinus on Matter and Evil." *Phronesis* 6 (1961) 154–66.
Robertson, Ritchie. "*On the Sublime* and Schiller's Theory of Tragedy." *Philosophical Readings* 5 (2013) 194–212.
Rockmore, Tom. "Analytic Philosophy and the Hegelian Turn." *The Review of Metaphysics* 55 (2001) 339–70.
Rogozinski, Jacob. "The Sublime Monster." In *The Sublime and Its Teleology*, edited by Donald Loose, 159–68. Leiden: Brill, 2011.
Römer, Thomas C. "Why Would the Deuteronomists Tell about the Sacrifice of Jepthah's Daughter?" *Journal for the Study of the Old Testament* 77 (1998) 27–38.

Roochnik, David. *The Tragedy of Reason: Towards a Platonic Conception of Logos.* New York: Routledge, 1990.
Rose, Gillian. *Judaism and Modernity.* Oxford: Blackwell, 1993.
———. *Mourning Becomes Law: Philosophy and Representation.* Cambridge: Cambridge University Press 1996.
Rosemann, Philipp W. *Omne Agens Agit Sibi Simile: A "Repetition" of Scholastic Metaphysics.* Louvain Philosophical Studies 12. Leuven: Leuven University Press, 1996.
Rösler, Wolfgang. *Polis und Tragödie: Funktionsgeschichtliche Betrachtungen zu einer Antiken Literaturgattung.* Konstanz: Universitätsverlag Kostanz, 1980.
Ryle, Gilbert. *Collected Papers, Volume 2: Collected Essays 1929–1968.* London: Routledge, 2009.
Sands, Kathleen M. *Escape from Paradise: Evil and Tragedy in Feminist Theology.* Minneapolis: Fortress, 1994.
———. "Tragedy, Theology, and Feminism in the Time after Time." *New Literary History* 35 (2004) 41–61.
Sarot, Marcel. "Does God Suffer?: A Critical Discussion of Thomas G. Weinandy's *Does God Suffer?*" *Ars Disputandi* 1 (2001). http://www.ArsDisputandi.org.
Schiller, Friedrich. *Sämtliche Werke.* Band 5. München: Hanser, 1962.
Schindler, David C. *Plato's Critique of Impure Reason: On Goodness and Truth in The Republic.* Washington, DC: The Catholic University of America Press, 2008.
Schmutz, Jacob. "The Medieval Doctrine of Causality and the Theology of Pure Nature (13th to 17th Century)." In *Surnatural: A Controversy at the Heart of Twentieth-Century Thomistic Thought*, edited by Serge Thomas-Bonino, 203–50. Florida: Sapienta Press of Ave Maria University, 2009.
Schwartz, Regina M. "The Ethics of the Tragic Imagination." *Modern Theology* 34 (2018) 273–79.
Scott, David. *Conscripts of Modernity: The Tragedy of Colonial Enlightenment.* Durham: Duke University Press, 2004.
Séguy-Duclot, Alain. "Généalogie du sublime: Le Περὶ ὕψους du Pseudo-Longin: une tentative de synthèse entre Platon et Aristote." *Revue des sciences philosophiques et théologiques* 88 (2004) 649–72.
Seifrin-Weis, Heike. "*Pros hen* and the Foundations of Aristotelian Metaphysics." *Proceedings of the Boston Area Colloquium in Ancient Philosophy* 24 (2009) 261–85.
Sellars, Wilfrid. "Empiricism and the Philosophy of Mind." In *The Foundations of Science and the Concepts of Psychology and Psychoanalysis*, edited by Herbert Feigl and Michael Scriven, 253–329. Minnesota Studies in the Philosophy of Science 1. Minneapolis: University of Minnesota Press, 1956.
Segal, Charles. "Sophocles' Praise of Man and the Conflicts of the 'Antigone.'" *Arion: A Journal of Humanities and the Classics* 3 (1964) 46–66.
———. *Sophocles' Tragic World: Divinity, Nature, Society.* Cambridge: Harvard University Press, 1995.
Seigfried, Hans. "Kant's Thesis about Being Anticipated by Suárez?" In *Proceedings of the Third International Kant Congress*, edited by L. W. Beck, 510–20. Dordrecht: Reidel, 1972.
Sgarbi, Marco. "The Spontaneity of Mind in Kant's Transcendental Logic." *Fenomenologia e Societá* 32 (2009) 19–28.

Shaviro, Steven. *The Universe of Things: On Speculative Realism*. Minneapolis: University of Minnesota Press, 2014.

Sherman, Jacob H. "A Genealogy of Participation." In *The Participatory Turn: Spirituality, Mysticism, Religious Studies*, edited by Jorge N. Ferrer and Jacob H. Sherman, 81–112. Albany: State University of New York Press, 2008.

Simon, Ulrich E. *Pity and Terror: Christianity and Tragedy*. New York: Palgrave MacMillan, 1989.

Smit, Bettine Van Zyl. "The Reception of Greek Tragedy in the 'Old' and the 'New' South Africa." *Akroterion* 48 (2003) 3–20.

Sophocles. *The Three Theban Plays: Antigone, Oedipus the King, Oedipus at Colonus*. Translated Robert Fagles. London: Penguin, 1984.

———. *Sophocles: Four Tragedies*. Translated by Oliver Taplin. Oxford: Oxford University Press, 2015.

Steel, Carlos, and Jan Opsomer. "Evil Without a Cause: Proclus' Doctrine on the Origin of Evil and its Antecedents in Hellenistic Philosophy." In *Zur Rezeption der hellenistischen Philosophie in der Spätantike: Akten der 1. Tagung der Karl-und-Gertrud-Abel-Stiftung vom 22.–25. September 1997 in Trier*, edited by Therese Fuhrer et al., 229–60. Philosophie der Antike 9. Stuttgart: Steiner, 1999.

Stein, Walter. *Criticism as Dialogue*. Cambridge: Cambridge University Press, 1969.

Steiner, George. *Antigones*. Oxford: Clarendon, 1984.

———. *The Death of Tragedy*. London: Faber and Faber, 1961.

———. *No Passion Spent: Essays 1978–1996*. London: Faber and Faber, 1996.

———. "A Note on Absolute Tragedy." *Journal of Literature & Theology* 4 (1990) 147–56.

———. *Real Presences*. London: Faber and Faber, 1989.

———. "Tragedy, Pure and Simple." In *Tragedy and the Tragic*, edited M. S. Silk, 534–46. Oxford: Oxford University Press, 1995.

———. "Tragedy, Reconsidered." *New Literary History* 35 (2004) 1–15.

———. "Tribute to Donald MacKinnon." *Theology* 98 (1995) 2–9.

Stevens, Wallace. *The Collected Poems of Wallace Stevens*. London: Faber and Faber, 1984.

Stoker, Wessel. "Culture and Transcendence: A Typology." In *Looking Beyond? Shifting Views of Transcendence in Philosophy, Theology, Art, and Politics*, edited by Wessel Stoker and W. L. van der Merwe, 5–28. Amsterdam: Rodopi, 2012.

Strawson, P. F. *Individuals: An Essay in Descriptive Metaphysics*. London: Routledge, 1959.

Surin, Kenneth, ed. *Christ, Ethics and Tragedy: Essays in Honour of Donald MacKinnon*. Cambridge: Cambridge University Press, 1989.

———. "Christology, Tragedy and 'Ideology.'" *Theology* 89 (1986) 283–91.

———. *Theology and the Problem of Evil*. Oxford: Blackwell, 1986.

Sutherland, Stewart R. "Donald MacKenzie MacKinnon, 1913–1994." *Proceedings of the British Academy* 97 (1998) 381–89.

Symes, Carol. "The Tragedy of the Middle Ages." In *Beyond the Fifth Century: Interactions with Greek Tragedy from the Fourth Century BCE until the Middle Ages*, edited by Ingo Gildenhard and Martin Revermann, 335–69. Berlin: de Gruyter, 2010.

Szondi, Peter. *An Essay on the Tragic*. Translated by Paul Fleming. Stanford: Stanford University Press, 2002.

Tanner, Kathryn. *Jesus, Humanity and the Trinity: A Brief Systematic Theology*. Minneapolis: Fortress, 2001.
Tarrant, Dorothy. "Plato as Dramatist." *The Journal of Hellenic Studies* 75 (1955) 82–89.
Tate, Daniel L. "Transcending the Aesthetic: Gadamer on Tragedy and the Tragic." In *Theological Aesthetics after von Balthasar*, edited by Oleg V. Bychkov and James Fodor, 34–50. Aldershot: Ashgate, 2008.
Taylor, Charles. *Sources of the Self: The Making of Modern Identity*. Cambridge: Harvard University Press, 1989.
Te Velde, Rudi. *Aquinas on God: The 'Divine Science' of the* Summa Theologiae. Aldershot: Ashgate, 2006.
Thacker, Eugene. *Cosmic Pessimism*. Minneapolis: Univocal, 2015.
Tilley, Terrence. *The Evils of Theodicy*. Eugene: Wipf & Stock, 2000.
Toole, David. *Waiting for Godot in Sarajevo: Theological Reflections on Nihilism, Tragedy, and Apocalypse*. Colorado: Westview, 1998.
Tracy, David. "Horror and Horror: The Response of Tragedy." *Social Research: An International Quarterly* 81 (2014) 739–67.
———. "On Tragic Wisdom." In *Wrestling with God and Evil: Philosophical Reflections*, edited by Hendrik M. Vroom, 13–24. Amsterdam: Rodopi, 2007.
Twetten, David. "Really Distinguishing Essence from Esse." In *Medieval Skepticism, and the Claim to Metaphysical Knowledge*, edited by Gyula Klima and Alexander W. Hall, 79–127. Proceedings of the Society for Medieval Logic and Metaphysics 6 Newcastle: Cambridge Scholars, 2011.
Van Der Kolk, Bessel A. "Trauma and Memory." *Psychiatry and Clinical Neurosciences* 52 (1998) 97–109.
Vernant, Jean-Pierre, and Pierre Vidal-Naquet. *Myth and Tragedy in Ancient Greece*. Translated by Janet Lloyd. New York: Zone, 1988.
Venard, Olivier-Thomas. "The Litany of Truth and the Scholia on Reason according to Radical Orthodoxy." *Ephemerides Theologicae Lovanienses* 90 (2014) 287–322.
Veyne, Paul. *Did the Greeks Believe in Their Myths? An Essay on the Constitutive Imagination*. Translated by Paula Wishing. Chicago: University of Chicago Press, 1988.
Villey, Michel. "Epitome of Classical Natural Law." *Griffith Law Review* 9 (2000) 74–97.
———. "Epitome of Classical Natural Law (Part II)." *Griffith Law Review* 10 (2001) 153–78.
———. "Remarque sur la notion de droit chez Suarez." *Archives de Philosophie* 42 (1979) 219–27.
Vlastos, Gregory. "The Third Man Argument in the Parmenides." *The Philosophical Review* 63 (1954) 319–49.
Vodolazkin, Eugene. *Laurus*. Translated by Lisa C. Hayden. London: Oneworld, 2015.
Vollrath, Ernst. "Die Gliederung der Metaphysik in eine Metaphysica generalis und eine Metaphysica specialis." *Zeitschrift für philosophische Forschung* 16 (1962) 258–84.
Waismann, Friedrich. "Notes on Talks with Wittgenstein." *The Philosophical Review* 74 (1965) 12–16.
Wallace, Jennifer. "Tragic Remembrance in the Era of Fake News." *Modern Theology* 34 (2018) 267–72.
Waller, Giles. "Felix Culpa? On Rowan Williams' *The Tragic Imagination*." *Modern Theology* 34 (2018) 243–51.

———. "Freedom, Fate and Sin in Donald MacKinnon's Use of Tragedy." In *Christian Theology and Tragedy: Theologians, Tragic Literature, and Tragic Theory*, edited by Kevin Taylor and Giles Waller, 101–18. Farnham: Ashgate, 2011.
Ward, Graham. "Extremities." *Modern Theology* 34 (2018) 235–42.
———. *How the Light Gets In: Ethical Life I*. Oxford: Oxford University Press, 2016.
———. "Steiner and Eagleton: The Practice of Hope and the Idea of the Tragic." *Literature & Theology* 19 (2005) 100–11.
———. "Suffering and Incarnation." In *The Blackwell Companion to Postmodern Theology*, edited by Graham Ward, 192–208. Oxford: Blackwell, 2005.
———. "Tragedy as Subclause: George Steiner's Dialogue with Donald MacKinnon." *Heythrop Journal* 34 (1993) 274–87.
———. "Transcendence and Representation." In *Transcendence: Philosophy, Literature, and Theology Approach the Beyond*, edited by Regina Schwartz, 127–47. London: Routledge, 2004.
———. "Transcorporality: The Ontological Scandal." *Bulletin of the John Rylands Library* 80 (1998) 235–52.
———. *Unbelievable: Why We Believe and Why We Don't*. London: Tauris, 2013.
Warner, Martin. "Literature, Truth and Logic." *Philosophy* 74 (1999) 29–54.
Webster, John. "Life in and of Himself: Reflections on God's Aseity." In *Engaging the Doctrine of God: Contemporary Protestant Perspectives*, edited by Bruce L. McCormack, 107–24. Grand Rapids: Baker Academic, 2008.
———. "Principles of Systematic Theology." *International Journal of Systematic Theology* 11 (2009) 56–71.
Weil, Simone. *Waiting on God*. London: Routledge, 1951.
Weinandy, Thomas. *Does God Suffer?* Notre Dame: University of Notre Dame Press, 2000.
———. "Does God Suffer?" *Ars Disputandi* 2 (2002). http://www.ArsDisputandi.org.
West, Philip. "Christology as 'Ideology.'" *Theology* 88 (1985) 428–36.
Wigren, Jodie. "Narrative Completion in the Treatment of Trauma." *Psychotherapy* 31 (1994) 415–23.
White, Roger M. "MacKinnon on the Parables." In *Christ, Ethics and Tragedy: Essays in Honour of Donald MacKinnon*, edited by Kenneth Surin, 49–70. Cambridge: Cambridge University Press, 1989.
———. *Talking about God: The Concept of Analogy and the Problem of Religious Language*. Farnham: Ashgate, 2010.
Williams, A. N. "What is Systematic Theology?" *International Journal of Systematic Theology* 11 (2009) 40–55.
Williams, Raymond. *Modern Tragedy*. Edited by Pamela McCallum. Toronto: Broadview, 2006.
Williams, Rowan. "Adult Geometry: Dangerous Thoughts in R. S. Thomas." In *The Page's Drift: R. S. Thomas at Eighty*, edited by M. Wynn Thomas. 82–98. Wales: Seren, 1993.
———. *Anglican Identities*. London: Darton, Longman, & Todd, 2004.
———. *Arius: Heresy and Tradition*. Rev. ed. Grand Rapids: Eerdmans, 2001.
———. "Art: Taking Time and Making Sense." In *Images of Christ: Religious Iconography in Twentieth Century British Art. An Exhibition to Mark the Centenary of St. Matthew's Church, Northampton*, edited by T. Devonshire-Jones, 25–27. Northampton: St. Matthew's Centenary Art Committee, 1993.

———. "Augustine's Christology: Its Spirituality and Rhetoric." In *In the Shadow of the Incarnation: Essays on Jesus Christ in the Early Church in Honour of Brian E. Daley, S.J.*, edited by Peter W. Martens, 176–89. Notre Dame: University of Notre Dame Press, 2008.

———. "Balthasar and the Trinity." In *The Cambridge Companion to Hans Urs von Balthasar*, edited by Edward T. Oakes and David Moss, 37–50. Cambridge: Cambridge University Press, 2004.

———. *Christ the Heart of Creation*. London: Bloomsbury, 2018.

———. "Christian Art and Cultural Pluralism: Reflections on 'L'art de l'icone,' by Paul Evdokimov." *Eastern Churches Review* 8 (1976) 38–44.

———. "Creation." In *Augustine Through the Ages: An Encyclopedia*, edited by Allan Fitzgerald, 251–54. Grand Rapids: Eerdmans, 1999.

———. "A Curious Novel: Postmodernism and Holy Madness." TEDx Talks. Uploaded July 5, 2016. YouTube video, 14:44. https://www.youtube.com/watch?v=6MCB9JuLFzo.

———. "Defining Heresy." In *The Origins of Christendom in the West*, edited by Alan Kreider, 313–35. Edinburgh: T&T Clark, 2001.

———. "The Deflections of Desire: Negative Theology in Trinitarian Disclosure." In *Silence and the Word: Negative Theology and Incarnation*, edited by Oliver Davies and Denys Turner, 115–35. Cambridge: Cambridge University Press, 2002.

———. "Dialectic and Analogy: A Theological Legacy." In *The Impact of Idealism: The Legacy of Post-Kantian German Thought*, edited by Nicholas Adams, 274–92. Cambridge: Cambridge University Press, 2013.

———. "Does it Make Sense to Speak of a Pre-Nicene Orthodoxy?" In *The Making of Orthodoxy*, edited by Rowan Williams, 1–23. Cambridge: Cambridge University Press, 1989.

———. *Dostoevsky: Language, Faith, and Fiction*. Waco: Baylor University Press, 2008.

———. *The Edge of Words: God and the Habits of Language*. London: Bloomsbury, 2014.

———. "The Four Quartets (1975)." Unpublished material.

———. "God." In *Fields of Faith: Theology and Religious Study for the Twenty-First Century*, edited by David F. Ford et al., 75–89. Cambridge: Cambridge University Press, 2005.

———. "Good for Nothing? Augustine on Creation." *Augustinian Studies* 25 (1994) 9–24.

———. *Grace and Necessity: Reflections on Art and Love*. London: Continuum, 2005.

———. "The Health of the Spirit." In *Public Life and the Place of the Church: Reflections to Honour the Bishop of Oxford*, edited by Michael W. Brierley, 217–22. Aldershot: Ashgate, 2006.

———. "Holy Folly and the Problem of Representing Holiness: Some Literary Perspectives." *Journal of Orthodox Christian Studies* 1 (2018) 3–15.

———. "Insubstantial Evil." In *Augustine and His Critics: Essays in Honour of Gerald Bonner*, edited by George Lawless and Robert Dodaro, 105–23. London: Routledge, 2000.

———. "'Know Thyself': What Kind of an Injunction?" In *Philosophy, Religion and the Spiritual Life*, edited by Michael McGhee, 211–27. Cambridge: Cambridge University Press, 1992.

———. "Language, Reality and Desire in Augustine's *De doctrina*." *Journal of Literature & Theology* 3 (1989) 138–50.

———. *Lost Icons: Reflections on Cultural Bereavement*. London: T&T Clark, 2000.

———. "Macrina's Deathbed Revisited: Gregory of Nyssa on Mind and Passion." In *Christian Faith and Greek Philosophy in Late Antiquity: Essays in Tribute to Christopher Stead*, edited by Lionel R. Wickham and Catherine P. Bammel, 227–46. Leiden: Brill, 1993.

———. "Mankind, Nation, State." In *This Land and This People*, edited by Paul Bellard and Huw Jones, 119–25. Cardiff: Collegiate Centre of Theology, University College, 1979.

———. *A Margin of Silence: The Holy Spirit in Russian Orthodox Theology*. Québec: Éditions du Lys Vert, 2008.

———. "The Nicene Heritage." In *Christian Understanding of God Today*, edited by James M. Byrne, 45–48. Dublin: Columbia, 1993.

———. "No More Happy Endings: Why We Need Fairy Tales Now More Than Ever." *New Statesman* (2015) 90–92.

———. "'Not Cured, Not Forgetful, Not Paralysed': A Response to Comments on *The Tragic Imagination*." *Modern Theology* 34 (2018) 280–88.

———. "Obituary: Donald MacKinnon." *The Tablet* (March 12, 1994) 31–32.

———. "On Being a Human Body." *Sewanee Theological Review* 42 (1998) 403–13.

———. *On Christian Theology*. Oxford: Blackwell, 2000.

———. "Origen: Between Orthodoxy and Heresy." In *Origenia Septima: Origenes in den Auseinandersetzungen des 4. Jahurhunderts*, edited by Walther Bienert and Uwe Kühneweg, 3–14. Leuven: Peeters, 1999.

———. "The Paradoxes of Self-knowledge in *De trinitate*." In *Augustine: Presbyter Factus Sum. Collectanea Augustiniana*, edited Joseph T. Lienhard et al., 121–34. New York: Lang, 1993.

———. "'Person' and 'Personality' in Christology." *Downside Review* 94 (1976) 253–60.

———. *The Poems of Rowan Williams*. Oxford: Perpetua, 2002.

———. "Poetic and Religious Imagination." *Theology* 80 (1977) 178–87.

———. *A Ray of Darkness: Sermons and Reflections*. Cambridge: Cowley, 1995.

———. *Resurrection: Interpreting the Easter Gospel*. London: Darton, Longman & Todd, 1980.

———. Review of *Augustine on Evil* by G. R. Evans. *Religious Studies* 21 (1985) 95–96.

———. "*Sapientia* and the Trinity: Reflections on *De Trinitate*." In *Collectanea Augustiniana: Mélanges T J van Bavel*, vol. 1, edited by Bernard Bruning et al., 317–32. Leuven: Leuven University Press, 1990.

———. "'The Sadness of the King': Gillian Rose, Hegel, and the Pathos of Reason." *Telos* 173 (2015) 21–36.

———. "Saving Time: Thoughts on Practice, Patience and Vision." *New Blackfriars* 73 (1992) 319–26.

———. "The Seal of Orthodoxy: Mary and the Heart of Christian Doctrine." In *Say Yes to God: Mary and the Revealing of the Word Made Flesh*, edited by Martin Warner, 15–29. London: Tufton, 1999.

———. "The Spirit of the Age to Come." *Sobernost: The Journal of the Fellowship of St. Alban and St. Sergius* 6 (1974) 613–26.

———. "The Standing of Poetry: Geoffrey Hill's Quartet." In *Geoffrey Hill: Essays on His Later Work*, edited by John Lyon and Peter McDonald, 55–69. Oxford: Oxford University Press, 2012.

———. "Suspending the Ethical: R. S. Thomas and Kierkegaard." In *Echoes to the Amen: Essays after R. S. Thomas*, edited by Damien Walford Davies, 206–19. Cardiff: University of Wales Press, 2003.

———. "'Tempted As We Are': Christology and the Analysis of the Passions." In *Studia Patristica: Volume LXIV*, edited J. Braun et al., 391–404. Leuven: Peeters, 2010.

———. "Tragedy and Redemption: A Response to Edith Hall." *Prospect* (December 19, 2016). https://www.prospectmagazine.co.uk/arts-and-books/tragedy-and-redemption-a-response-to-edith-hall-rowan-williams.

———. *The Tragic Imagination*. The Literary Agenda. Oxford: Oxford University Press, 2016.

———. "Troubled Breasts: The Holy Body in Hagiography." In *Portraits of Spiritual Authority: Religious Power in Early Christianity, Byzantium, and the Christian Orient*, edited by Jan Willem Drijvers and John W. Watt, 63–78. Leiden: Brill, 1999.

———. "To Give and Not to Count the Cost: A Sermon Preached at Mirfield in February 1976." *Sobornost: The Journal of the Fellowship and St. Alban and St. Sergius* 7 (1977) 401–3.

———. "To Speak Truly about God: Rowan Williams on Kevin Hector's *Theology without Metaphysics*." *Marginalia: The Los Angeles Review of Books* (May 27, 2014). http://marginalia.lareviewofbooks.org/speak-truly-god/.

———. "What Does Love Know? St. Thomas on the Trinity." *New Blackfriars* 82 (2001) 260–72.

———. "What is Catholic Orthodoxy?" In *Essays Catholic and Radical*, edited by Rowan Williams and Kenneth Leech, 11–17. London: Bowerdean, 1983.

———. *Why Study the Past? The Quest for the Historical Church*. London: Darton, Longman & Todd, 2005.

———. *The Wound of Knowledge: Christian Spirituality from the New Testament to St. John of the Cross*. Rev. ed. London: Darton, Longman & Todd, 1990.

———. *Wrestling with Angels: Conversations in Modern Theology*, edited by Mike Higton. Grand Rapids: Eerdmans, 2007.

Wisdom, John. *Paradox and Discovery*. Berkley: University of California Press, 1965.

Wise, Jennifer. "Tragedy as 'An Augury of a Happy Life.'" *Arethusa* 41 (2008) 381–410.

Wittgenstein, Ludwig. "A Lecture on Ethics." *The Philosophical Review* 74 (1965) 3–12.

———. *Tractatus Logico-Philosophicus*. Translated by D. F. Pears and B. F. McGuinness. Rev. ed. London: Routledge, 1974.

———. *Zettel*. Translated by G. E. M. Anscombe. Oxford: Blackwell, 1967.

Wood, Allen W. "The Emptiness of the Moral Will." *The Monist* 72 (1989) 454–83.

Young, Frances. *God's Presence: A Contemporary Recapitulation of Early Christianity*. Cambridge: Cambridge University Press, 2013.

Young, Julian. *The Philosophy of Tragedy: From Plato to Žižek*. Cambridge: Cambridge University Press, 2013.

Zachhuber, Johannes. "Transzendenz und Immanenz als Interpretationskategorien antiken Denkens im 19. und 20. Jahrhundert." In *Divine Presence and Absence*, edited by N. MacDonald and I. de Hulster, 23–54. Mohr Siebeck: Tübingen, 2013.

Author Index

Adams, Marilyn McCord, 198n121, 231n152, 254, 254n3
Adorno, Theodor, 11n38, 59n77, 241
Agamben, Giorgio, 178n47, 241, 241n178
Aristophanes, 21, 52, 221
Arnold, Matthew, 264n58
Aubenque, Pierre, 92, 92n3, 93n4, 96n22, 100n38
Augustodunensis, Honorius, 33, 162n221
Ayer, A. J., 102–3, 103n51

Balfour, Ian, 58n73
Balthasar, Hans Urs von, 3n5, 29n58, 34, 34–35n67, 68n28, 110–11, 113, 114n107, 159, 160, 189–92
Barish, Jonas A., 28n50
Barnes, Timothy, 28n51
Barrón, Jorge Uscatescu, 131n72
Barth, Karl, 12, 68n28, 106, 106n68, 108, 108n80, 184, 192–94
Beiser, Frederick, 56n67
Bengston, Josef, 77n46
Benjamin, Walter, 56, 242, 242n183
Benoist, Jocelyn, 114n111
Berlant, Lauren, xvi, xviin11
Berlin, Isaiah, 79n50
Bernhardt, Reinhold, 23n33
Bernstein, J. M., 53n54

Berti, Enrico, 93n4, 97n23
Betz, John R., 190n82, 191n86, 193n99
Bielik-Robson, Agatha, 242n183
Billings, Joshua, 52, 52nn49–50, 56n67, 58n73
Blackmur, R. P., 176, 176n39
Blanchette, Oliva, 13, 13n48, 54–55n63
Blowers, Paul M., 30–31n62, 32n63
Bohrer, Karl Heinz, 55n65
Bonino, Guido, 93n9
Booth, Edward, 92n2
Bornemark, Jonna, 41n2
Bottum, Joseph, 176n44
Bouchard, Larry D., 22, 22n30, 23n31, 29n58, 59n77
Boulnois, Olivier, 12n46, 97n23, 110n94, 113n106, 179n51, 181n58
Bourdieu, Pierre, 7n16
Bradshaw, David, 47n34, 137n115
Bowyer, Andrew, 70n29, 71n32, 121n16, 122n20, 124n26, 125n33, 137n116
Bradley, F. H., 93, 103, 156
Brand, Gerrit, 7n21
Brague, Rémi, 135n102
Breyfogle, Todd, 225n110
Brown, David, 1–2n1
Brümmer, Vincent, 7, 7n20, 8n22, 9, 11n39, 13n50, 16

Bulgakov, Sergei, 34, 159, 160
Burke, Edmund, 53, 53n55, 56n66
Burkert, Walter, 16n4
Burnett, Anne Pippin, 254n28
Burrell, David, 79-80
Burt, Donald X., 204n128
Butler, Joseph, 64n4, 68, 68n28, 70, 81, 82, 94, 94n11, 133, 137, 138
Bynum, Carolyn, 158n205

Cane, Anthony, 140n126
Caputo, John D., 34-35n67, 132n78
Carr, David, 3n5
Caruth, Cathy, 260, 260n37, 261n41
Cassin, Barbara, 11n39, 181n58
Cassirer, Ernst, 106, 111n98, 127, 127n54
Cavell, Stanley, 66, 66n11, 153n193, 235-36, 235n160
Caygill, Howard, 116, 116n118
Certeau, Michel de, 7n15
Charlesworth, James, 30n61
Cherniss, Harold, 196n116
Clements, Keith, 140-141n128
Clery, E. J., 56n66
Coakley, Sarah, 11, 12n43
Collingwood, R. G., 67, 91, 106, 106n72, 111, 122, 137, 165
Connor, Timothy G., 68n28
Courtine, Jean-François, 12n46, 54-55n63, 58n73, 97n23, 100n38, 110n94, 127n54, 181n58, 191n86
Cress, Donald A., 196n115
Critchley, Simon, xvi, xvin16, 5n9, 25n38, 26n42
Cunningham, Conor, 124n25, 133n86, 193, 193n96
Cupitt, Don, 82n57, 115, 115n115

Dalferth, Ingolf, 23n34, 41-42, 41n1-3
Dalin, David G., 145n155
Daniels, Joel, 142n140
Dante, 49n37
Davidson, Donald, 97n27, 170-171n4
Davies, Rachel Bryant, 30n61
Davis, Walter A., 241n177, 259, 259n32, 260

Dawe, R. D., 26n41
Deguy, Michel, 53n57
Dehart, Paul J., 9n29
Deleuze, Gilles, 132, 132n80
Derrida, Jacques, 11n40, 54, 150, 190, 190n81, 221, 241, 242n181
Descartes, René, 43, 53, 185
Desmond, William, 34-35n67, 260-61, 260n36, 261n38-39
De Libera, Alain 11n39, 12n46, 100n38
De Muralt, André, 79n51
De Vogel, C. J., 101n43
Diamond, Cora, 65-66, 65nn6-7, 66nn8-10, 66n13, 209, 209n14-15
Dominik, W. J., xvn9
Donini, Pierluigi, 26n42
DuBois, Page, 20n8

Eliot, T. S., 208, 208n10, 227-28, 227n126, 228n130, 228n134, 229, 255
Else, Gerald F., 19n3
Ernst, Cornelius, 67, 67-68n25, 208, 208n11
Esposito, Costantino, 12n46, 110n94, 114n109, 115, 115n114
Euben, J. Peter, 20n11
Evans, G. R., 196n115
Exum, J. Cheryl, 30n59
Ezekiel the Tragedian, 30

Farley, Wendy, 29-30n58
Farrell, Kirby, 261, 261n43
Felski, Rita, 23, 23n32
Feyerabend, Paul, 9n27, 124n27
Fichant, Michel, 114n111
Fine, Gail, 101, 101n42
Foucault, Michel, 13n47, 209n16
Fuchs, Thomas, 262n45

Gadamer, Hans-Georg, 10-11, 20n13, 22, 22nn24-29, 25n36, 53, 53nn51-54, 175n36, 176n43
Gasché, Rodolphe, 53n55, 54n58
Gavrilyuk, Paul L., 45n23, 160n216
Gellrich, Michelle, 20n12, 56-57, 57n69
Glock, Hans-Johann, 119n1

Goff, Barbara, xv
Goldhill, Simon, 20n9, 20n14, 21–22, 21nn20–22, 22n23, 233n158, 240, 240n174, 258
Goosen, Danie, 36n69
Gould, John, 21n16
Green, Ryan, 209n18
Gregory of Nazianzus, 33, 228n135
Gregory of Nyssa, 212, 212n37
Griffin, Nicholas, 93n8
Grondin, Jean, 12n46
Gray, Brett, 215–16, 216nn55–57, 216n60, 223n103, 225n109, 227n127, 241, 241n175, 246nn193–94, 255–56, 255n10, 256n11
Guyer, Paul, 53n56

Hall, Edith, 20n8, 231
Halliwell, Stephen, 19n4, 25–26, 25n38, 26n39, 50–52, 50n41, 51nn42–45, 51n47, 52n48
Hamilton, Christopher, xvi, xvin16, 139–40n122
Harman, John D., 27n48
Hartog, François, 3n5
Hauerwas, Stanley, 65n6, 156n196
Hebblethwaite, Brian, 64–65n1
Heidegger, Martin, 12, 12nn44–45, 13, 54n60, 54n63, 55n65, 56, 127n54, 191, 191n86, 192n89
Herman, Judith, 247n197, 261n40
Hick, John, 197–201
Higton, Mike, xxi, 207n4
Hill, Geoffrey, 146n166, 175n34
Hintikka, Jaakko, 112–13, 113n104
Hodges, H. A., 140
Hofstadter, Douglas R., 173n21
Holland, Henry Scott, 82n59
Holzer, Vincent, 192n89
Honnefelder, Ludger, 12n46, 114n111
Hösle, Vittorio, 132, 132n77, 132nn81–83
Houlgate, Stephen, 236–37; 236n162, 237nn163–67
Hughes, Samuel, 56n67
Hütter, Reinhard, 78n48
Hyland, Drew A., 27n47

Jakobson, Roman, 173n19
Janssens, David, 264n59
Janz, Paul D., 16, 23n35, 148n175, 255, 255n9
Jaspers, Karl, 28, 28n54
John of the Cross, 212, 212n38
Johnson, David B., 54n58,
Johnson, Luke Timothy, 145n156
Jüngel, Eberhard, 34–35n67, 43n10, 78, 115n116,

Kamerbeek, J. M., 21n17
Kelly, Henry Ansgar, 30–31n62
Kearney, Richard, 34–35n67, 54n58, 243n188, 243n190
Keller, Catherine, 48
Kerr, Fergus 34–35n67, 36, 67n20, 68n27
Keshgegian, Flora A., 61n85
Koselleck, Reinhart, 3n5
Krell, David Farrell, 57n71, 58, 59n74
Kruger, Jaco, 36n69
Kuhn, Helmut, 27n49
Kuehn, Manfred, 124n35

Lacan, Jacques, 61n84, 261, 261n44
Lacoue-Labarthe, Philippe, 54, 54n60, 57n70
Lash, Nicholas, xi, 8n23, 36, 67, 67n19, 74–76, 108n87
Lampe, G. W. H., 67n200
Lamanna, Marco, 12n46, 114n108
Landry, Bernard, 78n48
Laub, Dori, 261n40
Lear, Jonathan, 26n40, 26n42
Lefebvre, René, 97n23
Leonard, Miriam, 19n1, 20n15, 52n49
Lesky, Albin, 20n7
Lightman, Bernard, 82n57
Locke, John, 53, 96, 96n19, 185
Lonfat, Joël, 100n38
Longinus, 53, 53nn56–57
Longo, Oddone, 20n10
López, Leopoldo Prieto, 110n94
Lurie, Michael, 33n66
Lyotard, Jean-François, 54–55, 54nn58–60, 190, 221, 241, 242–43, 243n188–89, 260

Maltby, Michael, 172n15
MacBride, Fraser, 93n6, 97n26, 98n29
Manent, Pierre, 138n117
Mansel, Henry, 82, 82n57
Manser, A. R., 93n9
Maritain, Jacques, 105, 138, 180n52
Marion, Jean-Luc, 12, 13n49, 34–45n67, 112n102, 170, 170n1
Marx, William, 26n40
Masterman, Margaret, 186–87, 186nn69–73, 187n74–75
Maximus the Confessor, 47n34, 161, 174
McAleer, Graham James, 164n226
McCabe, Herbert, 192, 192n90
McCormack, Bruce, 106n68
McCurry, Jeffrey, 1–2n1, 8, 215n51
McDowell, John C., 62n90
Meagher, Robert Emmett, 247n198
Meillassoux, Quentin, 171, 171n9
Melnick, Arthur, 109n90
Merleau-Ponty, Maurice, 210
Metz, Johann Baptist, 59–60n82
Michéa, Jean-Claude, 138n117
Michel, Laurence, 28, 28n56
Millet, Louis, 78n48
Moltmann, Jürgen, 34, 59–60, 59n75–76, 59n78–81, 59–60n82, 160
Montagnes, Bernard, 78n48, 100n39
Moore, G. E., 70–71, 82–83, 89, 93–94, 94nn10–11, 94n13, 97, 97n26, 98, 103, 112, 122, 165, 171
Mulhall, Stephen, 65n6, 66, 66n12, 66n15
Muller, André, xxii, 66n16, 93n7, 106n72, 140–41n128
Murrmann-Kahl, Michael, 6n14
Murray, Paul D., 65, 65n5
Myers, Benjamin, xxi, 1–2n1, 207n4, 225n109, 255, 255nn6–7

Nancy, Jean-Luc, 54, 54n61, 55, 214, 214n49, 260
Narbonne, Jean-Marc, 196n116
Narcisse, Gilbert, 80n54
Nehemas, Alexander, 101, 101n42
Niebuhr, Reinhold, 143n146, 156, 156n196

Nietzsche, Friedrich, 23, 52, 85n65, 178n47, 238, 256, 264–65, 265n61
Novation, 28
Nussbaum, Martha, 234, 234n159

Ochieng, Omedi, xvi, xvin13
Opsomer, Jan, 196n116
Owens, Joseph, 92n2, 95n16, 95n18, 96n19, 96n22, 97n24, 99n34

Pabst, Adrian, 5n10, 77n47, 99, 99n33, 99n37, 138n117
Patzig, Günther, 96n22
Peperstraten, Frans van, 54n60
Perl, Eric D., 92n2, 96n19
Pieper, Josef, 80n54
Pietropaolo, Domenico, 30n60, 33, 33n65
Pickstock, Catherine, 26–27, 27n43, 79n52, 86n67, 124, 124n29, 171nn7–8, 171n10, 172nn16–17, 175, 175n37, 176n41, 177n45, 180n55, 190n83
Poole, Adrian, 21n18
Pound, Marcus, 162n220
Proclus, 198
Prynne, J. H., 96, 96n20, 173n23, 178nn47–49
Przywara, Erich, 100, 100n40, 113, 191n86, 193–95, 248
Pseudo-Dionysius, 46, 161
Puntel, Lorenz, 192n89
Putnam, Hilary, 170–71n4

Quash, Ben, 29–30n58, 225n109

Racine, Jean, 23
Rambo, Shelly, 261, 261n42
Rancière, Jacques, 54n58, 242–43, 242n185, 243nn186–87
Raphael, D. D., 28, 28n55
Rasche, Michael, 29–30n58
Richards, I. A., 28, 28n52
Riches, Aaron, 49n38, 162n219
Ritchie, Angus, 121n17
Ricoeur, Paul, 263, 263n54
Rigby, Paul, 32n63

Rist, John M., 196n116
Robertson, Ritchie, 56n67
Rockmore, Tom, 98n29
Rogozinski, Jacob, 55n65
Römer, Thomas C., 30n59
Roochnik, David, 27n46
Rosemann, Philipp W., 99, 99n35
Rösler, Wolfgang, 20n8
Rubenstein, Mary-Jane, 48
Ryle, Gilbert, 111, 111n100

Sands, Kathleen M., 14, 61–62, 61nn85–86, 62n87–88, 197, 201–4
Sarot, Marcel, 45n23
Schiller, Friedrich, 14, 22n24, 23, 53, 56, 56n67, 57, 167, 256
Schindler, David C., 27n45
Schmutz, Jacob, 48–49n35
Schopenhauer, Arthur, xvii, 62
Schwartz, Regina M., 225n109
Scott, David, xvn10
Séguy-Duclot, Alain, 53n57
Seifrin-Weis, Heike, 93n4
Sellars, Wilfrid, 98, 98n30
Segal, Charles, 21, 21n17, 21n19
Seigfried, Hans, 114n109
Sgarbi, Marco, 127n55
Shaviro, Steven, 171n9
Sherman, Jacob H., 3n3
Simon, Ulrich E., 29–30n58
Simpson, Michael, xv
Smit, Bettine Van Zyl, xvn9
Sorley, W. R., 125
Steel, Carlos, 196n116
Stein, Walter, 155n194, 163n225
Stevens, Wallace, 94, 94n12, 264, 264n57
Stoker, Wessel, 42n4
Strawson, P. F., 109, 119n1, 135
Surin, Kenneth, 30, 64–65n1, 67n24, 149n178, 157n202
Sutherland, Stewart R., 97n24
Symes, Carol, 30–31n62
Szondi, Peter, 57n72

Tanner, Kathryn, 49n38
Tarrant, Dorothy, 27n44
Tate, Daniel L., 22n24

Taylor, A. E., 84, 125
Taylor, Charles, 211n29
Taylor, Kevin, 30
Tertullian, 28, 31, 251
Te Velde, Rudi, 13n48, 34–35n67, 116n119
Thacker, Eugene, xvin14
Theodore of Mopsuestia, 30n60
Tilley, Terrence, 164n227
Tillich, Paul, 108
Toole, David, 29–30n58, 86n67
Tracy, David, 29–30n58, 51n46
Twetten, David, 114n110

Unamuno, Miguel de, 59, 139

Van Der Kolk, Bessel A., 260, 260n37
Vernant, Jean-Pierre, 19, 19nn2–6, 20n15, 50, 50nn39–40, 258
Venard, Olivier-Thomas, 77n46
Veyne, Paul, 19n5
Vidal-Naquet, Pierre, 19n2, 19nn5–6, 50n39
Villey, Michel, 82n58
Vlastos, Gregory, 100, 100n41
Vodolazkin, Eugene, 222, 222n98
Vollrath, Ernst, 114n108

Waismann, Friedrich, 119n2
Wallace, Jennifer, 225n109
Waller, Giles, 30, 139n120, 141, 141nn129–30, 143n144, 145, 145n154, 149n179, 150nn182–83, 225n109
Warner, Martin, 165n230
Webster, John, 11n42, 40, 42–44, 42nn7–8, 43nn9–16, 44n17
Weil, Simone, 207n3, 219, 219n81
Weinandy, Thomas, 45, 45n23, 160n216, 162n219
West, Philip, 157n202
Wigren, Jodie, 261n40
White, Roger M., 115, 116n117, 130, 130n70
Williams, A. N., 11n42
Williams, Raymond, ix, x, 57n69, 139, 139–40nn122, 223n104, 232n157, 239n170, 246, 261n39

Wisdom, John, 121n15
Wise, Jennifer, xviin17
Wittgenstein, Ludwig, xi, 119nn2–3, 121, 122n18, 123, 124n31, 166
Wood, Allen W, 132n79

Young, Frances, 161n217
Young, Julian, 56n68

Zachhuber, Johannes, 42n5
Žižek, Slavoj, 56, 243n188

Subject Index

Aeschylus, xvii, xvii*nn*17–18, 20, 20n7, 23, 31, 233, 262
Aristotle, 15, 20, 21, 22, 23, 26, 26n40–41, 31, 34–35n67, 52, 57n72, 89–101, 103, 108, 112–13, 116–17, 131, 131n72, 137, 165–66, 236, 247n198, 248
aseity (divine), 1–2n1, 3, 4, 14, 34, 35, 37, 39, 40–49, 50, 60, 62, 63, 88, 115n116, 160, 167, 169, 191, 251, 252
analogy, xi, 15, 62, 78–79, 80–82, 82n57, 91–92, 99, 101–17, 130, 165, 166, 169, 189–96, 251, 252, 253
   of attribution (*analogia attributonis*), 78, 81, 86, 102, 107–108n79, 113, 116
   of being (*analogia entis*), 1–2n1, 4, 15, 41n3, 55, 59–60n82, 73n37, 77, 87–88, 100, 104, 106, 108, 113–14, 117, 164, 164n226, 166, 170, 190, 190n82, 191, 191n86, 193, 194n109, 195
   of proportion (*analogia proportionalitatis*), 78, 123, 123n21, 192n92
Analogical metaphysics 4n6, 15, 34–35n67, 54, 101, 117, 163, 192n89, 251

Analogical participation, Being-as-analogically-participated-transcendental, 3, 42n4, 77, 81, 89–90, 99–101, 102, 103, 107, 109, 110, 113, 114, 116, 129, 163, 166, 168, 251
Aquinas, Thomas, 4n6, 11, 11n41, 13, 13n48, 34–35n67, 46, 78, 79–81, 79n52, 80–81nn54–55, 100n39, 102, 107, 110, 113, 113n105–6, 170n1, 184n64, 192n89, 192n92, 198, 210, 220
Attic drama, attic tragedy, tragic drama, xvii–xviii, 13–14, 16–17, 18–33, 50–52, 56, 72–76, 87, 138–39, 143, 221n93, 231–40, 246–47, 256–58, 260, 262–63n51, 263–65
Augustine, 16, 28, 31, 32n63, 60, 62, 162n222, 196–205, 211–16, 218, 223–24, 248, 251, 253,

Being, 5, 12–13, 15, 81, 96n19, 138, 174, 176, 188, 191, 197, 242, 243
   Infinite Being, 48, 49, 249
   Being-as-such, 55, 248, 249
   Being-in-itself, 55
   Being-as-*Ereignis*, 54n58, 55
   Being-as-*Anwesen*, 54n58, 55
   Being-as-predicate, 112, 113

Being (continued)
  Being-towards-death, 127n54
  God-as-Being, 73n37, 192n89

coherency, 2, 6, 8–9, 10, 11, 16, 37, 40, 137, 147, 164, 180n54, 205, 222
contingency, x, 4, 5, 13, 21–22, 42–43, 45–46, 47, 62, 80, 94, 100, 102, 105, 133, 141, 146, 150, 151, 153, 158n205, 169, 171n9, 174, 176, 191–92, 197, 198, 201, 203, 204, 210–12, 215, 220, 230, 231, 239n170, 246, 249
convertibility of the transcendentals: Being and the Good, 3, 5, 16, 48, 50, 197, 249, 253

Eagleton, Terry, ix, 29, 29n57, 39, 163, 163n224, 225n109, 262–63, 262nn46–47, 262nn49–50, 263n53
Euripides, xvii, 20, 23, 24, 31, 233, 259
evil, xi, 5n8, 15–16, 25, 27, 60–61, 62, 65, 66, 72, 73–75, 84–85, 144–45, 148, 149, 159, 161, 162, 164, 166, 169, 196–205, 222, 241–43, 253, 254–55
  evil-as-privation (*privatio boni*), 4, 5, 14, 15, 16, 40, 47, 48, 50, 60, 63, 73, 85, 87, 119, 132, 136–38, 144–45, 163, 165, 166, 167, 168, 169, 196–205, 251, 252, 254
  The problem of evil, 66, 140n126, 144, 148, 149, 231n152, 254n1
  radical evil, 60, 62, 85, 137n112, 168, 252

finitude, xviii, 4, 4n6, 5n8, 58, 70, 73, 80, 83, 91, 100, 102, 108, 131, 148, 151, 154, 161, 169, 191, 192, 215, 232, 245–46, 252, 254n1

the Good, 5, 26, 47–49, 62, 118, 119, 121, 131, 137, 138, 145, 153, 164, 166, 201, 202, 253, 254, 263
  ontological priority of the Good, 14, 62, 138, 204, 251

Hart, David Bentley, xi, 1, 3n4, 6, 9n26, 14–16, 29, 34, 35, 34–35nn67, 37, 38, 39–40, 63, 69, 72–76, 85, 86–88, 141–142n134, 155–57, 157n201, 165, 167, 196, 225n109, 244–45, 244nn191–92, 251, 252, 256–59, 262, 262–63n51

Hegel, G. W. F., xiii, 5–6nn11, 23, 52, 59–60nn82, 68, 76, 84, 97–98, 98n28, 106, 125, 132, 133n87, 135, 135n98, 141, 146, 156, 172, 182, 186, 193–94, 216–22, 224, 227, 231n154, 236–38, 244, 248, 253, 257n15
historicity, 3, 3n5, 4, 15, 35, 36, 37, 60, 80n54, 85, 86, 90, 107, 114, 116, 132, 137, 157, 166, 168, 169, 191, 192n89, 202, 219, 226, 243, 251–53
Hölderlin, Friedrich, 14, 52, 57, 57n71, 58–59, 58n73

impassibility (divine), *apatheia*, 3, 59, 73, 85, 85n65, 159, 160, 161, 161n217, 165, 251

Kant, Immanuel, 12n44, 15, 22n24, 42, 53–58, 60–61, 61n84, 68, 68n28, 71n32, 77–88, 89–92, 101–117, 118–19, 122, 125–38, 149, 151, 165–66, 171, 192n89

language, 7–8, 119–25, 172–89, 207–8, 210, 230–32, 235, 247–48, 253, 263–64
limit, limitation, xv, 6, 25, 41, 50–52, 55, 70, 80n53, 82, 82n57, 84, 85, 102, 104, 106, 107, 108, 109, 111, 115, 119, 125–26, 128, 134, 137, 146–48, 152, 154, 161–62, 163, 176, 178n47, 185, 198, 203, 206, 209, 210, 212, 215, 223, 230–31, 243, 245, 247, 248, 255, 264

SUBJECT INDEX 301

Milbank, John, ix, xi, 1, 5n10, 6, 9n26,
   14, 15, 16, 29, 34, 35, 34–35n67,
   36, 37, 38, 39, 40, 46, 54n62,
   55n64, 60–61, 61n84, 63, 68,
   69–70, 72, 76–88, 98, 98n31,
   99, 99n36, 115, 115n113, 124,
   124n25, 124n28, 124n30, 125,
   133n89, 134n96, 135, 135n101,
   136, 136n111, 137n112, 138,
   138nn117–18, 148n176,
   149n179, 149n181, 150–52,
   153, 155–59, 163, 165–66, 167,
   170n1, 172–73n18, 173n22,
   176, 176n38, 181, 181nn56–57,
   182n60, 185n66, 196, 225n109,
   231, 241, 244–45, 246, 251, 252,
   254n1, 255, 256, 262, 262n48
modern, modernity, 6, 6n12, 13–15,
   17, 18–19, 19n1, 27–30, 33–34,
   40, 42, 46, 50–63, 211, 238–39,
   250, 251

natural law, 53, 57, 82, 82n58, 119, 128–
   29, 137, 149, 163–64, 164n226

ontology, 96, 99, 100, 104, 110,
   114n111, 130, 170n1, 177,
   190n83, 192n89, 238
   ontology of violence, ontological
      violence, ontologization of
      violence, 5, 14, 15, 46–47, 74,
      87, 138, 164, 222, 238, 243, 245,
      249, 253, 260
ontotheology, 12, 12n44, 13, 13n49, 47,
   58, 59, 97n23, 191, 191n86

participation (ontological), participatory
   metaphysics, *methexis*, xi, 3n3,
   4n6, 54, 77, 78, 80–81, 86, 89,
   92, 99–101, 108, 112–14, 116,
   125, 138, 156, 162, 166, 168–69,
   174, 175, 179, 180–81, 184–85,
   189, 191, 204, 208, 224
pessimism, xiv, xvi, 5, 15, 37, 52n48,
   85, 137, 141, 142, 156, 163, 205,
   224, 226, 228, 232, 236, 242,
   246, 249

ontological pessimism, metaphysical
   pessimism, xvi, 5, 14, 37, 62,
   169, 204, 244, 247, 253
Plato, 13, 15, 16, 18, 23–27, 31, 36, 38,
   60, 89, 91, 92, 97n24, 100–101,
   108, 113, 118, 119–25, 131, 137,
   141, 146, 165, 166, 250
poetics, 15, 169–89, 253

Rose, Gillian, xivn3, 55, 162–63n223,
   216, 219–24, 229, 231, 231n154,
   235, 236, 236n161, 238,
   238n169, 241–42, 242nn179–84,
   253

sacrifice, x, 55, 61, 61n84, 72–73, 75,
   76, 85n65, 86, 86n70, 87, 131,
   141–42n134, 156, 205, 215, 242
   sacrificial economy, 75, 85, 87, 242,
      252
   sacrificial totality, totalitarianism
      14, 76, 141–42n134, 155, 156,
      251, 252
Schelling, F. W. J., 14, 52, 57–58,
   57nn71–72, 58n73, 59, 61
the self, 166–67, 204, 205, 206, 207, 208,
   209–24, 248–49, 253
Shakespeare, William, 66, 75, 138–
   39n119, 158–59n208, 235–36
substance, 5, 80, 83, 92–101, 113, 114,
   116–17, 132, 166, 174, 196, 198,
   200
Steiner, George, ix, x, xvii, 5, 14, 28–29,
   28n53, 36, 37, 62, 62n89, 65,
   65n2, 67, 67n18, 67n22, 76,
   106n72, 139, 238–41, 247, 256
sublime, sublimity, 4, 5, 14, 15, 16, 50,
   75, 151, 152, 169, 196, 253
   the (post-)Kantian sublime, 14, 40,
      47, 53–63, 76–88, 116, 119, 133,
      135, 138, 165, 167, 168, 174,
      184n65, 190, 190n82, 200, 205,
      217, 221, 241–43, 251–52, 256,
      258
   the tragic sublime, 5, 55, 148
Sophocles, xvii, xviinn19–20, 20, 23, 31,
   139, 138–39n119, 227, 237

SUBJECT INDEX

suffering, tragic suffering, x, xi, xii, xvii, xviii, 5, 5n8, 15, 22, 23, 26, 30n60, 31, 32, 33, 34, 51, 55, 66, 67, 71, 72, 86, 141, 145, 146, 148, 153, 154, 156, 157–59, 161–63, 166, 215, 223n104, 229–32, 233, 236, 238, 239, 241, 243, 245, 247, 253, 254–57, 260, 264–65

suffering, passibility (divine), suffering God, suffering Absolute, 4, 5, 14, 15, 29, 34–35, 40, 44, 44n20, 45, 46–48, 46n31, 50, 57–60, 59–60n82, 63, 73–74, 85, 85n65, 86, 87, 159–61, 165, 167, 251, 252

temporality, 22, 94, 111, 124, 127n54, 147, 176, 190n81, 191, 226, 228, 228n135

theodicy, 15, 51, 52n48, 71, 73n38, 85, 134, 145, 148, 149, 164, 198, 198n121, 203, 207, 215, 231n152, 254

time, 4, 7, 36, 58, 61, 70, 84, 106, 115, 130, 143, 147–48, 176, 179, 180, 183, 186, 188, 191, 195–96, 197n120, 198, 202, 203–4, 206, 209, 211–12, 214, 216, 218, 220, 224, 225, 227–28, 235, 244, 245–49, 254

transcendence, xiii, xvi, 1–6, 9–10, 12, 14, 15–16, 34–38, 39–63, 69, 73, 77, 81, 83, 87–88, 99, 100, 107, 117, 118, 121, 126, 128, 136, 140, 146, 149, 150, 151, 152, 160, 163–64, 169, 181, 191–92, 204, 205, 217, 224, 239, 241, 250–53, 255, 261

"The Transcendence of the Tragic", 16, 71, 138–55, 255

Ward, Graham, xxi, 7n17, 12n43, 29–30n58, 35, 36, 98, 98n32, 138–39n119, 184n65, 185n67, 205n131, 212n39, 225n109, 259–62

Scripture Index

Song of Songs
1:15—2:7	212n37

Mark
8:34	157

Matthew
10:38	157
16:24	157

Luke
10:25–37	153–54
14:27	157
15:11–32	152–53

John
3:13–14	156
8:28	156
11:1–44	143
11:45–57	144
12:27–33	156
13:31–2	156
17:1	156
20:24–29	255

Romans
6:1–14	156, 157
8:18–39	157

1 Corinthians
1:23	156
2:2	156, 157
10:1–33	156
11:17–34	156

2 Corinthians
13:4	156

Galatians
2:19–20	156
3:1	156
6:2	162

Ephesians
2:1–10	157

Colossians
1:24	162
2:8–15	157
3:1–4	157